role-playing
for
social values:
decision-making
in the
social studies

by **FANNIE R. SHAFTEL**

Associate Professor of Education
Stanford University

Stories by
GEORGE SHAFTEL

PRENTICE-HALL, INC., Englewood Cliffs, N.J.

© 1967 by PRENTICE-HALL, INC.
Englewood Cliffs, New Jersey

Current printing (last digit):

10 9 8 7 6 5 4 3 2 1

Library of Congress Catalog Card Number: 67:12247
Printed in the United States of America. C-78293

PRENTICE-HALL INTERNATIONAL, INC., London
PRENTICE-HALL OF AUSTRALIA, PTY. LTD., Sydney
PRENTICE-HALL OF CANADA, LTD., Toronto
PRENTICE-HALL OF INDIA (PRIVATE) LTD., New Delhi
PRENTICE-HALL OF JAPAN, INC., Tokyo

FOR OUR SON DAVID

FOREWORD

Twenty years ago Fannie and George Shaftel were invited to help prepare educational materials for the teaching of democratic ideals. With the understanding that comes from studying children in the process of learning, they realized that such abstract ideals as courage, virtue, integrity, or justice have little meaning for children. Therefore, they began to explore ways of relating democratic ideals to the everyday life of children. The results of their twenty years of thinking, creating, and experimenting with educational materials are published in this book.

During recent years the focus of our society has changed from ideals to values in action. Certain social values motivate human relations in a democratic society, and these values must be learned by each new generation. A child's personal needs for food, attention, acceptance, or status impel him to self-centered responses. He must learn gradually to find satisfaction in responses that are other-centered. One of the primary aspects of the socialization of children both at home and at school, therefore, is the inculcation of social values.

Although this book is addressed to teachers and to those preparing to teach, Part I includes a theoretical discussion of curriculum and methods in the social studies that should be of interest to all educators. Dr. Fannie Shaftel analyzes the place of interpersonal relations and social values in the social studies; she discusses the development of self-concepts and group relations during childhood and shows the importance of practice in making decisions.

The authors realize that there is more to education than merely teaching children such desirable characteristics as kindness, generosity, responsibility, loyalty, fair-mindedness, and so forth. They point out that situations in life are seldom simple and that values may often be in conflict. Mr. George Shaftel has developed a number of stories that simulate problem situations a child is likely to meet and end with a dilemma to be solved by the class. In general, the effort to find solutions to the dilemma stimulates children to choose between a social value and a personal interest: between loyalty to the group and honesty; between winning dishonestly and losing honorably; between concern for a friend and protection of self; between fairness to another child and fear of ostracism. The stories are pertinent, dramatic, and altogether charming.

Problem situations that motivate thinking were discussed by John Dewey many years ago. Modern psychologists also recognize the importance of the dilemma for learning: ". . . in order to get the individual to try a new response which it is desired that he learn, it is often necessary to place him in a situation where his old responses will not be rewarded. Such a situation may be called a learning dilemma." * In this way children are helped to see that there are alternatives in behavior, that choices can be made, that values motivate choices, and that consequences ensue from the chosen behavior.

The Shaftels realize that children with strong feelings of hostility will not be able to practice nonaggressive solutions to interpersonal dilemmas simply because of role-playing, just as children with extreme anxiety tensions will not be able to resist the taunts of the group after they learn social values. They do not purport to offer techniques for the resolution of personality problems of children. But they do provide these disturbed children with a clearer conception of the contrasts between egoistic and socially motivated behavior by letting them observe that some people do make choices on the basis of social values.

An outstanding feature of this book is the discussion of methods teachers may use to guide children in role-playing stories involving value dilemmas. The dramatic story situations provide motivation; role-playing provides practice in decision-making; the discussion stimulates evaluations of behavior related to other individuals and to peer groups. Specific suggestions are given in detail for conducting role-playing sessions, and the pitfalls for teachers are clearly identified.

Role-Playing for Social Values is unusual in combining the abilities of a master teacher with the creativeness of a sensitive writer. It will be of genuine value in the pre-service as well as the in-service education of teachers in relation to the social studies curriculum. Educators have long expected this book from the Shaftels; I am sure they will agree it was well worth waiting for.

Lois Meek Stolz
Professor Emeritus

Stanford University
April, 1966

* Dollard, John and Neal E. Miller, *Personality and Psychotherapy* (New York: McGraw-Hill Book Company, 1950), p. 45.

ACKNOWLEDGMENTS

Many teachers and colleagues have helped us prepare the materials for this book. To all of them the authors are sincerely grateful. To the following we wish to express specific appreciation:

To Lois Meek Stolz, Professor of Psychology, Emeritus, Stanford University, for her early and continued support in the development of this book.

To A. John Bartky, former Dean of Education, Stanford University, and Edward Krug, Associate Director of the American Ideals Project (1948) for encouraging us to study role-playing.

To Hilda Taba, Professor of Education, and Lavone Hanna, Professor of Education, Emeritus, both of San Francisco State College, for most helpfully reviewing our first manual on role-playing.

To Pauline S. Sears, Professor of Education, Stanford University, for her encouraging review of sections of this book.

To Herbert L. Seamans, formerly Director of the Commission on Educational Organizations, National Conference of Christians and Jews, and Franklin Patterson, Director of the Lincoln Filene Center for Citizenship and Public Affairs, for their guidance in preparing the booklet *Role-Playing the Problem Story*, from which we have borrowed liberally.

To the National Conference of Christians and Jews, who have urged us to continue to produce materials for improvement of intergroup and interpersonal relations.

To Jean Grambs, Associate Professor of Education, University of Maryland, who helped us in writing *Role-Playing the Problem Story* and who gave us a detailed critical examination of the whole manuscript, which was extremely helpful and encouraging.

To Stanford University for permission to use revised versions of some stories originally prepared for the American Ideals Project.

We are also indebted to Harcourt, Brace and World, Inc. for permission to reprint: *Spelling Bee* and *Finders Weepers,* from John Warriner, John H. Treanor, and Norman H. Naas, *Warriner's English Grammar and Composition 7, Teacher's Manual,* pages 126 and 128; and *Trick or Treat,* from John Warriner, John H. Treanor, and Norman H. Naas, *Warriner's English Grammar and Composition 8, Teacher's Manual,* page 136.

The story *George Wanted In* is reprinted by permission of the Association for Childhood Education International, 3615 Wisconsin Avenue, N.W., Washington, D.C.: "George Wanted In" by Marie Zimmerman Solt, from *Childhood Education* (April 1962), Vol. 38, No. 8.

CONTENTS

PART

II

materials:
problem stories for role-playing

"Peer-group experiences . . . can not only help members to work more effectively with others, but also to develop the basic attitudes and values that aid the growth of an autonomous and rational individual. Some of these values are an awareness and acceptance of self in its limitations and uniqueness; a validation of self as capable (within limits) of creative accomplishments; a commitment to build an interdependence with others, in which help can be both given and received; and a positive appraisal of the differences and conflicts among members as potentially productive of both growth and progress. These values are either absent or are being destroyed in many natural processes of socialization today. Yet the peer group, which is rising in importance as a means of early and continuing socialization, can strengthen a value system that supports creative individuality, the practice of liberty and genuine equality.

"People learn value systems, in the first instance, as they form relations with others. These relations in turn develop norms, with corresponding rationales, which the individual then internalizes. If people, young or old, can build groups with standards that reward and strengthen honest self-expression and self-acceptance, creativity, mutual helpfulness, and the capacity to cope with conflicts (within the self or with others), then the members of such groups will assimilate these values as conditions of membership."

> *Kenneth B. Benne, "The Uses of Fraternity,"* in Daedalus, *The American Academy of Arts and Sciences,* XC, No. 2 (Spring, 1961), 239-40.

theory and methodology

chapter

1

THIS IS ROLE-PLAYING

"——But I can't overlook your dishonesty and let *you* win by cheating," she said.

"You mean," Andy protested, "that you'll let *them* win by cheating?"

Miss Hendry started to answer, and could not; indecision held her silent. If she said nothing, she would be helping her students to profit from dishonest conduct. But if she made them confess their cheating, she would be helping the other group to win by dishonesty.

"What should she do?"

The sixth-grade class at A——School is listening to their teacher, Mrs. Gordon, who is reading a problem story to them. As they listen, they lean forward, gasp, react audibly, mutter to themselves. It is obvious that they are deeply involved in the events of the story.

"Paper Drive" is a problem story. In brief, it tells about a sixth-grade class who are caught, by their teacher, Miss Hendry, cheating in a frantic attempt to win a city-wide school paper drive that is being sponsored by the Junior Chamber of Commerce.

One of the sixth-graders says, "Oh, gosh!"

Mrs. Gordon asks, "What do you think will happen now?"

Johnny says defiantly, "It wasn't their fault! If the other class hadn't started it by wetting their papers and wrapping them in dry sheets so that their bundles would weigh more in the paper drive, this bunch wouldn't have hidden the metal junk in *their* bundles!"

"That's right," chorus several children.

"They might have won anyhow," Mary says.

"Are you suggesting," Mrs. Gordon asks in a neutral tone of voice, "that Miss Hendry should keep quiet and not do anything about this incident?"

3

There are nods in the class.

Someone says, "It isn't *really* right—"

A boy says, "They can't help it. The other class is forcing them to cheat—"

A girl adds, "No one really wants to do this; they can't help it."

Elizabeth says, "They don't really have to win—"

"Oh yes they do! Wilson School can't get away with this!"

Mrs. Gordon says, "Johnny, are you saying that the class has no choice?"

Johnny hesitates, then says firmly, "I think the class has to stick together against the Wilson School. They have to get Miss Hendry on their side."

"Johnny, will you come up here and play Andy and show us what you think will happen? Whom will you need to help you?"

Players are chosen: Miss Hendry, Sue, Pete and other children in the class. The other half of the class are instructed to act as critical observers. The time is delineated—Monday morning; the place—the classroom.

The Enactment:

Miss Hendry: "Boys and girls, I can't let you win by cheating."

Andy: "Miss Hendry, we're not cheaters, but when those other guys changed the rules, well, we just outsmarted them."

Pete: "They can't pull a fast one on us!"

Sue: "Miss Hendry, no one else will ever know, and it will be a good lesson for those Wilson kids!"

Mrs. Gordon steps in and ends the enactment: "If I understand you correctly, you are saying that because the other class cheated first, it's all right for this class to accept the prize."

She waits. There is silence.

Then someone says pensively, "I guess neither class should get the prize."

Reluctantly heads begin to nod. It is proposed that the next enactment should take Miss Hendry to see the teacher of the Wilson School sixth grade.

Mrs. Gordon: "Whom will we need for this enactment?"

Children: "The two teachers."

Mrs. Gordon: "When is this taking place?"

Student: "After school, in the other teacher's classroom."

Mrs. Gordon: "How was this arranged?"

Girl: "Miss Hendry called Mrs.—"

Mrs. Gordon: "You can give her a name."

Girl: "Mrs. Robinson."
Mrs. Gordon: "Who will be Mrs. Robinson?"
A girl volunteers.
Mrs. Gordon: "Mrs. Robinson, what are you doing?"
Girl: "I'm sitting at my desk and checking spelling papers."

Enactment:

Miss Hendry knocks on the door. Mrs. Robinson goes to the door.
Mrs. Robinson: "Come in, Miss Hendry. Please sit down. What brings you here?"
Miss Hendry: "Mrs. Robinson, my class cheated in the paper drive, and they say yours did too."
Mrs. Robinson: "Oh! How do they know?"
Miss Hendry: "One of the older brothers saw them doing it."
Mrs. Robinson: "This is terrible. What shall we do?"
Miss Hendry: "Well, I can't let my class win by cheating."
Mrs. Robinson: "I'll have to talk this over with my class."
(*End of enactment.*)

Mrs. Gordon: "What is happening?"
Boy: "The whole story is coming out in the open."
Mrs. Gordon: "What will happen now?"
A boy: "Mrs. Robinson's class will have to face up to it."
(The class quickly arranges an enactment in which Mrs. Robinson's class finally admits the cheating.)
Mrs. Gordon: "What do you think will happen next?"
A girl (*slowly*): "The two teachers will have to tell the Junior Chamber of Commerce."
Mrs. Gordon: "You think the teachers will do this?"
A boy: "Well, Mrs. Gordon, if it were this class, you'd make a committee of boys and girls go along!" (*laughter*)
(The final enactment is the confrontation. The children explain their actions, the Junior Chamber officials are shocked, sorry, but agree that neither class can win.)
Mrs. Gordon: "Well, we now have one way this situation might be resolved. What do you think?"
A boy: "Well, that's the way grownups do it. You have to take the punishment."
A girl says: "It could have ended differently."
Mrs. Gordon asks: "What do you mean, Angela?"
Angela: "The first time the others cheated, they could have been reported."

A boy protests: "But that would be tattling."

Mrs. Gordon: "You feel, John, that you can't tell on people who are cheating?"

(The discussion is on. Soon it will lead to exploration through further enactments.)

At B—— school, Mr. Lundberg stops reading.

Jody says, "They are gonna catch it!"

"Oh, no, they won't," insists Suzy, "Miss Hendry knows it really wasn't their fault."

"What will happen now?" asks John Lundberg.

"I know! Mr. Lundberg. Let me show you," volunteers Bill.

"All right, Bill. Whom will you need to help you act out your idea?" asks his teacher.

Roles are quickly assigned: Miss Hendry, boys in the class caught with the bundles.

Enactment:

Miss Hendry: "Boys, I cannot let you win by cheating. You will have to confess."

Bill (*playing Andy*): "Miss Hendry, I know we did wrong and will have to be punished, but *please*, let us go to the picnic and *then* we'll confess."

Others: "Yes, we will, *after* the picnic!"

(*End of enactment.*)

Mr. Lundberg comments, neutrally, "Well, we have now seen one way this might end. What do you think?"

There are nods. Children argue for this proposal.

Again, Mr. Lundberg asks, "If I understand you, you are saying that the class should go to the picnic and then take the punishment afterward."

Mary comments wistfully, "No, it ain't right, really. But you see, Mr. Lundberg, if that class is poor folks, like us, they've never been to a place like the Pink Horse Ranch. They oughta get a chance to go ..."

Let us shift the scene again. This time a group of adults—teachers, administrators, supervisors—are exploring the educational uses of role-playing. They have just heard the "Paper Drive" story read to them.

"How do you think children will end this story?" asks the role-playing leader.

After brief discussion of how the children feel, how Miss Hendry feels, a man comments, "I think they'll have to see the officials of the Junior Chamber of Commerce and confess."

This proposal is enacted.

Enactment:

Boy: "Mr. Morris, we are a committee from Glenwood school. We won the paper drive. We have something to tell you."

Mr. Morris: "You did a grand job! We're proud of you."

Boy: "But you see, it wasn't really like that."

(He tells the story of the cheating.)

Mr. S. (another J.C. member): "I'm surprised and disappointed."

Mr. Morris: "Well, of course, we can't give either class the prize. We'll have to decide what to do."

(The boys leave, with their teacher.)

(*End of enactment.*)

Role-playing leader: "What is happening?"

A teacher: "The Junior Chamber men are shocked."

An administrator: "The newspapers will get this and there will be talk about the failure of the schools to teach moral behavior."

A supervisor: "I think the immorality lies with the Junior Chamber of Commerce."

Role-playing leader: "What do you mean?"

A teacher (*quickly*): "She means that they had no right to tempt children with such glamorous prizes."

Another teacher: "Pitting children against each other to raise funds is a form of pressure on them."

A heated discussion follows. How should we teach responsible behavior to children? What is the effect of prizes on youngsters? Given such an outcome, how best help these youngsters? Punishment? Analysis of motives? Clarification of consequences? Heated arguments persist through the luncheon that follows the session.

In the three situations just described, human beings, children and adults, are struggling with the dilemmas of interpersonal relations, with the consequences of the choices individuals make as they strive to solve the problems of everyday life.

Some individuals learn in their daily life situations to be expedient, to "get by" somehow. Others, in a more benign and supportive environment, learn concern for others and sensitivity to the consequences of the choices they make. Although it is true that the pressures of poverty and slum conditions make for many expedient solutions, it is also true that in economically advantaged environments, expediency can become a way of life for children under pressure to achieve, to compete for grades and scholarships, to conform to expectations beyond their capacity.

The ability to handle problems which affect human relations cannot be left to chance. A positive development in ethical conduct is a process that can and must be acquired through thoughtful, planned experiences for children and youth—in homes, in the community, and *especially* in the school culture. This process does not happen in a vacuum. The culture imposes circumstances that must be resolved. As a young person learns ways of coping with his own crucial life situations, he develops the attitudes and values that shape his ways of behaving.

The children in the classroom sessions presented here were role-playing; they were participating in group problem-solving; they were practicing decision-making in areas typical of their own experience. Left to incidental learning, they may choose expedient solutions, and these may become a way of life. Guided to explore the consequences of their choices, to become sensitive to the impact of their decisions and actions on others, they may develop individual integrity and a sense of group responsibility.

WHY ROLE-PLAYING?

Role-playing, as presented in this book, has a variety of functions, but two are major: *education for citizenship*, and *group counseling* by the classroom teacher. Education for citizenship is an important goal of social studies. Group counseling is increasingly recognized as valuable to all children in their crucial transitions from one growth level to the next and also as helping disadvantaged children, emotionally disturbed children, and many other school populations.

At various times in the past, education for citizenship has been called "moral education" and "character education" and "social learning." Our focus in this present work is upon *educating for ethical behavior; more specifically, for individual integrity and group responsibility*; and this focus, we believe, covers much of the areas of behavior suggested by the other terms.

It is our conviction that a vital responsibility of education today is that of helping the individual child to become "inner-directed" at the same time that he learns to live well in groups and that he develops intelligent concern for others. This task has become an imperative in an industrial society in the Nuclear Age. Man cannot live for himself alone, or even for his culture group alone, and survive. The crucial question of our time is whether men, the world over, products of particular cultures, can overcome their ethnocentricity and act in terms of generalized ideals aimed at preventing wars, realizing human potential everywhere, and maintaining the integrity of the individual (Kenneth Benne, 1961).

It is the purpose of this book to analyze the need, to delineate the educator's responsibility, and to provide materials and methodology that we feel are unique contributions to this task.

Our materials: problem stories [1] that pose key dilemmas of middle childhood and early adolescence in American culture, in the solution of which young people discover their feelings, their modes of action, and their values, and learn to modify them intelligently.

Our methodology: role-playing, or sociodrama, a group problem-solving method that enables young people to explore, in spontaneous enactments followed by guided discussion—utilizing critical evaluation and full discussion in a supportive atmosphere—of how they tend to solve such problems, of what alternatives are available to them, and of what the personal and social consequences are of the proposals they offer.

Role-playing, when properly and skillfully used, is uniquely suited to the exploration of group behavior and of the dilemmas of the individual child as he tries to find a place in the many and increasing groups in his life and at the same time struggles to establish personal identity and integrity. When properly used, role-playing permits the kind of "discovery" learning which occurs when individuals in groups face up to the ways they tend to solve their problems of interpersonal relations, and which occurs when, under skillful guidance, young people become conscious of their personal value systems. As a result, young people are helped to develop a sensitivity to the feelings and welfare of others and to clarify their own values in terms of ethical behavior.

Role-playing, as employed in this book, is not aimed at achieving therapy; nor is it "creative dramatics" or incidental skits to highlight a discussion or lecture. Rather, it is a group of problem-solving procedures that employs all the techniques of critical evaluation implied in the terms "listening," "discussion" and "problem solving," and is akin to the research procedures which behavioral scientists term *simulation* and *theory of games*. Role-playing, as do simulation and gaming, utilizes a symbolic model (verbal rather than physical or mathematical). Role-playing (as do the others) proceeds into problem-definition, delineation of alternatives for action, exploration of the consequences of those alternatives, and decision-making.

MODELS, SIMULATION, THEORY OF GAMES, AND DECISION-MAKING

Researchers in the behavioral sciences borrow an important element of research from the physical sciences: the model. Engineers developing a

[1] The problem story was developed by the authors in the American Ideals Project of the School of Education, Stanford University, 1947–1948, and is reported in Fannie R. Shaftel, "Role-Playing in Teaching American Ideals," unpublished doctoral dissertation, Stanford University, 1948; and in George and Fannie R. Shaftel, *Role-Playing the Problem-Story*, National Conference of Christians and Jews, 1952.

new type of aircraft or ship hull build a scale model of the structure to subject it to intensive trials in wind tunnels or tanks. Similarly, behavioral scientists now develop not physical but symbolic models. Such models are then subjected to wide-ranging batteries of tests in an effort to achieve new learnings about people as reacting and interacting groups of individuals. This process, involving construction of a model, whether symbolic (pictorial, verbal, mathematical) or physical, is termed "simulation" (Guetzkow, 1962).

The behavioral scientist, of course, is not interested in ships or planes but in psychological and social processes; his interest is in the use of simulation as a research, training, and teaching procedure with human beings. To elaborate, simulation, in behavioral terms, refers to the "construction and manipulation of an operating model ... of all or some aspects of a social or psychological process" (Guetzkow, 1962, p. 3). It is of basic importance that such a model have a high degree of reality and that its components and variables respond in a manner comparable to that of the behavior of the real system.

The function of social science is, of course, to formulate theories that explain and predict human behavior. Simulation is a very useful device for this exploration of verbal theories and the testing of hypotheses, for the reason that it is often impossible to subject an actual group of human beings to experiments. By successfully simulating the significant variables it is possible to explore such phenomena by experimenting with the simulated system.

In other words, instead of subjecting a child to an actual crisis—of being rejected by a group, of having something cherished stolen from him, of being blamed for something distressing and disgraceful of which he is innocent, of being forced by his peers to commit an act of aggression or dishonesty or malice which he would never commit of his own volition—simulate the social situation and the psychological crisis by means of a model; i.e., a problem story. Then follow through on the simulated experience by exploring, through role-playing, its many facets of feeling and reacting behavior, of defining alternatives, of exploring consequences, and finally choosing a course of behavior in decision-making.

Role-playing focuses upon handling data (discussion of the details and issues in the problem-story model: problem definition), tentative decision-making in the choosing among alternatives, experiencing consequences (going through enactments in which the consequences attendant upon following through on various alternatives are undertaken), and making final decisions (choosing in the light of consequences).

The parallel between simulation (and gaming) and role-playing is clearly suggested in descriptions of the simulation procedure: Guetzkow's inter-nation simulation and the Carnegie Tech Management Game are used to help to teach college students about the behavior of complex systems by having the students make decisions, handle data, and experience consequences in the simulated systems, comparable to those which occur in the real system.

Parenthetically, some writers make no distinction between the terms *simulation* and *gaming*. Guetzkow does not consider them to be two separate techniques.

Games of strategy offer a good model of rational behavior of people in situations where (1) there are conflicts of interest, (2) a number of alternatives are open at each phase of the situation, (3) people are in a position to estimate consequences of their choices, taking into consideration the very important circumstance that outcomes are determined not only by one's own choices but also by the choices of others over whom one has no control (Rapaport, 1960).

The original approach to game theory was proposed by John von Neumann and Maurice Frechet in 1928 and 1937. Their now classic book, *Theory of Games and Economic Behavior*, elaborated the theory in 1944 and further treated gaming in a revised edition in 1947. Luce and Raiffa point out that in all of man's written records there has been a preoccupation with conflict of interest. The prototype, they say, is an individual in a situation from which one of several possible outcomes will result and with respect to which he has certain personal preferences. (This could be an abstract definition of a problem story dilemma.) And, although he may have some control over the variables that will decide the final outcome of the situation, he lacks full control. "Sometimes this is in the hands of several individuals who, like him, have preferences among the possible outcomes, but who in general do not agree in their preferences" (Luce, R. D. and Raiffa, Howard, 1964, pp. 1–2).

Sometimes still other individuals or even chance occurrences ("acts of God") may influence the end result. Game theory seeks to explain behavior in such situations and to formulate principles to guide intelligent action toward solving the complicated problems that result. Von Neumann and Frechet and subsequent researchers in game theory have developed mathematical models to handle such problems.

Gaming involves two or more individuals or teams with opposing points of view and purposes in conflict for stakes important to them. It is an excellent vehicle, when students are involved in realistic cases, for relating problem situations to the social studies. Because of this usefulness, in fact, the simulation of problems involving choice and decision has been used as an important training device in such different programs as those of the Northwestern University Graduate Program in International Relations, the Rand Corporation, the Harvard Graduate School of Business Administration, and many others (Gibson, 1964).

The parallels between simulation, gaming and role-playing may be summed up as a mutual concern in:

1. conflict of interest, personal or interpersonal or intergroup, in which players
2. face alternatives from which to choose, and
3. must make individual decisions.

Perhaps it should be pointed out that gaming may possibly place more emphasis than simulation upon solving problems of conflict of interest in mathematical models; simulation (as is true of role-playing) is helpful in solving problems of human interplay in which mathematical methods for considering all the desired factors are not available (Guetzkow, 1962, p. 13).

ROLE-PLAYING: A DECISION-MAKING PROCESS

There are numerous educational uses for role-playing or sociodrama. These will be discussed later in this book. But the one that looms high on the educational horizon today is its use as practice in decision-making. Through role-playing of typical conflict situations, children and young people can be helped to articulate the ways in which they tend to solve their problems. In the enactments, the consequences (social *and* personal) of the choices they make become more explicit. Analyses of these choices can lay bare the values underlying each line of action. Young people can thus learn that they act (make decisions) on the basis of the values they hold, which may be consciously, but most often are unconsciously, held. Once aware of their own valuing, they are in a position to modify their values.

ROLE-PLAYING: A BASIC SOCIAL STUDIES PROCESS

Perhaps the most important new frontier in the area of the social studies today is the contemporary research effort to bridge the gap between the social studies and the social sciences.

There have been two basic viewpoints expressed with respect to the nature and objectives of the social studies. One point of view has seen the social studies as essentially the same as the social sciences (Berelson, 1964). The other viewpoint has been concerned directly with developing the attributes of good citizens (Metcalf 1963). An aspect of the second position conceives of the social studies as essentially the process of decision-making under all the practical circumstances which confront the citizen (Engle, 1960; Massialas, 1963). This position sees the decision-making process and *the exercise of the process by which information and values are brought to bear upon the practical problems which citizens confront* as central in the social studies.

Gradually the two seemingly differing objectives just described are meeting on a common ground. The social scientists who have concerned themselves with the contributions of their scholarly fields to social studies education are urging a confrontation of youth with social realities. The historian urges a more realistic approach to human decisions in history texts (Stampp, 1964; Commager, 1965), the political scientist suggests the simulation of real political situations, and a social psychologist proposes a strand of learning experiences for elementary school focused on how individuals behave in groups and on learning to think consequentially about human behavior (Ronald Lippitt, U.S.O.E., 1964).

Not only do social scientists stress the key concepts of their field (structures of knowledge) but also their unique processes of inquiry as basic to sound social studies education. Therefore *inquiry* takes priority over acquisition of facts, key though they may be, in new social studies programs.

It is one of the myths of our time that one learns about society by making common sense judgments based upon one's life experiences and by adding simple information (facts) about human affairs. The argument goes something like this: "If you learn to read and then read widely in social materials, you become socially literate." Even C. P. Snow (1959) argues that the humanist cannot understand the world of science because he lacks the technical tools but that the scientist (since he can read!) can more easily cross over into the culture of the humanist.

This argument is naïve. To be socially literate today demands a long, careful, technical, social and philosophical education in the modes of inquiry of the various social sciences, in the dynamics of societal changes, and in the decision-making processes involving value choices.

The American child who is tomorrow's citizen is growing up in one of the most dramatic and crucial times in the history of the world. Suddenly we are confronted by changing conditions that demand unusual accommodations to new institutional arrangements and new human relations.

The most vital frontiers in the world today lie in the realm of man's relation to man and in the uses to which men will put their scientific and technological knowledge. We are realizing increasingly that social studies must draw not only upon the traditionally accepted areas of history, geography, political science and economics, but also on the behavioral sciences which help us to better understand the individual-in-society and group behavior. Thus, anthropology, social psychology and microsociology contribute content and methodology that help us to build the bases for healthy personal-social behavior in children. Classes can be helped to develop healthy group climates (Schmuck, Lohman, Lippitt, Fox, 1965) and in the process learn to understand group behavior in the wider society beyond the classroom. This personal growth is directly related to citizenship behavior.

In this time of great change and personal confusion, we must help children and youth to explore intensively and continuously their roles as individuals growing in changing and increasingly urban communities. Children must be helped to confront and cope with the realities of their own life space—the ways they make and relate to friends, the ways they behave in groups, how they reconcile personal desires with the social good, how they treat individuals who are different in some ways from themselves. It is in such a matrix that they will shape their own identity and character and become positive, constructive citizens rather than self-indulgent, non-involved individuals. (Benne, 1961). *These concerns are social studies content* and need a central place and focus in the curriculum.

Role-playing is an inquiry process; it is practice in decision making. The problem stories in this book are focused on personal-social decisions which reflect the American culture and the value choices which press upon children in the process of growing up in our society today. Explored through role-playing, under the guidance of skillful teachers, it is hoped that such problem confrontations can help children and youth develop the integrity that comes with value clarification and the group responsibility that results from sensitivity to the human consequences of the choices we make.

2

PROBLEMS AND CHALLENGES OF OUR TIME: NEW DIMENSIONS FOR EDUCATION

Are our cities committing suicide? Will automation throw men permanently out of work? Will the population explosion surpass our ability to feed the people of the world? Can free societies remain free? Can we survive a nuclear war?

These are some of the overwhelming problems of our time. They fill the headlines of our newspapers and the pages of our journals.

And, on a slightly different level, there are a host of other questions: Can man change his concept of significant work? Is it possible to create new concepts of "community" in urban life? Can we erase the liabilities of prejudice and ethnocentricity and develop a multicultural society?

Such questions are evoked by the scientific and technological revolution, the revolution of rising expectations, and the newly emerging world urban society. They delineate citizen tasks that go beyond any past conception of preparation for citizenship. The man of tomorrow must, to survive, be a problem-solving, innovation-minded individual. But he must also make his choices deliberately on the basis of consciously held, carefully criticized values.

Our entrance into the Nuclear Age has posed for us an immediate need for new human relations. Mankind is inevitably intertwined. The fate of men in obscure jungle villages and those in huge metropolitan centers depends on the ability of human beings everywhere to develop levels of cooperation across ethnic, racial and national boundaries.

There is a new moral climate in the world, a climate of high expectations, that stimulates the poor of the world, including our own, to

15

aspire to better realization of their human potential. We, the affluent members of American society, are morally committed to helping our fellow men at home and abroad to achieve a better life—hopefully a democratic one.

This revolution of rising expectations reflects the technological revolution that through such developments as automation changes our very basic concepts of work and of man's sense of identity and significance in a world of work. We are confronted by the possibilities and problems of a new leisure as machines displace men. How is man to develop a sense of worth if he is no longer needed in basic industries? Will we develop new concepts of significant contributions to society? Can men learn to shift their values as conditions change, or redefine them for modern circumstances?

Teachers of children and youth are entrusted with a key task in this challenge. Can they so guide the development of the young that these future citizens become problem-solving, humane individuals with high skills in the human encounter and an ability to adapt intelligently to changing conditions?

Most of us have drifted so casually into these profound societal changes that we have only dimly defined the problems and therefore are not clear about their educational implications.

THE NEED

One vital aspect of our societal situation is the need for the immediate development of a humane outlook and commitment on the part of all of us. This task requires thoughtful analysis of our ways of socializing the young child, and a thorough, clear-seeing evaluation of the social institutions and arrangements which permit or deny man a humane stance.

Man does not, of course, wish merely to survive. He wishes to realize himself as a creative individual who lives up fully to his potential. The irony of our time is that through the technology made possible by man's advances in science, there is available to human beings the means to free themselves from working each day solely to meet minimum physical needs. Man can, in fact, extend his life richly. Yet, this very technology has dislocated cultures, thrown our values into confusion and, possibly, provided us with the means for our own destruction. That destruction might take place not just in the physical sense of nuclear warfare but psychologically through the loss of individual identity and opportunity latent in the pressures of crowded mass-life in the urban complex awaiting us in the near future.

It is, of course, impossible in one or two chapters to pose adequate answers to the questions we have raised. However, we will make an attempt here to summarize some of the key conditions of modern life that have tremendous implications for education and demand new sensitivities and skills of our young people.

THE CHALLENGE

It is in the very nature of man to be conserving, to hold on to the ways that are stable and that help us to maintain equilibrium in the face of the many demands of living. Cultures, therefore, tend to change very slowly. Man adapts to new conditions cautiously; he often resists change.

The individual organism, at each stage in the process of growing up, must expend great effort to resolve the conflict between his inner drives and the modifications he must make to satisfy those drives in ways permitted by his culture (Frank, 1954). Yet, with each new stage in his development, the individual is confronted with new tasks: the crawling child must learn to walk, the tomboy girl of ten must become the adolescent "young lady" of twelve, and so on. At each stage, the culture imposes new demands on the child which require that he relinquish behavior he has but recently and painfully achieved and go through the struggles attendant on facing new situations which demand new learnings.

This personal growth is paralleled by similar conserving behavior in the wider culture. Institutions, customs, relationships that have evolved slowly through the rigors of facing and resolving problems of living in the physical and social environment are held to steadfastly as important values. They are changed reluctantly and, usually, only after long deliberation and much trial and error.

Now, quite suddenly, man is confronted by a qualitatively different set of circumstances. The changes posed by our rapidly developing technology are truly earth-shaking. Inventions are so revolutionary in nature that they do not permit gradual adaptation. One major change, such as automating an industrial process, sets off a chain reaction in a whole series of established cultural relations.

Such changes are profound and culturally disruptive. They call for more than trial-and-error adaptations. This dynamic, rapidly developing world technology makes great demands for adaptability, creativity, and problem-solving thinking in all human beings. It calls for new skills and attitudes in social behavior. It requires a sensitivity to the cultural perceptions and tasks of the many peoples of the world. It demands a commitment to the solutions of the problems of mankind over the earth— a recognition that there is no one way to solve our problems, that there may be many culturally different but acceptable solutions to man's needs.

Yet, above all, there is required a set of generalized ideals that will protect men everywhere from their predatory fellows and the threat of nuclear warfare.

URBAN LIVING AND GROUP LIFE

The United States, which is the most industrially advanced nation, clearly presents a trend in urbanization that is a forerunner of a phenomenon that is spreading around the world.[1]

All over the world nonliterate men, feudal men and industrial men are building new nations or developing old ones into modern, urban, technologically based societies. The tribesmen of Nigeria walk the broad boulevards and gaze at the skyscrapers of Lagos. The people of the village compounds of Malaysia find in Kuala Lumpur a fantastic city of Chinese bazaars, Moorish buildings, shining skyscrapers, and broad freeways. The Kentucky mountain hillbilly goes to Chicago to join Cousin Joe and lives in a "project" amid the many cousins from Southern towns and Appalachia. He faces an adjustment to weekly pay, installment buying —all the value shifts so vividly described by Harriette Arnow in her deeply moving novel *The Dollmaker. If he is lucky enough he may find a job.* But he is a rural man with little education and no technical skills.

One of the obvious facts of urban living is that the individual spends most of his life in many groups. Increasingly, these are not the intimate groups of small-town life and kinship families but the less personal groups of large schools, large churches, factories, corporations, huge business offices, and tremendous labor unions. In any given day, the average working adult takes on several roles in a variety of social settings. And, with the rapid obsolescence of jobs because of technological advances, the adults in families are facing the task of vocational re-education, the taking on of new roles, and often, the putting down of roots in new locations. Their children then confront not only adjustments to new family routines but also the task of winning their way into new child cultures in new neighborhoods and schools. Imbedded in such conditions, one can see, is the need for flexibility, ability to face and solve problems in new settings and under new conditions, skills for taking on a variety of roles. The rural person, moving into the city, must learn his way into the buzzing confusion of urban life; the big-city dweller moving to the suburbs needs skills for winning his way into the groups of his new community. Those who, through education and new opportunities, move into more skilled

---

[1] "The Future Metropolis," *Daedalus,* Journal of the American Academy of Arts and Sciences, Winter, 1961, p. 216.

or technical jobs also face the social requirements of a different (class) level than they have lived on in the past.

"COMMUNICATION OVERLOAD"

As newcomers enter the vast arena of a metropolitan area, they are confronted by a set of conditions that may be new to them. In the rush of people crowding into public transportation, the press of working in large organizations, the steeling of nerves against the dense background noise of the city, and the exposure to an overwhelming barrage of modern communication media—newspapers, journals, radio, television, advertising—urban man suffers what has been termed "communication overload" (Karl W. Deutsch, 1961). One has only to drive on a freeway, enter a subway train or walk on the streets in early morning, noon, or late afternoon to experience the impact of this nerve-battering excess of people, noise, constant movement, and verbal persuasions. In self-defense, the city dweller retreats. This retreat often takes the form of flight into television or other media that make few demands for immediate response and away from personal, intimate contact with people. He retreats from real "conversation" with his fellows to the impersonal, unreal world of commercial media (Huebner, 1963).

In a very real sense, he removes himself from people, especially from responsibility for his fellows at work, his neighbors at home, or for the man-on-the-street. Several years ago, *Life* Magazine featured pictures of a man lying on a subway stairway. In the several hours that the photographer watched, *not one person* stopped to see if the man was ill, dead, or drunk!

Newcomers to the metropolitan communities—confused, unsure of themselves, needing welcome and help and new affiliations—meet there the urbanites who have removed themselves from direct relations with other individuals and have repudiated any responsibility for their neighbors.

Rural folks who move into this environment suffer the confusion attendant on a new way of life, and encounter demands for behaviors they have had no preparation for, in apartment or tenement dwellings, in shopping, in employment agencies, and in getting medical help. Too often they are in financial straits when they arrive, and they and their children find themselves in the crowded slums of our big cities where neighborly concern for others is completely lacking. No one seems to care what happens to them. True, there may be social agencies to which they might turn if they knew about them, but often newcomers have no one to turn to for information and direction.

This lack of neighborliness, at one level, and alienation from others at a deeper level, does not hold promise for the emergence of a new, humane community. The urban newcomer finds that he has joined the "lonely crowd."

In contrasting circumstances, many city workers, as their earning power increases, move out to the suburbs, into the huge housing tracts that enable a skilled worker to provide a new way of life for his family.

But such people, too, must face a new set of cultural conditions and demands. The newly suburban family faces the need to adjust from the impersonality of city dwelling to the more intimate and more highly organized street and neighborhood communal activities of suburbia. The newcomers are suddenly confronted with new, local values (the well-kept front lawn, for example). Moreover, they tend to become members of homogeneous neighborhoods: the variety of people they encountered in the city, the range of differing subcultures they contacted in their former dwelling space, is now lessened and narrowed.

This homogeneity is even more accentuated in those suburban areas populated by the managerial and professional families of our society. In those areas, as Margaret Mead has observed, a family forms a close social relationship with five other families just like themselves; their children play together and go to the same school, the adults belong to the same church and clubs. By moving to the suburbs, the former city dwellers have, in a very real sense, removed themselves and their children from broad cultural contacts. Such exclusive relationships do not help them to relate themselves empathically to the many subcultures and groups in American life, let alone the many cultures of the world. Suburban life can be very provincial.

As a result, the schools face a new dimension of an old task: helping children to have the intergroup experiences that will enable them to know and respect the many groups that make up the subcultural strata that constitute so large a part of our democracy.

Such conditions as those described above suggest the need for planned community action to build neighborhood groups—even in the big city. Such groups can take responsibility for orienting newcomers and teaching them positive ways of living in the city in spite of limited means. Sol Alinsky and others in the city of Chicago have already demonstrated what can be done to mobilize leadership in slum areas to develop community action.

Schools have a role to play in this task, too. An alert school system can cooperate in community action, of course; but it also has its own unique contributions to make: School personnel can recognize the need to educate child groups to welcome and support the newcomer. They can teach, directly, the many positive, constructive ways of winning one's way into new groups. Furthermore, they can work actively to help children to relate themselves sympathetically to the child who may seem backward or a "country hick" in terms of the mores of the city.

THE IMPACT OF TECHNOLOGY ON THE INDIVIDUAL

The impersonalization of the metropolis is further reinforced by the routines of work of most people in a machine age. Charlie Chaplin's film *Modern Times* was satirically prophetic of what has come to pass as many people take places on assembly lines in factories or at desks in huge offices. Leisure time activities, as we have seen, tend to be passive participation in commercial media of entertainment.

These media, with their vivid presentations of many products of our affluent industrial society, entice people continually with new "things." All of us, from the most naïve to the most sophisticated, eventually persuade ourselves that we need many things we might otherwise not have desired if we had not been bombarded with enticements.

Such preoccupations tend to promote an atmosphere in which material things are more valued than relations with other people. We begin to value things by what they cost. Erich Fromm has pointed out that we even begin to value man by what his price (salary) is in the common market.[2] Thus we speak of a $10,000-a-year man or a $50,000-a-year man.

One cannot overemphasize the danger to real relationships among men if the market-place value of a man becomes the only criterion for valuing him. Is there not a tremendous task before us to help the young to a growing appreciation of the range and variety of abilities among people and to develop enjoyment of people as individuals—to promote genuine companionship and affiliation among children and youth that will carry over into adult relationships?

ORGANIZATION MAN

Another phenomenon of this organization life is the pressure to become a good organizational man (Whyte, 1956). It is obvious that working in groups demands some cooperation; it requires a host of communication and group-work skills to avoid snarls in the vast network of tasks necessary in large production or service operations. Gradually, in our society, a set of expectations has developed that shapes in powerful ways, both positive and negative, the behavior of the individual in the large organization.

On the positive side, we have gradually evolved, with some sys-

[2] Erich Fromm, *Man for Himself.* (New York: Holt, Rinehart & Winston, Inc., 1947), pp. 67–82.

tematic research, techniques for group-work and for leadership in large organizations. Cartwright and Zander (1958) have shown us the effects of various communication systems and small group arrangements, for example, that enable industrial organizations to improve morale, encourage intelligent leadership, and increase productivity.

On the other hand, sociological writers such as William H. Whyte and David Riesman (1950) view with alarm the tendency to crystallize a code of behavior for "organization man" and his wife—a code that rigidly delineates what is acceptable and proper role behavior in the "organization." This pressure to conform erases individuality and creativity as the ambitious person focuses on "cooperating" to such an extent that he relinquishes being himself. In such a subculture, one abdicates his responsibility for acting on his own judgment (and values) and, like a chameleon, seeks instead to take on the opinions and attitudes of "the organization."

This set of conditions filters down into the child-rearing practices of these adults as parents. They seek conformity for their children, so that they will be accepted in the right circles. Eventually, this driving need to conform expresses itself in such extreme behavior as occurred in a San Francisco suburb when neighbors demanded that one family replace the ivy ground-cover of their front yard with grass because everyone else on the block had grass! Other kinds of community incidents occur that reflect the abdication of common sense guidance by parents as they permit preadolescents to behave in precocious ways so that they will be acceptable in certain social circles. "Going steady" and attending unsupervised parties and drinking are matters that are causing concern to many parents.

There is a growing recognition in top managerial circles that this drive for conformity eventually robs their organizations of creative ideas and of the emergence of new leadership needed in business. Many raise these questions: "Can men be helped to be good organization men and at the same time maintain their individuality and creativity?" And, "What kinds of conditions must exist to make such individuality possible?"

THE INDIVIDUAL IN THE CULTURE

Many social scientists feel that it is unrealistic to ask the individual to go against the culture. They argue that it is the rare individual who is the rebel or is secure enough within himself to stand up against the groups within which he lives. Riesman, Fromm, Jules Henry (1963) are pleading for educative experiences that will help the individual to be "inner-directed," to be a "man for himself," to be "responsible for the well-being of others." They argue that only thus can man save his society, only thus can man make society truly humane.

Can children, in their most formative years, be guided toward an inner-directedness based upon personal integrity and an "intelligent concern for others"? Or is this asking for more than their immature egos can maintain?

It seems to us that we must set the feet of the young on this path, but do it in such a way that young people can maintain a healthy relationship with their culture and the subgroups that are their social base. *Can this be done?* It has been said that adults in our culture are characterized by their failure to face the realities of their dilemmas—that they give verbal allegiance to ethical relationships in a compartmentalized way (i.e., on Sunday, in church) and then are "practical" or "realistic" in their everyday affairs, giving in to the expedient values of the culture.

Perhaps, then, the first step in this educative process of ethical development is to help the children *to face up to and define the realities of the dilemmas confronting them in their everyday life situations.*[3]

SUMMARY

Children today, however, cannot be educated primarily for facing their local life situations. Their lives and needs are irrevocably intertwined with those of the entire nation and the world community. Across the nation and over the rest of the world, the vistas of a highly productive future based on scientific development has set in motion minority groups and peoples of underdeveloped areas who now dare to dream and work and to demand a better opportunity for all.

As Vera Micheles Dean has pointed out so vividly, the countries of Africa, Asia, and South America will solve their problems either with the realistic and sympathetic help of the Western world or, failing to receive this help, will tend to turn to the promises of the communistic societies. The strong authoritarian backgrounds of these underdeveloped nations make them especially prone to the latter solution. Both for humanitarian reasons and for survival reasons, we have no alternative but to concern ourselves with helping to improve the levels of living of the many peoples of industrially underdeveloped areas.

This task not only requires information about human circumstances but also demands an ability to relate ourselves to others who may look quite different, who live very differently and have different values from our own. It requires a realization that there are varied, yet acceptable, cultural solutions to common problems.

Can this be taught to children of the United States? We tend to think that our own ways are the best ways for everyone (Shaftel, 1962).

[3] Kenneth Benne, "The Uses of Fraternity," in *Ethnic Groups in American Life,* Journal of the American Academy of Arts and Sciences, Daedalus, Spring, 1961, pp. 233–46.

Bronfenbrenner, in a study of the American child, observes that children coming from achievement-oriented families excel in planfulness and performance, but that they are also more aggressive, tense, domineering, and cruel. He speculates that education for excellence may entail some sobering social costs (Bronfenbrenner, 1961). Else Frenkel-Brunswik reported an exploration of patterns of social, motivational, and cognitive factors in children that contribute to ethnocentricity as contrasted to those that develop the liberal child. After describing some of the contributing conditions in child-rearing, she concluded that "deliberately planned democratic participation in school and family, individualized approach to the child, and the right proportion of permissiveness and guidance, may be instrumental in bringing about the attitude necessary for a genuine identification with society and thus for international understanding." [4]

Certainly such evidence suggests that children will also bring prejudice and stereotyped thinking to the studies of people of other cultures. What educational experiences help children to step out of their own "culture shells" and see situations through the eyes of those with other cultural perceptions?

Many cross-currents are at work, both nationally and internationally, in these rapidly changing cultural situations. On the one hand, there are trends toward conformity in huge organizational structures; on the other hand, there is a breakdown of traditional ways in subcultures (for example, rural folk) and in societies (for example, Japan) as they move suddenly into industrial patterns of life. In addition, a new world outlook is developing—an outlook based on the concept that all peoples, of all races and groups, can participate in a good life based on the benefits of science and technology.

In past historical periods, social change evolved relatively slowly; and cultures adjusted, modifying their institutions and developing new perspectives over a long period of time. At times there was active resistance to change—for example, the disorders attendant on the Industrial Revolution in Europe—and frequently change was wrought by violent means. Today not only are changes occurring rapidly, not only are changes drastically out of key with "old ways" but they must take place under the cloud of possible nuclear war.

There was a time when war was deliberately used as an instrument of change, but that time has passed; today we dare not try to solve our problems by using war as a political tool (Jackson, 1959). Nor can we permit other nations, emerging from tribalism to nationalism, to solve

---

[4] Else Frenkel-Brunswik, "A Study of Prejudice in Children," *Human Relations* I, No. 3 (1948), 295–306.

their problems and unify themselves through war. We are confronted with the survival problem of helping one another, both at home and abroad, because no man or nation stands alone in the scientific age.

We are charged with the moral challenge of creating a humane world community in which all human beings can realize themselves. The anthropologist, Rhoda Metreaux, poses for us the challenge of whether we can "consciously, recognizing that cultures are man-made, take the responsibility of directing our social evolution." [5]

For educators who accept responsibility for participating in this evolution, many tasks exist. They must help to guide the development of young people into individuals of integrity who can face and tolerate the demands of a continually changing society, who can cope with emerging problems creatively and empathically, and who can commit themselves to responsible group behavior.

[5] Rhoda Metreaux, *New Insights and the Curriculum*, ASCD, Yearbook, 1963, p. 209.

3

EDUCATION FOR CITIZENSHIP: A MAJOR SOCIAL STUDIES EMPHASIS

EDUCATIONAL IMPLICATIONS

Education for the development of individual integrity and responsible group behavior is not a simple task, nor is it solely the school's responsibility. Certainly it begins in the early child-rearing practices in the home and is imbedded in family culture and neighborhood life.

The trends away from integrity and responsibility in urban life in an affluent technological society are strong; [1] in fact, so strong that it may seem mere sentimental idealism to propose a countervailing effort. Yet thoughtful social scientists propose that we must develop a definite program both for the preservation and enhancement of individual integrity and for the delineation of and commitment to responsible group behavior.

What does this commitment imply in the way of tasks?

The social conditions indicated in the previous chapter and the knowledge we now have of the dynamics of human behavior imply a number of major emphases.

THE "OPEN PERSON"

We must try to guide the experiences of children and youth so that, as a result of the inner security that comes of successfully meeting their

---

[1] John Steinbeck's novel, *The Winter of Our Discontent*, presents a dramatic picture of the self-seeking pressures in society today.

developmental tasks, they are "open" to new experiences—so that they can relinquish learned ways of behavior that are no longer appropriate, can tolerate the ambiguity of changing situations, can be challenged by the unknown and unresolved in the situations which confront them.

INNER-DIRECTEDNESS

As a child faces the many situations in his life that demand action and choice, he needs to be helped to become conscious of the values that guide his behavior, and *to learn to criticize those values in terms of their consequences to himself and other people.* Inherent in this process, if it is to be more than *self-centered,* is the development of a sensitivity to the feelings and welfare of others. An individual who clarifies for himself his values and beliefs is less likely to be swayed by others, or to be the victim of "unconscious" values (Taba, 1963).

The young child entering school builds a self-concept based on his past experiences and his evolving relations with others in his immediate life-space. If the adults in his early life have helped him to negotiate each crucial transition successfully, he builds a self confidence that enhances his growing ego. He feels adequate and competent; he is able, he can do things! If his experiences with parents, teachers, and friends have been positive and supportive, his self-concept is strengthened; he gains an inner security that enables him both to "be for himself" and to relate well to others.

It is out of healthy self-concept development and the gradual clarification of values that the quality of inner-directedness emerges: the individual's ability to act, despite outside pressures, in the light of ideas he respects.

A PROBLEM-SOLVING ORIENTATION

Highly related to an "openness" to new experience is the development of a problem-solving orientation. Ideally, not only should one be "open" to the new, but one should also acquire attitudes and specific skills for tackling problem situations. A "problem" has been defined as a situation in which old responses cannot be applied routinely, in which new elements demand definition, rethinking, and often call for creative responses.

ROLE-BEHAVIOR

Children and youth need guidance in learning appropriate behavior in a great variety of social and work situations. Never before in our history have families moved so often. Mobility is a reality of contemporary life. Never before have so many of us encountered such a broad range of social and work demands as we move from one community to another, as we improve in our jobs and professions or learn new work skills and take on heavier responsibilities. As our society has become more affluent for the majority, more and more of us have been required to take on new roles: as workers, as parents, as P.T.A. members, as residents of new communities, as members of civic committees, and so on. For an increasing number of us, as job requirements change swiftly because of automation and industrial rationalization, more and more of us become students and trainees again, or teachers and supervisors. Competence in a wide variety of roles requires flexibility, and flexibility in adapting to new roles is related both to "openness" and to the opportunity of practicing a wide range of different roles.

Young people who have the chance to *practice* many roles, to face the demands of new situations under conditions that do not penalize but maximize learning, will be better prepared for the demands of change in later life. Role-playing can provide such practice.

CROSS-CULTURAL PERCEPTIONS

Perhaps one of the most crucial needs of our time is keen sensitivity to the feelings and perceptions of others. The ability to place oneself in another's shoes and to sense how he sees the world and how he feels is a preliminary condition to the ability to move out of one's own "culture shell" and view events from the cultural outlook of someone raised in a subculture or national culture other than one's own.

As children explore open-ended situations and specific roles, they tend to respond to them in terms of their own cultural experiences. Thus a child playing a mother role in a story will usually behave in ways that reveal the values and role definition of her own family group. Occasionally, not often, children demonstrate a knowledge of other subcultural definitions of such roles. Usually, however, children express their own cultural experiences.

The realization that each one of us defines what is real and good in terms of our individual cultural perceptions is basic to real communication across cultures. It is only as we understand the other person's (or nation's) perceptions and assumptions, that we are in a position to come to mutually acceptable solutions of problems. Such an understanding does not necessarily imply abdication of one's own cultural values; it means, rather, that one gets into the other's frame of reference in order to think with him. It makes possible real communication about differences.

Out of a variety of experiences in discovering how individuals of different cultural backgrounds honestly think and feel, young people can be helped to realize that there are many different—and even acceptable—cultural solutions to common human problems.

It may be that only if we develop this empathic kind of cross-cultural communication, based on "I can see how you view this," may we then eventually evolve some generalized ideals that rise above cultural differences and enable us to create a genuinely humane world community.

The emphases outlined above are not accomplished through some one line of attack or a few specific media. They are actually fundamental orientations to learning and action that demand a comprehensive program, as well as specific skills and materials. Above all else, they require teachers who are committed to the values and insights underlying such conceptions as "openness" and "problem-solving" and "respect and concern for others" and "cross-cultural perceptions."

DEVELOPMENTAL CONSIDERATIONS

Every child learns his way into the culture into which he is born. In the process he builds a picture of himself, a self-concept that, to a great extent, is a product of how others react to his efforts to meet his needs. Teachers play crucial roles in this process; and teachers, knowing that the way in which the child comes to terms with the many developmental tasks he must accomplish goes far to determine whether he becomes a cooperating member of society or a hostile individual, can do much to help shape the kind of person he eventually becomes.

THE PEER CULTURE

The groups of which a young person is a member exert a tremendous influence on him. They are central in shaping his self-concept; they influence his motivation and values; they even assign him roles.

The group may decide that Johnny is "funny," a clown; that Elizabeth is a " 'fraidy-cat," or that Tim is the willing dupe onto whom the tedious jobs can be dumped. Often a group will glorify a popular leader and choose him over and over again for leadership roles even though he is not qualified by skill or merit for the positions allotted him. Ronald Lippitt and his associates have found that once a child has acquired a certain reputation within the group, the introduction of new data that should change their view of him is resisted (Lippitt and Gold, 1963). It is difficult for a young person to change the roles and esteem (or lack of it) that he acquires early in his relationships with a group; difficult, but not impossible.

Children are keenly aware of the power of the various groups in their life-space. They know who is influential and work very hard at winning their way into certain groups and maintaining a status in a group or clique. Individuals may even accept rather ignominious roles, such as that of the scapegoat, the butt of jokes, just to be "in" with an admired group. And, having won their way into a favored group, young people who are especially anxious and insecure will conform doggedly to the group code, even at times when such conformity means violating parental regulations. Some children, having achieved a comfortable place in a group, may lose their individuality. Other children, it is true, reject groups; rather than submit to group requirements, they become hostile and withdrawn.

A few children do not need groups. They are content with close affiliation with a single friend, or, being blessed with consuming interests, they prefer to go off on their own explorations.

In American culture, where adult social life is usually separate from that of children, the child culture becomes even more potent in young people's lives than in those cultures where large kinship families include children in adult activities. As a result, for most children, the values and codes of the peer culture tend to dominate their outlook and shape their actions. This results in the immature leading the immature! This condition is revealed in the sometimes dangerous and often cruel demands made by the group on its individual members.

A great need exists for constructive guidance of groups. *They need to be helped to an awareness of the consequences of their codes, their exclusion devices, their demands for blind conformity, their intolerance of deviant behavior.* James Coleman, in his study of social climates of high school groups, views with deep alarm the destructive aspects of peer groups in our culture (Coleman, 1961).

Just as the individual needs to be helped to sensitivity and concern for others, the group needs to be guided to concern for the individual. Ronald Lippitt speaks of the "cohesive group" as that group in which the individuals like one another and will support variability among its members. Such groups are sensitive to the ways in which their actions may affect others. When people work, live, or play together, there are times when team-work is necessary, and other times when divergence of opinion makes the difference between wisdom and folly. (When a popular leader suggests a rash or inconsiderate act, the member of the group with sounder judgment must feel secure enough to suggest cautioning second thoughts with force and confidence; when the imaginative member of the group suggests a plan involving effort and departure from cherished group plans, the group must feel that he deserves a hearing, however impractical his suggestions may seem at first glance.)

Such group attitudes must be systematically cultivated; we cannot depend upon their spontaneous emergence.

Studies in group climates (the emotional stress and harmony between the individuals who make up a group) suggest that educators need to plan specific experiences for the promotion of the kind of group climate in which the members respect and like and support one another (Jennings, 1950; Ralph K. White and Lippitt, 1960). Children need to be helped to explore the ways in which they resolve their group problems. They need help in becoming sensitive to how their decisions affect both their members and people outside their groups. They need to be encouraged to lend support to individuals who differ from the majority. Essentially, this is good citizenship; this is the Golden Rule in action; this is respect for the individual.

This is a goal that role-playing procedures are uniquely productive in helping to achieve.

VALUES

One of the great sources of stress and confusion in modern society is the fact that people act upon the basis of unconsciously held values. As a result, we are often the victims of our impulses, of our fears, and of external persuasions. We need to make our values conscious so as to be aware of what values we act upon (Taba, 1963). Once they are out in the open, they can be looked at, considered, compared with alternative values. Only then can one criticize, evaluate, deny or confirm and reconstruct one's value system.

Children can be helped to face up to the decisions they make, analyze why they made them, and develop an explicit set of values. In group discussions, in role-playing enactments, in individual writing, they can explore their values and learn the process of criticizing and reconstructing them in the light of tested experience. It is within such a process, under skillful guidance, that young people can develop a sense of responsibility for others as well as develop a core of values that becomes the basis for personal integrity.

TASKS

To use role-playing most effectively for teaching social studies, one must be aware of the purposes for which role-playing is especially helpful. Some of these purposes are described in the following sections.

TO HELP CHILDREN UNDERSTAND THAT BEHAVIOR IS CAUSED

When young people explore in action the consequences of choices they have made, they can more easily see causal relationships. In the discussions that follow enactments of alternative proposals for solving a problem there is opportunity, under guidance, for a classroom group to explore such questions as: "Why did they behave that way?" or "Why do mothers (or teachers) feel this way?" In such analyses, children can be helped to see the relationships in a group problem and to become increasingly sensitive to why individuals respond the way they do. Young people are in this way helped to move from a surface approach to explaining behavior to an approach that takes into account the basic, less obvious, dynamics of human behavior (Ojeman, 1963; Fox, Lippitt, and Lohman, 1964).

Children can be helped to see that (1) behavior is caused, (2) it occurs in a setting, (3) there are usually multiple causes for behavior, (4) behavior is usually not wholly "good" or wholly "bad" but just the best that the individual can manage at the time. (The consequences may be "good" or "bad"—for individuals, for society—but childish behavior needs to be viewed as efforts to be adequate in meeting the demands of circumstances.)

TO DEVELOP SENSITIVITY TO THE FEELINGS OF OTHERS

The egocentric young child is intensely involved with his own feelings. Gradually, as he interacts with others, he begins to relate to them. It is as he senses how they feel that he is enabled to step out of his own shoes into theirs, and to begin to feel with others. This capacity to imagine how another person feels—to "get inside his skin and move around"— needs to be nurtured. In role-playing, one is enabled not only to act out one's own feelings in difficult situations, but also to take on other roles and to feel how it is to be in someone else's shoes. The leader of a role-playing session often asks a player to switch roles so that he can experience the other person's reactions. This sensitivity to the feelings of others is the basis for the eventual development of concern for others and for responsible personal and group behavior.[2]

TO RELEASE TENSIONS AND FEELINGS

Teachers are not therapists, and most are not sophisticated in the clinical aspects of catharsis. They can, however, help children to find some release of tensions and outlets for feelings, even if only to provide a quarter-hour for folk dancing on a rainy afternoon. Children experience many frustrations in the process of socialization. One aspect of growing up is learning to deny some immediate, personal urges because the culture does not permit their expression or demands other forms of behavior.

[2] Roy Price, *Needed Research in the Social Studies*, National Council for the Social Studies, 1964, p. 30.

Young people need an opportunity to release the tensions built up by such restrictions.

It is a great relief to act out your feelings about younger brothers (whom, you are continually told, you must love—not beat) and to find out that others experience the same feelings. It is "safe" to role-play an angry or bitter response, and then go on to explore other, more socially acceptable solutions. How much better to siphon off the anger in role-playing than to have it find expression in making a scapegoat of some vulnerable child on the playground!

TO DIAGNOSE THE NEEDS OF CHILDREN

There is a growing body of procedures, in addition to conventional test materials, that help us to diagnose human relations needs (Taba, 1951). Role-playing is a potent member of this group of procedures; or rather, it is an especially fruitful and revelatory cluster of mutually energizing procedures.

As children portray roles and react to the enactments of others in discussion, they tell us much about themselves. One child always chooses to play dominant roles, another displays an obsessive awareness of antisocial solutions to human difficulties, and still another is invariably punitive when he enacts adult roles; still others similarly betray strong trends of impulse within themselves. As always, in speculating about human behavior, to jump to conclusions is risky; and yet, in evaluating the preponderant way in which an individual tends to solve problems, it can make good sense to consider that possible symptoms are being shown. Such symptoms can be followed up with further study through the use of other diagnostic procedures. And, when serious difficulties are suspected, the help of guidance personnel and clinical psychologists can be enlisted.

TO IMPROVE THE CHILD'S SELF-CONCEPT

Every child must, of necessity, learn his way into the culture in which he is born. In the process he builds a picture of himself, of who he is and what he is good for: he develops a self-concept. This image of himself is to a great extent a product of how people—adults and children —react to his efforts to meet his needs in the cultural environment. True, the self-concept is also a product of his innate abilities; but it is the environment that permits or blocks his efforts to realize those capacities. If he has the good fortune to experience much loving support from the adults who surround him in infancy and early childhood, he explores the world with confidence and eagerness. If he is helped to be successful in negotiating the cultural learnings required of him at each stage of his development, he builds a strong ego and has faith in his ability to face and cope with new tasks. In this process, his age-mates play a powerful role. If they accept him as a person and support his efforts at learning, whether on the playgrounds, in the streets, or in the classroom, they reinforce his perceptions of himself as an adequate person. As a result, he likes himself; and this self-esteem in turn frees him from preoccupation with self and enables him more easily to relate to others. Such a child can afford to be "open" to new experiences; he is not threatened by his environment.

Teachers have a key role to play in this process. They must be sensitive to the crucial transition points in the growth sequence of each child, and provide the necessary support as a child faces and comes to terms with new demands in the environment (L. K. Frank, p. 16). They must so arrange the teaching-learning situation that children can be successful and, savoring the mastery that comes with honestly earned success, be eager for more learning. In addition, teachers need to be highly alert to the inter-personal relations among children and plan situations which will teach children in their group life—on the playground, in the classroom, in their out-of-school group—to support each other positively. An increasing number of studies find that a child's success in school work, as well as his success as a social person, reflects the state of his self-concept (Sears and Sherman, 1964; Lippitt and Gold, 1959).

The growing child faces and comes to terms with many developmental tasks that are a product of his biological needs and the cultural demands of his environment. Coping with these tasks, he becomes a member of society. This can be a positive membership or a negative one. Because of loving help and adult and peer acceptance, he may become a "character-conditioned" friendly person, or—lacking such health-giving experiences—he can become a hostile person, one who never develops "trust" but always expects the worst from others (Erikson, 1950).

These socializing experiences shape his attitudes toward authority. Being sure of his own worth, successful in his efforts to learn his way into the culture, he can accept authority, he can accept guidance by adults, he can accept necessary restrictions; if hostile, however, he begins to view authority as something to be circumvented.

Such attitudes exert powerful influence in his relationships within groups.

If he is insecure, unsure of who he is, his anxiety may lead him to curry favor, to please the powerful children in groups he encounters. He becomes a conformist who is "other-directed," following the crowd or submitting to the powerful and influential. In the more exceptional cases, he will become a rebel. If he is developing into a hostile personality, his conditioning may take the form of defiance that eventually leads to delinquency. If he has a strong, healthy self-concept, some forms of rebellion may reflect a kind of independence and integrity that enable him to go against the group when necessary.

The child with a healthy self-concept can become Riesman's "inner-directed man." He can conform appropriately—that is, order his behavior to meet the demands and sanctions of his cultural group when he wishes to do so; but he has built an inner core of personal values that enables him to stand for his beliefs, even against the pressure of the group, if necessary, because he is secure in his ego-strength and can be himself.

A CHILD'S SELF-CONCEPT CAN BE IMPROVED

As we have noted, a child sees himself to a large extent through the reflected perceptions of the people around him, especially his peers. In some cases, age-mates provide strong support for a child; in many cases, peer groups arbitrarily assign demeaning and belittling roles to an individual. As a result, some youngsters—because they are labeled weak or timid or stupid or uncooperative—never have a chance to exhibit their actual capabilities to their peers.

Role-playing, used in a planned sequence, can do much to help change such an individual's underappreciated status in his group. The teacher can give such an individual opportunities to play roles quite different from the ones assigned him by his peers: roles in which an undervalued child can demonstrate a wider range of skills and perceptions and qualities than the group ever permitted him to exhibit. In this process, not only is the individual's status among his age-mates changed but, if he receives recognition and status from the group, his self-concept also is altered for the better. We have some initial, empirical evidence to support the belief that the teacher, by carefully selecting roles for an underappreciated individual to play, over the period of a planned sequence of role-playing sessions, can do much to help him win respect and sometimes even admiration from the classroom group; and, thereby, to help him acquire a higher degree of self-respect and confidence.

A frequent concomitant is an improvement in classwork (Sears, 1963). The more serene child usually works more effectively: Pauline Sears has commented that the strong interpersonal influence of the *opinions* of teachers and peers on the learning of the *less able* children gives food for thought. She observes that these children are the ones who are least likely to find inherent satisfactions in their schooling, and the ones who will provide a large proportion of the dropout group in high school. If it is true, as these results indicate, that their own self-esteem is associated significantly with the warmth with which they are regarded by the teacher and classmates, then opportunities for maximizing these personal relations should be provided.[3]

Another important consideration is the fact that as the individual is helped, the *group* is being helped to develop appreciation for individual differences in talents, in ordinary abilities, in ways of perceiving problems and interpreting data. Here again, we can encourage independent thinking and, along with it, respect for the "odd-ball" ideas that may be the creative aspects of problem-solving in emergent situations.

In addition, individuals and groups can be helped, through the use of problem stories, to explore their own feelings about themselves—to face up to and accept their limitations, to explore their strengths, to accept the reality that we all have strengths and lacks. In some of the materials in this volume (see the "Inside, Looking Out" stories) we have tried to provide opportunity for young people to face situations in which, because of poor self-concept, they tend to "over-read" others' responses and, in their anxiety, accept defeat or anticipate failure unnecessarily.

TO EXPLORE ROLES

Each child, in the process of growing up, learns many roles and discovers as he tries out various behaviors what is permitted and sanctioned by the culture and, especially, the subculture in which he lives. He is a son, perhaps an eldest son (with responsibility for younger siblings), a grandson, a brother, a pupil in school, a member of a gang on the playground, the captain of his baseball team at school, a newspaper delivery boy (with customers he must please and a boss to whom he must account) —and so on; and in each of these roles he is expected to behave in certain accepted ways, to live up to culturally sanctioned demands. In certain subcultures, for example, the eldest son is expected to start to work at an early age and to give his earnings to his parents; in other subcultures, he is expected to finish high school, go to college, and then to professional school, while his parents expect to support him all the way. The culture rewards him (or her) when he behaves in socially acceptable ways and punishes him for antisocial behavior.

As our lives become more complex and varied, the range of roles we take becomes wider. In addition, as life circumstances change, we are often required to take on new roles.

The city child, when his father starts earning more money and moves the family to a suburb, has to win his way into new groups, often in new

---

[3] Pauline Snedden Sears, *The Effect of Classroom Conditions on the Strength of Achievement Motive and Work Output of Elementary School Children.* From a report on Cooperative Research Project #OE 873, Stanford University.

subcultures. Not only does he have to learn the role behavior that is acceptable in this new subculture, he may also be assigned different roles in the new peer groups than those he held in his city play groups (Lippitt and Gold, 1959). Thus Tom, who was leader of his gang on the big city street by virtue of being a good fighter, may discover that if he wishes to be respected or a leader in the suburb he must be skilled in kickball. He may even have to struggle against the reputation he had acquired as a fighter and attempt to win the admiration of a group who value "interesting things to do."

Children need opportunity to practice the many roles which they must assume in the process of growing up. They also need help in exploring and defining appropriate role behavior for different situations. Frequently a child experiences rejection or failure in social situations simply because he is not able to differentiate between the role behavior expectations of several quite different situations. Off-color language and stories, while forgivable in one situation, are out of place in other situations; hilarious behavior, too, can be overlooked in one circumstance but frowned upon in another. Lack of social graces, similarly, can be ignored in some settings but is a glaring deficiency in others.

Groups also need help in order to become supportive of individuals as they seek new roles. Too often the group quickly assigns a reputation to a child and blocks his efforts to try new roles (Lippitt and Gold, 1959).

In role-playing, young people can be confronted with a number of situations in which to practice roles.

Moreover, an individual can be provided with opportunity to practice roles he would *like* to acquire, such as being the leader in a group, the expert who teaches others a skill. Furthermore, he can have the benefit of seeing numerous responses to the role as different members of the class demonstrate their ideas of how such roles are performed. The boy who is going to be master-of-ceremonies for a Boy Scout program, the girl who is going to teach clay modeling or folk dancing to small children in summer camp, can benefit from practicing the job ahead of time. Pupils who are going to be guides and ushers for a Parents Night, similarly, can be helped by practice in meeting problems that might arise.

TO EXPLORE THE CORE VALUES OF AMERICAN CULTURE

A young person growing up in a culture must, of course, learn the ways of that culture. He learns what is sanctioned and acceptable by imitation, by trial and error, and by instruction.

In American life, which is multicultured, the task is most complex. He learns some behaviors which are generalized as "American"; and he learns subcultural behavior, which may be ethnic (Italian, for example), regional (e.g., "Southern"), local ("our town"), or family (the Browns).

The teacher serves as a mediator between the child and the culture or cultures in which he is growing up. In this role, teachers help children to learn what is both negatively and positively sanctioned and, thereby, to acquire the core values of his culture. The teacher can also help the group (class) to accept the idea of subcultural differences and to value such differences as a positive quality in American life (Gordon, 1961).

In our technological society today, in which we are confronted with contradictions and ambiguities of a rapidly changing way of life as well as a strong heritage of American ideals of democracy, the task is indeed difficult (Henry, 1963; see also Goodman, 1960). Nevertheless, the task has an urgency that transcends the cost in effort; for, if we can help the young to know consciously the core values of our culture (including the contradictions) and to face the future aware of the moral choices available to them, then and only then can we create the humane community in an age of technology.

TO LEARN MORE ABOUT THE FUNCTIONING OF THE VARIOUS SUBCULTURES IN WHICH DIFFERENT CHILDREN LIVE

As children explore open-ended situations and specific roles, they tend to respond to them in terms of their own cultural experiences. Thus a child playing the mother-role in a story will behave usually in ways that reveal the values and role definition of her own family group. Occasionally, it is true, children do demonstrate a knowledge of other subcultural definitions of such roles, but usually children express their own cultural experiences.

Teachers tend to see children primarily in school situations. They seldom see the child as he faces and responds to the dilemmas of his life outside of school. Role-playing can bring outside situations into the classroom; and, as children enact their proposed solutions to problems, teachers can acquire much wider perspectives on the difficulties, perceptions, and values that shape the behavior of their students in their out-of-school life (Pettigrew, 1964; Landes, 1965).

TO HELP EACH CHILD CLARIFY HIS OWN FRAME OF VALUES FOR DECISION-MAKING

As children participate in role-playing sessions, each one has an opportunity to propose, through his role-playing and in the discussions that follow enactments, his own ways of solving human relations problems. Often his proposals are spontaneous and based on unconsciously held values. In the discussions following an enactment, and in the demonstration of next steps (or consequences) that may occur in further enactments, the teacher-leader, *with the help of the child's reacting peers*, may guide him to consciously face his choices. In this way he is helped to become aware of his values and, in a positive group climate, he can explore the effects of various choices upon himself and others.

Thus, for example, the urge to "get even" is strong in children (and in adults, too, all too often!) and usually not very discriminating.[4] Just suspecting that another boy has stolen a favorite jackknife or top or tool may induce a boy to steal something back from his suspected despoiler. The group may point out that (1) he has no positive evidence, only suspicion, (2) what he has stolen in retaliation may be worth far more than the article he has lost, and ask him if (3) there isn't a better way than retaliation to handle the problem and, (4) he is sure, positively sure, that his cherished possession is really stolen and not simply misplaced. How well has he actually searched for it? In other words, how fair is he being in judging and condemning his fancied foe? Is there no benefit of a doubt to consider? Has he really suspended judgment until all the facts are in? Has he let the fact that the other boy lives in a "bad" neighborhood, or speaks English poorly, or has a different color of skin influence his judgment? Knowing his dislike, shouldn't the accusing boy actually bend over backward in trying to be completely fair? All these facets of the problem may be pointed out by the boy's own peers; and, coming from them, they have unusual weight and persuasive power.

A further complicating factor, in a society of multiple values, is the contradiction in behavior that young people observe. To study the Bill of Rights and then discover the facts of segregation in any of its various applications, for example, creates bewilderment in logical young minds. Role-playing such conflicts in values can at least make the values visible. While we do not always find immediate solutions for such conflicts, the very fact that we are aware of our dilemmas often forces us to analyze and evaluate our choices. Such experiences may make possible future resolutions of value conflicts.

This process of delineating the many values and value conflicts confronting us also makes possible discussion and follow-up experiences in which young people can be guided to an alert awareness of humane considerations in problem situations. Expedient solutions can be weighed for their values: immediate personal gain can be set against possible long-range consequences to other people and even eventual emotional reactions of the actor himself. He can lie out of the fix he's in, Tommy reasons; he can say that Pete released the emergency brake when the two of them were playing in his father's car. But suppose Pete's father then has to pay

---

4 See "Money for Marty," page 288.

for the damage incurred when the car rolled down hill and hit a tree? Pete's father works as a gardener; paying for the damages would be a heavy burden on him. He has been kind to Tommy; he has often taken Tommy and Pete fishing when Tommy's own busy father couldn't find time. Tommy knows he'll feel like a traitor and an ingrate if he plays this dirty trick on Pete. But then Tommy thinks of his own father's stern wrath when he sees the damaged car, and Tommy gets a sick ache in his stomach. "Tommy, I've warned you time and again not to play in the car when it's parked on this hill!" He could escape this wrath, Tommy knows; a lie would work. Pete is so good-natured that, when accused, he'd just mumble that he didn't know whether he had released the car brake or not. *But I'd know,* Tommy realizes; *I'd know all right!*

But even this experience is not enough. In our world of rapid and often qualitatively different change, we need to re-evaluate our frame of reference continually; we need to develop procedures and attitudes that enable us to *reconstruct* our values on the basis of intelligent analysis.

Again, such reconstruction depends upon an openness to new conditions, a willingness to change, and a deep awareness of relationships. One of our problems today is the tendency to generalize for others our own personal and cultural values. This tendency needs the modification that results from a continual exploration of the many choices possible and of the reasons why people often make choices different from our own. (Some people will not eat meat on Friday, and others will not eat meat on any day. Some people will not call a doctor when ill. Some people will go to a baseball game on Sunday but not on Saturday. Some people take off their hats in church whereas others put them on. Some people will loyally die for their country if need be but will not fire a gun in anger against a foe. Some people let their parents choose their wives. Some people are proud of owning a big new car; among some Indian tribes, it is a disgrace to seem to brag or try to be better than one's friends. Cultures differ.)

Reconstruction of values can aid the individual to acquire the kind of maturity that enables him to hold general values and yet respect and protect other people's right to hold personal and private values so long as they do not work injury upon others.

Role-playing can rank high among procedures useful for value exploration.

TO IMPROVE THE SOCIAL STRUCTURE AND VALUE SYSTEMS
OF THE PEER CULTURE

One of the most important uses of role-playing rests in the opportunity it provides to help the group or class to develop healthy group structure. Since peer groups wield so much influence on the individual in childhood and adolescence, and immature but socially powerful children can and often do set the standards, we need to work with child groups in ways that help them to (1) become sensitive to the needs and feelings of individual children, (2) become aware of how a group can function positively to support an individual or negatively to deny him opportunities for self-realization, (3) grow critical of immature standards for selecting leaders, and (4) be appreciative and supportive of individual differences among their members.

As children become members of various groups they need to be helped to understand the interactions, or dynamics, of group behavior. If they explore problem-story situations in which the popular boy (a good athlete) is always elected to leadership roles, even when not qualified for them, or if the children face situations in which a powerful child wields autocratic leadership, *they can discuss such problems in the safety of a situation that is not actually their own.* They can thus afford to face the situation realistically and (a point which merits re-emphasis) *with the support of their peers,* begin to delineate what is good or destructive about certain kinds of group enactments of what happens in group behavior. Teachers can help children to analyze what happens to children's feelings about themselves (self-concepts) when they are excluded or ridiculed, what happens to the quality of experience when good ideas are ignored just because they have been expressed by certain children, and so on.

Eventually, in classes that are experiencing a planned sequence of problem-stories about group behavior, the time comes when children can draw up their own codes of constructive group conduct. With adolescents who are more advanced in their abilities to generalize, it is possible to follow up their new insights with specific content on small group behavior and effective group organization.

Teachers who use sociometric techniques to diagnose the social climate and structure of a class can use sequences of problem-stories and role-playing as a potent tool for the modification of relationships within the peer groups (Taba, 1951). When a group tends to exclude and deprive some children, for example, role-playing a series of problem-stories on the themes of *how it feels to be left out* or *how it feels to be different* can sensitize groups to the effects of their behavior on its victims. Or, a group that is blindly following the leadership of a boy simply because he is a good athlete may be helped through the discussion following a problem-story such as "The Squawk-Box."

Gradually, as a sequel to such role-playing sessions, groups can be led to analyze their own behavior. Are the talkative, assertive members of the class, by monopolizing discussion, preventing more timid youngsters from having a full say? Are cliques fighting each other, criticizing each other, and behaving so hostilely that they are disrupting class work? Are some quiet members of the class being excluded from activities because they are new, or of different race or religion? Is some youngster, because he limps or is extremely tall and thin—or short and plump—the butt of jokes? Such analysis can help groups to compare their ways of choosing leaders, selecting organizing committees, responding to others' ideas, and so on, to what is known about healthy group behavior. We have seen classroom groups—after undergoing such self-examination—become kinder, more inclusive, and even devotedly protective of individuals' rights.

The *cohesive group* is one in which the individual members like one another and will support variability (differences) among its members. Obviously, such classroom groups are a product of many factors: individual differences, past experiences, the social structure of the neighborhood subcultures, and general school and classroom policies. A teacher who is working to produce such cohesiveness in his classroom must work with all these factors.

Role-playing can be a useful tool for this task. By using a careful selection of problem stories, respect for individual differences can be cultivated in the group. How it feels to be different can be explored. Ways of helping the child who is different to win acceptance and inner security can be explored; ways of *using* individual differences, too, can be discussed and enacted. The boy from another country who dresses oddly and uses queer turns of speech, for example, can be helped to learn English. His knowledge of life in other lands can be utilized by the teacher to win respect for him instead of derision.

One of the major problems of developing cohesiveness is that of helping young children to move out of the narrow friendship cliques that are a phase of "learning to be and have friends" to a more inclusive awareness that some friendship behaviors ignore the feelings and needs of others in one's immediate environment; forming cliques, for example. Exclusive factions cause nonmembers to feel rejected. Exploring, through role-playing, how it feels to be left out would be one approach to counteracting cliques. Another would be to explore the conflict of loyalties to a friend (who may be unpopular) and to the wider group (which rejects that friend). It is in the struggle to reconcile one's need to have a personal friend, to belong to a small group, and at the same time to be a member of inclusive groups (the class, for example) that we can extend childhood sensitivities to the feelings and needs of others.

TO LEARN SOCIAL BEHAVIOR WITH THE SUPPORT OF A COHESIVE GROUP

Children will often learn through the *support* or *opposition* of their age-mates in areas where they reject help from adults. This is especially true in American life in which the peer culture of childhood wields such influence over the years of middle childhood and early adolescence.

When teachers have helped groups to develop a supportive climate in which they will help one another to overcome difficulties, role-playing becomes an excellent tool for the exploration of antisocial attitudes and responses to situations. Thus, when Johnny role-plays his tendency to try to "get the better of another person" his classmates, in the discussion following his enactment, and in the counterenactments they offer, may confront him with how his actions affect other people's feelings and circumstances and may propose other solutions that are more socially constructive. Cheating another person, allowing him to be blamed for something he did not do, letting a lie about him go unchallenged—such behaviors may have a trail of consequences far more destructive than the perpetrator may, in the sudden flush of angry impulse, foresee.

Admonition from adults is often not accepted by the hostile child; but when criticism comes in the nonjudgmental processes of role-playing as *observations of their own experiences by his peers*, it can be exceedingly effective.

TO TEACH PROBLEM-SOLVING BEHAVIOR

In our scientific and technological society, one thing is certain: there will be continual change. The chain reaction that sets in with new inventions creates for all people the necessity to confront, adapt to, or resolve problems for which they may have little or no precedent in past experience. We live in a world society in which problem solving is a necessity.

But culturally we have learned to act on the basis of past experience. There is a strong tendency in both individuals and cultures to hold on to old ways, to tried-and-tested solutions. We even attempt to define new situations in terms of what is familiar in our established culture. There is great danger in continuing this behavior today. It is true that we maintain stability in groups by conserving tested and established ways of behaving. But it is equally true, today, that we must learn to recognize developments that are of such new dimensions that they call for the creation of new solutions. Modern man must learn to be an intelligent and skillful problem-solver.

This calls for a very different orientation than we have emphasized in schools. Instead of setting up learning tasks that mainly call for known solutions and rote learning, we must set up an attitude of search, of hypothesizing (the "educated guess"), of speculating, of divergent thinking, in which the individual wanders down intellectual bypaths, *inventing* new approaches to problems.

Problem solving requires the ability to face a new situation, to define the problem in specific terms, and to assess the possibilities of solution. Problem solving demands the capacity to slough off old responses that are no longer appropriate and to create and test new responses. Problem solving, of necessity, involves the ability to tolerate ambiguity and to develop patience for trial-and-error searching. Problem solving requires the intellectual tenacity to follow through the possible alternatives of an hypothesis, to make choices based upon intelligent exploration of consequences. Such attitudes and skills can be learned by guided practice in meaningful problem situations.

In essence, this view of problem solving conceives of it as a discovery process, a search—one that often requires creative thinking and the eventual synthesis of many ideas. Such a procedure does not flourish in a school environment that emphasizes only the "right" answer and that is based on the intellectual authority of the teacher. It requires an atmosphere in which it is safe to speculate, to *guess*, to test out ideas, even at times to be *wrong*. It is a search in which all notions are respected for try-out, then critically evaluated for their consequences. Problem-solvers need a zest for exploration; they need to learn to really listen to each other's ideas before accepting or challenging counterproposals.

Children who have experienced only preplanned learning situations with predetermined outcomes do not develop this zest for exploration, nor do they usually acquire extensive problem-solving skills. Such skills are not learned through routine lessons in problem solving but *must be learned in problem situations that have meaning and importance to the young people involved.* Only then, as they face problems they sincerely *want* to solve, can teachers help them, gradually, to acquire the specific skills of the process.

Problem solving is both an orientation and a set of skills to be learned. The child in the classroom today needs much experience in facing situations that call for exploration, definition, invention, and synthesis of information and creative proposals.

There is at present a growing concern with developing new strategies for teaching and learning. Teachers of science, mathematics, and social studies are emphasizing problem solving and "discovery learning" in which the student is enabled to gather his own data, *put it together in his own way, and draw his own conclusions and build his own generalizations.* Researchers who have concerned themselves with creativity also emphasize the need for individual exploration and programming of ideas.

In working with interpersonal and intergroup behavior, we are confronted with the most difficult kinds of problem solving.

Individuals and groups face human situations that are much more elusive than the controlled experiments of the scientist because they involve *people in action*, human beings interacting with each other in emotion-laden difficulties. Problem solving in social situations is always variable, dynamic, complex. It is transactional in nature.

TO TEACH PROBLEM SOLVING AT THE ACTION LEVEL

One reason why human relations problems are more difficult to solve than problems dealing primarily with material things is the constantly changing and unpredictable behaviors of people involved in an emotional problem. Human responses are complex, often ambivalent, usually emotion-laden. Often we *intend* to solve a human problem one way but in action we *act* on the basis of feelings we cannot always rationally anticipate. Furthermore, in action, we act not only in terms of our own feelings and thinking but also in response to the feelings and behavior of the other individuals who are in the situation with us. The intellectual solution of a social problem situation often fails to cope with the feelings generated by the interactions of the people involved.

Because of these dynamic aspects of group behavior, we need much more practice in confronting, defining, and resolving problem situations on an *action level*. Role-playing enables us spontaneously to explore the interactions of people in situations that approximate the reality; it is active exploration.

TO TEACH GROUP PROBLEM SOLVING

When an individual considers a problem in solitude, he brings to bear on it the sensitivities and limitations of his own perceptions. Granted, creative insights are highly individual matters; nevertheless, researchers who are studying thinking processes are finding that the interaction that takes place in a group makes available a broader range of perceptions and definitions of a problem situation than occurs to an individual thinking alone. One person's response stimulates further analysis by another member of the group, and a third person adds refinement to their thinking, which elicits still further additions and insights, causing a spiraling of thinking in the group. Mary Follett has called this "circular response."

Furthermore, in human relations problem solving, interpersonal or group situations are involved and typically demand group action. We not only need to develop a sense of responsibility for decision-making in groups, we also need to help *individuals in groups* to "listen" to one another, to consider differing viewpoints, to develop ways of reconciling differences. Such skills demand both learned techniques and practice.

TO DEVELOP THE HABIT OF CONSIDERING CONSEQUENCES (CONSEQUENTIAL OR CAUSAL THINKING)

In the role-playing process, one person explores, with the help of participating observers, the consequences of his proposal of a way to solve a human relations problem. In an enactment, players put that proposal into action. In the discussion that follows, the leader guides the group to consider: "What happens now? How do these people feel?" In this process, impulsive and spontaneous actions can be "safely" followed to their consequences. In role-playing, it should be stressed, it is safe to make mistakes; it is safe even to explore an antisocial solution to a problem because everything is on a "practice" level. As a child asserts that one can "get away with" an antisocial solution, other children point out the consequences of that behavior, such as: "Even if you get away with it, you don't feel so good inside." Or the teacher, noting ignorance of social sanctions or insensitivity to the welfare of others, can so structure further enactments that the group is helped to a new awareness of the consequences of the actions proposed.

TO CONFRONT THE TYPICAL WAYS WE TEND TO SOLVE INTERPERSONAL AND INTERGROUP PROBLEM SITUATIONS

Children, even more than adults, tend to live on an impulsive and immediate level. When confronted with a dilemma or conflict of values, they often evade the realities and act on expediency, and then hope it will all come out all right. We can each of us remember that awful feeling in the pit of the stomach when choices made under such circumstances reached their social consequences.

Young people need help in facing up to the dilemmas and choices in their daily lives. They need help in becoming reality-oriented, in learning from their own past experiences. One of the focal contributions of role-playing is the opportunity to explore pertinent life situations, either actual or possible ones, in the nonjudgmental atmosphere of the role-playing session in which the fact is accepted that we all act hastily or impulsively at times, that sometimes we simply don't know what to do. In this atmosphere, with the emotional support of one's peers, under the skillful guidance of a leader (teacher) who does not punish but rather helps the group to delineate all the feelings, actions, and consequences inherent in the situation, children can and do learn to face up to difficult problems, and do eventually develop versatile and socially acceptable solutions to many human relations difficulties. Occasionally, and this is also important, they learn to live with problems for which there are no immediate solutions.

TO TEACH THE FEELING-THINKING-ACTING SEQUENCE

Our first tendency when facing a problem is usually to feel, to act on our feelings, then think about the way we tried to solve the problem. The result, often, is that we wish we had acted otherwise. Children especially need to examine their impulses to action and their tendency to use expedient solutions. As they explore the kinds of choices they make—in the safe, nonjudgmental atmosphere of the role-playing session—they can be helped to see the variety of alternatives available to them in specific situations if they stop to think *before acting;* moreover, they can be helped to explore the possible consequences of the various alternatives in a particular situation, so as to choose more wisely from among them. In this process, under teacher guidance and with the pooled thinking of the group, young people are helped to find socially acceptable solutions to problems which formerly they may have tended to solve by expedient or even negative solutions with antisocial consequences.

Instead of feeling, acting, then thinking, young people may be helped to acquire the habit of attacking problems in a feeling, thinking, *then* acting sequence: *acting in the light of considered consequences.*

SUMMARY

Children and youth need to be helped to face up to the ways in which they tend to resolve their social problems. Young people need to be sensitized to the feelings of others so that they become concerned about the consequences *to other people* of the choices they make.

When young people are enabled to confront and define the dilemmas in their daily life situations and to analyze their choices, they become more conscious of the values that form the basis for their actions. It is only as they learn to criticize and reconstruct their values that they can become responsible group members and individuals of integrity in their personal decisions.

Children need practice in facing problems at their level and in the safe, nonjudgmental situation of the role-playing session. If we are to make headway in solving the very difficult problems of living in urban society in a multicultured world community in the Nuclear Age, we must help young people to become intelligent, sensitive, responsible solvers of interpersonal and intergroup difficulties. We must help young people to become "open" persons who are inner-directed yet able to enter into responsible group behavior.

We can, in many ways, begin in schools. First of all, we can develop a problem-solving orientation to learning. Children can discover for themselves the challenge of the unresolved, can develop a zest for the search for solutions, and can experience the tremendous sense of achievement felt when a difficult problem has been intelligently explored and resolved.

Such a program calls for many strategies, materials, and media. Highly promising new approaches to learning in this area of concern are being developed by a number of experimenters, notably Torrance in his Creativity project and Richard Suchman in his Inquiry Training Program, and Hilda Taba in her study of children's thinking. The authors of this book have chosen one medium—role-playing—as the core around which to pattern a variety of communication techniques in a procedure that seems uniquely suited to educating young people for individual integrity and responsible group behavior.

Role-playing is an action problem-solving technique designed to explore human behavior situations.

4

SOME GUIDANCE FUNCTIONS
OF ROLE-PLAYING

THE TEACHER AS SUPPORTIVE ADULT

Most classroom teachers have not been trained as guidance workers; and yet, inevitably, the classroom teacher does much to guide and counsel her pupils both in individual instances and as a group. On the more obvious level, she administers various tests; and in many cases she identifies individuals with special problems and refers them to the guidance services of her school system. On the less obvious level, if she is alert and sensitive, she not only notices tensions between factions of her classroom group but catches minute reverberations of stress suffered by one or another individual; and often, either effectively or futilely, she makes some effort to erase or suppress the overt animosity between cliques, and to bring some measure of reassurance to the anxious, self-doubting individual. Children who are tranquil and unburdened are freer to learn; and when the teacher strives to help her young charges become zestful rather than doleful, she is functioning as a supportive adult: as a counselor.

Role-playing procedures can serve as aids in diagnosing tensions and sources of strain in her group; and role-playing, if skillfully structured, can be of major service as a procedure for helping the individual pupil to become more comfortable with himself and more confident in standing up for what he believes. Role-playing can help the classroom group to gain clearer concepts of its responsibility to support the individual. Role-playing, by helping to ease tensions between individual cliques and groups, can do much to aid the teacher in establishing an improved climate for learning (Trow, 1950; Lippitt, 1949–1950, Jensen, 1955).

This vital use of role-playing must have its base in an insightful appreciation by the teacher of its subtlety and penetration as a tool for aiding young people to acquire awareness of others as feeling, responsive individuals who share a common humanity, who wince at rebuffs, who react warmly to affection, who know self-doubt and self-blame, who long to cooperate and fear to dissent and must get courage to differ from the group, from the very group itself. Role-playing, as a group guidance procedure, can do much to help make the individual secure in his personal role as a thinking, feeling, cooperating, or dissenting member of the group.

THE CHILD'S OPINION OF HIMSELF

A child sees himself, to a large extent, through the opinions of him reflected by the people around him. If an individual is warmly regarded as estimable and competent by his teachers and friends, his self-esteem is likely to be high. It is important, therefore, to maximize the opportunities for individuals to earn the respect of peers and teachers.

If an individual is underappreciated in his group, a planned sequence of role-playing can do much to change his status with his peers. The teacher can give such an individual opportunities to play roles quite different from the ones assigned him by his peers, roles in which the undervalued person can demonstrate a wider range of skills and perceptions and qualities than the group ever permitted him to exhibit. And in this process, not only is the individual's status among his agemates changed but, if he receives a supportive response from his group, his self-concept also is altered for the better. The result is often a significant improvement in his learning achievement.

The undervalued member of the group may be the butt of jokes and pranks on the part of the others, or he may be simply ignored, always left out, treated as if he didn't exist. Role-playing, in which leading offenders are placed in the role of a person who is jeered at or pushed aside, often results in an awakening of sensitivity that changes scorn for the scapegoat or pariah into the beginnings of sympathy and acceptance.

The story of "George" provides an example. George was a "left-out" who was venting his anger and frustration so actively that he had become a nuisance and a disrupting influence. He was small for his age even in his class of first-graders. He was sullen, angry, and a problem.[1]

> George teased, punched, kicked, scribbled on other children's papers for no apparent reason. "He hurt me, and I didn't do anything to him," was heard all day long. Talking to him didn't help, for although he seemed to understand what I was saying, he was

[1] Marie Zimmerman Solt, "George Wanted In," *Childhood Education*, April, 1962, pp. 374–76. Quoted by permission.

unable to express more than the simplest thoughts in his new language. Nor did other plans to help him control his aggression, to give him status in the group, to find him a friend of his own. After several weeks of trying we reached an impasse. George continued to be George, and the children were as one in their refusal to have anything to do with him.

Then one day I had an opportunity to watch him on the playground. There were the usual hopscotch and foursquare games, cowboy-and-Indian and first-grade "chase" games. George stood on one side watching but going through the motions of the games. He ran along with the cowboys but a little distance away, until they were lost in the other activities. Then he wandered to the sandbox, the sparkle replaced by his more usual serious expression. He built sand castles which were knocked down by unobservant children. The third time he built his castles he saw a trio running toward him. What was in his mind I'm not sure, but as they approached he laughed and kicked over his own buildings. They charged on through as if he didn't exist. He stood quietly for a little while, then joined a group of children admiring another boy's new top. In a matter of seconds he found himself on the outside of the circle of boys. He stepped back, fury on his face, and kicked two little girls who were walking by.

"Teacher, George kicked me and I didn't do anything to him."

"George wants friends. He wants to be a part of the fun. Being ignored is what he can't stand." But how to break this continuing downward spiral of rejection—aggression—rejection? The previous year his kindergarten teacher told me that he had tried to play with the other children, but they couldn't understand him nor could he communicate with them. So they went their way and he either annoyed them or played by himself. George, with his limited English, had established a pattern of behavior which was going to be difficult to change.

But what about the rest of the class? Could they be helped to understand—to feel as George felt? Perhaps the medium of role-playing could help to put them in George's shoes.

The next day I told the class a story—a story without an end. I asked them to pretend that they were the children in the story and decide how it should be ended. It concerned Johnny's move to a new house, the loneliness he felt when he went out to play and saw no one he knew. They solved Johnny's dilemma very nicely by acting out the neighborhood children's inviting Johnny to play. The whole class agreed that this was good. A few days later I tried again, this time moving Johnny across the country. However, the story was complicated by the fact that the children were playing a game that Johnny didn't know. When he tried to play he made mistakes. Solutions offered were having him go away because he ruined the game and showing him how to play. These were acted out without any comment from me. The class decided that the second solution was better because it helped Johnny feel better. This indicated to me that most of the children identified with the boy in the story. The next week we talked about Johnny again. This time the setting was across the ocean in Germany, not questioned in our army-centered town. The first day he went to school he felt very lonely because they were playing games he did not know and speaking a language he did not understand. He asked to play and one of the children laughed at him. Then Johnny hit him because he didn't know what else do to. Now what?

There were different ideas. "Johnny shouldn't have hit the other boy—it only made him madder."

"Well, Johnny was mad, too. The other children shouldn't have laughed."

One solution tried was ignoring Johnny, but this didn't help him. The class recognized that. They also tried having a child explain the game, but the group protested—"Johnny couldn't understand him."

Then someone suggested that a child could show him what to do without talking. They tried this and decided it would work. Johnny could play and wouldn't feel like hurting anyone.

During this acting-out I weighed the children's feelings. They seemed ready to understand George, to realize their part in his problems, and to find some directions for helping him. I waited for a good day—a day when other things were favorable. Sunny weather to play outside, a day successful in other undertakings, a day when George had created a number of problems but none too serious. He left the room on a pretext arranged with the office. Then I told the class we were going to have another unfinished story—this time a true story.

The Johnny in today's story was born in Japan, a country far away. He had a big brother and sister who helped him learn many things, especially games that Japanese children like to play. They also taught him the games they learned at the schools on the army base—games that American children played. He knew London Bridge, Farmer in the Dell, and Cowboys and Indians. Then just before he was to go to school the family was transferred to America. Johnny wasn't worried. He knew all about American schools from his brother and sister. It would be fun—with lots of children to play with and wonderful things to do.

But it didn't work out that way. First there was no one to talk to, because no one spoke Japanese. When he tried to join the cowboy games he couldn't say whether he was a "bad guy" or a "good guy." The fun went on and he could only stand and watch. He knew how to play cowboy—he even brought his gun—but they didn't give him a chance. One day he felt so angry and unhappy that he used his gun—the wrong way—and the teacher took it away. He couldn't tell her what was wrong—that he only wanted to play.

Each morning he cried because he had to go to school. His father talked to the teacher and then told Johnny that if he didn't hit the children they would play with him and he would have a good time at school. He couldn't explain to his father that he had tried and it hadn't worked.

Then came first grade: learning to read and write and do arithmetic. It was better, but there was still no one to play with at recess. The boy who sat with him at his desk always turned around to talk to the girls on the other side, and he only turned back if Johnny pinched him.

About this time the story was interrupted by a quiet question. "Is this story really about our Georgie?"

"Yes, the little boy in the story is George. How did you know?"

"It sounds like him."

"George has been very unhappy since he came from Japan. He's unhappy most of the time."

"But he's a pest. He hurts us all the time and we don't do anything to him!"

"Let's see if you can tell why he hurts you." And I read the notes I had taken the day George had been in the sandbox.

"This is George's unfinished story. How do you suppose we can end it for him?"

"He can play with us. We're playing cowboys."

"We're playing kickball. He can play with us."

Out of the many responses I suggested the group I knew George wanted to play with most. When George returned to class, for the first time he was greeted with, "C'mon, George. We're going to play tether ball and if we don't hurry the courts will be gone." The smile on his face was a beautiful and fitting end to a long, unfinished story.

It was worth noting the academic success that followed on the heels of George's social success. In September he had tested high average on the Lee-Clark—even in the vocabulary—although I seldom heard him speak. He was in the lowest reading group because he simply did not respond to reading instruction. He either bothered everyone near him or stared into space. It was January before we finally were able to help him. At that time he was just starting the preprimers. He indicated that he wanted to join the top group with his new friends. They were half way through the primer. This posed a real problem, which I thought would be solved by having him visit. Within a few days I realized he was reading with them.

By the end of the year there was no difference between his work and theirs. He is now in third grade and has retained his place among the best in the class. Many times the sight of George running with his friends on the playground revives my sinking spirits in the morass of difficulties which face us each day.

IMPROVING THE EMOTIONAL CLIMATE OF THE CLASSROOM

Sometimes the various individuals and factions in a classroom are so hostile to one another that much disruptive clash of feeling and byplay occur, to the degree that learning is impaired. Role-playing can offer significant help in bringing harmony to the stormy atmosphere. Not a single session but a well-planned series of sessions is usually necessary. (See the example of such a situation and how role-playing was used to improve it in Chapter 10, page 162.)

Preliminary analysis of the group structure of the class is helpful in determining the causes of dissension. Identification of the individuals who are key persons in the tangle of hostilities is also a necessity. Role-playing can then be structured to show the class the results of their disruptive activity, the reasons for it, and ways of solving the issues that are making pupils lash out at each other. Such experiences can do much to bring calm and teamwork into the classroom.

Occasionally, in a classroom group, certain members who are outside the influential cliques are given no respect by their age-mates. In discussions, when these fringers make suggestions, their ideas are either ignored or mocked. An effective technique in such a situation is to bring awareness of what is happening to the group by playing a taped recording of a discussion in which the fringers' responses, although worthwhile, win no recognition from their classmates. A role-playing session then, in which influential members of the group (perhaps the actual offenders) take the roles of the individuals whose suggestions are ignored or belittled, can do much to help the offenders discover how their behavior is affecting the victims. The class is helped, too, to realize that they have all suffered by not utilizing the worthwhile ideas presented by the unpopular members of the group.

Sometimes a committee does not function well. A role-playing session, in which other people portray the committee in action, can do much to make the individual committee members aware of why they have not worked together well, of who have been disrupters and obstructionists and noncooperators, and can help the committee members learn to cooperate productively.

Sometimes a fight occurs on the playground, or a group of pupils get into a brawl over taking turns in the use of play equipment. After an incident of this kind, the teacher can bring the class to a focus on the problem of their behavior through discussion. Then the teacher can have the group re-enact the whole incident just as it occurred. Further discussion can analyze the causes of the rumpus, the lack of consideration shown by individuals involved, the errors in tactics committed by even the well-meaning participants. Discussion can then turn to sensible ways in which the problem could have been handled—and those ways can be tested out in role-playing that puts good sense and consideration for the other fellow into practice.

Another area in which role-playing can be a potent instrument for growth is in helping a group to learn to appreciate individuals who are different. Often young people need to be guided to awareness that everyone has something to contribute to the group. In fact, the odd-ball may have something very important to contribute. (See the story "The Squawkbox," page 343.)

Role-playing sessions can be set up to show, for example, that the shy, soft-spoken individual in the group who never pushes himself into prominence, never interrupts when someone else is sounding off, may be the person who has special knowledge needed by the group. If given a chance, he would share it; but he needs special consideration from the others before he can speak up. (See the story "Bandit Cave," page 336.) The youngster who has trouble speaking good English may be a newcomer from a foreign country who could teach the other children much about skiing or fishing with a butterfly net or gathering sea shells or what the ruins of Pompeii look like or what you can see from the Tokyo Tower or how the Haida Indians make canoes or dig for "gooey-ducks" or how you feed silkworms and treat cocoons to get the silk fibers or how sea shell is carved into cameos. The boy who limps because he had polio before the vaccines were developed may not be much of a runner when playing baseball but he may be a Dead-Eye Dick with a bow and arrow or a radio ham who talks to other hams a thousand miles away. Until you really get to know another person, you may be unaware of the talents he possesses; and when a group neglects or derides or rejects an individual who is in some way "different," it may be that the group is depriving itself of unsuspected riches. Role-playing can demonstrate this possibility to the class.

But, even more importantly, children must be helped to see all individuals as of worth, just because they are people, with feelings and desires, not alone because they have talents that may serve special causes. Everyone can contribute to and enrich life, in the cohesive group (Crosby, *Reading Ladders in Human Relations*, 1963).

PARENT-TEACHER CONFERENCING

Parent conferences can be prepared for through role-playing sessions. This is skills training for teachers. It can be done even as rehearsal for discussion with specific parents about the problems of a particular student. The young teacher who is shy, who tends to become tongue-tied with impressive people, who is naturally casual or brusque or sparing of words, can profit from role-playing with colleagues the act of greeting parents, of putting them at ease, the tactful presentation of the particular problems of classroom achievement their offspring is encountering. Such practice can be very helpful in learning how to win parents' understanding and cooperation in dealing with pupils' difficulties in the classroom.

HELPING A TROUBLED SECOND-GRADER

The following account shows how role-playing can be used to relieve a disturbing situation in a classroom, to bring help to a individual child, and to aid a whole class grow in tolerance and understanding.

Mrs. Nichols, who taught first and second grade in a suburban school, had nine-year-old Marilyn in her group. The girl should have been in the fourth grade, but had been put here in a combined first and second grade because she couldn't do fourth-grade work—and because the principal believed that Mrs. Nichols had the patience and warmth of personality to cope with Marilyn.[2]

On the playground, Marilyn was always a focus of trouble. She was the butt of playground mischief. Inside the classroom, she was still a center of furor: a disruptive clown, who would go through all kinds of antic movements with her hands and face and body, cavorting and mugging for laughs. She couldn't concentrate on work, and she kept the other children from doing so by annoying and distracting them until they lashed out at her in irritation.

Marilyn was deaf.

And the only talk of which she was capable was gibberish.

She had been almost totally deaf from birth, and had never learned to talk so that she could be understood.

She was not a drab, apathetic child but a bright and lively youngster acrackle with energy, keenly alive to sensation and impulse. The trouble was, of course, that her energy and curiosity had no constructive outlet. Frustrated, it found expression in mischief. She acted the fool. She stole things. Inside the classroom or out on the playground, she was always embroiled in excitement, either upsetting other children or being the butt of teasing that almost drove her into screaming hysterics.

Mrs. Nichols could have asked that Marilyn be removed from the class. But she knew that if this were done, Marilyn would be permanently excluded from school, for she had a record of trouble making. In the school which she had previously attended, she had repeatedly rebelled by

[2] The teacher in this true account of creative work is Mrs. Hildred Nichols of the Montebello Public Schools, Montebello, California. (See also H. Nichols and L. Williams, *Learning About Role-playing for Children and Teachers*. Association for Childhood Education International, Washington, D.C., 1960.)

running away. Several times she had not been found until help from the police had been enlisted. Here, Mrs. Nichols realized, with her, was Marilyn's last chance for an education. Her parents, with five other children to support, were too poor to provide special schooling for Marilyn.

Mrs. Nichols decided that she would *have* to help Marilyn become a cooperative member of the class.

But how?

First of all, Mrs. Nichols got the P.T.A. to buy Marilyn a hearing aid. For the first time in her life, then, Marilyn could really hear.

Next, Mrs. Nichols asked for help from consultants in the office of the County Superintendent. It was arranged for Marilyn to have some special tutoring in speech and reading at home.

Marilyn's problem, however, was not merely to become able to learn, but to become accepted by her contemporaries and to become a functioning and cooperating member of the class.

Mrs. Nichols decided to use role-playing to help her with this problem. She then discovered that the materials she needed did not exist at first- and second-grade level.

So Mrs. Nichols created them.

She wrote a series of two-minute stories on the general theme of "How it feels to be different." She selected the kinds of happenings which intensely arouse the feelings of children, the kinds of pressures which make them behave explosively and unacceptably. And this series of stories—over a period of several months—she read aloud to the youngsters seated on the floor in a circle before her.

The first story, "Play Ball," told about a crippled boy who could not run. He did take part in the ball games, however, for his classmates ran for him. They liked him, and they respected him: he was very skillful at making model planes.

Another story she wrote for her circle of rapt listeners was "A Big Boy Like You," about a child who was so shy and got so fussed when grown-ups questioned him that he couldn't answer. And she read to her class the story "There's No Room," telling how a child felt when he wasn't wanted, as Marilyn so often had felt. Mrs. Nichols read "The Lost Ring," about a girl who sometimes stole things—though she didn't really intend to: the act was unpremeditated, and afterward she was just sick over having committed it.

"Have you ever felt badly about not getting something you wanted very much?" Mrs. Nichols asked her youngsters before reading "What Did You Get?" The story was about a boy whose family gave no presents one Christmas because of lack of money. Meeting his friends, the boy lied about what wonderful gifts he'd received. "Why do you suppose Johnny did that?" Mrs. Nichols asked the class.

Usually, after reading a story, all she had to do was ask a question to release a flood of reactions.

Discussion would be excited and eager as the children told details from their own experiences or from those of friends. Mrs. Nichols achieved several goals simultaneously: as the weeks passed, she made the point—established and reinforced it, driving it home—that people may suffer not only from handicaps like a crippled leg which prevents running, but from other types of handicaps too, like shyness, or not being wanted, or not having money. Moreover, she was guiding the children into sharing experiences and feelings and ideas. Not only through discussion, but through role-playing.

Often she had the youngsters dramatize one of the stories, and act out roles in it, spontaneously, without structuring or rehearsing, just improvising as they went along.

They stepped into the story characters' shoes. They stepped into Marilyn's shoes. They "identified" with Marilyn, gradually and increasingly. They learned how much she wanted to be liked. They didn't know the words, but they grew aware of the frustration, the feelings of rejection and shame, which so often Marilyn had felt.

They made growth. Learning how Marilyn felt, they began to sympathize with her. It was only natural, then, that they began to ease up on her. They stopped teasing and prodding her into screaming outbursts. Instead, they began to accept her. They started including her in games. She was chosen on teams.

The result was, finally, that she—belonged.

All the careful work Mrs. Nichols had done paid off!

She had her class plan a culminating program for the end of the year, to which they invited the principal.

They showed him the things they had made in a construction unit. The pupils ran the whole show themselves. First and second graders! One would begin, would tell what he had made, how he had built it, and what tools he had used. Finished, he would call on another child to rise and perform.

And Marilyn took her turn with all the others.

Marilyn—the nine-year-old who hadn't been able to hear, at the beginning of the school term; who had been the disruptive element in the classroom, the child who had to vent the frustrated life within her in making trouble, the pathetic one who had run away when her helplessness got too intense for bearing—Marilyn rose when called upon, and took a turn like all the rest in explaining her project. She didn't mumble it, didn't do a fragmentary job, but gave a clear and logical presentation which the principal could easily understand. Marilyn could communicate now. Marilyn could talk intelligibly. When her turn was over, she called upon the next child and sat down. Just like anybody else.

Marilyn was no longer painfully "different."

An interesting footnote to Marilyn's story is worth adding. At the end of the year, Mrs. Nichols told the children that all had passed, and all were being promoted. "Me, too?" Marilyn demanded. "Yes," Mrs. Nichols assured her. And Marilyn wailed, "But I don't *want* to leave the first grade!"

Not only did Marilyn profit by this venture in teaching for better human relations, but the whole class was helped to grow in insight and sympathy. The effort Mrs. Nichols had made, to mold attitudes and values, *did* carry out of the classroom and onto the playground and into neighborhood and home.

ROLE-PLAYING WITH MENTALLY RETARDED CHILDREN

In the course of a research project in Special Education (Daley and Cain, 1953) it was decided to try role-playing with a group of mentally retarded ninth graders. The teachers concerned were devoted and conscientious, and eager for any help which held promise for their students. They were, however, frankly dubious about role-playing. They doubted that it was practical with their slow learners. They believed that any presentation which called for more than six or eight minutes of concentration on the part of their students would not work. The consultant urged them to try it, saying that she believed, out of her experience with the problem-story procedure, that even mentally retarded pupils would be able to participate for considerable periods.

The consultant came to one of the special classes, in a big city junior high school. The teacher was a skilled, sensitive person who had encouraged his students to develop spontaneity through use of a homemade puppet theatre.

He introduced the consultant by saying that, since they had had so much fun making up stories for their puppets, he thought that they'd like to hear another kind of story that Mrs. Jones had been using with other boys and girls.

The consultant set the stage for "Clubhouse Boat." This problem-story had not been tailored to meet the specific needs of mentally retarded students in junior high schools but was written for average fifth- and sixth-grade students.

Nevertheless, these members of the special class gave the consultant their full attention as she read the story. It took twenty minutes to tell, with some dramatics and elaboration of detail. No pupil became overtly restless. Many of the young people expressed their feelings, during the presentation, in whispers and quiet comments.

When the consultant stopped, and asked, "What do you think Tommy will do?" there was a long moment of silence. Then the students began to talk.

These mentally retarded youngsters had ideas. They explored the consequences Tommy would face if he kept the money. With a little encouragement, several students got up and role-played a solution to the dilemma. Even a brain-injured girl who, the consultant had been warned beforehand, was often irrelevant in her comments, made pertinent remarks.

The class not only offered as many real solutions as "normal" classroom groups, but added considerations the consultant had never before been given. Further discussion revealed that these mentally retarded youngsters understood the story dilemma very well—*because they had held jobs and had actual experience of similar conflicts themselves.*

The adults present who were observing, and who knew these young people well, were surprised and delighted at the amount of participation in both role-playing and discussion which this session brought forth.

Moreover, instead of showing an attention span of just six or eight minutes, this retarded group participated in the role-playing for almost fifty minutes. This tended to confirm the belief among the adults that mentally retarded youngsters have abilities that have not been tapped for lack of media that release their powers.

When the period ended, several students came to the consultant and told her, "That was a good story!" and they asked her to come back after lunch because they wanted to put on a puppet show for her.

At one o'clock she came back to the classroom. At the suggestion of their teacher, the group put on a puppet version of "Clubhouse Boat." And it was good! They recalled every significant element of the problem-story. In fact, they even inserted a scene which had been merely implied in the original. Their production was complete, the dialogue natural, and they acted out a sensible solution. And these were retarded youngsters!

When given material that touched upon the problems that were real for them in terms of the life situations they knew, they demonstrated a level of practical judgment that was considerably above the ability which the school had been able to elicit from them before. Role-playing, when structured through the problem-story, enabled them to perform in terms of the daily life experience they knew, and they had the exhilaration of success rather than the frustration encountered so often when dealing with academic materials.

EASING OUT-OF-SCHOOL PROBLEMS THROUGH ROLE-PLAYING

A teacher who works with role-playing for some time finds that she has released unexpected potentialities in her pupils which can help them to deal with some of their out-of-school problems.

For example, it was suggested to the members of two classes who had considerable experience with role-playing that they might like to write their own problem-stories.

The results were very satisfying. Pupils produced stories that were informative about the young people themselves, and therefore of help to the teachers in understanding their students. Some of the stories were used for role-playing. The two classes were so pleased with the results that they planned to do more writing.[3]

Several of these stories are reproduced below, with a record of how one class role-played one of the narratives.

1.

ROCK HAPPY JUDY

I was out in the backyard, playing with my friend Jack.... When my sister came up and hit me with a rock, and she ran around the house. Mother called Judy into the house and asked her if she hit me with a rock, and she said she didn't. There was a big argument between Judy and me. She said that somebody else must have thrown the rock from behind me. I didn't believe a word Judy said because it was all a lie. Of course just because Judy is a girl, I guess mother took her word, and told me to go outside and play and forget it. So I went outside and began to play, when up came my sister again and hit me. Then my friend and I went into the house together and told Mother. Mother called Judy in again and we had a nice little argument and Mother still wouldn't believe us. Now you try to solve this case for us.

2.

WORK AT HOME

My name is Jim and I want to tell you a story of my life.

My house has six living in it. They are my mother, father, brother, sister and brother-in-law. The reason my brother-in-law is living with us is because they are fixing their house.

I want to write this story because I don't think it's fair. Every night after six people have dinner at the house, they go to the other

---

[3] Guided and supervised by Barbara Celse Hunt, Supervisor, Orange County Schools, California.

part of the house. My mother says, "Do the dishes, son." I am the only living thing in the kitchen. I have to do the dishes and they go watch TV.

The class role-played this story. Jim, who wrote this problem, did not participate in the first enactment. However, he helped arrange the seating at the dinner table.

A. *Family around the table.*

(The adults did most of the talking. They tried to find someone else to do the dishes.)

Mother: "Well, I think Jean (older brother, aged 19) should stop gadding around every night with his girl friend. He should help, too. Now, Jean, you just stay home tonight and do the dishes. It won't hurt you."

Jean: "I got a date. Why doesn't Pat (married sister) help?"

(They suggested everyone in the family at one time or another. They also proposed:

That everyone take turns.

That a dishwasher be bought—but this was immediately vetoed because of cost.)

At this point, the class questioned Jim to get more information about the family. It was discovered that:

Sister had just had a baby.

Jean (the older brother) works all day and sometimes helps build a house at night. He's engaged.

Father and brother-in-law work on the house they are building at night.

Jim gets paid for doing the dishes.

B. *Family around the table.*

(In this second enactment Jim plays his own role.)

Father: "Well, I think the women should wash the dishes."

Jim: (to brother) "Why don't you help out?"

Jean: "I'm too busy."

Jim: "But I want to see my TV program. I think he should help."

Jean: "You need the money more than I do."

Brother-in-law: "I don't think Jim should have to do it all. Let's do them before we go to the house."

Father: "Well, you know, you aren't going to be living with us much longer. Your house is almost finished. It will be different then."

Then the class again began to question the family members.

To Jean:
   Question: "Why don't you bring your girl friend over and both of you help?"
   Answer: "We'll be all dressed up!"
   Question: "Well, she can wear an apron. I do."
   Answer: "Gosh, I work all day. I have to have some time for fun. Besides, I help on the house some nights, too."

To Mother:
   Question: "Why don't you help?"
   Answer: "I work all day, too. Jim gets paid for this job."

To Jim:
   Question: "How long does it take you to do the dishes?"
   Answer: "Last night it took me about two hours!"
   Question: "You don't know how to do them! I—"

The discussion then became a sharing of experiences in dishwashing, and rules for efficiency in doing the job.

The final consensus of the class's thinking was:

Jim should have help sometimes.
He needs to be more efficient.
He could arrange his time better.
Everybody has some job to do.
And, furthermore, Jim gets *paid* to wash those dishes!

SUMMARY

The classroom teacher, although in most cases not trained as a guidance worker, inevitably does much to counsel her pupils, both in individual instances and as a group. Role-playing can aid her in various ways: for diagnosing tensions and sources of strain in the classroom group, for helping individuals to become more self-assured, for helping the group to learn to accept and support the individual who is "different," for improving the emotional climate of the classroom.

A child builds an image of himself from the reflected opinions about him of others around him. It is important, therefore, to maximize the chances for individuals to earn the respect of peers and teachers. Role-playing can provide opportunities for the underappreciated individual to improve his status with his age-mates; and such improvement often not only betters a pupil's self-esteem but significantly improves his learning achievement. Role-playing, too, can help to build heightened sensitivity in the group for the feelings of the individual who is the butt of jokes, for the fringer and the isolate, and thereby can increase their chances for acceptance in the group. When cliques and factions cause a stormy emotional climate in the classroom, role-playing in which the effects of such strife are portrayed, and in which consciousness of the feelings evoked is awakened, can do much to produce peace in classroom relationships.

Role-playing can help the teacher in such aspects of guidance work as parent-teacher conferencing. The inexperienced teacher can *practice* consultation with other teachers, in order to acquire some skill and confidence.

5

ROLE-PLAYING: THE PROCESS

ESSENTIAL STEPS

Role-playing is a kind of "reality practice." It enables groups to relive critical incidents, to explore what happened in them, and to consider what might have happened if different choices had been made in the effort to resolve the problems involved. Such practice provides us with an opportunity to learn from our mistakes under conditions that protect us from any actual penalty and in situations in which we have the sympathetic help of group members in exploring the consequences of various choices of behavior we might have undertaken.

Role-playing can also provide a means of attacking new problems of human relations, of applying insights out of past experiences, and of trying out new methods to meet problems for which there may be no precedents in our past.

So often, faced with a problem, we have tried to resolve it with one line of behavior, then later wished we had made a different choice! Often, in discussing a decision with friends, their comments and wider insights have provided us with a better alternative than the one we had chosen—*because the experiences and sensitivity of other people added to our own* often help us to more productive thinking.

Role-playing as presented in this book employs the following steps: [1]

1. "Warming up" the group (problem confrontation)
2. Selecting the participants (role players)
3. Preparing the audience to participate as observers

[1] Adapted from Charles E. Hendry, Ronald Lippitt and Alvin Zander, "Reality Practice as Educational Method," Psychodrama Monograph 9 (New York: Beacon House, 1947). A fine discussion of role-playing.

4. Setting the stage
5. Role-playing (enactment)
6. Discussing and evaluating
7. Further enactments (replaying revised roles, playing suggested next steps or exploring alternative possibilities)
8. Further discussion
9. Sharing experiences and generalizing

This sequence of steps can perhaps be better grasped if the reader "experiences" a role-playing session, at least through a vivid illustration. (Of course, it would be better if you, the teacher, actually role-played a problem real to you.)

FIFTH-GRADERS ROLE-PLAY "CLUBHOUSE BOAT"

The following example is the record of a role-playing session in a school in which the faculty has become concerned over a sustained wave of antisocial behavior among pupils.

Role-playing is often used in a classroom to meet an urgent need. In this particular case the problem story "Clubhouse Boat" (one of the unfinished stories in this book) was selected because its basic issue, honesty, seemed to fit the troubling situation in the school. It was chosen also because it dealt with conflict between parental standards of conduct and the peer code, which was pertinent to the school situation.

The school is an attractive, modern building set in a rapidly growing suburban area. The families of the district consist of two distinct groups: former migrant workers, who have now settled down amidst the small farms into which the area was divided ten years ago and have built their own very modest homes, and a new population of middle-class families, who are building a district that is a typical big-city suburb.

The school faculty felt that the antisocial behavior of children of low economic background arose out of deprivation and a philosophy of get-what-you-can. Misbehavior among children of more privileged background was interpreted as often due to their being over-indulged and over-supervised. The teachers agreed that it was necessary to explore the human relations needs of their pupils.

Sociometric studies were undertaken. Some teachers were using stories selected from such lists as *Reading Ladders for Human Relations*.[2] It was decided that the fifth- and sixth-grade teachers would explore the contribution that the problem-story approach might make.

[2] Muriel Crosby, Ed., *Reading Ladders for Human Relations*, Fourth Edition, American Council on Education, 1963, 242 pp.

The following is a record of one of the fifth grades' experience with role-playing a problem-story focused on a need of this class.

ACTION	INTERPRETATION
Teacher: "Do you remember the other day we had a discussion about Janey's lunch money? Because she had put her money in her pocket and had not given it to me when she came into the room, it was lost. We had quite a talk about finding money: whether to keep it or turn it in.	*"Warming-up" the group* (Introducing the Problem): Utilizing an actual school incident to open up a problem area, sensitizing pupils to the problems.
"Sometimes it's not easy to decide what to do. Do you ever have times when you just don't know what to do?	Creating a permissive environment: recognizing that it is not always easy to find a socially acceptable solution to a dilemma.
(*There are nods in the group.*) "I would like to read you a story this afternoon about a boy who found himself in just such a spot. His parents wanted him to do one thing, but his gang insisted he do something else. Trying to please everybody, he got himself into difficulty. This will be one of those problem stories which stop, but are not finished."	Children indicate how meaningful the problem is for them by bodily and facial responses. Preparing the class to identify with the main character. This class had already experienced several problem sessions.
A Pupil: "Like the one we did last week?"	
Teacher: "Yes."	
A Pupil: "Oh! But can't you give us one with an ending?"	This response is quite typical. Children are used to the "happy ending" pattern. The satisfaction that comes with increased ability to tackle and solve problems develops slowly, and only through opportunity to face problems.
Teacher: "When you get into a jam, does someone always come along and tell you how your problem will end?"	
Pupils: "Oh, no! Not very often."	
Teacher: "In life, we usually have to make our own endings—we have to solve our problems ourselves. That's why I'm reading you these problem stories—so that we can *practice* endings—try out many different ones to see which work the best for us.	
"As I read this story, you might be thinking of what you would do if you were in Tommy Haines' place."	Preparing the class to listen purposefully. This is a very important part of the process.
(*Teacher reads the story, "Clubhouse Boat," here summarized*):	

ACTION

Tommy Haines belongs to a club which the boys have organized in the neighborhood, the Mountain Lions. An uncle of one of the boys agrees to give them a houseboat for a club if they will have it repaired and docked in the town's yacht harbor.

Tommy agrees to pay his share of the repair bill, twenty dollars. He is confident that he can manage this, because he is earning money as delivery boy for a drugstore.

To his dismay, his father refuses to let him participate, insisting that he must put his earnings in the bank.

This places Tommy in difficulty with his gang. They have had the boat repaired and owe money for it. Pete "borrows" the money for Tommy out of a purse which had been left in his Dad's taxicab by a patron.

Tommy, frantic to get together the amount he owes his gang, resorts to small subterfuges, deliberately working to talk people into giving him tips, not telling his folks that he has earned tips, or that he has been given a raise in pay, and even keeping several small sums given him in over-payment on orders.

Finally, the boys are in difficulty. The woman returns for her purse, and Pete's parents learn that he took money from it. They threaten to go to all the boys' fathers unless the money is returned by the next morning.

The boys manage to chip in some more money, but cannot raise enough. They insist that Tommy find the balance needed.

Tommy worries. Then, after delivering a package for the druggist, Tommy discovers that the customer had made a mistake and overpaid him $5. Enough to clear the debt to the gang!

INTERPRETATION

The story constitutes an extended warm-up or preparation for role-playing. Characters and actions are delineated and the problem situation is developed to its critical point.

ACTION	INTERPRETATION

Tommy is deeply tempted. He stands in front of the customer's closed door. Shall he knock and return the money—or shall he leave and keep the money he needs so badly?

Teacher: "What do you think Tommy will do?"

Stimulating the class to explore possible solutions.

A Pupil: "I think he'll keep the money!"

A spontaneous expression which probably reveals an impulse.

Teacher: "Yes?—"

A Pupil: "Because he needs to pay the club."

Analyzing the problem.

A Pupil: "Oh, no, he won't. He'll get found out, and he knows it."

Anticipating consequences.

A Pupil: "How can he? Nobody knows he has it."

Expressing a personal philosophy.
Selecting participants

Teacher: (to this last student) "Would you like to come up here, Jerry, and be Tommy?"

The teacher deliberately chooses the boy who expresses an antisocial solution.

(*Jerry comes to the front of the room.*)

"Jerry, whom will you need to help you?"

Jerry: "I'll need somebody to be the customer. And I'll need boys to be the gang."

Encouraging the pupil to describe his solution and situation himself.

(*Players are chosen.*)

The teacher invites several children to participate. The setting is arranged. One corner of the classroom is the school where the gang is waiting for Tommy to come with the needed money. A chair is placed in another corner to represent the door of the house to which the package is delivered.

While children are never urged to play roles which they do not "feel," occasionally a child needs to be encouraged to participate.

Setting the stage

The teacher helps describe the furnishings needed and helps arrange them quickly.

Teacher: "Where are you going to start, Jerry?"

Jerry: "I'll deliver the package."

Teacher: "Very well. Now, you people, as you watch, consider whether you think Jerry's way of ending the story could really happen. How will people feel? You may want to think of what will happen next. Perhaps you'll have

Preparing the class to be participating observers

ACTION

different ideas about it; and when Jerry's finished, and we've talked about it, we can try your ideas."

FIRST ENACTMENT

(*Tommy knocks on door. The boy playing role of old man "opens" the door.*)
Tommy: "Delivery from Central Drugstore, sir. Eleven dollars and twenty-eight cents due."
Man: "Here you are. And here's a quarter. Buy yourself a Cadillac."
(*Man closes door. Tommy counts money. Discovers he has been overpaid five dollars. Raises hand to knock on door and call man back—then turns away. Walks across the classroom to the waiting gang.*)
Tommy: "Hey, guys, look! I got the money we need. Here!"
Eddy: "Swell! Now we can pay for the boat. Come on, gang!"
(*End of enactment.*)

Teacher: "Well, Jerry has given us one solution. What do you think of it?"
A Pupil: "Uh-uh! It won't work!"
Jerry: "Why not?"
A Pupil: "That man is going to remember how much money he had. He'll phone the druggist about it."
Jerry: "So what? He can't prove anything on me. I'll just say he didn't overpay me."
A Pupil: "You'll lose your job."
Jerry: "When they can't prove it?"
Another Pupil: "Yes. Even if they can't prove it!"
Teacher: "Why do you think so, John?"
John: "Because the druggist has to be on the side of his customer. He can fire Tommy and hire another boy. But

INTERPRETATION

Role-playing
Pretend level.
A chair is used to designate the door.

This boy chooses to "get away with it." His enactment is an expression of the (ethical) value and the antisocial behavior that have been causing concern among the school faculty.

Discussing and evaluating
Encouraging an evaluation. The teacher is careful to be noncommittal.
A judgment.
It happens that Jerry is a boy of low mental ablity; he is quite sure of himself.
An analysis of consequences.

ACTION	INTERPRETATION
he doesn't want his customers mad at him."	
A *Pupil:* "He's going to feel pretty sick inside, if he keeps the money."	Other consequences are here foreseen —anxiety and guilt.
Teacher: "What do you mean?"	Encouraging further expression.
Pupil: "Well, it bothers you when you know you've done something wrong."	
Teacher: "Do you have any other way to solve this problem?"	*Exploring for other solutions*
Pupil: "Yes. Tommy should knock on the door and tell the customer about being overpaid. Maybe the man'll let Tommy keep the money."	A proposal with a wishful (fantasy) solution.
Teacher: "All right, let's try it your way, Dick."	The teacher follows through. The consequences of fantasy solutions should be explored.

SECOND ENACTMENT

(*New role-players are selected, and the scene is set.*)

(Tommy delivers the parcel, is paid; the door is shut. He discovers that he has been overpaid $5.)

Tommy: "Gosh, I better knock and call that man back!"

(*He knocks.*)

Man: (*opening door*) "What is it, son?"

Tommy: "Sir, you overpaid me five dollars."

Man: "I did! Well—you're an honest boy. Tell you what—You *keep* the change."

(*End of enactment.*)

ACTION	INTERPRETATION
	Further discussion
Teacher: "What about this solution?"	The teacher remains noncommittal.
Several Pupils: "It's all right! It's fine. That settles everything."	The class accepts a fantasy solution.
Teacher: "Do you think this could really happen?"	The teacher pushes for a realistic evaluation.
Pupil: "Yes. Because once I got overpaid for my paper delivery, and when I told the man, he said, 'Keep it.' "	Generalizing from personal experience.
Teacher: "How much money did he overpay you?"	Exploring the analogy for parallels.
Pupil: "A dollar and a quarter."	

ACTION	INTERPRETATION
Teacher: "Do you think it might be different with *five* dollars?"	Again pushing for reality.
Pupil: "Yes. That's too much. He might give you a dollar tip."	A more realistic evaluation.
Teacher: "How do the rest of you feel about this?"	Involving the rest of the class.
(The class agrees that few adults would tip five dollars.)	
"Then, how shall Tommy solve his problem?"	Guiding the class to see that they have not yet found a realistic solution to the story.
A Pupil: "I think he should talk it over with his mother."	This is probably the pupil's pattern of dealing with troubling dilemmas.
Teacher: "Why his mother, Alice?"	
Alice: "Well, when my Dad says no, I ask my mother."	The mechanisms that work for some?
(Grins and nods from the group.)	
Teacher: "Is that the way it works for you all?"	Again exploring with the class.
A Pupil: "No, it's the other way around in our house."	
Another Pupil: "My folks stick together. Kids just don't have a chance."	Different families have different relationships.
Teacher: "You feel that grown-ups just don't understand?"	Reflecting a child's thoughts so that he may explore further.
A Pupil: "Well, sometimes they jump to conclusions."	
Teacher: "Do you feel that Tommy's parents were wrong?"	Guiding the thinking.
A Pupil: "No. Tommy had no business promising so much money without asking his parents."	A judgment made.
A Pupil: "That was too much money for kids to spend."	
A Pupil: "But once he promised it, his dad should have helped him out."	A concept of the father role.
A Pupil: "My mother would help me out of a jam!"	A mother–child relationship expressed.
Teacher: "Would you like to play this, Sally, the way you think it could happen with your mother?"	The teacher seizes the opportunity to explore a constructive solution, now that the class has already explored an antisocial solution and a fantasy solution.

ACTION

INTERPRETATION

THIRD ENACTMENT

(The setting is Tommy's home.)

Another enactment

Tommy: "Mom, I'm in an awful jam!"
Mother: "What's the trouble, Tommy?"
(*Tommy tells his mother the whole story.*)
Mother: "Why, Tommy, you should have told me sooner. Here, you pay the money (opens purse) and we'll talk this over with your Dad when he comes home."
(*End of enactment.*)

Mother will help, but children do get punished, in this version.

Teacher: "What will happen now?"
A Pupil: "Tommy will get a licking!"
Teacher: "How do you feel about that?"
A Pupil: "It's all right. I'd rather have the licking and get it off my mind."

Probing for consequences.

Reaching a definite attitude on the problem.

Sharing experiences

Teacher: "Does this sound familiar, class? Do you know of an instance in which a boy or girl had to make such a decision?"
Jim: "Yes, it happened to me once. I was borrowing money from all the milk bottles on our street. It got so I couldn't sleep nights worrying about it. Finally, my Pop caught up with me and gave me an awful licking. And was I glad."
Teacher: "You mean, it was a relief not to have to worry about getting caught?"
Jim: "Yes."
Teacher: "Sometimes we get into things we wish we'd never started. Was that Tommy's trouble?"
Pupils: "Yes."
A Pupil: "But he should have told his Dad. He'd have helped him out."
Teacher: "Why was his father so strict?"

Tying the situation in with known experience in a nonthreatening way. If a child wishes, he may describe someone else's experience rather than admit his own mistakes.

This child chose to be direct and frank.

The teacher is careful to be noncritical and casual and to generalize. Any sort of discussion, in a permissive atmosphere, may elicit such admissions of individual behavior. The teacher should safeguard a pupil from any teasing or loss of respect from his peers.

Exploring the attitude of fathers.

ACTION

Pupil: "Because he wanted to teach Tommy a lesson from his own experience."

Teacher: "Do you think that a father should help his boy decide what to do with the money he earns?"

INTERPRETATION

Opening up a new phase of the problem.

This class, because of previous experiences with dramatic play and sociodrama, and because the teacher observed the principles of working with youngsters in a nonjudgmental and accepting situation, was very free and spontaneous in expression. The session lasted an hour, and was continued in discussion form the next day, centering around the topic: "Who decides how you can spend money you earn?" The majority of the pupils felt that children need supervision of their spending *but* that they should be allowed to spend at least half of their earnings.

AN ELABORATION OF THE STEPS:

Having followed the steps in role-playing through this actual classroom session, it may be useful to elaborate upon each step, its function, and the techniques used.

1. "Warming-up" the group (problem confrontation).

The "warm-up" serves several functions. It acquaints the participating group with the problem at hand. It arouses awareness of their need to learn ways of dealing with the problem. And it involves the group emotionally in a specific situation and thereby helps them to identify with individuals who are coping with the tangle of human relations to which the problem gives rise.

The teacher may begin her warm-up saying, "I'm sure that all of us, at some time or another, have been in an embarrassing situation—and felt that a lie was the only way out of it." Or, "Sometimes our friends want us to do something that our parents do not permit, and we get into a lot of trouble by trying to please *both* sides." Or, "You're not invited to a party because you are colored or go to a different church than your classmates."

The teacher's purpose in this "warm-up" is to get enough response from members of the group to make them realize that each of them, that everybody (the teacher included!) on occasion has had to face such problems. By *his* presentation, the teacher demonstrates that he is aware that children get into difficulties and is sympathetic and wants to help; that, in fact, most adults are on their side.

The problem under discussion must, of course, be one that is important to the young people. It must be one with which they can immediately identify; one that they feel a need to learn to cope with.

The next step of the warm-up is to express the problem in the vivid details of a specific example. Doing this will involve the children emotionally. Sometimes the group describes situations they have known that illustrate the problem. One of these incidents may then be selected for role-playing. Sometimes an actual incident that all the children know about or have experienced is recalled and structured for role-playing. At other times the teacher presents a problem situation which has been prepared in advance. A scene from a film, a television show incident, or a selection from literature can be used for this purpose.

An effective tool for the specific example is the *problem story* that is read to the class by the teacher and which stops at the dilemma point.

It is our belief that the problem story provides a structured situation which, while representative of children's actual experiences, provides an often necessary "remove" that makes exploration easier because the situation is not too close to be faced; one that is, in other words, not an actual threat in the lives of the group. Furthermore, such stories present dramatic springboards which quickly involve the group in role-playing, and do not demand as much initial skill in introductory warm-up techniques on the part of the teacher.

The problem story must deal with human relations in terms which are both believable and interesting. The basic situation must be real and important to the group. The more convincing the story is, the more excitingly it develops, the more strongly will the listeners identify with the fictional characters. They will participate in role-playing in direct proportion to the degree to which their sympathies and partisanship are aroused, or their convictions affronted.

When the story stops, a brief discussion period should be held, to lead into role-playing.

The teacher may wind up the initial warm-up comments by saying, "I'm going to read you a story about a boy who got into the sort of trouble we've been talking about. This story isn't finished. While I'm reading it, you may think of how it might end. When the story stops, some of you may want to show us some ways you think this boy may solve his problem."

This last point is important. It is a challenge to the listening group. Their attention is sharpened, and they will listen more alertly. They will identify themselves with various of the story characters and will try to get as much meaning as possible out of the situation, so as to be able to deal with it effectively.

After the problem story has been read, the teacher helps the group move into discussion and then into role-playing.

He may ask, "What do you think will happen now?" Or, "What is happening in this situation?" *And then he waits.*

Children are a wonderful audience. Less inhibited than adults, they vent their feelings, as they listen, with sighs and groans and comments and handclaps. Even their facial expressions and body postures are eloquent. After the reading is over (if the situation is meaningful for them), they usually have much to say and are in a hurry to say it. They are boiling over with responses.

Sometimes the situation may be meaningful in painful ways. There is silence when the story stops. The teacher, by waiting *serenely*, implies that he has confidence in their ability to face and cope with such a problem; and, gradually, the responses will come.

Usually, merely by asking "What do you think will happen now?" the teacher releases pent-up debate. Suggestions rain at him, often with much heat and emphasis.

2. Selecting participants for the role-playing.

In selecting participants, it is important to use individuals who have identified with the roles, who can see themselves as particular persons in the situation, who can *feel* the parts.

To do this, the teacher goes "fishing." He may ask the group to describe the various characters. He may ask, "What kind of a person is Johnny?" "How does he feel?" Children who seem identified with certain characters may be asked if they would play those persons. Sometimes volunteers are called for.

A caution is necessary at this point: *The teacher should avoid assigning roles to children who have been volunteered for those roles by others.* The situation may be punitive; or a particular child may not see himself in the role thrust upon him.

Usually a number of children in a group are quite vocal about what they think will happen and what specific individuals in the story will do. These responses give us clues not only as to *which* children are identifying with the various roles but also as to *how* they are identifying.

Often the teacher chooses children who indicate an antisocial solution to the problem so as to explore in action the consequences of such a solution. Or, he may select a child who will play an authoritarian or strict mother or father role, knowing that this role may typify a problem faced by a number of his young people.

Sometimes the teacher selects a child to play a part because he knows that the child needs to identify with the role, or needs to place himself in another's shoes, as a learning experience. This calls for much support and help in assisting such a child to get into the role. (Procedures for doing this are discussed in the chapter on techniques for the leader of role-playing.)

Primarily, the teacher chooses children who reveal by their remarks that they have identified with certain individuals in the story or have strong feelings about the behavior of specific characters. Usually he should avoid choosing, for the first enactment, an individual who will give an adult-oriented, socially acceptable solution. Using him first may result in shutting off exploration of what many children actually do think and feel in such situations. In "The Clubhouse Boat" session presented earlier in this chapter, you will recall that the teacher chose first to explore the temptation to keep the money and give in to expediency. It is by following through on such impulses and *exploring them for consequences* that children can learn from their own past experiences.

Usually, after a thorough investigation of the pupils' honest feelings and perceptions of the problem situation in which they have revealed, by their impulsive actions and expressions, the values they hold, the teacher may come back to the child who has a mature and socially acceptable solution to propose. By that time, the children may be ready to relinquish their opportunistic solutions since the role-playing may have revealed consequences they had not foreseen.

3. Setting the stage.

Before beginning the enactment, the role-players *very briefly* plan what they are going to do. They do not prepare any dialogue but simply decide in a general way on a line of action. They may decide to explore what happens if Tommy keeps the money. Or the teacher, in selecting a certain child's idea, may encourage that child to set the line of action in accordance with his own idea.

Each player is then reminded of the role he is to take. The role-playing has most value when completely spontaneous and each child taking part responds to the action of the other role-players. There are no set speeches and no detailed plotting.

Once a simple line of action has been selected for exploration, the teacher may ask the main role-player whom he needs to carry out the action. After the players are chosen, the teacher helps the actors to get "inside" the situation. He may ask, "Where is this taking place? What is it like in this place?" Or, "Where is the door?" or "What time of day is it?" or, "What are you doing, Mother, when Johnny comes home?"

In this way he settles the players into their roles and situations.

4. Preparing the audience to be participating observers.

The next step is to prepare the observing group to participate actively and intelligently.

Here some of our skills in "listening" come into play. Uninstructed observers may watch passively, or may be hyper-critical, or can be so consumed by their own ideas that they merely wait impatiently and inattentively for the enactment to finish so that they may get turns.

We wish to help young people to become good listeners to other people's feelings and ideas, to "place themselves in the other person's position" in order to look at it *with* him, and see what he sees. It is only as you understand another's viewpoint that you are in a position to agree or disagree with him. Furthermore, if you are observing from a true listening stance, you may learn from the other person's perceptions and ideas. Too often most of us are so busy expressing our own ideas that we are closed to any benefit from real interaction with others.

At the same time that we want to achieve this alert and receptive listening to the other fellow, we also want children to go beyond grasping the other fellow's ideas to the exploration of alternative proposals to solving the problem under attention.

Therefore, in instructing the observers, the teacher may begin by assigning the group to various observer tasks. If he is working with a beginning group, he may suggest to the entire group that they judge the realistic quality of the solution that is being proposed; that is, he tells them to ask themselves as they watch the enactment: could this really happen? *Do you think, as you watch the actors, that they are behaving in a way they would really behave in similar situations that you know about?*

The teacher may, after initial experience in reality testing, divide the group. He may ask certain children to concentrate on particular actors and decide whether those roles are being played in a way that is true to life. He may ask other children to observe how certain players feel as the action progresses. Or, he may ask some children to be thinking of the next steps (consequences) of the action.

After such instructions, the teacher keeps the way open for further solutions and enactments by saying to the group that he feels sure that some of the group members have other ideas about the way the situation problem should be solved, and that after this first idea has been explored in role-playing, other members of the group will have a chance to try out their alternative suggestions.

It may be wise for the teacher to warn a beginning group that laughter spoils the role-playing and that attentive observation *helps* the role-players.

5. *Role-playing (the enactment).*

The role-players then put on their enactment. They assume the roles and "live" the situation, responding to one another's speeches and actions as they feel the people in those roles would behave. Since there is no set plot, only a situation—a time, a place, and, perhaps, one person's line of action should be indicated (Johnny will keep the money!)—each player must think and feel on his feet, spontaneously reacting to the developing situation.

No role-player is expected to present his role flawlessly. Slips or awkward moments are taken for granted; so are occasional lapses into less than formal language and gesture. When real feelings are being portrayed, language may become quite vernacular. At this point the teacher needs to use discretion; while extremes in language may not be acceptable, too much censorship will destroy the spontaneity and sense of reality.

In responding to an enactment, the group should be helped to understand, too, that the way an actor portrays a role has no reflection upon him as a person. He is simply presenting a role as he sees it. He will not be condemned for his interpretation by the teacher or anyone else. He is presenting what he has seen or felt is the role behavior of such a person as the situation character has been indicated to be. This is a very important precaution.

Moreover, no role-player is evaluated for his acting. An enactment is not a play with focus on theatrical performance; it is reality exploration. Our only test is whether the group feels that the portrayal is true to life in some place or situation which they have experienced.

6. *Discussion and evaluation.*

The discussion that follows an enactment is one of the most vital phases of role-playing. While research has indicated that the actual taking of roles may have greatest influence on attitudinal change,[3] it is in the give-and-take of discussion that problem-solving procedures are refined and learned.

Usually, at the close of an enactment, there is no need for prompting by the teacher. Discussion is fast and furious. The young people are keyed up. They bubble over with comments. They pour out their opinions of the

[3] Pearl P. Rosenberg, "An Experimental Analysis of Psychodrama," unpublished doctoral dissertation, Harvard University, 1950; Bert T. King and Irving L. Janis, "Comparison of the Effectiveness of Improvised Versus Nonimprovised Role-playing in Producing Opinion Changes," *Human Relations*, Vol. XIX (1956).

portrayals. "I don't think a mother would say that! Mine wouldn't," is countered by, "Well, mine *would!*" Or someone else may say, "That kind of mother would behave that way." And, even more importantly, observations are made on the consequences of the actions taken. Thus one boy may observe that Tommy will lose his job because the druggist can hire another boy but doesn't want to lose a customer. Another youngster is concerned with how it feels to live with a bad conscience.

It is in such discussions that a child learns, *with the support* and often *with the opposition of his age-mates,* to consider the consequences of the choices he proposes.

The teacher guides the discussion with stimulating open-ended questions such as, "What is happening?" Or, "How does Jane feel?" Or, "Could this happen in real life?" Or, "What will happen now?" The questions guide toward consequential thinking, toward looking ahead to the consequences of behavior.

At first, the questions are focused on helping the observers to think *with* the role-players. Such questions as "How is Mary feeling?" or "What is Tom thinking?" help to focus on the action that has been presented. Later, the teacher picks up comments that lead to alternative proposals. As Mary says, "I don't think I'd do it that way!" the teacher responds with "What would you do?" If no alternatives are offered, he may ask, "Is there some other way this situation might be resolved?"

The initial role-players have stimulated further thinking in the observers, and the group of observers, in their responses, broaden the perspectives of the role-players. Because the observers are not as emotionally involved and committed to a line of action as the actors, the observers are in a position to see consequences to proposals more easily and to see many more alternatives.

The entire group experiences, in a very active sense, the stress and satisfaction of problem solving.

7. *The re-enactment (further role-playing).*

Re-enactment is the next step in role-playing. So often, in real life, one wishes for a second chance to solve a dilemma. In role-playing, this second chance is now forthcoming. So is a third and a fourth chance. *Facing problems on a "practice level," you have all the chances you need.* This is the great value of role-playing. *You can arrive at a good solution to a human difficulty through as much trial and error as is necessary.* You "discover" for yourself the complex dimensions of a problem situation and the personal and social considerations inherent in various solutions.

The role-players may play their roles over and over again, changing their interpretations in the light of the suggestions they receive from their fellow group members.

Or, new actors may take over the roles to demonstrate other interpretations and solutions.

Sometimes a role-player precipitates a situation which leaves another role-player at the end of his ideas. The teacher may then have to (1) guide him indirectly into further action by asking questions, such as, "How are you feeling now?" or "What kind of person are you?" or (2) select another pupil to pick up the role who seems to have ideas on how to respond to the altered situation, or (3) cut the scene short and start class discussion.

FURTHER ENACTMENTS GIVE OPPORTUNITY FOR A VARIETY
OF APPROACHES TO SOLVING THE BASIC PROBLEM

New actors may take over the roles and portray them differently, or the original role-players may be asked to switch roles (that is, the "son" of one enactment may play the "father" in a succeeding one) in order to get *inside* roles with which they were in conflict, so as to get a better understanding of other facets in the tangle of human relations and of other people's feelings and views in the situation.

A surprising number of episodes may be enacted and re-enacted in a short period of time. It is possible for five or six versions of a situation, with intervening discussion, to take place within an hour. Of course, the length of a discussion, or the length of an enactment, cannot be foreseen. A discussion may last two minutes, or possibly a full hour. As long as a discussion is fruitful, as long as an enactment is moving productively, it should be allowed to continue. This is an area in which the teacher must use his best judgment.

This moving back and forth from acting to discussing to acting again can be a most effective learning sequence. An individual who thinks he has a rational solution to offer may find, in actual role-playing, that *his feelings get in the way of his rationality*. He may find, on the action level, reason often giving way or find himself so affected by his emotional response to the behavior of the other role-players that he *acts* differently from the way he had intended. Such an experience gets close to reality and gives the teacher an opportunity to help the group to face up to the complexity of human relations problems. Gradually, under skilled leadership, young people are stimulated to analyze their feelings and impulsive responses and thereby to bring the emotional and rational aspects of behavior into closer relationship.

There is also a kind of insight that comes to the individual as he moves back and forth from being a role-player to being an observer. *This insight permits each child to come to his own conclusions on his own thinking* schedule. He programs his conclusions when ideas fall into place *for him.*

8. *Sharing experience and generalizing.*

The last step in a role-playing session may be termed a period of general discussion, sometimes of sharing experiences, and, if the enactments and insights of the group promote it, a time of generalizing from the exploration.

After a number of alternatives and their consequences have been enacted and discussed, the teacher may ask, "Do you think this problem is one that is true to life for young people like you?" Or, "Has something like this ever happened to someone you know?"

Often, individuals will volunteer examples of incidents they have known about. *Occasionally they offer personal experiences, but this should not be urged actively by the teacher since it may invite a child to expose himself to the group in ways that will harm his reputation. Therefore the teacher avoids asking, "Did anything like this ever happen to you?" unless it is in an area that is not likely to rebound on individual children.*

This sharing of experiences, this exploration of consequences of behavior, achieves several important objectives:

It helps anxious young people to discover that their problems are shared by other people—many other people. In this awareness a worried individual finds relief and reassurance.

It brings the classroom experience and the child-life outside of school into closer relationship and provides opportunity for the teacher, through his supportive leadership, to gain the confidence of the group.

Out of the enactments, out of the criticisms and suggestions and re-enactments, out of the excited clash of opinions, the group hammers out some general principles of conduct. They may conclude that "Even if you get away with it, you don't feel so good inside," which may be translated to mean, "Opportunistic solutions are not worth the loss of self-respect that often results." They may see that leaders should be selected for their ability to guide the task at hand rather than on the basis of hero-worship.

In this period of sharing and generalization, such principles gradually emerge. They are especially influential to the individual child because they bear the authority of his own peers.

We must be prepared to accept the fact that some role-playing sessions do not reach the level of generalization. Sometimes a session may do no more through a series of enactments than delineate in full detail the nature of the problem. It is important for young people to learn that superficial definitions of a problem situation may overlook significant facets that must be considered.

The teacher too must often content himself with a session that may go no farther than numerous attempts to solve the problem-story situation itself. Often it requires many role-playing sessions on a specific problem, using different stories, before a group develops insights that promote generalization. We cannot command generalization; it is a product of individual insights based on much meaningful experience.

ROLE-PLAYING IS A FOCUSED TOOL

The experiences inherent in the role-playing process have their own rewards. There is much to be gained from the spontaneity training, the interaction of feelings and ideas, the stimulation of group interaction.

But the really significant educational outcomes of role-playing lie in their focused use for clearly delineated educational purposes. It is as we use role-playing as a keenly sharp tool, for thoughtfully conceived educational programs, that its best functions will be achieved.

SUMMARY

WHAT IS ROLE-PLAYING?

Role-playing, in its simplest sense, is the spontaneous practice of roles—assuming them in order to practice the behavior required in various cultural situations.

In psychotherapy, role-playing has a special and clinical meaning that is outside the scope of this book. (Role-playing intended as therapy may be termed *psychodrama* [4] and should, of course, be attempted only by the trained clinician. Role-playing that is intended to provide practice in dealing with group social problems is sometimes labeled *sociodrama*.) Role-playing is an important group guidance procedure.

Here, we present role-playing as an elaborate social-learning method, and as a basic decision-making skill in the social studies program. Role-playing is a group problem-solving method involving a variety of techniques—discussion, problem analysis and definition through (1) initial en-

[4] The uses of role-playing in psychotherapy, initially as psychodrama, and later in education as sociodrama, were conceptualized by Jacob Moreno, who developed and expressed his creative ideas in the now classic volumes, *Psychodrama*, and, *Who Shall Survive?* We are deeply indebted, as are many others, to Jacob Moreno for his theories of spontaneity and his development of the field of sociometry. He conceived the spontaneity theater and took the early theories of role and developed them into the basic work on role-playing.

actment of proposals (taking on of roles), (2) observer reactions to the enactments (discussion), (3) exploration of alternatives through further enactments and discussion, and often (4) the drawing of conclusions or generalization and decision-making.

To describe role-playing in still other terms: it is the opportunity to explore, through spontaneous (that is, unrehearsed) improvisation and carefully guided discussion, typical group problem situations in which individuals are helped to become sensitive to the feelings of the people involved, where the consequences of choices made are delineated by the group and where members are helped to explore the kinds of behavior that society will sanction. In this process, young people are guided to become sensitive to feelings, to the personal consequences of the choices they make, and to the consequences of those choices for other people. The group members practice many roles, or different approaches to roles; and gradually they develop skills for solving problems of social conduct and interpersonal relations.

Perhaps the most important aspect of the role-playing process is the fact that individuals, with the help *and* opposition of their classmates, *gradually face and make conscious the choices they make in situations crucial to them,* and, through the experience of articulating, testing, and criticizing their motivations, develop a system of consciously held values.

Role-playing, as presented here, employs the following steps:

1. Warm-up (teacher introduction and reading of the problem story)
2. Selecting role-players
3. Preparing the audience to observe
4. Setting the stage
5. The enactment
6. Discussion and evaluation
7. Further enactments
8. Further discussion
9. Generalizing

Out of the enactments, out of the discussions and the excited clash of opinions, the group often hammers out some general principles of conduct.

chapter

6

GUIDING ROLE-PLAYING

SOME BASIC ASSUMPTIONS

Underlying successful guidance of role-playing is a set of basic assumptions about human behavior and the teaching-learning process. Most central is the belief that each individual has the ability to cope with his own life situations and to grow in his capacity to deal with his problem intelligently (Rogers, 1951). This is so deceptively simple that it may seem like belaboring the obvious, but let us probe its significance.

If you really believe in the individual's capacity to solve his own problems, *you have to permit him to make his own decisions and learn from his own mistakes.* This means that we, the teachers, often have to be willing to go along with very low-level attempts to solve problems, not showing children the right ways, but rather, *patiently guiding enactments and discussions in such ways that children make their own discoveries and gradually move to higher levels of decision-making because of their increased awareness of alternatives and consequences.*

Another basic assumption in role-playing is that the behavior that is enacted is not good or bad; it is simply the best idea that is available to the child at the time that he makes his decision. True, his first decision may not be socially acceptable; but he must come to terms with that matter *himself*, as he is faced with the analysis of consequences.

Back of this assumption is the proposition that we only change our behavior as we change our insights. Individuals often know intellectually what is "right" but act on feelings or past behavior patterns. The role-playing leader operates on the commitment to the principle that behavior is caused and that, typically, there are multiple causes. Human problems are seldom as simple as they may seem at first glance. Furthermore, behavior occurs in a setting; the history of an incident, its background of

85

emotional climate, the matrix of circumstances, all must be taken into consideration in order to understand the behavior.

When we follow through, in the discussion of motive and reason and impulse in role-playing, by analyzing the *causal* aspects of behavior (Fox, Lippitt, and Lohman, 1964, pp. 32–43), the human dynamics involved, we help children to cope with reality rather than merely to verbalize overly simplified judgments which, too often, are little help in real situations.

Still another assumption that promotes spontaneity and sincerity in role-playing is that teachers can accept negative feelings and behavior from children, temporarily, for the purpose of helping children to accept themselves and their past experiences, and to make these experiences available for further learning. The teacher therefore permits more open expression of feelings, even hostile ones, than we ordinarily accept in classroom behavior on the basis that this is exploration of reality. At the start, this acceptance of perhaps hostile or crude behavior can seem, for some teachers, very difficult; nevertheless, this acceptance can be learned, and it is important that it be acquired.

ESTABLISHING A CLIMATE

Given these assumptions, the teacher who guides role-playing is then committed to certain conditions and procedures.

It is necessary that he create an environment or "climate" that encourages frank expression of ideas and feelings, one in which:

1. It is "safe" for students to explore behaviors (both antisocial and socially acceptable)
2. It is permissible for strong feelings—even "bad" feelings—to be expressed. (We teachers are often afraid of children's feelings.)
3. The group is helped to respect the ideas and feelings of all members

How does one create such an atmosphere?

The effort poses special problems for teachers. We have been taught to punish wrong behavior and reward proper behavior. We have been charged with the character education of our students, with their learning of socially sanctioned behavior. In the classroom we set limits and do our best to promote positive behavior. Children quickly "learn the teacher," what his or her goals are, and how to respond in terms of teacher expectations. Children gradually cease to express their own feelings and ideas; instead, they respond in terms of teacher demands.

Role-playing, if it is to have worth, must explore the *children's* honest feelings and ideas. We must encourage sincere, frank expression so that their feelings and perceptions may be brought to the surface for exploration in an environment where it is safe to examine both their social and antisocial efforts to meet somehow the demands that circumstances place upon them.

This position is the reverse of the traditional teaching approach that assumes that the child does not know and *we* will show him how. It is based instead on the belief that the individual needs opportunity and support (from his teacher and from the group) in facing and working through the life situations in which he must act, in which he must make decisions.

The teacher who uses this approach recognizes that whereas the child may begin at a low level of coping (just getting by somehow), he has the capacity to weigh alternatives and to move to more productive solutions *when he has been helped to extend his awareness of the possibilities available to him in the culture.*

In this procedure, the decision on which he acts (even in role-playing) *is always the child's.* Not the teacher's or the group's! True, he never acts alone, inasmuch as he is confronted with situations involving other people; the procedure helps him to learn to make intelligent choices in real life; he can practice that choice-making in role-playing.

This commitment on the part of the teacher *not* to direct the action, but rather *to make it possible for children to choose their own behaviors,* is the critical aspect of role-playing. The teacher is directive in selecting role-playing situations, in deciding whom to involve, *but is nondirective in the role-playing enactments.*

How does the teacher establish a "safe" climate for role-playing? Several procedures are effective.

Since, in most classrooms, students are oriented to cues (listening for goals voiced by the teacher), one of the first steps is to demonstrate another point of view and establish at least a time in the day (or week) when students can express any and all ideas with no resulting penalties.[1]

It will do little good to tell your class that there are new ground rules. They will have to be shown: the rules will have to be demonstrated in the teacher's behavior.

Simple ways to start are by providing literature for human understanding for the class and by using the discussion techniques developed originally by Margaret Heaton and others in *Reading Ladders for Human Relations* (Crosby, 1963). In this procedure, children are encouraged to read stories or books centering around a common theme; for example, relations between generations. Those pupils who have read a story or book

---

[1] One might well argue that the teachers who start down this road will increasingly find more times in the school day when teaching–learning situations become more learner-centered and are taught through "discovery" procedures.

on this theme (they may have read the same book or different ones focused on the same theme) are then guided by the teacher to discuss the key relationships and conflicts.

The teacher demonstrates that he *understands* why the characters in books behave the way they do by such comments as "It isn't always easy to do what adults expect of you," or "Sometimes you just don't know which way to turn," "He was desperate, wasn't he?" or "She was so angry, she didn't care what happened." Such comments tell children that the teacher *feels with children* as they confront dilemmas (Crosby, 1963).

After children have experienced the relatively "safe" procedure of talking about characters in books over a period of weeks, gradually the teacher can begin to use more direct, and sometimes more personal, techniques. Writing private themes about personal dilemmas may be appropriate. Using completion sentences is helpful, such as "One time when I got very mad . . ." or, "Once, I just didn't know what to do when. . . ."

After such experiences, the teacher can much more easily set the stage for role-playing. Again, it is wise to begin at a nonthreatening level. First role-playing may center on "skills training" that does not demand much risk-taking. The class may invite an expert in to talk to them on some subject related to their studies. Role-playing may be used to practice greeting the visitor and making him comfortable. Then the class may role-play the opening of discussion with the visitor, what questions they might ask, how they will share their concerns with him, and so on. Or, the class may role-play a committee going to the principal to ask permission to go on a field trip.

Such skills practice encourages spontaneity and thinking-in-action. It prepares the way for deeper explorations.

When, finally, the teacher introduces real dilemma situations, his approach to the class in the warm-up is a further demonstration that it is safe to risk oneself with this teacher. He may begin by saying, "Have you ever gotten yourself into a jam in which you just didn't know what to do? I have, and it's a very frightening feeling sometimes. Once, I . . ." Or, he may say, "Sometimes we all are faced with choices that are very difficult to make. Each alternative may have advantages. How do we decide? Have you ever made a choice, then wished you had done it another way? I have!"

Children, responding to this new teacher–pupil relationship, gradually build a trust in the teacher as one who values them as persons, regardless of their behavior. This relationship, often called the therapeutic relationship, is summed up in the writings of Carl Rogers and his former student, Virginia Axline. Axline states: "It is the permissiveness to be themselves, the understanding, the acceptance, the recognition of feelings, the clarification of what they think and feel that helps children retain their self-respect; and the possibilities of growth and change are forthcoming as they all develop insight." [2]

The classroom teacher borrows some useful techniques from the therapist. He reflects back to role-players the feelings they are expressing in their actions. As an enactment ends, the teacher may say, "You are really angry, aren't you?" (He says this only if the child reveals anger, not to lead the child to play anger.) This enables the child to say, "Yes, I am! He's been taking things from me for a long time!"

Or, the teacher may say, "It seems to me you are saying that you don't know what to do next." The child may thus be helped state his dilemma more fully. Sometimes, after a series of enactments, the teacher says, "It seems to me that all of you are saying that adults just don't care." This summary may lead to further expression, at a verbal level, of feelings that, up to this point, have been only intuitive. By such responses, over and over, the teacher is demonstrating his sympathy and understanding to the class.

When the teacher waits patiently for a child to think through a proposal (rather than turning quickly to another child), when he is warm and relaxed and friendly, he demonstrates his awareness that ideas sometimes come slowly, *but will emerge* if waited for. Sometimes he says, "Think it through, John. I'll come back to you in a minute."

Occasionally, as a child stumbles, hesitates, as he struggles with an idea, the teacher helps by asking enabling questions, such as: "Do you mean that you think he will want to do *both* things? Do you think he can?" Or, "Are you wondering if this can be worked out?" In this process, the teacher must be careful not to ask leading questions, but rather to know intuitively what the child is feeling and thinking.

Perhaps the one major difference between therapist and teacher lies in the limit which must be set in a classroom. Teachers can accept negative feelings *temporarily* for the purpose of helping the child to accept himself. The teacher is permissive of feelings, somewhat permissive of verbal behavior (certain limits must be set for language in the classroom), less so of physical behavior. The teacher encourages, stimulates, and sometimes directs.

The teacher retains the role of guide, of one who (1) has knowledge of subject matter and professional competence, (2) helps children anchor in reality (by accepting contributions, but raising questions), and (3) helps children to focus (order) their experiences.

In role-playing, the teacher can permit much freer expression than in other classroom activities, since this is "reality practice." The teacher

---

[2] Virginia Axline, *Play Therapy* (New York: Houghton-Mifflin, 1947), pp. 75, 77.

must be willing to follow untraveled pathways, to let one thing lead to another. By expressing *genuine empathy*, the teacher demonstrates that he can view things from the internal frame of reference of the student, that he tries to imagine how the student feels.[3]

The leader of role-playing is not concerned with coercing the student into predetermined behavior. He *is* concerned with creating an openness to experience in which all known behavior can be examined, explored for consequences, and pondered on. The teacher, therefore, remains nonjudgmental, objective, one who facilitates the open exploration of life-situations under the assumption that all possible alternatives are available for examination. He assumes, at this point, that there is no one right answer, although the child may eventually choose one that is right for him or may accept the fact that society defines what is "right" quite specifically in certain areas.

Just as the teacher avoids the use of coercion, so must he, at the same time, protect the child from the coercion of the class group. Children are often made to feel that they are "out of step," that they ought to fall in with the dominant beliefs (especially those voiced by popular children).

Children do need to be accepted members of many kinds of groups, and the effort to maintain one's position in a group may be quite healthy. Torrance points out that cliques may be needed by groups and by the individuals who compose them, as defenses.[4] Sometimes the destruction of such cliques may rob the group of healthy modes of adapting to the demands of a situation. Unhealthy conditions develop when one clique is used, by adults, as a model for others. The group can provide the child with supporting ground to stand on, *if* the group is helped to support variability among its members.

To protect the individual child from group pressure, the teacher supports his right to do his own thinking by asking the group such questions as: "Do you think——must see this the way you do?" And, "Can we gain something from one another's ideas, if we explore our different ways of seeing things, rather than insisting on agreement?" Or, "Why do you suppose——sees this differently from most of you? Can you tell us more about your view ... ?"

---

[3] E. Paul Torrance writes, "The strategy of genuine *empathy* is necessary to replace the strategy of *identification*. Try to view things from the internal frame of reference of the student. Try to imagine how the student feels about things. This is then the basis for helping the student meet the requirements of the situation, as something he is doing for himself rather than as an accommodation to a powerful person." From *Guiding Creative Talent* (Englewood Cliffs, N.J.: Prentice-Hall, 1962), pp. 172–73.

[4] *Ibid.*, p. 183.

Gradually, in such a classroom climate, children feel safe holding different views, in being honest in their opinions. And, hopefully, the class gradually begins to cherish and support the search for many points of view. They learn to "listen" intently to varying opinions, ideas, proposals, to ponder them, to engage in a real encounter with one another.

To sum up, ways in which the teacher, by his *demonstrated behavior*, sets the climate for role-playing:

TEACHER BEHAVIOR

A NONEVALUATIVE POSITION

The teacher demonstrates such a position by accepting all suggestions for solving a problem in role-playing (including antisocial ones) as legitimate material to be explored. Thus a child may say, "I think Tommy should keep the money [paid him by mistake] and pay his debt to the club." The teacher then may say, "All right, Tom, come up here and work out your idea so that we can see what you mean." Instead of condemning the proposal as dishonest, the teacher is trusting to the process of group examination of the proposal, in the light of considered consequences, to reveal how antisocial and impractical it is. By this behavior, the teacher makes it safe for children to risk expressing their impulsive reactions.[5]

A SUPPORTIVE ATTITUDE

The teacher accepts negative feelings temporarily, for the purpose of exposing "real" situations. Feelings are facts that need to be brought to the surface. The recognition of feelings by the teacher helps the child to recognize and release tensions.

Thus, when a child, playing a role, yells "I hate you!" or "You dirty guy!" the teacher may say, with sympathy: "You are really angry." This is an invitation to the child to explore his feelings about the situation.

In making the judgments necessary to such support, the goal is to create an open, nonthreatening, creative relationship rather than to coerce the child (in however kindly a fashion) into socially acceptable behavior. The teacher is warm, relaxed, nonpunitive. He can wait for responses and thus reflect confidence that pupils have the ability to cope with the situation.

[5] Arthur Foshay, "The Creative Process Described," in Alice Miel (Ed.), *Creativity in Teaching* (Belmont, Calif.: Wadsworth, 1961), p. 27.

A "LISTENING" FOR UNDERLYING MEANING

Perhaps one of the most needed and *subtle* orientations that promotes successful leading of role-playing is real skill in listening for underlying meanings. Teachers are habituated to "telling" in most of their teaching. Modern concepts of listening demand a full giving of oneself to *listening for the underlying meaning of what the other person is saying— listening to understand his words as the other person means them.*

Dwayne Huebner has given a description of the climate necessary for real listening.

> The listener . . . establishes the climate for conversation, for it is he who determines whether the words addressed to him are simply to be acknowledged as words or as signs indicating the willingness of the speaker to bridge the gap separating them. He may shrug off the words, listen for information, categorize the speaker, or wait to say his piece; or he may listen to the speaker, plumbing the words for the speaker's meanings, feelings and thoughts, which are only partially symbolized. He must be open to the speaker; the speaker senses this openness as an invitation to forsake his clichés, to expose his thoughts, to prove his own unformed notions, and to shape them so that he too gains new insights and satisfactions from the poetic form which they might take.[6]

The teacher who guides role-playing is *listening* in the fullest sense of the word; he places himself at the disposal of the role-players, trying, with all his senses, to feel and think *with* the child about what he is saying. The test of this listening quality in the leader rests in his ability (1) to reflect back to the students what they are trying to say, and (2) to summarize from time to time the many perceptions that have been accumulating in the various enactments.

In such leader behavior as we have been describing, the teacher is constantly *demonstrating* his willingness to explore openly and sympathetically *all* the children's meanings without attaching value to some and ignoring others.

LEADING ROLE-PLAYING

THE LEADER OF ROLE-PLAYING

The teacher directing role-playing must be clear about what his function is as a guide. He is not completely nondirective. It is his respon-

[6] Dwayne Huebner, "New Modes of Man's Relationships to Man," in *New Insights and the Curriculum*, Chap. 7, p. 149, 1963 Yearbook, Association for Supervision and Curriculum Development, NEA.

sibility to select the problems to be explored. (Exceptions occur. Occasionally a class that has experienced the role-playing approach to problem-solving will suggest that they role-play a problem that has arisen.) The teacher leads the discussion, chooses the actors, decides when to cut enactments, develops the design of enactments and probes for and selects which suggestions to follow through on. The types of questions he asks may be very decisive in pointing the direction in which the explorations of behavior will go.

However, to borrow a phrase from Paul Torrance, the leader of role-playing is a guide, not God.

PURPOSES DETERMINE PROCEDURES

Spontaneity Training. The decisions made by the teacher will be determined by the purposes he has for the role-playing session. If his purpose is simply spontaneity training—to release inhibitions and to invite active exploration—then he may be very open in his strategies and tactics. He asks only enough questions to help the children get into the role, but not enough to "set" the role in a detailed way. Thus he asks, "What is Pete like?" and accepts any useful definition. He encourages wide variety.

Skills Training. If his purpose is skills training, his questions help the children to focus on acquiring skill in the task that is contemplated. He may ask children preparing to interview a resource person, "How do we make this person feel welcome?" and "How do we help him to give us the information we need? What kinds of questions do you need to ask him?" and so on.

Sensitivity Training. If his focus is on sensitivity training, he necessarily spends time on questions about *feelings*, both in helping the children to delineate a role and in exploring an enactment. He may ask (in working on role delineation), "How does this person feel? Why does he feel this way?" And, after an enactment, he may ask, "How is——feeling toward——?" Or, "What are Nora's feelings now?" Further, "Who will be affected by this action? How will they feel?"

Problem-solving. If the major purpose of the session is problem-solving, he may focus on both feelings and alternatives. He may spend more time on delineating the problem—through many beginning enactments—focusing on "What is happening?" And he may probe for many alternative proposals, in an effort to get many brief enactments of alternatives; and then he will help the group to choose one or two alternatives to explore in further detail. He will also spend more time in summarizing proposals for behavior, and in discussing the enacted consequences.

Subject-matter exploration. If the purpose of the session is to explore an area of special subject matter—a social studies historical study, for example—the teacher spends time in a preliminary warm-up, for example, reviewing the events that led to the Boston Tea Party. The class discusses what it must have been like to be a colonial, how it felt to be taxed without representation. Then the teacher can ask, "What do you suppose the various points of view were among different colonists? Describe one man and his possible viewpoint. Describe another." A situation is thus gradually delineated, and a role-playing presentation may result in which the events leading up to the Boston Tea Party are enacted.

The questions the teacher asks in this type of session are focused not only on feelings and dilemmas but also on the historical realities of the time. He may ask, "How did prominent men feel about these issues?" And, "Did ordinary working people feel differently? How could we find out?" In such content uses, follow-up research is implied.

It should be pointed out here that although such varied purposes help to determine the kinds of questions asked, *the questions must always be as open-ended as possible.* They should suggest wide exploration and decision-making by the students rather than requiring answers that are predetermined by the teacher. True, the social realities are determining factors; but the role-playing teacher must always recognize that what is accepted as fact also depends on the perceptions of individuals.

INTRODUCING CHILDREN TO ROLE-PLAYING

If the teacher's group of children have never participated in role-playing before, he must be prepared to accept crude initial enactments.

Results will depend greatly on the nature of the rest of the curriculum in which the children are participating. If the school program is informal, uses group work, encourages much discussion and interaction among young people, then the class will probably move easily into role-playing. But if the students are used to a highly directive, very controlled classroom environment, it will take time to establish a safe climate and to encourage spontaneity.

SO YOU ARE GOING TO LEAD ROLE-PLAYING!

It is best to minimize the process at first. Simply say, after the warm-up discussion, "This story stops, but it is not finished. When it stops, you may finish it the way you think such a situation would be finished in real life."

As the children react, in the discussion, invite someone up to work out his proposal for finishing the story. Be matter of fact. Just say, "Well, let's try it out and see what might happen." You will need to help beginners to feel the role by asking numerous small questions, such as, "How are you feeling,——(use the name of the person in the story)?" and "Where are you now?" and "What have you been doing?"

Spend some time preparing the class to be observers. Remind them that they can help explore each person's idea for solving the problem by cooperating with him. Instruct them as to what to observe for.

As leader, enter quickly to help reset the stage if there is uncertainty about time, place, or who is involved. If a child fumbles, stop the role-playing briefly and ask a helping question, such as, "Who are you working for, Johnny? Do you like him?"

One real problem, for beginners, is that everyone wants to instruct the role-players to act as he would act. You have to say to the class, over and over again, "Let's help Marvin to work out *his* idea. I'll give you a chance to work out yours later."

Initial role-playing is laden with self-consciousness, so the children tend to get silly. When this happens, stop the role-playing and ask, "Are you playing this true to life? How would people *really* behave in such a situation?" Turn to the actors and ask them questions that settle them back in their roles: "Mother, what kind of person are you? What are you doing now?" and so on.

Avoid scolding or being judgmental about silly behavior. You may have to say, "You're having fun, but we're not really working on this problem, are we?" Your attitude of *positive expectancy* that they will be serious and productive will help.

Do not be discouraged if first enactments are fragmentary, or even irrelevant. Simply thank the role-players, turn to the class, and ask for other ideas. Help the children to become more spontaneous by encouraging many quick, brief enactments and *accept all ideas.*

Do not expect to move in an orderly sequence from definition to alternatives to consequences.

Perhaps the most useful advice for beginning sessions is to avoid too much preliminary discussion and move quickly to enactments. Even the follow-up discussions should be brief, at first. After many enactments, the time may be right for an extended discussion of what was proposed, how well it worked, how real it was.

One characteristic of children who have not worked actively with problem-solving is that they tend to stay at a very concrete or operational level of thinking. By this we mean that they continually manipulate the specific incidents in the story rather than generalize about behavior in such situations. For example, they will insist that Tommy knock on the door and return the money (in "Clubhouse Boat"), or they will suggest that he pay the gang, but they will seldom say, "He's caught between his knowledge of what is right and what he feels he has to do to keep his place in the club." Often, one or two children work at this more abstract level, but that does not mean that the rest of the class is thinking with those few. The class may still need to work with the specific incidents in order to think things through.

This need to work at the operational level is characteristic of most young children. It is our goal increasingly, as children progress into the upper grades of the school, to help them move toward generalizations that can serve as guides to behavior in new situations.

Some children will hesitate to participate in beginning role-playing. A little "friendly persuasion" is helpful, such as saying, "How about it, Jane? Don't you think you can be the teacher this time?" But, as a general rule, allow those children to watch the role-playing. Eventually they will involve themselves. Occasionally you may have children whose experience in dramatics leads them to put on "performances." You will need to explain that we are not putting on a play, we are simply thinking things through in action.

Never evaluate the quality of performance. Instead, focus on how real the enactment was, what ideas and feelings were presented, what will follow, and so on.

The teacher of beginning role-playing need not be discouraged at seeming wild behavior: hands waving madly, everyone talking at once, children issuing orders to each other and laughing hilariously at an enactment. This shows involvement. It also is the product of a first effort. Each session will bring more order and self-discipline as the teacher helps the group to focus on thinking, feeling, listening to one another, doing the job. You may say, "I can't hear you all at once!" Or, laughing, you say, "Calm down, so we can hear one another."

When selecting first role-players, it is wise to choose children who are demonstrating by their comments that they visualize the roles. This will require much support from you. Help each child to see his role. Ask him what kind of person he is to play, what such a person characteristically does in such situations. Conjecture with him about what this person may be thinking.

Spend more time setting the stage in initial role-playing. Visualize in some detail what the place is like, who is doing what, where doors are, furniture, other details.

Occasionally, the first session may be too much for a group—they may become overexcited, or extremely noisy. Simply terminate such a session, saying that this will be all for this time. Then, the next time, remind them what happened and suggest that they try *really* to explore seriously the new problem story. End the session by commenting on all the useful contributions, such as "Marie helped us to see how angry some people can get," or, "You had so many different ways that this situation could end."

In this initial experience, you, the teacher, are walking a tightrope. You wish to release the children to express their feelings honestly and spontaneously; at the same time, you must set some limits on behavior. Since first efforts release feelings in an area of low skills, you control the situation by permitting only short enactments, by asking key questions, by ending the whole session early, finishing with praise for the positive elements that emerged. You avoid scolding or criticizing. Later, after the children sense your openness to their experiences, you can set limits by helping them to decide on what helps and what gets in the way of good role-playing.

PATTERNS OF ROLE-ENACTMENTS

As you lead role-playing, you are confronted with a number of decisions: When shall I cut an enactment? Shall I follow through on one proposal to its consequences, or shall I call for an alternative proposal? Should I keep one actor in his role and change the others, or should I change them all?

The following guide lines may be helpful:

1. Allow an enactment to run only until the behavior that is being proposed is clear. Cut the enactment when you have enough data for discussion, or when actors and audience seem to have gained some insight, or when a skill has been practiced.

   Sometimes you cut when an impasse has been reached and the actors need help, or it is time to let another actor take over. Occasionally, you cut in order to rescue a child who is becoming emotional. Always cut when it is obvious that the action is continuing too long—that it is going nowhere, or when the group has obviously become bored and restless.

   Remember that an initial enactment is to help the group to define the situation further, and to identify with the characters; it does not always have to be completed to be useful.

2. You may choose to re-enact the same scene if discussion of the first enactment reveals confusion about the details of events or ambivalence about the roles of the various characters. Thus, if a discussion centers on what a boy like Tommy Haines would do (in "Clubhouse Boat"), there may be several conceptions of what Tommy is like, of what kinds of people his father and mother are. This may lead you to invite the child who sees Tommy differently to play the same incident out as he sees it.

   A first session may actually do no more than explore thoroughly the dimensions of the situation in terms of the many perceptions the children bring to the roles. This is a vital learning to achieve—to learn that the solution of a problem is highly dependent on the wide range of human responses that can be made to any given situation. Tommy may be seen as a boy who is afraid of his father, or as one who wants his father's trust, or as a boy preoccupied with his friends.

3. You may choose to keep the same subordinate actors but to change repeatedly the person playing Tommy so as to demonstrate the range of behaviors different children will bring to the role. Or, you may find that a child simply cannot manage a role—that of the mother, for example—so you change her, keeping the other players constant.

4. In other instances, an enactment may so clearly define the situation and imply next steps that it is best to let the same players follow through to another enactment, perhaps through several enactments, until consequences are fully delineated.

   Then the guided discussion can focus on: "What happened? Do such situations in real life sometimes work out this way?" And, "How is —— feeling now?" Or, "Why does —— behave this way?"

   In the lively discussion that follows, you, the teacher, have still further choices to make. Has this series of enactments and discussions plowed up enough ground for one session? Is your allotted time up? Or should you finally ask, "Is there some other way this situation might be resolved? Would other people act differently?" Or, "Is there some place earlier in this story where some other kind of action could have been taken?"

   Such questions take you off into a new series of enactments.

5. If you are guiding the enactments so as to reveal the consequences of a chosen line of action, it is best to help the children to reveal the consequences in action rather than through discussion alone. (Their actual behavior often differs from their verbal actions, that is, from their stated purposes.) Therefore you ask, "What happens now?" And, as quickly as a next event is dimly delineated (do not allow solution at the verbal level only, if possible) you say, "All right, let's see what happens next. Where does this take place? Whom do you need?" and so on.

   After the enactment of consequences, which may be at an intuitional level, you help the class to discuss the meanings of the presented actions. "What really is happening here? What does Mona mean? Why do you suppose she behaved this way? Will this solution work? Why?"

6. Throughout the enactments, you are careful to give the audience active roles. Pearl Rosenberg's study, mentioned earlier, has shown that role-players experience more change of attitude, but that instructed observers see more alternatives, and that uninstructed observers gain the least from a role-playing session. The class can be asked (1) to observe as a whole group, in order to test the reality of the proposed behavior, (2) to divide into groups, each group watching one role in order to define the feelings or ways of thinking of the person being portrayed, or (3) to comment (in a skills training session) on what the role-player did that helped or did not help.

   Before asking for group comments after an enactment, it is

useful to ask the actors to comment on their own behavior. Thus actors can express their own feelings, and this interval gives the class time to think about their own responses.

7. A key decision for you is the timing of the positive solution to the story problem. After a series of enactments that explores impulsive and expedient behaviors, probe with questions for positive solutions. Ask, "Are these the only ways out?" Or, "Could other ways of behaving earlier in the story have helped?" If possible, enact several of the positive suggestions for solution.

    But do not say, by your tone of voice, facial expression, or actual words, "So, you see, boys and girls, there *are* better ways to solve this problem!" By doing so, you will imply that you have been straining to reach a preordained conclusion. Instead, you review matter-of-factly what the many explorations seem to have said. You may say, "It seems to me that you have been saying that in troublesome situations like this, many different kinds of action are sometimes taken." You ask the class to restate the several proposals. Write them on the chalkboard. Ask, "Why do you suppose people behave one way rather than another?" (Remember: *behavior is caused.*)

This is a good time for analogies. You may ask, "In your experience, could this kind of situation happen to someone you know?" Applications can now be made, closer to home.

If in your judgment the time is right, you may finally ask, "If you could manage this situation as you wished, what would you choose to do?" You may also ask, "Why do you suppose that——didn't choose your way?" Or you may use this question—if it is in a sensitive area, for individual, private writing.

Again you have demonstrated to your pupils that it is all right to risk themselves in the presence of a teacher who is not trapping them into a confession and then leading them down *one right path.* Instead, you, the teacher, confirm the principle that behavior is caused, that children do the best they are able to manage at the time, but that other alternatives (with other consequences) may be available. *The judgment remains the children's.*

GUIDING DISCUSSIONS

Much has already been suggested to improve discussions. A few more guidelines may be helpful.

A good rule to observe is that lengthy discussions *follow* enactments rather than precede them. Another is that in the early phases of a role-playing session anything that can be explored by enactments rather than through lengthy discussions should be so managed. Thus, when a child says, "I think the class won't give Andy a chance to lead [in "Squawk Box"]," you invite the child up to enact what he thinks will happen rather than, at this point, discuss his idea. The reason for this is that experience has shown that the actual role-playing evokes real feelings, expresses the interactions and further delineates the situation.

After such enactments, real discussion can be encouraged.

As has been emphasized previously, the teacher's role is to guide, not direct, the discussion. To do this, you:

1. *Listen with all your being to what each child is trying to say.* When a child hesitates, you may try to reflect back to him his feelings or thoughts. You may say, "You're angry at this group . . ." And wait to see if this is what the child means. If he does not respond to this suggestion, you may say "Oh, are you wishing they would like Jimmy more. . . ." Such statements may help the child to bring to a verbal level feelings he has been unable to express.

2. *Your responses are always in line with what the student is trying to say.* You respond by a nod, a comment, that shows that his contribution is genuinely accepted. (You do not turn away and call on some other child if his contribution is trivial; you try to find meaning in his effort.)

3. *You select some comments for immediate consideration, because they hook on to the action or elaborate on a previous contribution.* As ideas rain down upon you from many children, you good-humoredly sort them out, help the children to take turns and stay in focus.

   You tell other children to hold their comments a while because they are new ideas that will be dealt with later.

4. You guide children to think *with* one another. "Let's help Mary work out her idea. What did she tell us in her acting? What do you think about it?" Or you suggest, "Carmen, tell Louis your opinion," in order to stimulate the class members to talk to each other.

5. Certain questions help to lift the children out of their preoccupation with their own immediate proposals to wider considerations. You may ask:

   "Do you know someone who would have handled this situation differently?"

   "Why does — behave the way he does?"

   "Why were our ways of solving this situation so very different?"

   "Why do you suppose problems like this arise?"

   Some groups (or children within a group) respond to such questions and move up to analogies, speculation, or some level of generalization. Others remain able only to cope with the specifics of the story. This tells you that much more experience with confronting problem situations is needed and much more comparison and speculation should be encouraged in other role-playing sessions.

DEVELOPMENT IN ROLE-PLAYING SESSIONS

As you lead role-playing sessions, you will find that different groups of children (and subgroups) respond at different levels to the problem stories. What should you do about this?

First of all, as you become more experienced, you will become increasingly able to diagnose a situation. You may have to decide on a slow, easy exploration of a problem through a number of planned story sessions, or you may conclude that a particular group of children need only limited warm-up through one or two stories that delineate an issue before they are able to move to broad considerations and generalization.

It may help you, as a role-playing leader, to think of your task along the lines of the five levels in the following scheme:

1. *First enactments:*	A further definition of the specific events (a form of beginning problem analysis)
2. *Second, third enactments:*	An exploration of roles and feelings (*who* is involved, *how* they feel; data collection)
3. *Later enactments:*	A delineation of events leading to consequences, personal and societal (social sanctions become clear)
4. *Final enactments:* (not always achieved)	Decisions are made (values are brought to bear on the situation)
5. (Sometimes) *generalization* is achieved through discussion:	Conclusions are drawn, applications made, and generalizations are verbalized.

With some groups of children and with some problems in many groups, an entire role-playing session may remain at Level One. You yourself may choose to focus a group on Levels One and Two, with certain stories, in order to develop needed sensitivities for a given class. Some stories, with some classes, will move easily through all the levels in one story session. With many classes, it may take much practice in problemsolving through role-playing before children can consciously, deliberately, and with a maturing sense of values arrive at Level Five.

From time to time, after many comments, enactments and discussions, you help the class to order their thinking by asking if someone can put together what has been suggested, or summarizing for the class saying, "It seems to me you people have been saying ..." (in a mild, open, not final, tone). If you are *listening* to your children—their voices, actions, words—you can lift their thinking by reflecting back to them in summary form their thoughts and actions.

PROMOTING SENSITIVITY:

There will be moments when certain children reveal themselves as insensitive to the feelings of others. Some children may consistently reveal this trait. Several devices will help you with such children. You may ask such a child to switch roles with the role to which he has been insensitive. Thus the boy who has been playing the classroom leader suddenly finds himself in the role of the unwanted boy. You may have to help him step into this role by asking, "What is——like? Why is he left out? What does he do that annoys other boys and girls? How is he feeling now? How does he see his situation?"

You may have to switch roles—to the roles to which he has been insensitive, using literature for human understanding, placing this particular child on the receiving end of thoughtless treatment in other role-playing sessions, and planning a role-playing sequence that focuses the entire class on feelings.

MEETING INDIVIDUAL NEEDS:

As you, the teacher, diagnose the needs of individual children, you may find role-playing useful in specific areas. For example: 1. You may select a problem story because it supports a child's need to be accepted *with* his differences—Hildred Nichols did this when she developed short situations to help second graders to accept and understand Marilyn, the deaf child.[7] 2. You may use a story like "Bandit Cave" because Bobby, who is poor at sports and gets left out of games and is shy, you know to be a good story-teller; you can improve his status with the group by casting him (with preparation) in the key role. 3. You may choose a role and a story that will help an insensitive child to identify with others. 4. Or, you may use a story (as did Marie Zimmerman Solt in the story of "George"), to help a group understand a troubled child.[8]

SOME PROBLEM AREAS:

From time to time you will meet problems that call for special consideration. What shall you do with the child who never participates in role-playing? He may have deep-seated problems that need careful diagnosis. You may, considering all that you know about him, decide this child needs special help from the school guidance services. Sometimes, however, simple devices are helpful. Perhaps he is self-conscious and shy. Selecting a role that calls for a special skill and *teaching him that skill in advance* may help. Then, when you call for someone who knows how to do this particular activity, he may volunteer. Sometimes structuring a role

---

[7] See Chapter 4, p. 56.

[8] See F. Shaftel and G. Shaftel, "Role-playing the Problem Story," National Conference of Christians and Jews, 1952, pp. 61–65.

for him, asking him to play the boy who returns the money to the white-haired man (in "Clubhouse Boat") will enable him to participate. Other times, when several roles are called for, inviting this child and someone who is his close friend gives him the support he needs.

What do you do when extreme feelings precipitate highly unacceptable language? The use of nondirective techniques can help. You can say to the child (or children) kindly and sympathetically, "I know you are furious. He's really made you furious. But," and here your voice is firm, "in this classroom we can't speak that way. Can you express your feelings in other words?"

What do you do to protect a child who portrays a highly unacceptable solution? You accept his enactment matter-of-factly, saying, "Henry has shown us what some people do in this situation. He is reminding us that these things do happen." In this way you remove the implication that this is the way Henry himself would behave.

What do you do when a child reveals too much of himself? For example, Therese says, "I lie, and it works for me all the time!" This is the time to accept the comment, nonjudgmentally, to turn the discussion to other matters, and to take note of Therese's need—to be followed up with further diagnosis. *Do not confront her with her admission.* To do so would be to jeopardize the trust the class holds in you.

What do you do when you sense that a discussion has aroused guilt feelings in the group? The problem may be one of lying to get out of a deserved punishment. Such lying may be attacked vehemently by some members of the class. This is an opportunity for you to help the group to acquire a healthy perspective on the matter. You may say, "We all lie at one time or another. Sometimes it is to keep from hurting someone. Sometimes it is because we are afraid, or desperate." You may encourage children to talk about why people lie, how it feels to lie, what can be done to find more comfortable and more adequate ways of solving problems.

By so guiding the discussion, you can replace guilt feelings with the reassurance that none of us is perfect but that we can improve with experience. Here discussion can provide a release of tensions.

IN CONCLUSION:

While much can be gained from even random uses of role-playing, teachers will be using a much sharper tool if they recognize that this useful medium serves best the teacher who uses it diagnostically. You need to know your group, its social structure, its individual needs, the dynamics of social interaction that help or deny children opportunity in interpersonal situations. Each group of children reveal their own needs to the skilled and observant teacher. Sociometric data are helpful. Role-playing programs can be planned for specific classes in terms of:

1. Groups that lack cohesive structure: where there is social competition, or a power cluster, or neighborhood conflicts
2. Individuals who need help in building up their self-esteem
3. Provincial attitudes born of suburban or small-town isolation that accentuates poor attitudes toward differences
4. Lack of opportunities for experiencing decision-making because of a highly traditional curriculum, authoritarian subcultural components, or the presence in a class of many dependent children

There will be other needs, of course. What is important, to our viewpoint, is a realization on the part of the teacher that role-playing is a focused tool, most useful when used appropriately.

OUTCOMES

As you do role-playing, how do you know that you are successful? How do you know when you are getting worthwhile results? How do you know when you are achieving some of the goals described earlier in this book? How are you to judge your effectiveness in leading the kind of role-playing described here?

Often, successful results in role-playing are not immediately obvious; sometimes, luckily, they are. But human beings are complex; values and attitudes, culturally imprinted outlooks and determiners of behavior are not transformed as if by the magic of a push-button or the adding of a new chemical to a mixture. However, to the role-playing leader who has some training and experience, the effects of role-playing are often quickly apparent.

> A large body of psychological research convincingly demonstrates the power of role-playing to change deeply-held attitudes, values, and even conceptions of self. . . . Recently, social psychologists have subjected the process to intensive laboratory investigation in their study of attitude-change.[9]

What are some of the outcomes of the role-playing process herein described?

1. Problem confrontation

An important value of role-playing lies in problem confrontation and definition. If a group listens to a story, reacts earnestly, and proceeds to

[9] Thomas F. Pettigrew, A Profile of the Negro American (Princeton: Van Nostrand, 1964), p. 5.

analyze it, showing that they have grasped the essential problem involved and perceive its richness of implications, this alone (even if no other insights and conclusions are immediately expressed) is an achievement of real value.

For example, in the story "Trick or Treat," two boys induce two younger lads to play a Halloween prank that unexpectedly results in serious property damage and in injury to an old man. The older boys, who are actually to blame, are safe from exposure, however; their younger dupes are the only ones who have been identified as at fault. By saying nothing now, the older boys can remain unsuspected and unpunished for their actions. If a classroom group, after hearing this problem story, realistically defines the problem and expresses awareness of the issues involved—that the younger boys, who committed the mischief, were put up to it by the older boys and were, besides, too immature to foresee the possible consequences; that the really guilty pair, even if they escape exposure and punishment, will not escape their own consciences; that the younger boys, who have been misled, will probably retain resentful feelings of mistrust— then the pupils have had an important growth-giving experience in problem definition.

2. *Sensitivity to others' feelings: awaking empathy*

The *feelings* involved are, naturally, of basic importance in studying behavior. Too often, however, as we make decisions as to courses of action to be pursued, we either fail to foresee the emotional concomitant of given behavior, or we fail to estimate the full weight of doubt, self-blame, or remorse it may inflict upon us. Similarly, we may fail to foresee the impact of our behavior upon others; for example, the possible sense of belittlement and rejection it may inflict upon them.

Thus, in the "Finders Weepers" story, three boys who have damaged a boat lack the money to pay for repairing it. They find a wallet. It contains the sum they need and a little more. They are torn between using the money to pay for repairs to the boat and returning the money to its owner, whose name is in the wallet. A group role-playing this story enacted the alternative of keeping the money. They repaired the boat, returned it to its owner, were thanked and told they could use the boat whenever they wished. They felt a great sense of relief upon extricating themselves from trouble, but, *afterward*, doubt spoiled their happiness. They had been dishonest. They *felt* guilty. As one boy expressed his feelings, in discussing the aftermath of such behavior, "You don't feel so good inside," and another youngster said that after he had confessed such an act to his father and had been punished, he felt much better.

Such responses reveal that role-playing pupils are *relating the trial behavior to their own past experiences. They are finding answers from reality.* Clearly this is a worthwhile outcome to the role-playing, perhaps even a truly important outcome.

The role-playing group may come to a generalization: behavior often exacts a toll of feelings, and if these feelings are painful, the consequences of questionable behavior may be far too costly. When such a generalization is arrived at through an interchange of opinion among peers, it carries far more weight and is far more likely to influence future choices of behavior than if it comes as a moral or directive from an adult exhorting a group "to be good."

Sensitivity to others' feelings is, of course, the other face of this coin. In the story, "The Prize," a student committee selects a boy as the outstanding Student Citizen of the Year to be given an award offered by an out-of-school donor. When this donor discovers that the winner is a Negro boy, he is angry; he tells the committee that he will provide another prize to be awarded to the outstanding *white* citizen of the year. The selection committee of three boys debates the matter. One says that they must refuse the second prize; another judge asks what's the harm in taking a second prize so that another student can win a valuable award? The harm is, of course, the fact that awarding a second prize to a white boy in this situation serves to set the Negro apart as different and is an indirect belittling of Negro people, that such an experience sharpens the long-felt feelings of being treated as inferior and of being rejected. If the role-playing group, through discussion and enactments, sharpen each other's insights to the point where they become aware of the fairly subtle ego-erosion this second award will cause, they will have made significant growth in sensitivity to others' feelings.

In the story "Bandit Cave," a youngster is ignored by the group. He is too quiet, too retiring, to assert himself. He has no athletic skills, no skills in clowning, no ingratiating skills for making friends, and has no close friends in the camp group.

In one session of role-playing this story, during discussion on how it felt to be left out of activities by the group, one child said of the rejected boy, "He feels like nothing, like nothing at all." Further discussion brought suggestions on ways the lonely boy could win his way into the group: learning to be a good athlete, wearing the kinds of clothes that are popular, being a good sport, and so on. Such discussions may be the beginnings of empathy. Such responses often have their origin, of course, in feelings of rejection that had been experienced by the speakers. Role-playing that evokes awareness of such feelings and responses of sympathy— especially in a group situation, where the voiced opinions of peers give immense authority and sanction to values—is role-playing that is achieving results.

3. *Considering the probable consequences of behavior*

Still another vital goal of role-playing is developing a habit of taking forethought, of considering alertness to the probable consequences of behavior. If a role-playing group—after exploring the consequences of alternatives of behavior in a problem situation—comes to the realization that they should have taken thought before acting, they are learning a vastly important lesson.

In the story "A Pistol for Pete," for example, a boy has received a gift of a fifty-cent piece. Indifferently—after all, it's just a half-dollar—he leaves it lying on his bureau top. Later, he learns that it is not just an ordinary half-dollar but a rare coin worth quite a bit of money. When he goes to hunt for it, it is gone. Then he discovers that his younger brother —wanting a cap pistol like the ones his friends had—saw the coin, picked it up, and bought a cheap cap gun with it. Outraged, the older boy's first impulse is to expose his brother to his parents and to go to the seller of the gun and reveal how the coin was stolen and get it back by repaying the seller with an ordinary coin. If in role-playing this story the members of your group, through discussion and enactments, show (1) an appreciation of what temptation that half-dollar lying there on the bureau was to the younger brother, (2) how badly the younger boy wanted a cap gun just like his friends' pistols, and (3) the consequences of disgrace and self-blame that will be experienced by him, they will have had a worthwhile experience of looking ahead to consequences.

Another example may be helpful. In the story "Mr. Even-Steven," twelve-year-old Ken is severely scolded by his father for riding his bike through the wet concrete of a driveway newly poured by a neighbor, and is told that he will have to draw out his savings to pay for repairing the driveway. But the boy is innocent. He discovers that a neighbor boy is actually to blame. The latter denies it, and Ken can't prove the other's guilt. Ken is outraged, but helpless. Then something happens that gives Ken a sudden chance to get even with the culprit by having blame fall on him for an act of malicious mischief. The impulse to get revenge is strong; and as Ken foresees how much punishment the other boy will get, he is sorely tempted. Ken has to make a quick decision.

If, in role-playing this story, your group explores the consequences of Ken's revenge, and decides that they are too drastic, that the punishment far outweighs the crime, that Ken, before getting even, should have paused to consider what the results might be, your group is becoming sensitive to the results of a behavior and is acquiring the judgment to weigh probable consequences. In discussion, if your group points out (1) that the guilty boy might have accidentally ridden across that new driveway, and (2) that his father is harsh and the punishment might have been very severe, they will be actively pursuing the feeling, thinking, *then* acting sequence. This is a worthwhile outcome.

4. *Ethical development: personal integrity and/or group responsibility*

At one time or another, every young person finds himself at odds with his group of close friends; he may wish to do one thing, but his group has decided on another. He has decided to go to a concert conducted by Leonard Bernstein, but his friends have arranged for them all to hear the Beatles that night. Then again, his small group of close friends may decide upon a Halloween prank which he foresees can cause real harm. Does he go along, or stand out against the group in spite of being called "chicken"? The latter sort of dilemma is particularly difficult for anyone, young or old; but the ability to say no to one's own group, when the group plans behavior that goes against an individual's sense of right or justice, is a very important strength. Conversely, the ability to set aside a cherished goal in order to go along with a group decision that is truly worthwhile is also, in many instances, a most difficult choice to make.

The individual, in relation to his immediate group, must develop the skill to distinguish between conformity to group will and cooperation, between personal integrity and abject surrender. Practice in making such distinctions is important; it enables the individual gradually to acquire the judgment to guide him in his relations with any group of which he is a functioning part.

If the group, while role-playing a story, comes to some awareness of how difficult a choice is, yet sees that sometimes the individual must say no, real growth in judgment and in integrity has occurred. Then, again, if your pupils can recognize that personal interest may be a matter of self-indulgence, that the group activity may be a far worthier goal, then the role-playing young people have had a worthwhile experience. And the opposite, too, may be true: If the individual has an important personal goal, and his group of cronies plan a trivial activity that could interfere with the individual's worthy goal, then again—if the pupils can see that the personal goal is more important, *in this instance,* than the group purpose—your pupils are acquiring insights into relative values; and this is significant growth.

Thus, in the story "Sacrifice Hit," Danny faces a difficult choice: his ball team votes to buy a present for a man who has helped them. But pitching in his share of money for this present will mean a real sacrifice for Danny. Certainly the group's desire to show their appreciation to their friend is worthwhile, but Danny has been saving the money to buy glasses that he badly needs for distant vision, and that his parents cannot afford to get for him. If the role-playing group can see that, in this instance,

Danny's need outweighs the group's purpose, they are acquiring judgment. They are learning to discriminate between human values. And if they can appreciate what a struggle this is for Danny, how difficult it is for him to stand against group pressure, to hold out for his personal need against their strongly expressed consensus, they are acquiring sensitivity to others' feelings. Moreover, the teacher can help the group to recognize that they can support an individual rather than function only to coerce him into group conformity.

SUMMARY

Role-playing need not result in solutions that fully resolve the story problem. Instead, the goal is to achieve some growth on the young people's part in sensitivity to others' feelings, and to achieve responses that reveal growth in personal integrity and group responsibility. If the group's response reveals that the young people are becoming increasingly aware of the humane issues involved in the social problems they are analyzing, if their choices indicate that they are choosing to support such issues, they are making important growth.

The role-playing leader carefully avoids imposing his answers on the group. The young people, it is hoped, develop insights from discussion and enactments. These insights, which they may enlarge into generalizations, are their important learnings; such generalizations may guide them in making future decisions.

In guiding role-playing, the teacher must bear in mind a set of basic assumptions about behavior and the teaching–learning process. Most central is the belief that each individual can cope with his own life situation and can grow in his capacity to deal with his problems intelligently. Accordingly the individual must be permitted to make his own decisions and to learn from his own mistakes. In guiding young children, the teacher must tolerate low level efforts to solve problems; she must not show children how to cope but should make it possible for them to *discover* better ways to handle their difficulties, and thereby to grow in ability to make decisions based increasingly on insightful awareness of alternatives and consequences.

Another assumption basic to role-playing is that behavior is not good or bad but the best that the child can think of at the time. Moreover, the teacher temporarily accepts more open expression of feelings than is ordinarily permitted in the classroom.

On the basis of these assumptions, it is necessary for the teacher to establish a "climate" for role-playing in which (1) it is "safe" for pupils to explore behavior, (2) it is permissible for strong feelings to be expressed, and (3) the group is helped to respect the ideas and feelings of all members. The teacher creates such a climate by taking a nonevaluative position (that is, accepting all suggestions for solving a problem), is *supportive*, and *listens sensitively* in an effort to plumb the full meaning of what pupils try to express.

Research bears out the effectiveness of role-playing in changing deeply held attitudes, values, and even self-concepts (Janis and King, 1954). Such results, however, are not always obvious. Role-playing is achieving some measure of success when it (1) helps young people to analyze a problem of personal relations, (2) helps them to gain increased sensitivity to the feelings of others, (3) helps them to become alert to the need for weighing probable consequences before acting, (4) gives them practice in judging when to relinquish a personal desire for the good of the group—or to stand against the group when its goal is trivial or malicious, (5) alerts young people to increasing awareness of the humane issues in a problem of relationships between human beings.

When planning to hold a role-playing session, the teacher new to the procedure is wise to make a bit of preparation.

1. Read the problem story carefully to become familiar with it before reading it to the group.
2. Prepare a list of the characters, with a few identifying notes and comments, to make it easier for you to cast pupils in various roles.
3. Make a check list of the steps involved to keep before you until the procedure is so familiar and automatic that no reminders are necessary.

7

ROLE THEORY

Any teacher who conducts role-playing sessions soon observes certain interesting variations in the enactment of a problem situation.

First of all, different individuals delineate the same roles differently. Yet at the same time there are certain expectations regarding specific roles, which are expressed in such comments as "That isn't what a father would say," or, "Students don't act that way." In other words, there are certain common expectations regarding roles, at the same time that there are individual variations in interpretations of those roles.

In addition, there seem to be highly varied proposals for solutions of problem situations and differing perceptions of consequences.

How shall the teacher interpret these role behaviors? Are there certain regularities in role perception or expectation? When do these occur? How much do individual personality characteristics affect role behavior? Do groups have unique standards (norms) and role expectations? In what respect do classroom groups have elements in common? What is the role of the group in the life of the child?

Social psychologists have concerned themselves with similar questions to those we have just raised and, in recent years, have developed their speculations and research in *role theory*. Role theory gives us a way of viewing the behavior of individuals in groups and of groups as they respond to and make demands upon individuals in the group. We can understand children better if we see each child and the group behavior in our classrooms in the matrix of role behavior.

One of the provocative and valuable concepts in contemporary psychology is that of "role" (or "social role"). Sarbin develops the following concept of role expectation: Each society may be regarded as structured into a number of positions, statuses, or offices. Each of these positions is a collection of rights and duties designated by a term such as mother, policeman, son. The actions of the individual are organized around these positions and comprise the role.[1] The role is linked with a position and not with the person who occupies the position. Thus we think of the role of mother not in terms of the behavior of Mrs. Jones, Terry's mother, but as the common elements in the behavior of all the mothers of Terry's playmates—women who are caring for, feeding and guiding the behavior of children. In Terry's group, a mother who does not carry out these actions in expected ways is not "behaving like a mother." We speak of Mrs. J. or Mrs. M. as being "a good mother" or "a bad mother" in terms of how she fulfills her social group's expectations of the position of "mother."

"To the extent that the actions of a person in a particular position are perceived as conforming to the expectations (preferences) of the members of his society, he may be said to be successful in fulfilling that role. To the extent that he fails to behave in the prescribed manner, that he does not conform to role expectations, he is subject to censure." [2]

In middle-class American society, there are certain expectations for father and mother roles—direct responsibility for rearing their offspring for example—that are quite different from that of a Polynesian society where children may be given away to adults who have no children of their own.

In all societies there are some roles that are highly formalized and well defined (behavior in wedding ceremonies, for example), whereas other roles may permit a wide variation of behaviors.

Some roles are carried by an individual for a lifetime (male, female roles) or for long periods of time (father, wife, husband). Others may be of shorter duration (member of a teen-age group, debutante).

THE INDIVIDUAL AND THE GROUP:

Perhaps one of the greatest contributions of role theory is the concept of the *interaction of the individual and the group*. Newcomb, Turner, and Converse view the individual as a group member responding both in terms of his unique individuality and of influences that the group brings to bear on him.[3] His unique individuality accounts for his behavior in the group in terms of the personal characteristics and attitudes he brings to the group situation. He may, for example, bring to the role of chairman attitudes of trust and confidence in the ability of the committee members to work out their own plans, or he may bring distrust and fear and a need to control every decision made.

[1] Theodore R. Sarbin, "Role Theory," in *Handbook of Social Psychology* Vol. I: *Theory and Method*, G. Lindzey (Ed.) (Addison-Wesley, 1954), 226–58.

[2] *Ibid.*, p. 289.

[3] Theodore M. Newcomb, Ralph H. Turner, and Philip E. Converse, *Social Psychology* (New York: Holt, Rinehart & Winston, Inc., 1965), pp. 322–56.

The other facet of this interactional relationship between individual and group is that each group member's behavior is also to be understood in terms of the influences exerted or mediated by other persons with whom he is interacting. In the same committee alluded to above, there may be persons who will reduce the anxiety of the fearful chairman by the way they carry out supporting roles, thereby changing his attitudes in the process of interaction. There will also be expectations of how a chairman should behave.

Role theories lean heavily upon the interaction theory formulated by George M. Mead (1934), who regarded role as the unit of socialization, a pattern of attitudes and actions that a person takes in social situations. The "self" internalizes these roles in ways that are consonant with that self's experiences. A person cannot enact a role for which he lacks the necessary role expectations.

Cottrell states that "a role [is] ... an internally consistent series of conditioned responses by one member of a social situation which represents the stimulus pattern for a similarly internally consistent series of conditioned responses of the other[s] in that situation...." [4] It requires that any item of behavior must always be placed in some self–other content.

Newcomb points out that the relationship of two persons depends on what each contributes to it—what he does to create and maintain that relationship may be regarded as his role.

The role of an older brother, in general, is that of guide and protector of a younger sibling. We think of an older brother as one who sees that a younger child does not play in the street, is not "picked on" by other children, who calms and cheers the younger when he is in trouble. In many cases, however, an older brother may consider a young sibling merely as a pest and nuisance to be disciplined or avoided. Thus we have *idealized roles* and *actual roles*. Some roles that evolve out of the specific interaction are termed *emergent roles*.

DIFFERING ROLE EXPECTATIONS:

In our society, with its rapid mobility and continual social shifts, there are many roles for which people from varying cultural and socioeconomic backgrounds hold widely different expectations. For example, the student role in an upper middle class suburban community may be perceived quite differently from that in a lower class ghetto with a high incidence of drop-outs. However, a mobile, lower class student may develop the role expectations of the middle class.

To complicate this picture further, any one individual carries a num-

[4] L. S. Cottrell, Jr., "The Adjustment of the Individual to His Age and Sex Roles," *Amer. Sociol. Rev.*, 7 (1942), p. 617.

ber of roles (son, member of a peer group, employee), and may find one role in conflict with another of his roles,[5] or may even find that different people expect him to behave differently in the same role.

A girl going to college may find her student role (as a high achiever) in conflict with her dating role (as a subordinating feminine companion). Must she pretend to be "dumb" when she'd like to discuss ideas with her date? In classes, she may find one instructor encouraging her to speak her mind, and another one irritated by her "feminine garrulity." Such varied expectations can be very confusing to a young person.

A person's several roles occasionally conflict. One may be participating in two different groups, each having different standards. A college freshman may come from a home with strict religious commitments against smoking and drinking. He may seek membership in a college group where he is expected to demonstrate his manliness by smoking and drinking. Trying to meet both standards may place him in emotional conflict.

Anyone occupying a position is bound to be influenced by the expectations (or prescriptions) that are held for the role that accompanies that position. Often one faces conflicting kinds of influence. Sometimes personal characteristics may be incompatible with the role prescription. A public administrator, for example, may resign because he finds the role of stern, impersonal keeper of the public funds incompatible with his self-concept as a paternal, helpful friend of the poor.

Each person adapts to the role prescription in his own way. Accordingly, we must take account of these personal influences as well as the regularities of role expectations in understanding the social behavior of individuals.

Most of us, most of the time, tend to conform to role prescriptions. The group provides sanctions for markedly conforming or deviating behavior. If the individual internalizes the group norm, he finds rewards in role conformity.

One reason for failure to conform may be that membership simultaneously in different groups with differing prescriptions, which are actually in conflict with one another, make it necessary for an individual to choose between two demands. A teen-age boy may come from a very religious home where riding in cars, going to movies and dancing are forbidden. His teen-age group may focus on all these activities as symbols of manliness and adulthood. He cannot meet both demands.

In some conflicting role prescriptions, deviant role behavior may not necessarily be the result. It may be possible to work out compromises, to conform to different prescriptions with different groups. It may be pos-

---

[5] S. Stanfield Sargent, "Conceptions of Role and Ego in Contemporary Psychology," in *Social Psychology at the Crossroads*, John H. Rohrer and Muzafer Sherif (Eds.) (New York: Harper, 1951), p. 363.

sible for a child to be the daring innovating member of a play group and, at home, be the quiet, conforming son of a stern father. The problem for the individual is that of adapting in some way to the group's prescription (peer group, family) as long as he holds a position in that group. *His manner of adapting is his role behavior.*

For the most part people seem unaware that they are playing roles. As Sargent describes it, "they are not conscious of the way their behavior is patterned and delimited within particular social situations.... Our customary life situations—in home, school, office, and community—are well-defined and understood and our behavior within them is performed without reflection or conscious decision." [6]

In new or unusual situations, however, where one's role is not clear, one may suddenly become aware of role demands and consciously consider what may be appropriate. For example, a person who carries a high status role (a diplomat, a community leader) is quite likely to be conscious of role expectations.

When there is a change in position, we see a change in role behavior. It has been said that "the role makes the man." So often the student who is elected to a school office takes on new dignity. Social position determines role behavior. Once one takes on a social position one is subject to the role expectations that accompany that position. One tends to conform to those expectations. A position is thus a center of influences that impinge on the person occupying it. Once one becomes a police officer, or teacher, or parent, the numerous expectations the community holds for these positions tend to shape the role behavior toward the norm.

It has been emphasized that every society develops a series of role expectations, of "positions" that specify the kinds of roles expected of the various persons in that society. But there is added to these role expectations and the reciprocal action between persons another interaction, between "self and role." There is structure within the environment and structure within the organism (the self). It has been said that the self is what the person "is," the role is what the person "does." Role theory, in broad perspective, is concerned with human conduct as the product of the interaction of self and role (Sarbin, 1954).

Each individual is characterized by an internal organization of qualities or dispositions that are the residue of that person's experiences as a participant in the culture. Each unique person, then, brings his personal interpretation, based on his experiences, to a role. A *person cannot enact a role for which he lacks knowledge of the necessary role expectations. These must be acquired through experience* (Sarbin, 1954).

[6] *Ibid.*, p. 363.

INDIVIDUAL INFLUENCES (ROLE AND SELF):

Consciousness of one's roles also may be related to individual differences in insight and self-awareness, or in anxiety. Harrison Gough in discussing deficiency in role-playing abilities has commented that "that part of the personality which links an individual to the social community, often referred to as the 'self,' is a product of social interaction." [7] Self-conceptions are in large part determined by the responses of others. George H. Mead has said that "The self arises in conduct when an individual becomes a social object in experience to himself. This takes place when the individual assumes the attitude or uses the gesture which another person would use and responds to it himself or tends to so respond. . . . The child gradually becomes a social being in his own experience, and he acts toward himself in a manner analogous to that in which he acts toward others." [8] The self thus has its origin in communication and in *taking the role of the other*. The way in which each child develops his self-concept is unique. The amount and kind of social interaction experienced will highly influence the quality of sensitivity toward others which a person develops. *To the degree that a person is able to take the role of the other, he is enabled to predict the other's behavior*. If he has this sensitivity, he is able to anticipate the reactions of others. Some individuals are so preoccupied with themselves (their own unresolved problems) that they are limited or unable to take the role of the other. Gough concludes, in his study of such deficiency, that in the extreme case, the psychopath is unable to foresee the consequences of his own acts, especially their social implications, because he does not know how to judge his own behavior from another's standpoint. [9] These variations in insight will be influential in determining one's consciousness of one's role or one's ability to adapt to role expectations.

Various psychologists have concerned themselves with this relationship between role and ego or self (Sargent, Sherif and Cantril). Sherif and Cantril in their *Psychology of Ego-Involvements* define the ego as a cluster or constellation of attitudes related to what the individual considers "I," "me," or "mine." These attitudes "prescribe the individual's relationship, status or role with respect to other individuals or groups."

[7] Harrison Gough, "A Sociological Theory of Psychopathy" (an abstract), *American Journal of Sociology*, LIII (July 1947–May 1948), 359–66.

[8] George H. Mead, "A Behavioristic Account of the Significant Symbol," *Journal of Philosophy*, XIX (1922), 160.

[9] See Gough, *op. cit.* See also Leonard Krasner, Leonard Pullman, and Robert L. Weiss, "Studies in Role Perception," *Journal of General Psychology*, 71 (1964), 367–71, and Margaret A. and N. A. Cameron, *Behavior Pathology* (Boston: Houghton Mifflin, 1951).

They state that "attitudes related to role or status are ego-involved." [10] We all know the individual who leaves a game or group when he is denied a leadership role. He sees himself as a leader and will accept no other role.

Thus one can conceive of role in terms of ego-involvement (or self-concept) or one can define role in broader terms as patterned forms of social interaction (dependent on situations).

Sargent points out that the "self-image" is definitely based on roles. The individual's idea of himself depends upon his "subjective" roles—his conceptualization of his relationship with others. If, for example, a child feels inadequate in physical games and conceives of himself as unable to be a good baseball team member, he may take on the role of clown and helper, subordinating himself to the team, running errands, carrying equipment, being "funny." This perception of himself can serve as a self-fulfilling prophecy—others come to see him as he sees himself.

Roles are linked to social situations, but are learned, perceived, and often conceptualized by individuals. [11]

INTENTIONAL INSTRUCTION AND INCIDENTAL LEARNING

We learn our roles through *intentional instruction* and through *incidental learning*. Families teach their children how to behave in social situations. The school also teaches certain modes of behavior quite deliberately. The child learns that other persons have expectations into which his overt acts must fit. He also learns what to expect in response to his behavior from others, thus developing his own system of expectations. Perhaps an awareness of role theory would enable the school to be more deliberative and selective in its intentional instruction and the kinds of reinforcement it provides.

Intentional instruction and incidental learning can and do go on simultaneously. The child adopts the ways of others in his environment. As he observes the actions of others around him, he imitates those actions in play, "trying them on for size." Sarbin identifies several forms of acquiring role behavior through incidental means. He comments that among them play is probably the most widely observed and emphasizes its importance in the adoptive learning of social roles.

> At least two resultants follow from the play acting of children: (a) the acquisition of roles (truncated, of course, because of maturational limitations), and (b) the acquisition of skill in shifting roles. In play, the child can shift from role to role without observing the formal logic

[10] M. Sherif and Hadley Cantril, *Psychology of Ego-Involvements* (New York: John Wiley, 1947), p. 134.

[11] S. Stanfield Sargent, *op. cit.*, p. 369.

of the adult. This movement from role to role leads to oscillatory shifting of sets, thus enabling the child to take both his own role and the role of the other. . . . The absence of a number of different standard roles, as well as the absence of skill in taking-the-role-of-the-other, retards socialization and leads to invalid role enactments.

The imaginative processes are central in play acting. They are likewise central in covert processes, such as fantasy. The silent rehearsal of roles appropriate to real or imagined positions, and the roles appropriate to the position of the other, provides a large reservoir of experience. . . . The imaginative process is central likewise in the form of acquiring roles which have been variously named identification, introjection, empathy, and taking-the-role-of-the-other. Dependent on the ability of the person (child or adult) to engage in "as if" processes, identification provides numerous avenues for acquiring roles. The number and kinds of persons with whom one may identify, of course, is limited by the number and kinds of persons in the environment and by cultural practices. . . .[12]

If an individual's experience has been severely limited (our so-called "culturally deprived," for example) or different (minority groups who live with different cultural expectations, or lower class children entering middle class groups), then such a person is unlikely to know the role expectations of the new (or major) group and cannot respond to their norms. We may say, "He doesn't know how to behave." What we should add is "in this situation." He may be very effective in meeting the role expectations in his own subgroup.

ROLE CONFLICT AND COMPLEX ROLE RELATIONSHIPS

In a society as open as ours, where access to new positions and roles is ever present, *ambiguity of role expectations* is often the source of conflict for the individual. He may not only be meeting new role expectations, but he may also be confused by contradictory expectations. Newcomb has said that problems of role adaptation arise when one is confronted with role prescriptions that are personally unacceptable; when the nature of the demands is either unclear or too difficult and confusing; and when several sets of demands are mutually contradictory. There may be present in many classrooms or families *ideal* expectations of role and *actual* expectations. A parent, for example, may wish her child to be honest, yet may set the example of the "social lie." [13] Children may be told by teachers, "We don't fight." Yet those same teachers may tell a child to "stand up for yourself."

Conflict may arise from contradictory demands on the part of differ-

[12] Sarbin, *op. cit.*, pp. 226, 227.
[13] See the story "Little Echo," p. 221.

ent members of a single group of which one is a member. For example, Jane may demand that Mary prove her friendship for Jane by excluding certain other girls from her birthday party. Elizabeth, also Mary's friend, may remind Mary of how it feels to be left out. What should Mary do? There are, of course, many other elements as well at work in such a situation. How central is Jane (or Elizabeth) in the life of the group? [14] (What is her "position" in the group? Leader? Small clique leader? Aspirant to leadership?) How does Mary see herself in the group? What are her role perceptions and/or aspirations?

Perhaps the most serious conflict arises for most individuals from simultaneous membership in different groups. If a child is an accepted member of a neighborhood group that has one set of standards for being a "good guy" and is at the same time an accepted member of another group, a school club, for example, with quite contradictory standards, he may find himself in real conflict. Can he be a tough, daring, aggressive guy on the street, and be at the same time a thoughtful, sensitive member of a service club? Sometimes such dual membership is possible, especially if neither group demands denial of the behavior required of the other group. Sometimes one is forced to choose; one cannot survive in both, at the same time. And sometimes, even if one can manage both, one's inner convictions make such a compromise acutely uncomfortable. Our story "Clubhouse Boat" is an example of such a dilemma.

MEMBERSHIP NEED

It is important to remember that the alternatives are not always choosing between "good" and "bad" groups. The street group's standards may be realistic for the inner city situations in which this group lives. True, they are not ideal, but neither is the life situation ideal. In time, under skillful guidance or changed social conditions, such street groups may develop other norms; at present the ones they have may spell survival for them.

Gross, McEachern, and Mason (1965) speak of the *moral solution*, the *expedient solution*, and the *moral-expedient solution*. Not only children, but also adults, struggle constantly with these alternatives. Again this struggle is dramatically delineated in such stories as "Paper Drive" and "Clubhouse Boat." The child, however, is in the process of shaping his values, of developing his own sense of integrity. He is most likely to respond to the standards set by his reference groups. A knowledge of the complex role demands of those groups is therefore vital to guiding his development.

[14] See "The Birthday Present," p. 274, and "The Un-Invitation," p. 329.

Sometimes individuals are borderline members of different groups. Such membership is considered marginal if one is a full member of neither. Perhaps the most dramatic example of this is the first-generation child of immigrants who does not participate fully in his parents' ethnic group but is not accepted fully by his age groups in the neighborhood or school because he is a "hunky" or a "dago" or a "Dutchy."

The consequences of marginality are especially difficult to bear when one membership group is more privileged than the other and when, at the same time, it is impossible to escape from the less attractive one. This we see poignantly illustrated in the plight of such minority groups as the Mexican-Americans in the Southwest,[15] and in the Negro Americans who are not content to settle for the ethnic or racial ghetto.

Newcomb differentiates between (1) marginality, and (2) dual membership in society at large and in smaller groups from which it is difficult to escape. There may be similar consequences in both sets of circumstances. However, in dual membership (most Negroes and gang delinquents, for example) the individual has full membership in the smaller if not the larger group. The marginal has full membership in neither group.

The minority group has to cope not only with conflict, but also with feelings that they are expected to comply with the standards of the larger society without having access to the means of doing so. This situation is dramatically illustrated in a field study of a California town, Guadalupe (an assumed name), in which the "Anglos" carry certain stereotypes about the "Mexicans" and assign certain roles to them.[15] They expect the "Mexicans" to comply with Anglo norms, criticize them for not doing so, but treat them differentially in church, in schools, in the courts.

The Mexican-American in Guadalupe has a series of role expectations which are the result of his interactions with his own ethnic group (the Mexican-American family and community), his self, and his interactions with the Anglo community. Thus, at home, as eldest son, he is head of his family (after his father), but he is submissive to the padre (the priest) and his boss (patron). In his encounters with Anglos, he expects to be given subordinate roles: to be told what to do in community affairs, to sit at the back of the church (a so-called integrated church), to be told what the school board has decided is good for his children. It can be said that he has many roles, some of which can be in conflict with each other, especially if, as head of his family, he chooses to challenge the role expectations of the Anglo community about his children's education. If the Mexican-American goes against the Anglo-American expectations he is punished by differential legal treatment (in the courts, etc.). If his devi-

---

[15] See Theodore Parsons, "Ethnic Cleavage in a California Community," unpublished doctoral dissertation, Stanford University, 1965.

ation is in the direction of Anglo-approved behaviors (not "Mexican") he is no longer identified as "Mexican." He becomes a "Latin American" or a "Spanish-speaking" person.[16]

In the same way, we have seen the role expectations for Negroes, as held by the Southern white community, being challenged by an emerging conception of community roles on the part of Negro Americans, northern and southern. Traditionally assigned positions (citizen, for example) are being given new role definitions by Negro Americans.

We can thus say that in the Civil Rights movement we have a number of historic role expectations (rights and obligations) being challenged, with resulting conflict.

MULTIPLE ROLE RELATIONSHIPS:

In some situations, it is possible for an individual to manage multiple role relations because he shares expectations with different role partners that he will maintain distinctive kinds of relationships with them. Juan Garcia, for example, may be a highly prized member of the baseball team, but the team may also understand that outside of team activities, Juan must play with and go to movies and picnics with his brothers and cousins (the extended family). If this is not understood and tolerated by both the team members and the family members, Juan may be forced to choose between the groups. We have seen similar problems of dual membership in the role of the "A" student versus that of being a good pal in the crowd. In some school groups at present, it is all right for a boy to be an "A" student in mathematics and science, but not in English or art, if he wishes to maintain his role relations with certain boy groups. Teenage girls who are "A" students in mathematics and science may be dropped from certain "popular" dating groups. We see some girls resolve this by becoming "A" students who are not popular dates, or by deliberately becoming "B" students and avoiding being called "square."

Many other examples could be cited to illustrate how such dilemmas have been resolved or conflict reduced. We are all familiar with the social class barriers that result in insulation of class groups from one another, with the result that each group lives in a homogeneous world of common role expectations. Many suburbs and the inner city ghettos are illustrative. Marie Fielder recounts how cliques develop as homogeneous groups in her study of the social structure of a mid-West high school.[17] The suburban school is often a graphic illustration of homogeneity, in which families

[16] Ruth Landes, *Latin Americans of the Southwest* (New York: Webster Division, McGraw-Hill, 1965).

[17] Marie Fielder, "The School As a Social System," unpublished dissertation, University of Chicago, 1960.

with similar role expectations have grouped together to form a community and school district where conflict is reduced to a minimum. Everyone knows what is expected in the way of appropriate behavior and has shaped his role behavior to the group norm.

Now, however, in our exceedingly mobile and prosperous society, the barriers between social classes are breaking down, and so-called homogeneous suburbs find a new heterogeneity as people of different social backgrounds "buy in" to a community. This new heterogeneity will bring a variety of role expectations into play, and there is a strong likelihood that we will see an increase rather than a reduction of role conflict. For schools this represents a new challenge and task.

GROUPS AS SYSTEMS OF ROLES

The very complex role behavior we have been exploring always occurs in an interactional situation, where an individual responds to the behavior of one or more persons. Since an important aspect of role behavior is the response the individual develops to the role expectations of others, the groups to which one belongs become a strong determinant of role behavior.

A group is what its role relationships are; it is a network of role relationships. Such a total set of roles can be thought of *as a system.* Newcomb, Turner, and Converse state:

> *What distinguishes one group from others is its members' behavior, and not just who its members are—that is, their names, faces, and personal idiosyncrasies. And any member's behavior, as we have seen, is strongly influenced by the positions as centers of influence—both from and upon the occupants of related positions—that he occupies. Thus the role relationships within a group represent the ways in which its members adapt to their positional relationships with each other.*[18]

Each group responds to individuals and situations both in terms of societal expectations and in terms of their own history of interacting with each other. Their responses contain both positional and personal elements. To understand the behavior of individuals in specific groups, one needs to analyze the structure of those groups as well as to know the individual histories of the members.

Groups have many properties. The size of a group may be very influential in establishing the qualities of the interactions that occur. A group that is very large may have difficulty in establishing real communication among its members. In an effort to reduce complexity, demands may

---

[18] Newcomb, Turner, and Converse, *op. cit.,* p. 350.

emerge for a high degree of conformity, while smaller groups, knowing each other well, can develop a liking for one another that tolerates variability in behavior among its members. Small groups tend to participate more in group relevant tasks.

Some groups have a high degree of consensus about role behavior. They have common expectations that reduce the possibility of role conflict among the members. Their common expectations may consist of general acceptance of conventional role behavior. Or they may agree to allow a high degree of variability in individual role behavior. Some groups assign roles and reputations to certain individuals and refuse to change these, even when data is presented that should change their perceptions of an individual (Lippitt and Gold, 1959). Others may have conflicting norms operating within the group, with consequent ambiguity and dissension regarding role prescriptions.

COHESIVE GROUP STRUCTURE

Perhaps the most crucial quality in the life of a group is its degree of cohesiveness. Ronald Lippitt has described a cohesive group as a cluster of individuals who like one another and will support variability among their members.[19] Newcomb, Turner, and Converse describe cohesiveness as the degree to which members of a group stick together so that the group has unity.

Cohesiveness is a very complex property of groups, consisting of interpersonal attraction, individual loyalty to group tasks, and pride in group membership. The ability to share is a necessary precondition. Some degree of common agreement as to role expectations is also essential.

In commenting on role relationships of cooperation and competition, Newcomb, Turner, and Converse state that "a system of role relationships is a cooperative one insofar as the behavior of any one of the interacting persons, or any combination of them, affects all members in the same way with respect to goal attainment. By the same token, a role system is competitive to the degree that behavior on the part of any interacting person which brings him closer to his goal moves one or more others farther from their goals." [20]

In cooperative groups, there is a high mutual attraction, status differences are relatively slight, and members have ready communicative access to one another.

In competitive groups, mutual attraction is low, status differences

[19] Speech delivered before ASCD Research Conference, Palo Alto, 1961.
[20] Newcomb, Turner, and Converse, *op. cit.*, pp. 350–51.

tend to be created by the fact that some individuals appear to be achieving more success than others, and communicative access is limited by the fact that each member is motivated to offer his best ideas as his own rather than as a contribution to a group product.

The group can become the focus of role relations. Muzafer Sherif has commented on the problem of restructuring perceptions of individuals and the pressures that are exerted upon them by the social groups to which they belong—their reference groups. He poses the task of changing the attitudes of *groups* as the challenge.[21]

To sum up, role theory gives us a way of viewing the behavior of individuals in groups and the behavior of groups as they influence and respond to the behavior of individuals. It is a study of the interaction between persons as their actions are organized into roles. It is also an interaction between the role and the self, which adds the unique personal element. Role theory, then, is a study of structure within the individual and structure within the social environment.

SOME IMPLICATIONS OF ROLE THEORY

Education, if it is to be systematically adequate, must be concerned with the role-taking process. Mead stated that "education is definitely the process of taking over a certain organized set of responses to one's own stimulation; and until one can respond to himself as the community responds to him, he does not genuinely belong to the community." [22]

Earlier he had given this definition of *self*. "The self arises in conduct, when the individual becomes a social object in experience to himself. This takes place when the individual assumes the attitude or uses the gesture which another individual would use and responds to it himself or tends to so respond.[23]

The *self* thus has its origin in communication and in *taking the role of the other.*

In *role-playing, we are taking the roles of others as well as our own, as we explore situations in group life.*

Role theory thus provides us with a theoretical basis for analyzing the role needs of children and youth in society and for explaining behavior of our own students in their life space.

Certain interesting propositions appear to flow from role theory.

21 Muzafer Sherif, "The Problem of Inconsistency in Intergroup Relations," *Journal of Social Issues*, V, No. 3 (1949), 32–37.

22 George H. Mead, *Mind, Self and Society* (Chicago: University of Chicago Press, 1934), p. 265.

23 George H. Mead, "A Behavioristic Account of the Significant Symbol," *Jrl. of Phil.* XIX (1922), 160.

Proposition One

If the individual tends to adopt the code of the group, and finds or makes a role for himself in the group, then the climate of group life becomes highly influential in the self-realization of individuals. Lippitt's concept of the cohesive group suggests to us that teachers can actively promote positive group climates that support variability among their members.

1. Role-playing presents us with a medium which provides individuals with the opportunity to try many roles, *with the support of their classmates.*
2. The teacher, by guiding the role-playing, provides the child with the opportunity to play roles that can break down initial, negative reputations often assigned to individuals by the group.
3. The individual, by playing many roles, can acquire skills that may encourage him to seek new roles in his real life situations.

Proposition Two

If one tends to internalize the group's expectations and make those expectations one's frame of reference, one can lose freedom of value choice. It therefore becomes imperative for teachers to help children to become aware of this process and to deliberate on when it may be appropriate to be *with* the group and when it may be necessary to stand alone.

This confrontation with the dynamics of group conformity can be furthered by careful use of problem stories focused on individual integrity and group cooperation. The role-playing of actions that represent the many facets of cooperation, conformity, independent choice, and group pressures make it possible, under skilled teacher-guidance, to make explicit the bases upon which choices are made. It can be hoped that individuals can thereby gain the strength to stand alone as well as cooperate when that is appropriate and that groups can be helped to become sensitive to the demands they make upon individual members.

Proposition Three

Since situational conditions (past experience, the present structure of the group and one's position in the group) influence one's perception of one's role and of the role of others, teachers need to analyze their classroom group structure in order to understand and sometimes seek to modify the role expectations of individuals and of the group. Both the subjective and the cultural demands of the situation need to be diagnosed.

Proposition Four

If a person must have the appropriate role expectations in order to respond to the norm of the group and yet lacks the experience that will delineate such expectations, then such experience must be provided.

Role-playing enables individuals to participate in *reality practice* in which such role expectations are delineated in various enactments with follow-up discussions (Lippitt, Henry, and Zander, 1947).

Proposition Five

Since roles are patterned (1) through *intentional instruction* and (2) through *incidental learning*, it is important for teachers to analyze when each occurs.

In our rapidly changing society, schools need to provide intentional instruction for the changing and emerging roles in our society, especially for children whose families are mobile and unfamiliar with the role expectations of new situations. Thus schools may very well need to help rural children whose families are entering urban life to explore and practice new roles.

In role-playing sessions, the role expectations of the community can be explored and practice provided in appropriate role behavior for key situations. For example, the new child can play the role of shopper in a supermarket or applicant for a job in a store.

Since play is an important means to incidental learning for young children, schools must incorporate play as an educational tool in the curriculum. As children observe adults carrying out their many roles, they "try them on for size." The tricycle becomes a truck with which fires are extinguished or milk is delivered. As he tries the many roles he observes, the child is putting himself in the role of the other. Teachers, understanding this rich medium for role exploration, can provide opportunity, materials, and enriching follow-up experiences for dramatic play in the school curriculum. This spontaneity leads naturally into the more structured procedures of role-playing.

Proposition Six

In the process of growing up, children need help in confronting the contradictory expectations held for certain roles.

In our society, which makes accessible to the individual many positions and roles, this multiplicity of roles at times forces inconsistent behavior even on those who have attained a level of logical and psychological consistency.[24] Role-playing, under an aware teacher, can be a means of exploring the variety of expectations held by different individuals and groups. For example, teachers expect boys to resolve their differences rationally, to "talk it out"; some fathers expect boys to defend their positions by "fighting it out." While we may not always be able to help children to choose lines of action in our inconsistent society, the very awareness of that inconsistency and analysis of alternatives and their consequences may reduce tensions and contribute to stability.

Proposition Seven

The accuracy of one's role perceptions and functional adaptations to the social world are highly related (Sherif, 1949). If a person's perception of the position of the other is unrealistic, then his location of his own position is likely to be unrealistic. His role enactment, then, will be inappropriate and he will have difficulty in relations with others.

Role-playing can be used as a tool to locate such unrealistic perceptions, and appropriate re-educative experiences can then be provided.

Proposition Eight

Maladaptive behavior may be related to inability to take the role of the other. While we see this in a pathological state in some adults, it may very well be a developmental stage in a child. Opportunity to "put oneself in another's shoes," to play at being someone else, is a necessary part of healthy growth. Teachers can provide this in planned programs for sensitivity training, in which role-playing along with dramatic play, literature for human understanding, and curricular content focused on human behavior are basic means.

Proposition Nine

In organized social living, the tendency to act immediately upon presentation of an annoying stimulus is constantly upon us. This is even more true of chidren. What Sarbin has called "tension binding"—the inhibiting of inappropriate role behaviors—needs to be learned through practice. Some individuals need more help in this than others.

In role-playing, one may act on annoyances, with no threat to oneself, and *then* explore the consequences. One may thus practice both immediate reaction and restraint and, hopefully, learn to control impulsiveness.

[24] Marie Jahoda, "The Problem," Journal of Social Issues, V, No. 3 (1949), 5.

Proposition Ten

When an individual occupying two or more positions simultaneously experiences role conflict, he needs help in analyzing his role behavior in terms of *moral responses, expedient responses,* or *moral-expedient responses.* Role-playing provides us with an excellent tool for making these choices explicit.

Proposition Eleven

An individual's willingness and capacity to learn what the role prescriptions are in his group life and how to adapt to them is a determinant of his adjustment to that group life. The objective nature of the role system is also a determinant. An understanding of the system can sometimes make it possible to change it.

The role-playing of incidents in which decisions are made in the daily life of children's groups can be used to make the role system obvious. The teacher is then in a position to diagnose needs and plan a program for change in the climate and structure of the classroom group.[25] Teaching procedures that promote competition or cooperation or that affect communication may also need to be studied.

Proposition Twelve

If positions in a group affect the nature and frequency of communications, then this will affect role relations. The less the distance between people, the greater the possibility of role relationships characterized by shared interests and interpersonal attraction. Such considerations make it imperative to analyze the borderline membership various children have in school and neighborhood groups. Planned intergroup and interpersonal experiences, in which children of various subcultural backgrounds are placed in positive communication with one another, need central consideration in curriculum planning.

Here, again, role-playing is one of several tools for reducing distance between individuals and making possible a sharing of perceptions of subcultural definitions of common situations.

[25] The teacher may find helpful illustrations of diagnosis and program in: H. Taba et al., *Elementary Curriculum in Intergroup Relations,* American Council on Education, 1950; and F. Shaftel and G. Shaftel, *Role Playing the Problem Story,* National Conference of Christians and Jews, 1952.

chapter

8

DRAMATIC PLAY:
GROUNDWORK FOR
ROLE-PLAYING

Sociodrama has been called a spontaneity technique.[1] It is a structured extension of play itself.

Play is a basic means by which infants and young children begin to explore their world. It is a process of coming to terms with reality, in which the young child is beginning to manage his inner world in relation to the world outside him. He constantly revises his ideas of reality by playing them out, by testing them in action.

Erik Erikson proposed the theory that the child's play is the infantile form of the human ability to deal with experience by creating model situations and to master reality by experiment and planning.[2]

Barbara Biber described this interaction:

> The free dramatic play of children during their early years serves as an extraordinarily effective mechanism by means of which they find release from emotional pressures at the same time that they clarify their understanding of their own objective experience in the world.[3]

Early childhood specialists have long understood the educational role of play. In recent years, however, as we have become more concerned with improving cognitive learning, there has been a tendency to retreat from the use of play in elementary education. We simply do not have

[1] Jacob Moreno, *Psychodrama*, New York: Beacon House, 1946; and *Who Shall Survive*, New York: Beacon House, 1953.

[2] Erik Erikson, Childhood and Society (New York: Norton, 1950), p. 195.

[3] Barbara Biber, *The Five to Eights and How They Grow*, undated paper (New York: Bank Street Publications), p. 4.

time for "play" in our hurry to effect means for more efficient cognitive learning.

Ironically, this attitude is a disservice to our concern for cognitive learning. Our interest in simulation and gaming is growing precisely because the utilization of spontaneity techniques enables teachers to make elaborate, complex systems more explicit to the learner.

It is important to remember that children need to learn by analogy, demonstration, and active exploration, *with all their senses*, if we are to help them become imaginative, sensitive, and creative thinkers. There is danger that, in our haste to develop their intellectual capacities, we may narrow the channel of learning to symbolic forms only, and since they would then lack a solid, meaningful base in personal experience, such learning could become a mere manipulation of forms. The industrial arts processes, when done as experiences in unit-of-work studies where children are reconstructing a way of life for themselves *so that they can visualize that way of life, at their own maturity level*, can become the bridge to real understanding.

Jerome Bruner reminds us that "research on the intellectual development of the child highlights the fact that at each stage of development the child has a characteristic way of viewing the world and explaining it to himself...." [4] Reviewing the work of Piaget, Bruner emphasizes the need for children of elementary school age to go through (1) the stage of establishing relationships between experience and action and (2) the stage of concrete operations. In this latter stage the child is getting data about the real world into the mind and then transforming them so that they can be organized and used selectively in the solution of problems. He is building an internalized structure with which to operate. Finally, sometime between ten and fourteen years of age, the child passes into (3) the third stage of formal operations where he is able to operate on hypothetical propositions and is able to give formal or axiomatic expression to concrete ideas.

LEARNING THE PLAY WAY

Long before children have mastered language in order to share the cultural experiences of their environment, they begin to explore the world around them through play.

Children would like to be participants, to engage actually in the adult work that they see about them. Unfortunately, one of the first

---

[4] Jerome Bruner, *The Process of Education* (Cambridge, Mass.: Harvard University Press, 1960), pp. 33–35.

phrases the child in our culture learns to respond to is "No! No!" [5] In addition to our cultural prohibitions, so often derived from middle class concern for property, there are maturity limitations. It is not possible at two years of age, or four, or even ten years of age, to get into the family car and drive it off to "adventures unknown." Children solve this impasse for themselves by reproducing what they see by "playing it out." They dramatize life as they encounter it.

Corinne A. Seeds gave us a very fine definition of dramatic play:

> ... When experience, firsthand, vicarious, or imaginary, stimulates children to an expression of it, through the identification of themselves with the persons or things involved in it, in order that they may get on the inside of the situation and find out how it feels to be there and control it, such activity is called dramatic play.[6]

SPONTANEOUS PLAY OF BACKYARD AND FIELD

In their free play in fields, streets, and backyards, children dramatize their every feeling and impression. They explore the roles of mother, father, the new baby, the big brother—often venting their frustrations in aggressive play toward a play mother, as they might not dare to do in the actual home situation. The doll is spanked, the mother is defied, the father goes off gaily to work on his tricycle.

Children dramatize everything that catches their fancy, improvising equipment and organizing into groups as those are needed. Four-year-old Jimmy on a trip downtown with his mother sees a man being given a ticket for traffic violation. This dramatic episode stimulates Jimmy to organize a game of "traffic" that afternoon on the empty lot next door. Bobby, excited by the play, contributes his experience of watching fire engines go weaving and screaming through crowded intersections. Other children add their experiences—and dramatic play is on!

In such play children inevitably discover needs and meet difficulties. They are eager to understand the world into which they are growing. They have an intense curiosity about life as it unfolds for them. This drive to find out spurs them into great ingenuity in surmounting obstacles and meeting the needs of their play. Jimmy and Bobby will devise traffic signals, will hunt up whistles, and will turn tricycles into motorcycles and wagons into ambulances. Their intense desire to make the play effective

[5] W. Allison Davis and Robert J. Havighurst, *Father of the Man* (Boston: Houghton Mifflin Co., 1947), p. 171.

[6] Corinne A. Seeds, "Newer Practices Involving Dramatic Play," in *Newer Instructional Practices of Promise*, 12th Yearbook, Dept. of Supervision & Directors of Instruction, National Education Association, 1939, p. 122.

will even act as a mediating influence upon individual ego expressions. Jimmy will reluctantly learn to give in and let Bobby be the traffic cop, if this is a necessary condition for the maintenance of the play. These children will continue their active pretending to the limits of their experience, and then play will end for lack of further enrichment. New experiences will set off new play patterns, momentary or extended, depending upon the maturity of the children and the depth of experience involved.

This intense drive to dramatize life activities is a powerful educational tool. Creative teachers have long recognized the contribution that dramatic play can make to growth and development and the learning process (Wright, 1932; Bouton and White, 1935).

DRAMATIC PLAY IN THE CLASSROOM

If a stimulating environment, designed to arouse the interest of children in an area of human experience, is arranged in the classroom and the children are encouraged to respond in their own characteristic ways, they often explore the area through dramatic play.

Kindergarten and many primary teachers long ago recognized that play was an educative tool (Pratt, 1948). They frequently did not know the specific functions of dramatic play but they had learned that if they created play centers in their rooms and allowed small groups to use them, the children gained satisfactions that seemed to aid the processes of socialization that so often are traumatic experiences for the child entering school. These primary teachers used the play centers as a release technique but did not attempt to manipulate the situation for intellectual development.

In the classroom today, dramatic play differs from the casual play of yard and field and the earlier practices in the primary grades in that the teacher feeds it with developmental experiences until it assumes a sequencing that leads children to ever-expanding understandings and skills. Not only is it used to help young children explore and experiment with the social relations of their own immediate environment under teacher guidance, but it is also used as a social studies technique to help children acquire concepts in and identify themselves with cultures and events that may be at a remove in time and space. For example, a group of children respond with enthusiasm to an arrangement of pictures and books about pioneer life in the time of Daniel Boone and to an exhibit of a replica of a long rifle, a candle mold, a hunting knife, a powder horn, and a suit of pioneer clothing. The group's immediate response is to take the gun and hunt Indians. Their concept of a pioneer is a man with a gun, hunting savages.

In the sharing period, afer playing, the teacher asks how the gun was used, and if this method of use was the way the real pioneer gun was actually employed. Pursuit of these questions leads to seeking authentic answers, which necessitates reading for further information about pioneer weapons. The children learn that not only was the pioneer gun used for protection, but also that it provided a means of procuring meat. This new understanding leads to a study of pioneer hunting, to care and preparation of the meat, to pioneer cooking, and to a study of foods other than meat. With each addition of information, dramatic play proceeds on progressively higher levels in terms of activities portrayed and accompanying satisfaction for the players.

In the course of playing the "massacres," the teacher has the opportunity to help the children explore how it felt to be in strange country and to be attacked, why the Indians attacked the white men, how it felt to be an Indian when your land was being overrun by another culture. As the experiences are played and further questions are raised under teacher guidance, the entire culture of pioneer days is explored. Moreover, as the children seek "props" with which to make their play increasingly lifelike, they manufacture rifles, powder horns, costumes and other realia as needed. They undergo the life processes of cooking over open fires, building cabins with logs, and spinning wool thread. These enterprises, of course, involve them in learning to plan, to do research, to use tools and materials appropriately, to measure and estimate, to learn to work and live together cooperatively.

This interweaving of many learnings is the great merit of dramatic play. Such play satisfies children's needs for play and for manipulating materials and for activity and communicational goals. At the same time through this play, the teacher is guiding the children into acquiring concepts that lead to extended knowledge, skills, and attitudes that are important for individuals growing up in our American culture but that children in their immaturity may not see as important.

The success of dramatic play in the classroom is dependent upon a clear definition by the teacher as to the goals of this "educational play."

Its purpose is to provide an environment that will stimulate children to explore, *in their own way*, to the limits of their experience, the activities of a selected social studies area. It is designed to help children identify themselves emotionally with the people whose lives they are adopting, their life activities, and the time and place involved, so that they may develop *real interest* in the activities being experienced and *real felt needs* that will impel them forward to vital learnings. Another major concern is to involve children in common enterprise in which they can learn to work and live together democratically and meet their own basic personality needs.

To achieve these goals the teacher works for spontaneity of expression on the part of the children. He gets this spontaneity by:

1. Providing some vivid contacts with the selected social studies area through an arranged environment of things that children can handle and use, and, sometimes, by introducing a dramatic story about the selected area

2. Allowing the children to explore the environment, and begin to play in their own way, *with no instructions from the teacher;* by permitting them to *discover* their own difficulties and *feel* the need for better organization and further knowledge

3. Avoiding an audience situation. (This is not a stage play or the presenting of a story to an audience; it is the reliving of an experience, each child trying to be a person or animal and *think* his way through the developing situation.)

4. Avoiding criticism of the children's activities. It is important that *the children shall not try to do what they think the teacher wants them to do, but rather that they reveal in their own way* what they know or think they know about the area. By a technique of sharing experiences and by discussion, the teacher will get them to question their own procedures and to want to find out more in order to improve the hunting, cooking, or building activities. Then the enriching experiences the teacher provides as a follow-up of the discussions will not be teacher-imposed, but rather a means of meeting the children's own felt and expressed needs.

In summary, dramatic play in the classroom is an educational technique in which children explore an area of human experience (1) by reliving the roles, activities, and relationships involved in that experience in their own way, and, (2) by acquiring, under teacher guidance, needed information and skills and, (3) by increasing the satisfactions inherent in play that is meaningful and extensive. Dramatic play encompasses the following procedures.

1. The introductory situation is an arranged environment planned by the teacher.
2. Children explore the arranged environment and are permitted to respond in their own way, to manipulate tools and materials and discuss them.
3. A story may be read by the teacher to further the interest of the children in the selected area and to provide initial data for use.
4. Children are invited to play any part of the story or set their own situation.
5. First play is spontaneous and unguided, but is carefully observed by the teacher.
6. Play is followed by a sharing period in which satisfactions are expressed and dissatisfactions are clarified, under teacher guidance, into statements of questions and expressed needs.

7. Planning for meeting the expressed needs includes the processes of problem-solving, making of rules, assignment of work to be done.
8. A period of extension of experiences through such activities as research, excursions, firsthand processes and utilization of multimedia ensues before, and beside, further play.
9. Play proceeds on higher levels (involving more accurate activities and more interrelationships and interpretations) as a result of enriched experience.
10. This is a continuous and expanding procedure, progressing on an ascending spiral that may, in the upper elementary grades, eventuate after weeks of growth into a structured drama.

Thus dramatic play in the classroom utilizes improvisation, discussion, research, problem-solving, and generalization and employs many separate subjects and the entire gamut of educational media (paints, musical instruments, recordings, costumes, literature, films, etc.) as needed.

ORGANIZATION AND PROCEDURES

What are the techniques and procedures involved in dramatic play?

There are no absolute rules or methods for dramatic play. It is essentially a dynamic process. As children interact with ideas and experiences, they shape them into play patterns. The play is always new, spontaneous, evolving. It has a quality of its own because children feel free to *be* the people and the animals as they see and feel them, in their own way.

The maintenance of that unself-conscious freedom of expression should be a guiding principle for the teacher. The way in which this is done will vary with the play situations and the individual teacher, but this quality of spontaneity should be maintained.

With this always in mind, the teacher should feel free to make those changes, suggestions, or arrangements that her particular play situations seem to require.

While there are no absolute procedures in the guidance of dramatic play, there are some techniques that have been found successful by teachers who have worked experimentally with this medium of expression. We present them here with the hope that they may be of help.

THE ARRANGED ENVIRONMENT

The arranged environment, previously described, serves to arouse the immediate interest of the children in the area of experience presented. Usually, if there are realia such as a gun, a metate, chop sticks, or a loom in the exhibit, the children respond by wanting to handle them and to demonstrate their use to each other.

If the children bring to these articles a sufficient background of experience and information, they are ready immediately to launch into play. For instance, the long rifle usually evokes immediate action—Daniel Boone is off to kill that bar! Or, if a little boat is in the exhibit, it is at once put into action by being pushed along the floor with accompanying "toot-toot" sound effects.

However, if the meanings of the articles are meager for the children, they may begin by handling the articles curiously and asking questions. Then the teacher's next step is to enrich the children's knowledge by means of a vivid story, one that will quickly involve the children in the activities of the period concerned. Thus, in a Hopi unit, reading the beginning of Grace Moon's *Chi-Wee* may be advisable.

Enough of the story is read to develop a full incident. Then the teacher invites any who wish to play out the incident.

BEGINNING PLAY

Usually, after the reading of a story, in an area for which the children have meager background, the play takes the form of actual reproduction of the story itself. The teacher helps to organize the first play by asking who the people and animals are that the children will play and by guiding the choice of players. The other children are then permitted to go on to other activities—drawing or painting, looking at books and pictures, and so on. An audience situation is avoided.

If *Chi-Wee* is used, for example, the first play might be the incident of Chi-Wee's finding the red clay for the making of the fine pottery the trader wanted. The children would probably attempt to play the finding of the clay, the sharing of the meal, and the mother's procedures in making the pottery. The children would soon find that they did not know enough about the ways of serving and eating a meal in a Hopi home and the process of pottery making to make the play interesting. The children may become self-conscious as a result, and even silly. This is the teacher's signal that they have reached the end of their knowledge and play must stop for further enrichment.

The first time the play may be stopped after five or six minutes. It has lasted long enough to make the children aware of their difficulties, but has ended before it deteriorated into confusion and disorder.

In beginning play, children often use the few realia at hand and even improvise equipment to help establish the reality of the play.

During this play time the teacher has taken notes on what the different children did and on evidence of further needs. For example, she notes how Jack threw the rabbit stick while hunting, and that the women left in the pueblo "set a table" for dinner.

When the teacher calls the group together, she may begin a sharing period by a casual comment such as "That looked like fun." The children may respond by telling some especially good incidents they acted out in the play. Then the teacher may say, "Mary, I noticed you serving the meal. Just what did you do?" Mary is encouraged to show how she served the meal. This enables the teacher to guide the group into a discussion of how the Hopis prepared and served meals.

What the teacher is doing is to help the group to realize that they need to know exactly how Hopis served meals. This leads to a *"We Need to Find Out"* list with an Item 1 of: "How Do the Hopis Serve Meals?" Item 2 on the list may be "What Utensils Do the Hopis Use?"

Gradually, the teacher guides the discussion: (1) to give satisfaction and recognition for the fun and good thinking that went into this first play; (2) to build an attitude of dissatisfaction with sketchy information and a desire to obtain accurate information and items for use in the play; (3) to make definite plans for obtaining that information and for making the items needed; and (4) to help the group to begin to formulate rules for better social interaction as they play.

For several days, during dramatic play time, the children may continue to use the plot of the story read to them as the basis of their dramatizing, enriching it with the details they are learning through reading, looking at pictures and films, undergoing industrial arts experiences, taking excursions, and through other activities the teacher provides to meet their growing needs. Gradually, as they acquire wider knowledge of Hopi life, they may suggest other episodes to play, or the teacher may herself suggest that they might enjoy making up new incidents about life in a Hopi pueblo. While the story is used to initiate play, the children are encouraged to deviate from it and to develop new play patterns continually. Our purpose always is not the perfection of a story, but the wide exploration of the life of the people being portrayed.

Dramatic play on the primary level operates on the same principles as with older children. The starting point with young children, however, is usually their own immediate environment. They are ready to build and play immediately since they work with manipulative materials such as blocks, toys, and wood for construction. A group of primary children react to an arranged environment of a dairy farm, for example, with a response similar to that of the Hopi situation, except that they may begin at once to run the trucks, use the blocks to build corrals for the animals, and use apple boxes for barns and houses. *They build and play simultaneously.*

It is only as the unit plans develop that the building that becomes construction work with wood is assigned to a work period separate from the dramatic play period. Even then, the primary child who is making a truck for the farm will stop work when he has nailed the engine to the truck body and will take time to run his truck (and deliver some milk) before he has the wheels on the vehicle. Older children, on the other hand, can wait and plan. They often postpone dramatic play for several weeks while making the things with which to play. Thus an upper grade group will work long, hollowing out boats for harbor play, and will wait for the unfinished vessels before playing. In contrast, again, primary children would use blocks for tugs and liners until their constructed craft were ready for service.

In such an industrial arts program, the firsthand experiences are concerned with real processes that illumine the intellectual concepts of man's relationship to his environment, of his institutions and processes, and of other men. Each activity is selected for its significant contribution to important ideas. Construction, in this framework, is subordinated and modified. It is done simply, on a child's level, to facilitate his thinking, to create an atmosphere in which to take on the roles of people. It contributes, as does a stage set, to identifying with a time, a place, and a people, but does not dominate the program.

FOLLOW-UP

After the first play time, as we have seen, the teacher works for the emergence of felt needs in the sharing time.

It is in this sharing time that the teacher guides the group.

This is the opportunity for *the asking of provocative questions,* for the pointing up of attitudes of inquiry, for skillfully assuming that of course "we want to do this the way it is really done," and for helping the children decide how they can find out the actual processes and relationships. This sharing period is a golden time for developing techniques of problem-solving, critical thinking, and other aspects of democratic living.

The teacher plays a positive role as leader, drawing as many ideas from the group as possible, adding others herself, and then helping the children decide which ones are best for them to use.

The quality of the dramatic play and its growth to ever higher levels depends on how the teacher follows up the play needs expressed in the sharing time, and on what plans the group makes.

Let us consider the Hopi play a little further. After the two items were listed on the board, the teacher did several things. (1) She helped the children list sources from which they could find the answers to their questions. (2) She had a reading lesson in which the children read about making pottery and rabbit hunting and then discussed their findings. (3) She shared with the children books and pictures of the women's work in the pueblo. (4) She provided a pottery lesson for the class so that they could experience a major activity of the women in the village and make dishes for use in play. (5) She planned a corn-grinding experience for the same reason.

Now the types of experiences which the teacher can provide for meeting the children's needs are almost endless and depend upon her knowledge of the field and her judgment of what should be fed into the growing unit as a "next" experience. They are a series of teaching strategies. That judgment, of course, is based upon her teaching goals.

There are times when she provides a carefully planned excursion to a direct center of experience, such as the harbor, the freight yards, the farm, or a newspaper plant. Sometimes the excursion may be to a museum. Or an expert may be brought in to share his knowledge with the group. At other times, or even in conjunction with these activities, the teacher may use instructional aids. Always she seeks to weave in the use of significant reading material so that the children may have a growing awareness of the importance of reading. At the primary level she frequently guides the development of an experience chart or presents an informational chart to the group.

Another procedure that pays high learning dividends is that of providing direct experiences with the life processes of the area—the industrial arts experiences such as grinding corn, weaving, making paper, or making boats that float. Then the children learn to do things as they were really done by people striving to meet their basic needs. Properly guided, these activities help children to relate historic and geographic conditions and anthropological conceptualizations.

And always, as children plan, work, and develop the dramatic play, the teacher guides them to see the necessity of improving their skills in order better to achieve their goals. She provides specific learning periods for this purpose. These specific learning periods are kept separate from the dramatic play time to safeguard the spontaneity of the play period and to promote serious study habits.

If the procedure of (1) responding to a stimulating environment, (2) playing dramatically, (3) sharing experiences, defining and planning to meet felt needs, is followed up by the teacher with enriching and specific learning experiences, children will play on increasingly higher levels. Though the first play period can end after five minutes for lack of sufficient knowledge, the second period can go on for fifteen minutes because the children know more and can actually do more. Increasingly, the tendency is to extend the length of play time until, toward the end of the curriculum unit, there are occasional play periods for summarization purposes that last an hour. Moreover the play grows qualitatively. This gain is the fruitful result of deepened and extended understandings.

SOME PRACTICAL CONSIDERATIONS

1. *How many children shall participate?* Ideally all the children in the class should play at one time. At the start, only a few may desire to participate. But as the play goes on, others enter in as their interest is caught and grows. Also, as they make tools or ships or trucks, children will put them into use and are thus naturally swept into the group activity. When all the children play at one time, a common sharing period enables the teacher to guide the development of the same felt needs for the entire group.

Sometimes it is not possible, however, to have the entire class in one play group. Space limitations or the nature of the play may limit the number of participants. With young children it is not advisable to divide the class into more than two groups. If every day one group has a dramatic play period, each group is able to play every other day. An interval of more than one day between the periods is not advisable, since young children forget quickly and continuity of expression is lost.

With intermediate grades, however, it has been found practical to use three groups, each one participating in play every third day.

It is best to keep the group membership as constant as possible, so that the same children work out the play sequences together long enough to get a continuity of experience.

When classes are divided into groups, needs that emerge from one play group may not necessarily be felt by the rest of the class. It then becomes necessary to arrange class sharing periods, from time to time, in which all groups discuss together the important needs that have emerged in any one group or in all groups. This procedure will help to knit the class needs together into a common set of purposes.

2. *When shall dramatic play occur?* The play period is a matter of convenience of schedule. Some teachers prefer to have it during the latter part of the morning, following a reading or research period, when enriching ideas have been explored. This also enables her to plan follow-up activities, when advisable, that afternoon while questions are clear and immediate.

With primary children, dramatic play ideally is provided for as a daily routine, unless other needs interfere. In the intermediate grades dramatic play may be stimulated by the arranged environment and then postponed for several weeks, while the children concentrate on construction and industrial arts activities in order to make the things with which to play. Then play may proceed intensively for many days, with construction and industrial arts at a minimum or standstill.

3. *How long shall the dramatic play period be?* In its early stages, dramatic play should last from five to fifteen minutes at the primary level. Gradually it may grow to thirty minutes. Fifteen minutes or more should be provided for sharing time, varying with the need and the ability of the children to concentrate and sit still. It is significant to note that, as interest rises and the children develop driving purposes, their interest span lengthens and even young children will often sit, absorbed in thinking and sharing together, beyond the usual time span for their age.

In the intermediate grades, play may grow to forty-minute periods with at least twenty minutes for sharing time. There will come climaxes in play patterns, especially toward the end of a study, when these older children will have so much to share that occasional long periods of an hour or more should be provided to enable them to use their knowledge and materials to full satisfaction.

Actually, there are no arbitrary rules on the length and frequency of dramatic play periods. Each teacher adjusts the time in terms of the growing curriculum unit, the developing patterns of play, and the possibilities and requirements of his program. If this media is looked upon as language development as well as social studies, the teacher may feel more justified in the time taken.

4. *Where shall dramatic play be done?* Most teachers have to operate almost entirely within the confines of their classrooms. This necessity does not rule out dramatic play. As some types of social studies units develop, a space may be cleared on the floor so that the growing farm or harbor or community or log cabin can be arranged for use. Dramatic play can be done in that space.

In some areas of the United States it is often possible to use the out-of-doors even more than school people are inclined to do. Some teachers have been quite successful in building and using out-of-door harbors or in carrying out of the room much of the play paraphernalia for pioneer life studies. Going outside enables the entire class to play and helps to relieve much of the tension that arises when we must continually restrict expression because the noise may disturb the class next door.

If the classroom is small and yet must be used, much ingenuity is possible in turning desks into trees in a forest, aisles into roads, and so on.

5. *How much shall the teacher enter into the play? What is her role?*
The teacher's role is that of *facilitating*, not directing, dramatic play. She assists with the minimum organizing needed to get a group started.

She may *help* to decide who will play which roles. (She does not order the choices!) She may ask leading questions to help limit the area of play. For example, if it is a pioneer play period she may ask who the people are in the hunting expedition, what time of day and year it is, and where they plan to hunt.

She guards against making too many suggestions, however, because then the play pattern becomes hers rather than the children's. Her real guidance comes in what she provides in the way of follow-up experiences.

The test of the meaningfulness of those follow-up experiences is whether they emerge spontaneously in later play. *If the learning was meaningful, it will be used by the children;* if it is never used, we may question the significance of the experience or how well done the teaching was.

In the primary grades, the teacher may sometimes casually enter the play and participate, in order to indicate some things that are fun to do. For example, the six-year-olds are building houses and stores with blocks. No play between children has emerged. Miss Brown takes a miniature man and walks him into a store and asks Gordon, the boy builder, if he has some tomatoes for sale. This starts interplay in a situation in which the children have been playing in isolation before.

Sometimes the teacher steps over quietly to a group or to a child to settle a minor difficulty. Sometimes she has to stop play to discuss a major difficulty with the entire group. Such interference should be used only when absolutely necessary as it may spoil the spontaneity of expression. The teacher at all times, however, maintains the standard that "we do this play as it would really be done, seriously, or it isn't fun." Play should always be stopped if the children become silly or disorderly. Silliness is a reminder that children have reached the limits of their knowledge and need further enriching experiences.

The teacher's main role is that of quiet observer. She jots down in a small inconspicuous notebook items that will help her guide the sharing period. She may note (1) interesting and significant play incidents, (2) evidences of partial understandings that need elaboration or evidences of need for new information, (3) need for further play materials or facilities, (4) difficulties in social behavior, and (5) evidence of individual personality needs. Then, at sharing time, by casually glancing at her notes (but not reading them as a judgment!) she can weave into the discussion the points she has noted.

In order to be alert to the emerging needs, the teacher must be observing and noting actively while a play period is on. She cannot assign a group to play and then go off to help a reading group! This would nullify the educative value of the play, for she will not know what has occurred and therefore cannot give appropriate guidance.

This does not mean that two or three children cannot play quietly in the harbor or farm at other times when the teacher is busy elsewhere. But regular dramatic play periods must be actively observed by the teacher.

6. *On what basis shall we group children for play?* When dramatic play is in its formative stage, it is wise to let grouping occur spontaneously and naturally and to allow those who wish to participate to come together, make their decisions, and begin to play.

As this initial play expands in form and group size, it is advisable for the teacher to call the class together and to help the children to divide into regular play groups, if grouping is necessary.

There are many considerations that determine the grouping of a class. It is well to divide the highly creative individuals among all groups. Often it is wise to separate conflicting personalities. Sometimes if an aggressive new leadership individual is removed from a group, qualities may develop in children who have theretofore been shy or reserved.

Occasionally a group just doesn't develop interesting ideas because it lacks highly creative members.

Always the teacher works for the kind of grouping that will permit the maximum development for each child. This may mean that she experiments by shifting individuals from group to group. She tries always to guide for (1) democratic leadership and followership opportunities for all children, (2) the emergence of good ideas, and (3) the personal–social development of each child.

7. *What shall we do with the child who does not wish to participate?*

Occasionally there are children who do not wish to play. Since wholehearted participation is basic to the concept of dramatic play, forcing this child to take part would violate our goals.

Let him observe. Try to involve him in making things that serve the play. The time will come, for most children, when they enter the play of their own accord. If it does not come, it is best to permit such children to do other things.

8. *What shall we do with disrupters?* This is a difficult problem to solve. Since one of our purposes is to promote individual growth, eliminating a disrupter from the play may be a way of denying him opportunity to solve his problem. Why does he disrupt? Does he crave attention? Perhaps a good role may aid him. Is he insecure? Helping him to acquire some special skill or information that improves the play may be a solution. All possible factors should be explored.

Sometimes, however, an individual child's needs are too complex to be met by simple solutions and he actually and persistently spoils the experience for the other children. It may become necessary to remove him temporarily or permanently from the dramatic play group. Of course the teacher continues to work on his needs. The welfare of the group as well as that of any individual must be considered by her.

9. *Shall we develop large constructions in which to play, or "miniatures"?*

The choice of large or small should depend on what the teacher wishes to accomplish.

In the first and second grades, where we try to help children understand their extending immediate environment in its many relationships, the miniature community or airport or harbor offers better opportunities than the large play house or store. Since these children are just beginning to learn cooperative behavior, the small houses, boats, farm tools and machinery enable them to begin individually and gradually to learn to play together. As the child with a small house plays in that house, he learns to cooperate with the child who has built a store and to *see* the relationships involved.

The miniature or small construction at either primary or intermediate level offers far greater opportunities for promoting interrelationships and many varied social understandings.

The large construction serves others important functions. The Hopi puebo built of packing boxes large enough for families to live in can promote the growing social relationship of the children and permit them to carry on the roles and rituals and real life processes of cooking, weaving, pottery making, and the like. This is also true of the colonial or pioneer home.

Sometimes it is advisable to use both. A class may build the interior of a colonial home at the same time that they develop a miniature of a Pilgrim village, shifting from actual living in the large room to using miniature people to carry on community affairs.

There are no hard and fast rules as to large or small. They should be used to promote the needs of the group and the area of experience under exploration.

10. *When does dramatic play become dramatics?*

Those teachers who have worked with dramatic play have come to prefer it to dramatics as a major medium of expression because it is so creative for all its participants and promotes real emotional identification and understanding. Children are really *living* an experience rather than merely telling a story to an audience.

From a literary point of view, dramatics with older children certainly has its own unique contribution to make. But as a means of developing social studies concepts and social adjustments and learnings, dramatic play offers far greater possibilities.

Even from a literary point of view, dramatic play has rich potentialities. In order to enrich play, the literature of the cultures studied can be used extensively. Children will respond to the vivid descriptions in poetry and narrative of how people lived, talked, and dreamed in a given time and place. The arts, in all their aspects, serve this cause.

It is gratifying to see the growing pattern of oral expression in children who participate in dramatic play.

As children grow older, from ten or eleven years on, they have increasing ability and interest in organizing ideas. Often, from about the sixth grade on up, we see them begin with spontaneous dramatic play, then choose the events they particularly like and define them into definite patterns. And sometimes those patterns become "fixed" in form and emerge as "plays" to be presented to other groups, parents and community. It is always important, however, to safeguard the preliminary spontaneous dramatic play and let the dramatics emerge as an outcome.

SOCIODRAMA: AN EXTENSION OF DRAMATIC PLAY

Dramatic play, if properly done, offers the school a method of guiding children into social studies experiences in a way that satisfies their basic needs as children to be active, to have contact with reality, to try out roles, to belong to a group, to learn the techniques of democratic group life, and to express themselves emotionally and aesthetically. Dramatic play becomes a means of integrating both cultural and personal experiences in the task of promoting wholesome child growth.

We have said that sociodrama is an extension of dramatic play. Essentially, sociodrama is the role-playing of human relations problems with the help of a critical, evaluating audience.

How does it differ from the dramatic play procedures we have discussed in the previous section? It would be possible to define dramatic play and role-playing in a very broad way, but for the purposes of a social studies program we find a definition geared to social studies objectives more immediately useful.

In a social studies program *dramatic play* is used to encourage children to explore an area of human experience by reliving the activities and relationships involved in it. Its major purpose is to help children identify emotionally with the people, their life activities, and the time and place involved, so that they may develop real *interest* in the activities being experienced and real *felt needs* that will impel them forward to vital learnings. A major concern is to involve children in a common enterprise in which they can learn to work and live together democratically and in some measure begin to meet their own basic personality needs. Thus children playing pioneers or firemen have a chance to enjoy the feeling of being firemen or trappers or Indian Scouts or bullwhackers, and, at the same time, to gain understanding of the data they use through actual experience. Actually churning butter is, for some, a more effective way of learning than merely reading about churning.

The teacher guides her pupils into discussion, into raising questions about *content*, into planning and making artifacts and props, and into carrying on life processes, first, to enrich their experiences and second, to increase the pupils' satisfaction and aesthetic pleasure in dramatic play. Perhaps, to emphasize the point being made here, it should be said that dramatic play, as used in social studies, is focused on a *continuity of content*. Unlike sociodrama, dramatic play does not have as a chief goal the solving of problems and does not necessitate an observing and reacting audience.

Sociodrama, on the other hand, is primarily a group problem-solving tool, focused on human relations. Usually in a sociodrama session, a problem is either presented by the teacher or emerges from the group. Solutions are proposed by various members of the class in the form of spontaneous enactments of the situation. The class serves as active observers of the actors, evaluating and criticizing the playing of the roles, offering other enactments, continuing discussion until a variety of possible solutions and their consequences have been explored. The enactments are focused on exploring alternative solutions and their consequences.

Perhaps the difference between dramatic play and sociodrama can be illustrated in the following way:

Children studying pioneer life choose to portray, in dramatic play, many situations that arise as a wagon train moves westward out of Independence. The boys and girls elect a wagon train captain, divide into families, and dramatize a day on the trail. The events are unspecified. Each child decides for himself what he will do and the kind of man, woman, or child he will be, within the general framework of the wagon train set-up agreed upon. As the play progresses, the action of the individual players will precipitate events. Continuity emerges from the spontaneously expressed ideas of the players.

The teacher's primary objective is to guide the evaluation of the play in such a manner that children will feel the need for more accurate and detailed information so that they can better identify with the time and people. This, of course, is *content*.

In a sociodrama session, however, the material is structured into a definite situation involving a problem of interpersonal relations. For example, it would be possible to develop a problem situation out of the dramatic play just described. As the wagon train moves westward through the mountains, a crisis occurs. (This problem may be presented by the teacher, or may arise spontaneously in the dramatic play, or is deliberately set up by the pupils.) A wagon breaks down, because it is overloaded, while the train is moving through a narrow pass and is endangered by Indians or by a snow storm.

The wagon captain orders a halt so that the damaged vehicle may be repaired. Members object. The whole party may be snowbound in a narrow, inhospitable pass if the train is held up in order to repair a wagon that would not have stalled if the driver had just used ordinary common sense in loading. The captain insists that all must stick together. Protests arise, argument grows heated. Finally one man refuses to comply with the captain's decision and declares that he will pull his wagon out of the long line and crowd his way past the file of wagons in order to escape from the dangerous pass.

This foolhardy attempt may cause a jam in the pass that will delay the entire wagon train for an even longer period and needlessly add to everyone's peril.

The class discusses the problem briefly, defining the problem, and the various roles involved are described. Some children volunteer to play the parts; the rest of the class act as critical observers as the situation is enacted.

After the first players have offered their unrehearsed enactment, the class discusses the presentation and evaluates it in terms of: *Could it have happened this way? Why did the characters behave as they did? Is another solution possible?*

Perhaps a child playing the wagon train-master decides to abandon the disabled wagon. This solution will be discussed by the class. What will be the consequences of this act? Is it practical? Could it have happened? How will the people affected feel about this? Is there another solution possible?

Another youngster may suggest a different action. She will be invited to enact her proposal. Whom will she need to help her? Where does this action take place?

The first actors are replaced by the new ones who have different ideas of how the roles should be played. Again the enactment is evaluated. And still a third group of actors play out their version of the conflict, and for a third time the solution is analyzed and modifications suggested.

The focus of the group, under teacher guidance, is on the human relations involved in the crises faced by the wagon train as it makes its hazardous trip westward and on the consequences of the behavior of the people. The class may eventually generalize on the need for cooperative attitudes and skills in pioneer life.

In such a sociodrama session the emphasis is on exploring why the people behaved as they did, and on trying out many possible solutions to the problem situation. *The session is deliberately structured for experi-*

ence in specific problem-solving in human relations. Children who have explored their world through play, both in school and in their neighborhood life, develop the capacity to enter freely and imaginatively into the more structured explorations of sociodrama or role-playing and other forms of simulation. Teachers who are interested in the educational usefulness of role-playing would do well to reconsider dramatic play as an educative medium that is the initial spontaneity technique of childhood.

To sum up, *dramatic play* is a spontaneity experience focused on exploring roles and acquiring content. Sociodrama is a group learning procedure focused on providing practice in solving problems of human relations.

chapter

9

OTHER USES OF
ROLE-PLAYING

ROLE-PLAYING AS A LEARNING METHOD FOR
DISADVANTAGED CHILDREN

Role-playing can serve a most useful function as a method for enabling slow learners to improve their classroom achievement markedly.[1] Role-playing can be used to help young people to acquire a better self-image and more personal security. Acceptance of self is basic to acceptance of others, which is implicit in group responsibility.

Our disadvantaged children [2] present us with a difficult problem. As our cities become urban complexes so large that they are thought of as "regional cities," and as automation—in the period of lag between the vanishing of old jobs and the development of new large-scale work requirements—causes increasing unemployment, the number of low-income families in our country is multiplying.

In 1950, out of every ten children in fourteen of our large cities one was culturally deprived; and in 1960 the number had risen to one in three. It is predicted now that the percentage will increase. By 1970, one in every two children in these cities will come from environments that can be described as culturally deprived.[3] In addition, in big city elementary schools, from 40 to 70 percent of the students will be from minority groups.[4]

[1] Frank Riessman, *The Culturally Deprived Child* (New York: Harper & Row, 1963), p. 77.

[2] Disadvantaged or culturally deprived children are those who come from lower-class, socially impoverished circumstances.

[3] Frank Riessman, *op. cit.*, p. 1.

[4] Martin Deutsch, "The Disadvantaged Child and the Learning Process: Some Social, Psychological, and Developmental Considerations," a paper prepared for

A great many low-income families today are of rural background and minority origin: Negro, Puerto Rican, Mexican, and so on. For the most part, they live in very crowded slums. The young people of such families are labeled low-income, culturally deprived, disadvantaged, slum, lower-lower class, underprivileged, and in some contexts, dead-end kids.

Disadvantaged children are usually economically deprived. Many suffer from poverty so unrelieved that it is overwhelming. Their housing is poor and inadequate. Some have never known what it means to go to sleep for the night with full stomachs. Their only complete meal each day is the "free lunch" they receive at school.

Among such deprived children, physical survival blots out all other needs. In many families, the mother is the sole breadwinner. With long work hours in unskilled employment all that is open to her, she is required to be away from home during most of the child's waking hours. It is impossible for such mothers to meet all the needs of growing children. In many instances, even family meals are unknown. The oldest children in such families handle the food budget, prepare whatever food is available for younger children, and take on full responsibility for them, assuming the burdens of maturity too early in life.

"Among the economically deprived are many whose health has been crippled. Poor nutrition, inadequate clothing and housing, and lack of simple routine medical care have made deep inroads prior to school entrance. In one typical city, 65 percent of all public school children have never known what it means to have a family doctor or any medical service, except emergency clinic care.[5]

"Many disadvantaged children are the victims of a poverty so crushing that early in life poor health not only drains the energy but blights the spirit."

One result of such poverty is that deprived children acquire a self-image of worthlessness. Thousands of boys and girls, entering school at five and six years of age, have already learned that they are of little worth. This is understandable in the light of their lack of family security. Many children do not know who their parents are, and know only that they have been shunted around among adults and have lived in a succession of homes. Many have no father but live with their mother and siblings in a fatherless home or in a home to which the mother brings a series of men in temporary alliances. Such children lack the stability of a normal home in which a child is made to feel important and wanted.

the Ford Foundation Work Conference on Curriculum and Teaching in Depressed Areas, Columbia University, July, 1962.

[5] Muriel Crosby, "A Portrait of Blight," *Educational Leadership*, February, 1963, p. 300.

Children whose parents are competent and self supporting live in an environment that fosters self-esteem and independence. Unfortunately, many children grow up in homes in which the chief source of income—in many cases, over a period of several generations—comes from public and private welfare agencies. To such children it is the accepted and normal pattern to receive financial support without individual effort or initiative from social agencies. In addition, for many low-income children, awareness comes early that racial discrimination will close the door to many kinds of work opportunities. The results, the all-too-understandable results, are a general attitude of defeatism and a generation of children without self-reliance or optimism or sense of personal dignity. Instead, far too many low-income children acquire a value system that is in sharp conflict with the established middle-class values of school and community.[6]

SLOW LEARNERS

The demands that middle-class schools make upon deprived children are out of harmony with their cultural experience, and because most deprived children come to school with deficits of attitude, preparation, and skills, they do not fit readily into the school culture and find meeting its demands too difficult to accomplish. They lack the skills even to meet the expectations of conduct in school. Hilda Taba has observed first-grade classrooms where the children do not even distinguish one piece of paper from another one. "They might tear out a page from a book to make a marker for another and cherish a piece of toilet paper. They have had no training in disciplined group behavior, such as the middle-class child gets around the dinner table, because they seldom had dinner as a family group. Consequently, they lacked the habits and skills necessary for reading in groups .... Similar observations abound about difficulties with speaking or being spoken to in groups, and such virtues cherished in school as cleanliness, punctuality, and orderliness." [7]

Deprived children, in general, are expected to do badly in the classroom. Actually, some 10 percent do well. But the majority *expect* to fail, to meet frustration and defeat; and this expectation engenders in them such fear of failure that it is a great handicap to adequate performance.

> ... *The disadvantaged child becomes the victim of the group intelligence test. Lacking the experiences and the language tools which are incorporated in the typical group intelligence test, the child emerges from*

---

[6] *Ibid.*, p. 302.

[7] Hilda Taba, *Cultural Deprivation as a Factor in School Learning*, mimeographed lecture delivered at the Merrill-Palmer Institute, Detroit, Michigan, March, 1963, p. 6.

this measurement of experiences he has never known as a 'slow learner,' one whose potential is severely limited. And his teacher proceeds to build his curriculum upon a false diagnosis, thereby making certain that a low ceiling for potential is permanently established. In many schools the matter is confounded by rigid segregation based on the findings of group intelligence and achievement tests, thereby blocking the deprived from the stimulation of association with more fortunate children.[8]

There are clear reasons why deprived children make low scores on tests. They have extremely limited horizons. Many have never traveled more than two blocks from home before entering school.[9] Little reading is done in their families, and little informal discussion takes place on a literate level. Such children reach school with a serious deficit in formal language which affects their ability to grasp what they hear and to learn to read. Their response to questions is fragmentary and poor. For many, even as they move up through the grades, taking an oral or written test is a hazard so frightening that it stultifies learning effort. Their performance in intellectual tasks is so much slower than that of middle class children that their achievement is humiliatingly inferior.[10]

"The net result is that these young people are labeled uneducable and treated as such. Little is expected of them and little is offered. The pupils, in turn, expect little and get little. Comparatively speaking such pupils 'get dumber' as they grow older. By the fifth grade they are three years behind. This, in turn, adds to lowering of self-expectation, and generates hostility to school, teachers, and the whole business of learning. This is probably the dynamics which turns the children, who in kindergarten are described as curious, cute, affectionate, warm, independently dependent, and mischievous, into ones described in the fourth grade as alienated, withdrawn, angry, passive, and apathetic." [11]

So, from the very start, deprived children are stigmatized as *slow learners*.

The label *is* a stigma, for our schools stress speed in learning. Schools focus on providing maximum opportunity for learning to those children

---

[8] Muriel Crosby, *op. cit.,* p. 302.

[9] Warren G. Cutts, "Reading Unreadiness in the Underprivileged," *National Education Association Journal,* April, 1963, p. 24.

[10] This section owes much to the mimeographed records of two speeches by Dr. Frank Riessman: (1) *School Culture, Learning Culture, and the Learning Style of the Disadvantaged,* delivered at the Training Program for Mobilization for Youth Staff, September, 1962; and (2) *The Culturally Deprived Child: A New View,* the opening address to the Conference on Education of Disadvantaged Children, U.S. Office of Education, Washington, D.C., May, 1962.

[11] Hilda Taba, *op. cit.,* p. 17.

talented in terms of speed in performing intellectual tasks, especially in taking tests.

POOR SELF-CONCEPT

Another block to learning for disadvantaged children lies in the realm of attitudes, their own, and their teachers'.

Such children are expected to do badly in school, and know it, and foresee frustration and failure for themselves. As a result, they fear and detest school. Such a set alone is almost enough to insure that school will be for them little more than custody with scheduled humiliation.

Teachers often bring to their profession a middle-class value system that is poles apart from that of residents of low-income areas. Yet, teacher attitude toward slow learners can be quite crucial. The teacher who expects her disadvantaged pupils to be slow, nonparticipating, and troublesome does much, in the silent language of emotional perception, to create a self-fulfilling prophecy. The children learn quickly how she feels about them, and accept her judgment as fact, and, in hopelessness and resentment, passively do little to prevent it from becoming fact.

To sum up, then, disadvantaged children come to school burdened with blocks to learning in the school culture. They may be slow, suffer a very real deficit in formal language, have poor ability to listen and answer, have limited readiness for reading as it is typically taught, lack test-taking skill, and expect to fail humiliatingly.

The result is just what can be expected: a large proportion of future citizens grow up poorly equipped academically. Moreover, the effectiveness of the school as a socializing agent is diminished. "...In 1950 Allison Davis made a dramatic impact on the audience at the White House Conference on Education by declaring that 40 percent of children go through school untouched by it except for acquiring a meager literacy. As characters, as persons, as possessors of academic competency they might just as well not have been in school. From this population we get disproportionate contributions to delinquency, particularly among the bright ones because their genius and energy turns to organizing delinquent activities to express their antisocial feelings." [12]

THE SLOW GIFTED

And yet—this is not the whole picture.

Disadvantaged children, handicapped by deficits as they are, nevertheless have some strengths. The picture is not entirely negative.

[12] Hilda Taba, *op. cit.*, p. 19.

Frank Riessman contends that our understanding of the culture of the deprived child is too limited; that our term "deprived" carries a middle-class bias that skews our perception from the full truth. The child living in a city slum is not deprived of awareness of life; on the contrary, he is subjected to an onslaught of sensation and stimuli that is exceedingly varied.

St. Clair Drake describes vividly what life is like in the Black Ghetto.

> *For the average Negro who walks the streets of any American Black Ghetto, the smell of barbecued ribs, fried shrimps and chicken emanating from numerous restaurants gives olefactory reinforcement to a feeling of "at-homeness.". . . The insouciant swagger of teen-age drop-outs (the 'cats') masks the hurt of their aimless existence. . . . The spontaneous vigor of the children who crowd streets and playgrounds (with Cassius Clay, Ernie Banks, the Harlem Globe Trotters and black stars of stage, screen and television as their role models) and the cheerful rushing about of adults, free from the occupational pressures of the 'white world' in which they work, creates an atmosphere of warmth and superficial intimacy which obscure the unpleasant facts of life.*[13]

It is a different environment from that of the advantaged child, of course; nevertheless, it is not poor but opulent in color and insights. A city street busy with traffic, sidewalks flanked with stores and flats and jammed with pedestrians, is a lively substitute for a suburban backyard or a rural roadway. Street play is highly resourceful and inventive; one researcher counted fifteen varieties of games that slum children had developed at one brick wall.

It is true that, in the classroom, the deprived child lacks verbal ability. Nevertheless, he is not characteristically nonverbal. Outside of school, on the playground and in the home, his verbal ability is more than adequate—rapid, fluent, forceful. It may well be that slum children do more actual talking, arguing, exhorting, scolding, cheering and jeering than do their better-mannered, more supervised, book-reading and theater-going and music-lesson-taking contemporaries of middle-class families.

The Spanish-speaking areas of New York City, for example, are no lunar landscapes of silence but compressed babels of laughter and radio music and talk—constant talk, talk, talk. In such districts, taciturnity is not a folkway.

Irving Taylor suggests that not only are slum children not nonverbal but that they are less word-bound than advantaged children; and moreover, that the language habits of slum children are endowed with considerable creativity. He notes that the "mental style of the low-income youngsters

---

[13] St. Clair Drake, "The Social and Economic Status of the Negro in the United States," in *The American Negro*, Fall, 1965, *Daedalus*, p. 777.

strongly resembles the mental style of one type of highly creative person." [14] On word association tests he found that deprived children give responses that are less conventional, more unusual, original, and independent than the responses of advantaged children. Deprived youngsters tend to permit language to interact more with nonverbal forms of communication, such as gestures and pictures. Taylor believes that the wide range of associations for slum children indicates a freer use of language. He points out that studies of creative people show that they have greater "semantic flexibility" than noncreative people and that they respond well to visual, tactile, and kinesthetic cues.

Frank Riessman stresses the point that disadvantaged children, although slow in getting involved in problems, are able, once their interest is engaged, to work intensely and patiently for long hours at a stretch. In fact, once interested in a task, they typically want to stay with it and dislike working in short spurts with frequent breaks. Moreover, they have real contributions to make to society. "Many of them are talented in music, in art, in athletics, and in other fields, but few of them have had the opportunity to reveal these talents." [15]

In concluding from these characteristics, Riessman makes a basic point: *A child who is slow is not necessarily stupid.*

Slowness in performing intellectual tasks is not necessarily a weakness. One person may require five minutes to learn something another person learns in one minute; nevertheless, the slow person may acquire the skill or information wholly and satisfactorily. The slow child may be "extremely careful, meticulous, or cautious. He may be slow because he learns in a one-track way; that is, he persists along one line of thought, and does not readily take on other frames of reference. He may be slow because he cannot understand a concept unless he does something physically (e.g., with his hands) in connection with the idea he is trying to grasp." [16]

In fact, Riessman suggests, often the single-minded individual has considerable creative potential which, unfortunately, too often fails of reinforcement in school and remains unrealized. Rather than equate slowness with stupidity, it would be well for school people to be alert to the fact that there are many *slow gifted children.* Among college students, many who are slow are also very persistent when interested and do creative work too outstanding to be ignored. Among such students are many who take five or six years to complete a college education; nevertheless, they do earn a degree and their contribution, although requiring more time in conception and realization, is of high quality.

[14] Frank Riessman, *The Culturally Deprived Child*, pp. 77–78.
[15] Cutts, *op. cit.*, p. 23.
[16] Frank Riessman, *The Culturally Deprived Child*, pp. 77–78.

Learning Styles Differ. Certain points here need to be stressed. Learning styles differ; speed is not essential to learning; slow learning does not necessarily mean inadequate learning; the disadvantaged child comes to school not only with deficits but also with strengths that are assets that should be made use of in methods of teaching practiced by the teacher.

Among the strengths are various factors which should not be overlooked. Many slum children are members of extended family groups and are used to, and rely upon, the cooperativeness and mutual aid of such a group. Slum children, not constantly under the pressure for achievement so characteristic of upwardly mobile middle-class families, are not under the high order of nervous tension characteristic of the more competitive and individualistic children. Slum children enjoy one another's company with humor and informality. They live in an intensely egalitarian atmosphere. Not so hedged in with precept and moral teaching as more privileged children, they are far freer of guilt and self-blame. They are free of the sometimes paralyzing overprotectiveness of middle-class parents. They know less sibling rivalry. They possess a high degree of spontaneity and are uninhibited in expressing and draining off anger.

To minimize the deficits of disadvantaged children and to maximize their learning strengths, the classroom teacher must use newer approaches and methods.

Deprived children do not learn readily from the printed word and from abstract principle; rather, they learn from concrete detail, from use of the senses, from touching, seeing, acting, making. Teaching methods should fit this learning style.

> Deutsch points out that the greater the variety of stimulation and the number of situations which challenge modification of conceptualization, the more mobile and differentiated the mental structure becomes. In other words, the more the child hears, sees, and interprets, or is being helped to interpret, the more likely he will want to see and hear, and the more he will get from what he sees and hears. The greater the variety of reality situations with which the child has coped the greater his ability to cope.[17]

ASPECTS OF A TEACHING PROGRAM FOR THE DISADVANTAGED

Muriel Crosby suggests some principles for a teaching program for the disadvantaged which have been effective in helping them to improve

[17] Hilda Taba, *op. cit.*, p. 8, referring to Martin Deutsch, "The Disadvantaged Child and the Learning Process: Some Social, Psychological, and Developmental Considerations," a paper prepared for the Ford Foundation Work Conference on Curriculum and Teaching in Depressed Areas (Columbia University, July 1962).

their academic achievement and their sensitivities and their human relations skills: [18]

1. Planning experiences which change the self-image of the disadvantaged child [Role-playing provides opportunity for offering such
   experience]
2. Assuring that they gain enough fluent and correct English to prevent
   language lack from being a handicap in job hunting
3. Planning a curriculum high in expectation but realistic in nature
   a. Devising a curriculum that is rooted in use value for children
   b. Basing the curriculum on children's perceptions of their own needs
      through the use of diagnostic instruments that reveal their per-
      ceptions, concepts, and needs and lead to changing attitudes of
      teachers toward children
   c. Providing many experiences in seeing the relationships between
      cause and effect. (Making wise choices depends upon foreseeing
      probable consequences. In a sense, this means establishing habits
      of forethought.)

Role-playing provides rich opportunities for gaining these ends. Frank
Riessman recommends role-playing as a method of great usefulness in this
context.

Children from low-income families respond more fully and directly
to action than to talk, and role-playing provides action. Through its
movement, informality, humor, and empathy-arousing drama, role-playing
catches young people's interest, involves them, and holds them attentive.[19]
Slum children, whose crowded homes and play settings condition them to
working together, find the group aspects of role-playing natural and con-
genial. In contrast to their lack of attentiveness to ordinary discussion,
their halting ability to answer questions in a formal situation, they respond
to role-playing with a heartwarming fullness, spontaneity, and enthusiasm.

A research team, planning to do role-playing with a slow group in a
San Francisco junior high school, were warned that the class (consisting
of mentally retarded and culturally deprived youngsters) averaged an attention span of but six to eight minutes. Nevertheless this group, after a
warm-up that caught their interest, did role-playing for a full and busy
fifty minutes. Moreover, some hours later, this group reenacted the whole
story in a puppet theater performance for an excited and vociferous hour
and twenty minutes. This was a "slow" group but they were not tongue-

18 Muriel Crosby, *op. cit.*, p. 303.

19 Jean Goldfarb and Frank Riessman, *Role-Playing with Low Income People*,
outline prepared for Mobilization for Youth Training Department, November,
1962; and *The Culturally Deprived Child: A New View*, address given at the
Conference on Education of Disadvantaged Children, U.S. Office of Education,
May 21, 1962, Washington, D.C.

tied, nor slow or halting or dull of speech in this situation, but bubbling over and at times even eloquent. Furthermore, they made good sense.[20]

Frank Riessman, working with a group of disadvantaged children, asked them, "Why are you sore at the teachers?" He got little response. Then he set up a role-playing session with some of the youngsters acting the role of teachers and others the role of pupils. A sharp interchange resulted. The young people had much to say and gave sensitive answers to the questions he had raised earlier.

In the role-playing session, the informality and permissiveness and security allow self-conscious and uneasy children to respond with a spontaneity that permits them much fuller expression than does a formal classroom recitation. Riessman describes this process in action.

> *In role-playing sessions we have had occasion to observe that the verbal performance of deprived children is markedly improved in the discussion period following the session. When talking about some action they have seen, deprived children are apparently able to verbalize much more fully. Typically they do not verbalize well in response to words alone. They express themselves more readily when reacting to things they can see and do. Words as stimuli are not sufficient for them as a rule. Ask a juvenile delinquent who comes from a disadvantaged background what he doesn't like about school or the teacher and you will get an abbreviated, inarticulate reply. But have a group of these youngsters act out a school scene in which someone plays the teacher, and you will discover a stream of verbal consciousness that is almost impossible to shut off.*[21]

All these considerations imply ways in which the guidance worker especially can greatly help the busy classroom teacher. It is essential for the teacher to be reminded that learning styles differ; that speed is not essential to learning; that slow learning does not necessarily mean inadequate learning; that new approaches and methods of instruction exist which promise more success for the slow learner. The guidance worker can do much to construct a bridge of understanding between the teacher and her group of disadvantaged pupils by enlarging the teacher's understanding not only of the deprived child's blocks to learning but also of the positive elements on his side, the psychological assets that he brings from his cultural background, assets which can provide guidelines for methods of teaching and for curriculum making.

[20] George and Fannie R. Shaftel, *Role-Playing the Problem Story*, National Conference of Christians and Jews, 1952, p. 65.
[21] Frank Riessman, *The Culturally Deprived Child* (New York: Harper, 1963), p. 77.

ROLE-PLAYING FOR SKILLS TRAINING: VOCATIONAL, SOCIAL

It may come as a surprise to many of us in education to learn that role-playing has been used, for a comparatively long time, in industry. Role-playing is used as a group problem-solving device to some extent in industry, but for the most part it is used as a procedure for training people to cope with typical problems they are likely to meet in doing their jobs. This type of role-playing—focused on the purpose of *training* people to perform work routines—is a kind of rehearsal of how-to-do and should, in our opinion, be more precisely labeled under the term "skills training."

To gain some notion of just how widely industry uses "skills training" it is helpful to glance over a four-page bibliography on role-playing published by the Cleveland Public Library.[22] This bulletin refers to role-playing as a "recent medium in behavior training for manpower management." The bibliography is subdivided under headings entitled: *Role-Playing as a Training Technique, Application of Role-Playing,* and *Psychodrama and Sociodrama Therapy.*

Good human relations are recognized as being vitally important in business management, naturally; and role-playing, in the opinion of N. R. L. Maier, may serve the same function for human relations training that clinical experience does in serving the young doctor of medicine. Maier refers to role-playing as "acting that teaches how to handle people." Stuart Chase, in his *Roads to Agreement,* calls role-playing a dress rehearsal for real life. In the *Michigan Business Review* for November, 1950, R. P. Calhoun writes that "The techniques of practicing and demonstrating are rising in importance as methods of training people to meet typical problems." The journal *Factory Management* for January 1954 tabulates the experiences of over one hundred training directors in using role-playing in training supervisors.[23]

Such role-playing in industry involves helping personnel to develop skills in training other employees in doing specific jobs, handling a lathe or a drill press, for example, and in coping with problems of workers expressing grievances. Sales people, too, are training in how to make an ingratiating approach to potential customers, how to answer expected questions, and how to placate individuals who make angry complaints. Not only sales people but other personnel who deal directly with the public—telephone operators, information clerks, want-ad solicitors, for example—also benefit markedly through *rehearsals* in doing their tasks.

[22] *Role-Playing or Dramatization in Training Methods,* Bulletin of the Business Information Bureau, Cleveland Public Library, February, 1955.

[23] See Alan Klein, *Role Playing in Leadership Training and Group Problem Solving,* New York: Association Press, 1956.

Students in school, too, can benefit greatly from skills training in such matters as making introductions; applying for part-time jobs; asking a girl for a date or for a dance, and in accepting or rejecting such a request; making an apology when in the wrong—and in accepting such an apology; baby-sitting—caring for an ill or unruly child, answering the phone or the doorbell; and presenting a visitor or new member to the class.

To Provide Practice in a Social Skill. The group may be making an historical study of the community and preparing, in order to gather information, to interview long-time residents. Practice in interviewing will be helpful. Or, the class may practice techniques for applying for delivery jobs with local merchants. Younger children may practice ways of involving the cooperation of the older children of the school in organizing a 4-H Club.

SUMMARY

Role-playing can serve a useful function as a method of helping slow learners to improve their classroom achievement. The typical deprived child has a poor self-concept, due to difficult family relationships and living conditions. When these children come to school, they have such deficits in readiness for learning under ordinary school conditions that they find meeting school demands much too difficult. While some 10 percent of deprived children actually do well in school, the majority expect to fail, and most do badly. However, disadvantaged children do have some strengths. Researchers point out that their *learning style* differs from that of middle-class children—that, although slow in learning, deprived children are in many cases gifted.

Various teaching programs planned for deprived children suggest experiences that (1) improve the self-concept of such pupils, (2) provide them with chances to gain fluency in language, (3) deal with a curriculum that is clearly useful in their understanding of their own needs, (4) provide opportunities in seeing the relationship between cause and effect.

Role-playing is recommended by researchers as a procedure that can contribute much toward these goals. Moreover, slum children respond warmly and fully to role-playing.

Industry has long used role-playing as a "skills training" procedure for providing employees with practice in meeting typical problems. Foremen practice teaching a crew how to handle a machine; salesmen practice approaching customers. Young people in school, similarly, can practice social skills.

chapter

10

EXTENDED ROLE-PLAYING

THEMATIC SEQUENCE IN ROLE-PLAYING

Although even a single session of role-playing can often help a group confronted with a problem of human relations, far more growth in insight and empathy is achieved by *role-playing that extends through a series of sessions focused upon various aspects of a single theme.*[1] Role-playing can be most effective when a group deals with a general problem through sessions that have been carefully planned as a *cumulative sequence.* In such a sequence each successive role-playing experience reinforces and enriches both the emotional impacts and the understandings and generalizations of previous sessions. This means, of course, that each new session should build on the preceding experience; this is another way of saying that the goal of role-playing experience is growth in maturation. An effective impetus for changed behavior is awareness of probable consequences, and extended role-playing upon a crucial theme offers optimum potential for growth toward behavior that can change in the light of foreseeable results.

An example may be helpful.

Occasionally the members of a class are an uncongenial, quarrelsome group, and the classroom climate is charged with tension. Personality clashes between key individuals are frequent; conflict between factions

---

[1] In support of this hypothesis, see Jerome S. Bruner, Jacqueline J. Goodnow, and George A. Austin, *A Study of Thinking* (New York: Science Editions, Inc., 1962), p. 242. "First of all, to understand the intelligent or adaptive nature of behavior, one must work with units larger than a single response, no matter how 'molar' that response may be. One must, moreover, work with *sequences* of response if one is to appreciate the unfolding interplay between successive responses in reaction to prior consequences."

causes so many daily eruptions that costly delays in the learning process utterly dishearten the teacher.

> The establishment of effective working relationships in the classroom has traditionally held high priority for teachers concerned with promoting educational achievement among their pupils. Although much of learning is ultimately an individual task, in the modern school it takes place in a social environment. Pupils learn through interaction with the teacher, by working in committees, by discussing with classmates, by checking homework assignments over the telephone. Their motivation to learn is influenced by their position in the classroom social structure, by the peer group standards toward classroom activities, and by the supporting or conflicting pressures from a great variety of forces which are a part of their life space.[2]

A sixth-grade class in a laboratory school was causing their teacher a great deal of anxiety. So much strife was flaring up between rival groups and individuals in her classroom, so much spiteful bickering occurred that the orderly learning process was disrupted and the basically able group was failing to make normal progress. As members of one group attempted to recite when called upon, others would make jeering comments; naturally, the first group would retaliate in kind.

Especially distressing to the teacher was the fact that a number of vulnerable youngsters were having a severely damaging experience. One girl, who had had difficulty in previous grades, was becoming increasingly frightened and unhappy and hostile; her present experience, the teacher suspected, might set so bitter an edge of failure upon her aspirations that she might never regain confidence in learning. One particularly withdrawn boy, similarly, had stopped making any effort to participate. And others, the teacher realized, whose problems she had not yet fully learned, were receiving an experience that might become an irreversible setback.

The teacher was spending far too much time and effort in maintaining discipline. Repeatedly she had tried to make the class see how destructive their behavior had become, but without success. She could have enforced discipline by a stern use of authority; but this she was reluctant to do, for she foresaw that it would leave her, metaphorically, holding down the lid on a cauldron of seething, barely suppressed feeling. Rather

[2] Robert S. Fox and Ronald Lippitt, "The Innovation of Classroom Mental Health Practices," in Matthew B. Miles, ed., *Innovation in Education* (New York: Bureau of Publications, Teachers College, Columbia University, 1964), p. 271. Chapter XI, reviewing an extended research project, is very helpful for it describes a teacher's effort to improve the climate for learning in her classroom. "She saw as a possible source of the problem the pupils' failure to accept individual differences in classmates, and their failure to recognize the importance of all members of the group." Difficulties in interpersonal relationships among her pupils were evidenced by expressions of intolerance, unhealthy boy-girl competition, ambivalence toward others in the group (p. 287).

than force an outward compliance, she preferred, if possible, to change the troubled classroom climate.

She discussed her problem with a consultant. In answer to questions, she explained that her pupils were children of professional and academic people and were highly competitive. They had had a teacher, the previous year, who pitted them against each other for achievement and, as a result, they were set in a critical attitude toward everything said and done in the classroom. To this dour, grudging outlook the rancor of rival cliques added a shrill quarrelsomeness.

"In some way, I have to calm this group down," she told the consultant. "But I want to do it in a way that leaves them comfortable with me and with one another."

"It may help if you can get the individual members of the group to realize what feelings they are arousing in each other."

"How can I do that?"

It was decided to try role-playing. A series was planned that resulted in a sequence of role-playing stories all of which dealt with the same theme: how a person feels when he is rejected by his group. Five such stories were used in the sequence.

USING A THEMATIC SEQUENCE OF ROLE-PLAYING STORIES

The consultant directed the sessions while the classroom teacher observed from the back of the room. In the first session, the story entitled "The Squawk Box" was used.* In this story a very able youngster is denied a chance to use his knowledge in a classroom project. He is rejected by the children because he is different: he has formal manners, uses adult language, and dresses very neatly. Moreover, instead of trying to overcome this hostility of the group by being ingratiating, he fights back by being sarcastic, at which he has more than a little skill.

The consultant read the story to the group, and stopped at the dilemma point. Discussion, then role-playing followed. The session proved surprisingly diagnostic: the teacher learned important facts about the group.

The pupils who volunteered to play roles were the members of the class who were suffering most from rejection; and in the role-playing they reflected their own experiences in this classroom. They knew what it meant to be rejected! On the other hand, the influential members of the class—leaders of cliques, and their close friends—refrained from taking roles. Instead, they made critical comments to one another about the individuals who did play roles.

"Isn't he something?"

* The stories used are included in Part II of this volume.

"Thinks he's smart."

After the enactment, the role-playing was discussed, and the central issue raised: How could the rejected boy (Andy) be helped to win acceptance from the classroom group? Among the suggestions offered by the children were that *he should dress like the others.* And that *he should learn to play games.* And that *instead of becoming so sarcastic, he should learn to take a joke on himself.*

The role-playing leader then asked the children if they thought that these suggestions would solve Andy's problem. A boy said, very emphatically, that this would *not* solve his problem, that Andy would not be permitted to be the equipment engineer unless Jerry (the power clique leader in the class) would let him. Another boy supported this statement, saying, "Jerry is the power in that bunch, and everyone knows it!" Another child added that Jerry would never let Andy in and no one else would if Jerry wouldn't.

These comments were most significant; for this troubled class had a clique leader like Jerry, and the boys who made the comments were his satellites. There was a cynical acceptance in this class of the role of influential persons and the need to get along with them. These youngsters were really speaking about their own classroom situation. It is important for the teacher to know who are the most influential individuals in the classroom group. Research provides some support for the hunch that individuals who play active roles in role-playing undergo more change of attitude through the experience than do individuals who sit in the audience and observe.[3] If key students were given roles as the sessions proceeded, chance of changes of attitude in the group would be improved; for not only would the influential individuals be given the most chance to learn how it feels to be rejected, but their consequent changes of attitude would tend to bring on changes of attitude among their close followers.

In the next role-playing session, the second problem story of the thematic sequence was used, "Bandit Cave." In this story, the boy who is rejected by the group is a quiet youngster who reads a great deal and who would have much knowledge to contribute to the group if he were given a chance. He does not fight against the treatment he is receiving, either constructively, or by being sarcastic and hostile; instead, he withdraws, participating less and less in the activities of the camp.

Again the consultant read the story to the group, and invited discussion and role-playing. Surprisingly, the role-playing aroused very strong feelings in the listening group. For them, the lot of the rejected boy was

[3] Pearl Rosenberg, *An Experimental Analysis of Psychodrama,* unpublished doctoral dissertation, Harvard University, 1950.

deeply poignant; to them, he seemed so very alone, and so deeply hurt. The leader of one clique summed up the feeling of the class by saying, "He feels like he is nobody. Just nobody at all."

The fact that this classroom leader, one of the "chief stars of attraction" among the pupils, voiced his own feelings in public this way set a seal of approval on openly expressing sympathy for the rejected boy in the story; in effect this authoritative reaction freed this influential boy's followers to avow their own feelings publicly. The result was that this role-playing session aroused a high pitch of empathy in the classroom group that was not kept private but was frankly stated.

Feelings of rejection were explored still further in the succeeding sessions, in which a group of three stories called "Inside, Looking Out" were used.[4] In the first story of this little group, a girl returns with her family to a community from which they had moved two years previously. She had had many close friends here before the family moved away; and while absent had missed her friends intensely. Her unhappiness was so deep, in fact, that it had been one of the chief reasons why the family had returned to the town. But now, back again, she suffers acute disappointment. Her old friends have acquired new cronies. Increasingly, during the first days of her return, she feels left out of things. And, when the members of her group are invited to a party and she is not, she feels bereft and heartsick. She no longer has any friends, she realizes; her former friends, on whom she had counted so heavily, no longer care much about her.

She is mistaken. The night of the party, to which she has not been invited, finally comes. Her mother sends her out on an errand. When she returns home, she finds the house full of young people—all her old friends. They are waiting for her, and when she enters, noisy greetings welcome her. The party to which she had not been invited along with all her former friends is her own party—a surprise party given to welcome her back home.

In the discussion that followed the reading of this story, almost every pupil in the classroom stated that he or she had had just such an experience of feeling left out when not invited to a party. And they were delighted by the happy ending to the story: it obviously soothed a common hurt.

More importantly, of course, this discussion alerted the group to another aspect of common behavior: Sometimes we *expect* to be mistreated; sometimes *we are too quick to jump to conclusions about other people's behavior.*

---

[4] This series uses two preliminary complete stories as preparation for role-playing the third story of the group. They are studies in perception.

In the next session, a second story of this "Inside, Looking Out" group in the thematic sequence was used.

In this story a boy who is the star pitcher for his sixth-grade baseball team is a candidate for captain of the team. When the election is being held, Johnny Kotowski overhears the teacher-coach of the team listing his (Johnny's) defects to his teammates: Johnny is hot-tempered, he stutters, he cannot run as fast between bases as the bigger boys, he tends to slow up in a tight spot, and so on. Johnny is crushed. To him, this is a betrayal. The fact that everything the coach has said is true only makes the hurt keener. Johnny slinks away, feeling humiliated and rejected. Later, however, Johnny learns that the coach was listing his handicaps only to show the group how much Johnny had learned to overcome; the teacher had been making the point that Johnny had had the strength of character to overcome even such a burden of defects. The result had been that Johnny had been chosen team captain.

The final story used, from the "Inside, Looking Out" series, was Jimmy Garrett. Briefly, in this story a young Negro boy comes to believe that he has been rejected for a job as delivery boy, and blamed through prejudice for stealing a bike which he had actually retrieved for its owner. But the policeman who he thinks is coming to arrest him has come, instead, to thank him for saving the bike and to help him get the job he wanted.

What, then, were the results of this sequence of role-playing experiences?

This sequence of role-playing played a part in changing the climate of this particular classroom. The teacher expressed it in this way: "Before, they were beastly to each other, but now they are decent human beings." The isolated youngsters had been given a chance to take part in an absorbing group activity; their status with the group improved, and their self-concept and morale had consequently become healthier as the other children extended friendship to them. The girl who had hated coming to school because she had been so bitterly unhappy now was bringing classmates home to play. The withdrawn boy, still quiet, was participating more and more in classroom activity. Toward the end of the term the class was functioning productively at a very satisfactory level.

The basic strategy used to bring about this improvement in interpersonal relations in this formerly troubled classroom had been to induce the influential leaders of cliques *to play roles that helped them to gain insight into how it feels to be rejected.*

The experience had sensitized them, had given them heightened empathy for their isolated classmates. Of course, this experience was not the only factor that operated to transform these warring cliques into a more "cohesive" group; the fact that they all participated in an exciting project that involved them emotionally, that they shared a common experience in problem solving, was of real importance; also, as the weeks passed, they grew to know each other better under "action" circumstances that provided reasons for them to appreciate individual abilities. The personality and ethical feeling of the teacher, too, was a potent influence for change. Role-playing is not a magic cureall; it cannot be given all credit for improving the learning climate of this classroom; but it is only reasonable to assume that role-playing may have helped significantly to bring about this needed and welcome change.

To sum up: It is unreal to hope that a problem of social relationships can be solved in a single role-playing session. A change of attitudes and values requires growth. Time and emphasis and reinforcement are necessary. Extended role-playing, a sequence of problem solving and projective experiences on a strong central theme, is far more likely to be effective.

Role-playing (thought of as a complex involving discussion, problem solving, and often research as well) should be supplemented by other classroom procedures such as the use of audiovisual materials—films, tapes, records, and the use of carefully selected books, various testing instruments, and sociometric techniques. For her own guidance, the teacher should learn who the leaders, followers, isolates, and rejectees are in her group; she should learn the individual needs and aspirations of her pupils. With such knowledge, she can structure role-playing experiences that will have sharp focus on meeting those needs and aspirations.

SOME THEMATIC SEQUENCES FOR EXTENDED ROLE-PLAYING
FROM THE MATERIALS IN THIS BOOK

Some of the themes into which the stories presented in this volume can fit are listed below. In general, these themes touch upon aspects of ethical behavior; their focus is upon use in helping young people to mature in terms of individual integrity and group responsibility.

Just how attitudes and values are acquired is not obvious; perhaps they are absorbed, or, better yet, *achieved* by an extended process of heightening awareness and empathy that come from poignant experience that is critically, sensitively understood.

Such experiences can be provided in the classroom by role-playing situations that are structured upon the generalizations implicit in these listed themes: experiences that are immediate yet removed enough so that they exact no penalties for mistakes and provide a second—even a third or fourth—opportunity to make a choice of behavior over again.

The role-playing process provides time to mull over new insights, chances to explore and *test* the consequences of decision-making, and opportunities to utilize continuous feedback for *revising* behavior.

The stories in Part II were written to implement a number of ethical themes. The stories are listed in groups or patterns to support these ethical considerations. The themes are listed below. However, the stories are sufficiently varied and numerous to fit a much wider range of themes than those we have listed. When a problem of human relations arises in the classroom, the concerned teacher can select specific stories from these groups that may fit the problem troubling her class. The stories can be rearranged in a wide variety of patterns to fit themes applicable to many classroom situations.

THEMES FOR EXTENDED ROLE-PLAYING

1. Honesty
2. Fair-mindedness
3. Unfair revenge
4. Rules are for everyone
5. Self-acceptance
6. Prejudice
7. Feelings of rejection
8. Anticipation of rejection: sometimes mistakenly we expect to be rejected
9. Integrity in friendship
10. Responsibility of the group to respect and support the individual
11. Responsibility to others: the individual of integrity feels intelligent concern for others
12. Cooperation within the group: dilemmas of when, and when not, to cooperate with the group. When is cooperation just cowardly surrender to the group? When is refusal to cooperate mere self-indulgence?

SELECTING A THEMATIC SEQUENCE OF STORIES FOR EXTENDED ROLE-PLAYING

To illustrate how stories are selected for extended role-playing: Suppose, for example, you wish to help a group of young people develop a more conscientious regard for rules. The theme for the sequence of role-playing experiences could be as follows:

I. Theme: Rules are for everyone.

Three stories in this volume fit this theme:

1. "*Blind Fish.*" In this story, boys on a hike with a youth leader find some blind fish in a pool in a cave. Several of the boys catch some of the fish. Other boys enter, learn what has been happening, and start

to try catching some of the rare fish for themselves. But the adult forbids this, pointing out that the entire group' of fish could be taken out and no survivors left in the pool. Some of the boys protest. Other boys had taken some specimens, so why couldn't they? He wasn't being fair!

2. "*Frogman.*" This story elaborates the same theme on a more serious level. Teen-age boys go spear-fishing at night in a trout pool below a dam where fishing is forbidden by law. They spear a huge trout and bring it back to their summer camp, where the trout will be cooked and enjoyed by all. But next day a game warden arrives; he has been tipped off that somebody from this camp had speared trout in the protected pool. Who did it? Some of the boys lie to protect the culprits; even the camp cook evades telling the truth. The warden leaves without discovering who is guilty. Later, other boys come to the culprits and ask to borrow the spear guns and diving masks: *they* want to go spear some big trout too. But one of the guilty boys, thinking of the lying and law breaking that he has already been guilty of, and how others were involved in falsehood and trickery to protect him, and of the possible consequences if these boys go to the pool and are caught, refuses to lend the equipment. Angrily the other boys say that they have as much right to spear trout as he had.

3. "*Deep Snow.*" This story presents another aspect of the need to observe rules, an even more serious one, for in this case human lives are endangered. Eddie has been the victim of a number of pranks perpetrated by Toby, but when Eddie complains to the camp counselor, Mr. Lorton, he is sternly scolded for carrying tales, for tattling. Mr. Lorton takes a group of the boys, Eddie and Toby among them, on a ski trip into the mountains with two snow-surveyors. Again, Toby plays a trick on Eddie, but Eddie, still smarting from being called a "snitch," says nothing to Mr. Lorton. Then Toby tries to involve Eddie in a prank that could possibly be dangerous, and Eddie angrily refuses and reminds Toby that Mr. Lorton had warned them that, on trips into the mountains, the rules about hiking and skiing must be carefully observed. Toby poohpoohs him. And, a little later, Toby starts a big snowball rolling down the slope upon the rest of the party. That snowball, growing in size as it rolls, becomes big, and starts an avalanche that engulfs the party. Luckily, Eddie and Toby manage to dig them out, unhurt. Then Mr. Lorton, who has scolded Eddie for tattling, turns to him and demands to know what happened.

As these stories are read in successive sessions, discussed, and role-played, and replayed, the consequences of failure to observe rules can be envisaged and elaborated upon in the light of particular circumstances. The young people's own experiences can be drawn upon to build and reinforce lasting awareness that rules set for the safety and best interests of all should be observed by all.

II. *Theme: Honesty*

A dozen stories in this group deal with problems of honesty. From among these stories, the teacher can select three to five (or more) that seem particularly applicable to the needs of her group. The aspects of honesty touched upon are lying, cheating, hiding someone else's possessions, letting another person take the blame, social lying, not returning a found article.

Lying:
1. "Boy Out on a Limb"
2. "Lost Ball"
3. "Little Echo"
4. "The Un-Invitation" (social lying)

Cheating:
5. "Boy and Girl"
6. "Paper Drive"

Letting Another Person Take Blame for Your Wrongdoing:
7. "Rocket Shoot"
8. "Heavy, Heavy, Hangs Over Your Head"
9. "Trick or Treat"

Not Returning a Found Article:
10. "Money for Marty"
11. "Clubhouse Boat"
12. "Finders Weepers"

III. *Theme: Responsibility to Others*

These stories overlap in the ethical considerations with which they deal. For example, stories listed above as dealing with aspects of honesty can also be listed as concerned with the responsibility to others that an ethical individual must feel. Sometimes, merely to point out that it is dishonest to let another person take blame for a wrong you committed keeps the matter on a vague, abstract level; whereas pointing out just how that other individual is injured by a damaging act for which you are responsible puts the matter on a plane of individual feeling that is far more real and meaningful.

This aspect of human relations—responsibility to others—is, of course, an area of vast dimensions; many of the stories included in this volume bear upon facets of individual and of group responsibility: "intelligent concern for others." The teacher planning to provide her group with a sequence of experiences in role-playing responsibility in human relations may select from the list those stories which best apply to the concerns of her group and should present the stories in the sequence that seems most logical to her at the time.

Letting Other People Take the Blame for Your Wrongdoing. Such behavior is, of course, dishonest; but involved, also, is failure to face up to your responsibility to others. Stories dealing with this problem include:

1. "Trick or Treat"
2. "Heavy, Heavy, Hangs Over Your Head"
3. "Rocket Shoot"
4. "The Letter of the Law Series."

In these stories, the person who has committed a wrong can, *by keeping silent*, evade punishment for that wrong, but, by keeping silent, he is failing to establish the innocence of the person who is wrongly blamed for the misbehavior.

Setting a Bad Example. Sometimes young people can break rules (like going swimming, fishing, or hunting in places marked *Keep Out*) and have much fun and safely evade detection. But, often, when this occurs, other young people will observe, take note, and decide to imitate. Usually there are good reasons for prohibitory rules: beaches, for example, marked *No Swimming* may be subject to dangerous undertows, and young people imitating older individuals' behavior in ignoring signs may get into serious trouble. This matter of setting an example is an important facet of the individual's responsibility and concern for the welfare of others.

5. "Blind Fish"
6. "Frogman"

In these two stories, the central character commits an act that breaks the rules and safely gets away with it. But other youngsters then want to imitate his behavior. The central character can foresee the possible harm that might come to them, but if he does not permit them to do what he has done, he is a spoilsport, a hypocrite who is bitterly resented by his friends.

Setting Temptation in a Younger Child's Way.

7. "A Pistol for Pete"

A teen-ager leaves a coin on his bureau. His much younger brother, who yearns for a toy pistol of a kind popular among his friends, picks up the coin and buys the toy. He doesn't know that the coin, a present to the older boy, is a rare coin. The older brother, on discovering what has happened, ponders: Should his kid brother be punished? But who is really to blame? Isn't he himself at fault for leaving the coin where it became an irresistible temptation? And yet, taking the coin without permission, wasn't that the same as stealing? Not exactly; the family were pretty free and easy about small matters; and *all* the other small boys had those toy guns. But because the coin *was* a gift, and *was* valuable, his parents might severely punish his young brother.

This, too, is an area of responsibility toward others, especially those younger or particularly vulnerable. The responsibility lies in not permitting situations to arise in which they will find easy opportunity to break rules, to "borrow" a bike or a fine ball glove or rifle a candy box, just because the valued item was left lying in the open. And, once an older person has been careless in this respect, he must assume some share of responsibility for the happening.

Cruel Pranks. Sometimes a group or individual plans or commits a prank on others that is cruel or even potentially dangerous. For the ethical individual, an aspect of intelligent concern for others is the preventing of such pranks going beyond the bounds of mere humor or mischief.

8. "The Junior Cavemen"

A group of boys, hiking into rough hills, plan to run off from one of their number who is not popular. He would have to spend the night alone in the hills, and would be frightened almost beyond bearing. The chief character is reluctant to take part in this cruel joke, but if he stands out against it he knows that the group will have nothing more to do with him.

9. "Deep Snow"

This story was described in the section on the need to observe rules. It concerns a reckless youngster who endangers the lives of his whole group by heedless mischief. The chief character of the story is a boy who has been the butt of a number of cruel pranks on the mischief maker's part. The guilty boy *should* be exposed; but, the other boy realizes, if he does reveal who was guilty, he will be carrying tales, tattling.

Accepting an Honor or Prize or Gift Which More Properly Belongs to Someone Else

10. "The Big Comic"

Accept a position of responsibility for which you are not the most adequate person, knowing that others may suffer as a result?

11. "Big Shot"

Accept an honor, granted you mistakenly, when someone else merits it more?

12. "Fast Ball"

(Same theme as in 10)

13. "Winner Take All"

Accept a much-wanted prize although you did not really earn it and others did?

IV. *Theme: Being Fair*

Fair play has an infinitude of aspects, of course; many of the stories in this volume deal with dilemmas of being a good sport, being honest with people, taking one's fair share of responsibility, avoiding behavior that damages other people undeservedly, and so on. (Many of the stories listed below as focusing on the theme of *being fair* also bear upon other themes, such as honesty, being loyal to friends, prejudice, and cooperation.)

The "Getting Even" Sequence. At times, when we feel that we have been unjustly wronged, we want revenge, we want to "get even," and in the hot rush of indignation that overwhelms us, we may do cruel things. The issue involved may be stated in this way: Is it being fair to inflict upon a person who has wronged you a far greater wrong than the one he committed? Is revenge fair? A sequence dealing with this problem can consist of the five stories listed below.

1. "Money for Marty"
2. "Mr. Even-Steven"
3. "Eye-Witness"
4. "You're Not Invited"
5. "Tell-Tale"

The "Outside, Looking In" Sequence. In these stories, the chief character can accept a fine reward or opportunity that he or she wants very much, but the dilemma arises in each case: Will he be fair to other people if he accepts the honor?

6. "The Big Comic"
7. "Big Shot"
8. "Fast Ball"
9. "Winner Take All."

Letting Innocent People Be Punished for Your Misbehavior. Sometimes punishment for some misbehavior can be evaded because an innocent person is wrongly blamed for it. By keeping silent, you will escape severe loss or disgrace; but, and this fact troubles you, you will unfairly let an innocent person pay the penalty. The stories in this sequence are represented by

10. "Trick or Treat"
11. "Heavy, Heavy Hangs Over Your Head"
12. "Rocket Shoot."

The Prejudice Sequence. In this sequence, the unfairness of discrimination against an individual on the basis of race or religion is the issue.

13. "Second Prize"
14. "No Trespassing"
15. "Keep Out: This Means You."

(This last story has the same theme as number 14, but is for somewhat older children.)

Dishonesty Is Unfair. Often an act of dishonesty inflicts unfair treatment upon an innocent person. The following stories develop this issue.

16. "Boy and Girl"
17. "Lost Ball"
18. "Finders Weepers"
19. "Clubhouse Boat."

A Rejection Sequence. In this sequence, the unfairness of rejecting an individual because he is different in some way is explored.

20. "Bandit Cave"
21. "The Squawk Box"
22. "Birthday Present."

The Letter of the Law Series:

23. "Spelling Bee"
24. "The Treasure Out in Left Field"
25. "A Long Nose Has a Short Life."

V. *Theme: Self-Acceptance*

It is difficult to help young people to accept themselves, especially if they suffer some sort of serious disadvantage, real or fancied, inherent or imposed by the culture, such as having red hair or being crippled or cross-eyed or being of Indian or Negro or other racial background in an environment where the Caucasian is dominant, or belonging to a religion which seems exotic to the dominant culture. The approaches to this problem are many, of course, ranging in variety from in-service training for teachers that focuses on training the teacher to warmly "accept" pupils who are different to the varied cultural activities of "higher horizon" programs.

The various themes presented in this volume impinge on this problem. An individual's self-concept depends very much upon the way other people treat him, whether with liking and respect or dislike and indifference. Accordingly, when the group acquires attitudes of fairness to people who are "different," attitudes of responsibility, attitudes of acceptance, the individual in that group has a better chance for good mental health.

The sequence of stories presented here deal with just one approach to self-acceptance:

1. "The Big Comic"

Tom has a chance to win acclaim in school by performing on a program, showing off a very special skill, but doing so will necessitate revealing that he has trouble in learning to read.

2. "Big Shot"

Nora is a bright girl, eager to be prominent in school affairs. On the basis of an essay she has written, she is elected to editorship of the school paper, but she knows, in her heart, that she would not be as good in the job as the girl who is runner-up.

3. "Fast Ball"

Eddie, who has a crippled foot due to polio, is a fine baseball pitcher. So good, in fact, that he enables his scrub team to beat a good Little League team. The Little League group invite him to join their team, to his great delight; but, although he can pitch very well, he can't run bases; all in all, he knows that he would be a handicap to a really good all-around team.

4. "Winner Take All"

Lucia has a fine singing voice and has received excellent training from her father, who is a voice teacher. She enters a local beauty-talent contest, although she knows that she is plain. She discovers that the sponsors of the contest have decided in advance to award her the prize, because they believe that she needs the encouragement. Thinking about it, she is very upset; she is not pretty; she does not deserve to win a beauty contest; yet, she does have an outstanding talent.

VI. *Theme: How It Feels to Be Different, to Be Rejected*

This, too, is an important theme that is touched upon in many of the stories in this volume; how it feels to be left out, rejected, because one is somehow different from most people in race, religion, or social background, or because one has interests, or handicaps or skills, or backgrounds of experience that mark one as unusual in some way.

1. "The Un-Invitation"

The issue: not inviting someone to a party because she goes to a different Sunday school, or is of a different race.

2. "Bandit Cave"

The quiet, shy, studious child is often ignored by a boisterous group.

3. "You're Not Invited"

A child of poor family is not included by the more privileged children in their social life.

4. "Second Prize"

Adults treat a child as different because he is of a different race.

5. "Birthday Present"

The unpopular or minority group child is left out by a prestige group.

6. "The Squawk Box"

Often the studious child is branded "teacher's pet" and made the butt of jokes in a classroom.

7. "No Trespassing"

The child who is different in race or religion may meet discrimination not from his peers but from adults dealing with his age-mates.

8. "Keep Out: This Means You."

Same thesis as that in 7 above, but the story is for an older group.

9. The "Inside, Looking Out" group of stories.

These three stories deal with youngsters who, because they are "different" and because of previous experience, are too quick to anticipate rejection. The stories should be used as a group. Because they do treat, strongly, with feelings of rejection, they can be used in this sequence.

a) *Judy Miller.* A girl feels rejected because she thinks she's not pretty, or doesn't dress well enough, or because her family isn't important.

b) *Johnny Kotowski.* A boy believes he is not being elected to a position he merits because he's little, awkward, and hot-tempered—because of his faults.

c) *Jimmy Garrett.* Jimmy believes that he is being rejected and mistreated because of his race.

Although this group of stories overlaps stories of rejection because of prejudice, it has utility because it shows that people often differ in other ways than in color or religion, and that feelings of rejection can be felt by any of us, and felt deeply.

VII. *Theme: Prejudice*

A main focus of the following stories is prejudice. Most of these stories are listed in the previous section, under the theme of how it feels to be different. In the present sequence, the focus is upon young people who choose whether to participate in the rejecting behavior born of prejudice or to refuse to reject their friends who are different in race or religion, even though it means that they too will suffer some loss.

1. "The Un-Invitation"
2. "No Trespassing"
3. "Keep Out: This Means You"
4. "Second Prize"

VIII. *Theme: Anticipation of Rejection*

See the "Inside, Looking Out" group, story 9 of Theme VI.

This sequence can either be used as a part of a longer sequence on *How it feels to be different,* or used alone as a short sequence on hypersensitivity that results in self-inflicted damage. The question is not one of whom to blame for discrimination, but of maintaining a sensible outlook. Discrimination does exist, yes, but not all one's peers are guilty of it.

IX. *Theme: Integrity in Friendship*

Young people often cause each other heartache by immaturity in friendship relations. One boy may insist that another reluctantly accompany him in an act of mischief in spite of his strong dislike of participating; or one of two girls who have been best friends will suddenly pair off with another girl, and the new pair will not only exclude the forsaken girl but belittle her as they reject her. A basic aspect of integrity in friendship is, of course, loyalty, dependability. Another aspect is concern for a friend's feelings and well-being. (Such concern, naturally, is part of the general "intelligent concern for others" felt by individuals of integrity.) Some stories from which a sequence on this theme could be selected are:

1. "Birthday Present"

A popular boy, who has been best friend to a shy, quiet boy, is invited to go on an exciting trip with a prestige group. The group dislike the shy boy and won't invite him. The popular boy accepts the invitation —then is reminded that he has already accepted an invitation from the shy boy to attend his birthday party on the same day as the day on which the trip will occur.

2. "Lost Ball"

This story involves lying: One boy, out of fear of punishment for causing some damage to a car, puts the blame on a friend.

3. "The Un-Invitation"

In this story, the issue is: Get out of an embarrassing situation, that is entirely your own fault, by hurting a friend's feelings?

4. "Trick or Treat"

Participate, out of loyalty to a friend, in an act that hurts other people?

5. "Second Prize"

Accept a reward although it means that a friend will be belittled, because of his race, as a result?

6. "No Trespassing"

Accept a fine reward, although a friend who deserves it as much as you do will be denied a share in it?

7. "Keep Out: This Means You."

Same theme as story 6, but for somewhat older children.

X. *Theme: Cooperation Within the Group:*

When does the individual within the group cooperate with it, when does he refuse?

This question of the active relationship of the individual to his group is one of increasing importance as more and more the individual is a member of a group in almost every aspect of living. Dilemmas become more frequent and more crucial. When is conforming to group will an act of honest cooperation, and when is it an act of abject surrender? When is refusing to cooperate with the group an act of courage and independence, and when is it an act of selfishness? Developing the clarity of judgment to differentiate between these aspects of group living is important not only to a maturing sense of the obligations of citizenship but also to the developing of self-reliance and personal integrity.

The following stories provide opportunities to grapple with these dilemmas. Most of these stories occur on lists applying to other themes—responsibility to others, concern for others, integrity in friendship, fair play, honesty, and so on.

1. "The Junior Cavemen"

Dilemma: Join the crowd in a cruel prank on an unpopular member?

2. "Paper Drive"

The group is in a contest with another group, and the other group has cheated. The first group members decide to fight fire with fire and cheat too. Individuals are troubled: Go along with the group in cheating?

3. "Clubhouse Boat"

The club insists that a member make up a deficit of money he has failed to pay. He can do so, by keeping the money of a customer who has overpaid.

4. "The Menace in the Trees"

The group is playing a prank that may result in harm to an old person. Go along with the group?

5. "The Un-Invitation"

The group of girls who are invited to a birthday party number seven —one too many for the six tickets to a show the hostess has received. The group says to phone the one absent girl and tell her the party is off, otherwise none can go to the show. But the hostess foresees that the girl who is "un-invited" will soon learn that she was lied to, and rejected.

6. "Deep Snow"

Obey the group code, even though this means endangering the group? Don't tattle, even though someone may get hurt?

7. "Blind Fish"

Go along with the group on an act of vandalism?

8. "Frogman"

Cooperate with the group in breaking game laws?

9. "Shutter-Bug"

Give up a cherished gift because the group wants to make a good showing in a money-raising effort?

10. "Sacrifice Hit"

Give up something honestly and badly needed just because the group wants to do something nice?

11. "Birthday Present"

A boy has a chance to become a member of a popular group, but to do so he must cooperate with them in rejecting a friend.

XI. *Theme: A responsibility of the group to respect and support the individual*

Our country is composed of peoples whose ancestors have come from a wide variety of nations, of people who differ in race, religion, social and economic background. Even so, our land has grown great because many diverse peoples have, for the most part, learned to live together in productive harmony, to respect and support each other's rights as individuals and citizens. However, the struggle for civil rights for *all* Americans is far from full achievement. It is imperative for young children, as they meet one another in school, on neighborhood playgrounds, on family picnics, and so on, to make this basic American tradition an essential part of their value systems. The individual owes his cooperation to the group in activities that are worthy. Conversely, the group owes respect and support to the individual in activities and aspirations that are sincere, worthwhile, and not injurious to other people, however "different."

The following stories provide experiences in confronting this issue:

1. "Spelling Bee"

Here, we spell the word *labor* without a *u*; but in England, it is spelled *labour*. Which is right? In other words, do we make allowances for cultural differences?

2. "Bandit Cave"

The indifference of the group to a quiet member may rob the group of worthwhile experience; it also robs the individual of self-respect.

3. "The Squawk Box"

Because a boy is unpopular, the group may deny him recognition that he merits, and as a result, both the group and the individual suffer.

4. "Second Prize"

A Negro boy is discriminated against because of his race. Will his group support or reject him?

5. "No Trespassing"

A Jewish boy is discriminated against because of his religion. Will his group support or reject him?

6. "Keep Out: This Means You."

(Same as theme in story 5, but for somewhat older children.)

7. "Josefina"

A Mexican-American girl wonders if she should accept a date with a Caucasian boy. Will their respective groups ostracize them afterward?

8. "Seed of Distrust"

This is another expectation of rejection story. It deals with the way that expectation is sometimes established. Negro educators say that one of the chief problems in Negro–White relations is Negro distrust of Whites.

XII. *Theme: Sensitivity-training*

9. "Eeny-Meeny-Miney-Mo"

Often, with utterly no intention of hurting another person, we use "hurt words" that do insult them. It is important for children to develop an alertness to the way in which expressions in common use can hurt other people's feelings.

10. "But Names Can Never Hurt Me?"

This story deals with the same theme as that in story 10. Sometimes individuals of similar racial or family background will use insulting language to each other. The "hurt words" are accepted. But if a person of another race or background uses the same words, it may be bitterly resented.

SUMMARY

Even a single session of role-playing, in some instances, can help a group working to solve a problem of human relations. In general, however, far more growth of insight and empathy is achieved by role-playing that extends through a series of sessions focused on a single theme. Such sessions should be planned as a cumulative sequence in which each successive role-playing experience with various aspects of the general theme reinforces and enriches with meanings the understandings of previous sessions. A change of attitudes and values requires growth; time, emphasis, and reinforcement are necessary. Helpful for planning a thematic sequence is knowledge of the social structure of the classroom group—the leaders, followers, fringers and isolates. A sociometric study of the class before role-playing is started can contribute such information.

The problem stories in this book are listed in patterns to implement a number of ethical themes; moreover, the stories are varied and numerous enough so that many teachers, dealing with a problem not listed here, may be able to select stories to make a pattern that will better apply to the specific problem causing concern.

A CHECKLIST FOR
GUIDING
ROLE-PLAYING

PART A

1. PROBLEM DEFINITION

After reading the story, wait for volunteered responses: *wait for the children to think.*
This is a process of recall. After a bit, you may ask:
"What is happening here?"
If the children still seem to have difficulty in moving into the situation, to evoke responses you may ask further recall questions. Who is involved? How are they affected by this situation? Then:

"How is—(Chief character)—feeling?" and
"Why is he feeling this way?"
"How are—(some of the other characters)—feeling?"
"Why are they feeling as they do?"

2. DELINEATING ALTERNATIVES

This is a process of projection. Ask:
"What do you think will happen now?"
(Note the use of will, not "should.")
Invite ideas from the children. Do not go on to role-playing until you have a number of solution proposals from the group. Both antisocial and socially acceptable solutions will usually be offered. Sometimes only one kind of solution is offered; if this happens, you may need to ask:
"Is this the only way in which such a situation usually ends?" If still no other kind of solution is proposed, go into role-playing.

3. EXPLORING ALTERNATIVES

Negative solutions: Members of your group may offer impulsive, negative, or antisocial proposals for solving the story dilemma, as well as socially sanctioned solutions.

183

1. *Select a negative solution* for first consideration.
2. *Hold brief discussion.*
3. *Select a volunteer* to role-play this proposal. Ask him:
   "Whom will you need to help you?"
   With him, select other role-players from volunteers.
4. *Set the stage* for the role-playing by asking:
   "Where is this happening?"
   "What time of day is it?"
   "What is each of you doing?"
   If necessary, remind each actor of the role he is to take.
5. *Prepare the audience:*
   If you have a beginning group, instruct them to judge, as they watch the role-playing, how realistic the enactment is.
   "Ask yourselves as you watch:
   Could this really happen?
   Are the people behaving as they would really behave in life?"

If the class is experienced in role-playing, divide them into two or three observer groups.
You may ask Group I to observe for true-to-life behavior, Group II, to observe how individual players feel, Group III, to think ahead for next steps in solving the dilemma.

6. *Start* the role-playing.
   Stop it as soon as you think the acting has delineated the proposed solution.
   (It is not necessary to come to a complete ending.)
7. *Start discussion* by asking:
   "What has been happening?" and, if needed,
   Ask chief character how he is feeling; then ask group:
   "How is—(chief actor)—feeling?"
   "Why does he behave in this way?" and
   "What will happen now?"

(At this point it will be necessary for you to decide whether it is worthwhile to go on to further enactment exploring this negative, socially unacceptable solution, or to go on to explore proposals that offer alternative courses of behavior.)

(*If you have time for elaborated role-playing, see Part B, following.*)

Positive solutions:

Ask the group: "Do some of you have ideas about other ways in which this story could end?"

1. *Select a positive, socially acceptable solution* from the proposals offered.
2. *Hold brief discussion.*

3. *Select a volunteer* to role-play this proposal. Ask him:
   "Whom will you need to help you?"
   With his help, select other volunteers to role-play.
4. *Set the stage* for the role-playing by asking:
   "Where is this happening?"
   "What time of day is it?"
   "What is each of you doing?"
   If necessary, remind each actor of the role he is to play.
5. *Prepare the audience:*
   If beginners, ask the group to judge how realistic the role-playing is, as they watch.
   "Could this really happen?"
   "Are the people behaving as they would really behave in life?"

If the class is experienced in role-playing, divide them into observer groups. Ask Group I to observe for true-to-life behavior, Group II, to observe how individual players seem to feel, Group III, to think ahead for next steps in solving the dilemma.

6. *Start* the role-playing.
   Stop it as soon as you think the acting has well delineated the proposed solution.
7. *Start discussion* by asking:
   "What has been happening here?"
   "How is —— feeling?"
   "Why does he behave in this way?" and
   "What will happen now?"

4. DECISION-MAKING

A. If the group has reached some clear understanding of the alternatives that have been explored and of the consequences they engender, ask:
   "Which of the solutions to this problem do you think is best?"
   "Why is it best?"
   "For whom is it best? Who will benefit?"
   "Who will be unhappy with this solution?"
   "How do you choose if you can't make everybody involved happy?"
   "If you were so-and-so (a person in the story) how would you choose? If you were (another person in the story) how would you choose?"

B. Ask: "At what point in the story could a choice have been made that would have enabled an acceptable solution to be reached?"

PART B

If you have time to guide your group into role-playing with some depth, you can add several extra steps to the process.

1. *Extend exploration of the consequences of a proposed solution* to the dilemma by suggesting another scene to be role-played. This scene should follow logically from the premise of the alternative being enacted; that is, it could logically be an aftermath of the proposed behavior.

(For example, in "Little Echo," Nora has told her mother that she is going to Marylee's house to study; instead, she and Marylee go to a movie, which is forbidden by Nora's parents on a weekday night. After the group has role-played this behavior, suggest to the group that

 a) Nora's mother, who has to leave the house for some reason, telephones Marylee's home to tell Nora that the doorkey will be under the front doormat. Nora's mother thus learns from Marylee's mother that the girls, instead of studying, have gone to a movie.
 Or:
 b) Marylee's mother, called to an ailing sister's bedside, telephones Nora's mother to ask which movie the girls went to, so that she can pick up Marylee before leaving.

The result is, of course, exposure of Nora's lying; the consequences can be explored in enactments.)

2. *Reverse the roles* of the chief characters in the problem story.

It is often effective, in order to bring home to an individual unaware of the effect of his behavior upon others, to put him in the shoes of a person who is affected by his behavior.

(For example, in the story "Birthday Present" the chief character, Susan, had promised to go to her friend Wendy's birthday party. Then Susan has a chance to go on a clamming trip with a group of the most popular girls in school. Wendy is a lonely, rejected, unpopular girl. Susan wants very much to be included in the popular group. She tells them she'll go clamming with them—although this means she will have to disappoint Wendy. She tells Wendy she will not come to her birthday party. Wendy asks why.
Role-play this scene.
Reverse roles: put Susan in Wendy's role—and role-play the scene with the former Wendy now telling the former Susan that she will not come to her birthday party.)

3. *Search out the implications of the proposed alternative* by means of analogy; that is, suggest a situation *outside* the story, in another time and place and activity, in which an individual behaves in the way indi-

cated by the proposed behavior; in other words, apply the principle suggested by this alternative to other situations.

(For example, in "Paper Drive," Miss Hendry's class hears a rumor that their rival class is cheating in the paper drive: wetting their bundles of paper to make them weigh more. Miss Hendry's class counters this rumored cheating by cheating in turn: hiding junk in their bundles of paper. When role-playing this story, if the group justifies this behavior, suggest a scene in which this principle of countering dishonesty with dishonesty is applied:

a) The school is voting on student body president. Rumor spreads that friends of one candidate are forging ballots in his favor. Friends of a rival candidate start forging ballots.

b) A follow-up situation for this one: discovery that the rumor of cheating was just that—a mere rumor without basis in fact.

GUIDING THE ROLE-PLAYING
A Shorter Check List of Steps in the Process

1. PROBLEM DEFINITION:

After reading the story, *wait for volunteered responses.*

2. DELINEATION OF ALTERNATIVES:

Ask: "What do you think will happen now?" and, if necessary, "Is this the only way such a situation usually ends?"

3. EXPLORING ALTERNATIVES:

A. *Negative proposals:*
   1. Of the offered solutions, *select a negative proposal.*
   2. *Discuss.*
   3. *Select* volunteers to role-play.
   4. *Set the stage* for role-playing.
   5. *Prepare the audience.*
   6. *Start* the role-playing.
   7. *Discuss* the enactment.
   8. (If desirable, undertake further enactments.)

B. *Positive proposals:*
   1. *Select* a positive proposal.
   2. *Discuss.*
   3. *Select volunteers* to role-play.
   4. *Set the stage.*

   5. *Prepare the audience.*
   6. *Start role-playing.*
   7. *Discuss the enactment.*
   8. (If desirable, undertake further enactments.)

4. DECISION-MAKING

A. Ask: "Which of the offered solutions to the problem do you think is best? Why?"

B. Ask: "At what point in the story could a choice have been made that would have enabled an acceptable solution to be reached?"

BIBLIOGRAPHY

ALEXANDER, JEAN, *"Let's Get Down to Cases"* (rev. ed.). New York: Anti-Defamation League of B'nai B'rith, 1957. A series of role-playing situations in the field of intergroup understanding.

AMBROSE, GERTRUDE and ALICE MIEL, *Children's Social Learning*, Association for Supervision and Curriculum Development of National Education Association, 1958.

ARNOW, HARRIETTE, *The Dollmaker*. New York: Collier Books, 1961.

AXLINE, VIRGINIA, *Play Therapy*. Boston: Houghton Mifflin Company, 1947.

BANDURA, ALBERT and ALETHA C. HUSTON, "Identification as a Process of Incidental Learning," *Journal of Abnormal and Social Psychology*, LIII, No. 2 (1961), 311–18.

BANDURA, ALBERT and RICHARD H. WALTERS, *Social Learning and Personality Development*. New York: Holt, Rinehart & Winston, Inc., 1964.

BENNE, KENNETH, *Education in the Quest for Identity and Community*. Columbus, Ohio: Ohio State University Press, 1961.

———, "The Uses of Fraternity," in *"Ethnic Groups in American Life."* *Daedalus*, Spring, 1961, 233–46.

BENNE, KENNETH and BOZIDAR MUNTYAN, "What Is Role Playing?" and "The Uses of Role Playing," *Human Relations in Curriculum Change*. New York: Dryden Press, 1951, pp. 223–49. The examples are concerned primarily with adult groups, but discussion of the technique, its methods and possibilities, is applicable to all age levels.

BERELSON, B., *The Social Studies and the Social Sciences*, The American Council of Learned Societies and the National Council for the Social Studies. New York: Harcourt, Brace & World, Inc., 1962.

BERNADETTE, SISTER, D.C., "Social Development in the Elementary School," *Catholic School Journal*, LX No. 7 (September, 1960), 29–31.

BERNARD, E. J., "Teach Retail Selling Through Role Playing," *Journal of Business Education*, XXXIX (November, 1963), 61–62.

BIBER, BARBARA, *The Five to Eights and How They Grow*, Bank Street Publications, New York (undated pamphlet).

BLAIR, ARTHUR and WILLIAM H. BURTON, *Growth and Development of the Pre-adolescent*. New York: Appleton-Century-Crofts, 1951.

BONIFACE, JENORA, "Role Playing in Kindergarten," *Grade Teacher*, LXXVI (October, 1958), 31.

189

BOYD, GERTRUDE A., "Role Playing," *Social Education*, XXI (October, 1957), 267–69.

BOYD, GERTRUDE A. and MYRTLE R. YOUSSI, "Role Playing Reveals Language Levels," *Elementary English*, XXXIV (October, 1957), 388–93.

BRONFENBRENNER, URIE, "The Changing American Child," *Journal of Social Issues*, XVII, No. 1 (1961), pp. 6–18.

BROWN, CORRINE, *Creative Drama in the Lower School*. New York: Appleton-Century-Crofts, 1929.

BROWN, IDA S., "How We Act in Groups," in *Childhood Education*, XXVII (December, 1950), 156–60. Outlines a plan for improving the role-taking abilities of primary school children.

BRUNELLE, PEGGY, "Action Projects from Children's Literature: An Indirect Approach to Intercultural Relations in the Elementary School," *Sociatry*, II (December–March, 1948), 235–43. Examples of episodes from children's books which can be utilized for sociodrama at various grade levels.

BRUNER, JEROME S., *The Process of Education*. Cambridge, Mass.: Harvard University Press, 1960. 97 pp.

BRUNER, JEROME S., JACQUELINE J. GOODNOW, and GEORGE A. AUSTIN, *A Study of Thinking*. Science Editions, Inc. New York: John Wiley & Sons, Inc., 1962.

California State Department of Education, "Education of Mentally Retarded Minors in California," *Department of Education Bulletin*, XIX (January, 1950).

———, *Teacher's Guide to Child Development, Intermediate Grade*, "Creative Play as an Integrating Activity." California State Printing Office, Sacramento, 1936, pp. 501–16.

California State Department of Education, BOUTON, H. and NATALIE WHITE, "How The Pioneers Moved Westward," *Bulletin* No. 1 (April 1, 1938).

———, BURROW, CLAYTON, "Community Life in the Harbor," *Bulletin* No. 16 (August 15, 1935).

———, MALONEY, GERTRUDE, "A Study of Pueblo Indians," *Bulletin* No. 10 (August 15, 1938).

CAMERON, EDWARD HERBERT, "The Psychology of Behavior Disorders." Boston: Houghton Mifflin Company, 1947.

CAMERON, N. A. and MARGARET A., *Behavior Pathology*. Boston: Houghton Mifflin Company, 1951.

CARTWRIGHT, DORWIN and ALVIN ZANDERS, *Group Dynamics*. New York: Harper & Row, Publishers, 1958.

CHASE, STUART, *Roads to Agreement: Successful Methods in the Science of Human Relations*. New York: Harper & Row, Publishers, 1951. Popular account of use of role-playing with adults.

CLARK, MARGARET W., "Role-playing in a Group Guidance Class," *California Journal of Secondary Education*, XXVI (January, 1951), 34–36. Tenth-grade guidance class uses role-playing to gain insight into some elementary psychology concepts.

COLEMAN, JAMES SAMUEL, *The Adolescent Society*. New York: Free Press of Glencoe, Inc., 1961.

COMMAGER, HENRY STEELE, *The Nature and the Study of History*, Charles E. Merrill Social Science Seminar Series. Columbus, Ohio: Charles E. Merrill Books, Inc., 1965.

COREY, S. M., "Experiment in Leadership Training," *Educational Administration and Supervision*, XXXVII (October, 1951), 321–28.

COTTRELL, L. S., JR., "The Adjustment of the Individual to His Age and Sex Roles," *American Social Review*, 1942, 7, 618–25.

CROSBY, MURIEL, *An Adventure in Human Relations*. Chicago: Follett Publishing Co., 1965.

———, "A Portrait of Blight," *Educational Leadership*, February, 1963, 300.

CROSBY, MURIEL (ed.), *Reading Ladders for Human Relations* (4th ed.). Washington, D.C.: American Council on Education, 1963.

CULBERTSON, FRANCES M., "Modification of an Emotionally Held Attitude Through Role-Playing," *Journal of Abnormal and Social Psychology*, LIV (1957), 230–33.

CUNNINGHAM, RUTH AND ASSOCIATES, *Understanding the Group Behavior of Boys and Girls*. New York: Columbia University, Teachers' College Bureau of Publication, 1951.

CUTTS, WARREN G., "Reading Unreadiness in the Underprivileged." *National Education Association Journal*, April, 1963, 24.

DALY, FLORA and LEO CAIN, "Mentally Retarded Students in California Secondary Schools," in *California State Department of Education Bulletin*, Vol. 20, No. 7 (October, 1953).

DAVIS, W. ALLISON and ROBERT J. HAVIGHURST, *Father of the Man*. Boston: Houghton Mifflin Company, 1947.

DEAN, VERA MICHELES, *The Nature of the Non-Western World*. New York: The New American Library, 1957.

DEUTSCH, KARL W., "On Social Communication and the Metropolis," in "The Future Metropolis," *Daedalus* (Winter, 1961), 101–5.

DEUTSCH, MARTIN, "The Disadvantaged Child and the Learning Process: Some Social, Psychological, and Developmental Considerations." Paper prepared for the Ford Foundation Work Conference on Curriculum and Teaching in Depressed Areas. New York: Columbia University, July, 1962.

———, "A Theory of Cooperation and Competition," *Human Relations*, II (1949), 129–52.

———, "The Effects of Cooperation and Competition upon Group Processes," *Human Relations*, II (1949), 199–231.

DOBSON, CAROLINE, The Effect of Problem-Story Role-Playing by Fifth-Grade Children. Unpublished doctoral dissertation, Stanford University, Stanford, Calif., 1952.

DRAKE, ST. CLAIR, "The Social and Economic Status of the Negro in the United States," in "The American Negro," *Daedalus* (Fall, 1965).

EDWARDS, WARD, "The Theory of Decision Making," *Psychological Bulletin*, LI, No. 4 (1954), 380–417.

ENGLE, SHIRLEY, "Decision-Making: The Heart of Social Studies Instruction," *Social Education*, XXIV (November, 1960), 301–4, 306.

ERIKSON, ERIK HOMBURGER, *Childhood and Society*. New York: W. W. Norton & Company, Inc., 1950, 397.

FIELDER, MARIE, *The School as a Social System*. Unpublished dissertation, University of Chicago, March, 1960.

FLANDERS, NED A., " Diagnosing and Utilizing Social Structures in Classroom Learning," *National Society for the Study of Educational Yearbook*, LIX, No. 2 (1960), 187–217.

FLANDERS, NED A. and SULO HAVUMAKI, "The Effect of Teacher-pupil Contacts Involving Praise on the Sociometric Choices of Students," *Journal of Educational Psychology*, LI, No. 2 (1960), 65–69.

FOLLETT, MARY, *Creative Experience*. New York: Longmans, Green & Co., Inc., 1930.

FOSHAY, ARTHUR, "The Creative Process Described," in Alice Miel, ed., *Creativity in Teaching*. Belmont, Calif.: Wadsworth Co., 1961.

Fostering Mental Health in Our Schools. Association for Supervision and Curriculum Development of National Education Association, 1950.

FOX, ROBERT S., RONALD LIPPITT, and JOHN E. LOHMAN, *Teaching Social Science Material in the Elementary School*, Cooperative Research Project No. E–011, U.S. Office of Education, Department of Health, Education and Welfare, 1964, pp. 26–44.

FRANK, L. K., *Feelings and Emotions*. Garden City, N.Y.: Doubleday & Company, Inc., 1954.

FRENKEL-BRUNSWIK, ELSE, "A Study of Prejudice in Children," *Human Relations*, I, No. 3 (1948), 295–306.

FROMM, ERICH, *Man for Himself*. New York: Holt, Rinehart & Winston, Inc., 1947.

GIBSON, JOHN S., *New Frontiers in the Social Studies*. Address to the Summer Workshop on Curriculum for the High School. New York: Columbia University, Teachers College, 1964.

GOLDFARB, JEAN and FRANK RIESSMAN, *Role Playing with Low Income People*. Outline prepared for Mobilization for Youth Training Department, November, 1962. Mimeographed material.

GOODMAN, PAUL, *Growing Up Absurd*. New York: Random House, 1960.

GORDON, MILTON M., "Assimilation in America: Theory and Reality," in "Ethnic Groups in America," *Daedalus* (Spring, 1961), 263–85.

GOUGH, H. G., "A Sociological Theory of Psychotherapy," *American Journal of Sociology*, LIII (1948), 359–66.

GRAHAM, GRACE, "Sociodrama as a Teaching Technique," *Social Studies*, LI (December, 1960), 257–59.

GRAMBS, JEAN D., "A Psychodramatic Approach to the Teaching of Personnel Relations in a Course on Supervision." Unpublished doctoral dissertation, Stanford University, Stanford, Calif., 1948.

———, "Dynamics of Psychodrama in Teaching Situations," *Sociatry* I (1948), 383–99.

GREENLEAF, WALTER J., "Sociodrama as a Guidance Technique," in *California Journal of Secondary Education*, XXVI (February, 1951), 51–55. Specific guide for classroom use of sociodrama, giving step by step directions for the teacher-director.

GROSS, NEAL, ALEXANDER W. MCEACHERN, and WARD S. MASON, "Role Conflict and Its Resolutions," in *Readings in Social Psychology* (3rd ed.). Eleanor E. Maccoby, Theodore M. Newcomb and Eugene L. Hartley (eds.). New York: Holt, Rinehart & Winston, Inc., 1965, pp. 447–59.

GUETZKOW, HAROLD (ed.), *Simulation in Social Sciences: Readings*. Englewood Cliffs, N.J.: Prentice-Hall, Inc., 1962.

GUILFORD, JAY PAUL, "The Structure of the Intellect," *Psychological Bulletin*, LIII, No. 4 (July, 1956), 267–93.

HAAS, ROBERT B. (ed.), *Psychodrama and Sociodrama in American Education*. New York: Beacon House, 1949. Many examples of classroom practices using these techniques.

HAAS, ROBERT BARTLETT, "Sociodrama in Education." Unpublished dissertation, at Stanford University, Stanford, Calif., 1949.

HAIMOWITZ, MORRIS L. and NATALIE R. HAIMOWITZ, *Human Development, Selected Readings*. New York: Thomas Y. Crowell Company, 1960.

HARRISON, GOUGH, "A Sociological Theory of Psychotherapy," *American Journal of Sociology*, LIII (1947–1948), 359–66.

HARTLEY, RUTH E., LAWRENCE K. FRANK, and ROBERT M. GOLDENSON, *Understanding Children's Play*. New York: Columbia University Press, 1953.

HAVIGHURST, ROBERT, *Human Development and Education*. New York: Longmans, Green & Co., Inc., 1953.

HEATON, MARGARET M., *Feelings Are Facts*. National Council of Christians and Jews, New York, 1952.

HEILIZER, FRED, "Conjunctive and Disjunctive Conflict: A Theory of Need Conflict," *Journal of Abnormal and Social Psychology*, LXVIII, No. 1 (1964), 21–37.

HENDRY, CHARLES E., RONALD LIPPITT, and ALVIN ZANDER, "Reality Practice As Educational Method," Psychodrama Monograph No. 9. Beacon, New York: Beacon House, 1947.

HENRY, JULES, *Culture Against Man*. New York: Random House, 1963.

"How to Use Role Playing and Other Tools for Learning," Leadership Pamphlet No. 6. Adult Education Association of the U.S.A., Chicago, 1955.

HUEBNER, D., "New Modes of Man's Relationship to Man," in *New Insights and the Curriculum*, Association for Supervision and Curriculum Development *Yearbook*, 1963.

HUTT, MAX L. and DANIEL R. MILLER, "Value Interiorization and Democratic Education," *Journal of Social Issues*, V–VI (1949–1950), 31–42.

JACOBS, A. J., "Sociodrama and Teacher Education," *Journal of Teacher Education*, I (September, 1950), 192–98. Use of technique with a group of teachers, and an analysis of the reasons for the effectiveness of this procedure.

JANIS, I. L. and B. T. KING, "The Influence of Role-Playing on Opinion Change," *Journal of Abnormal and Social Psychology*, XLIX (1954), 211–18.

JAHODA, MARIE, "The Problem," *Journal of Social Issues*, V, No. 3 (1949).

JENNINGS, HELEN HALL, "Sociodrama Teaches Democratic Living," *Journal of Home Economics*, XLIV (April, 1952), 260–62.

———, *Sociometry in Group Relations: a Manual for Teachers*, 2nd edition, American Council on Education, Washington, D.C., 1950.

———, "Sociodrama as Educative Process," in *Fostering Mental Health in Our Schools*. Washington, D.C.: Association for Supervision and Curriculum Development, 1950 *Yearbook*, pp. 260–85.

JENSEN, GALE E., "The Social Structure of the Classroom Group: An Observational Framework," *Journal of Educational Psychology*, XLVI (1955), 362–74.

JERSILD, ARTHUR, *When Teachers Face Themselves*. New York: Columbia University, Teachers' College Bureau of Publication, 1955.

JOHNSON, E., M. PETERS, and W. EVRAIFF, *The Role of the Teacher in Guidance*. Englewood Cliffs, N.J.: Prentice-Hall, Inc., 1959.

JOHNSON, MEAD R. and GILBERT G. RAU, "Sociodrama Applied on a Teacher-training College Campus," *Peabody Journal of Education*, XXXV (September, 1957), 93–96.

Journal of American Academy of Arts and Sciences, "The Future Metropolis," in *Daedalus* (Winter, 1961).

KEAN, CHARLES, "Some Role-Playing Experiments with High School Students," *Group Psychotherapy*, VI (January–March, 1954), 256–65.

KELLEY, HAROLD H. and JOHN W. THEBAUT, "Experimental Studies of Group Problem Solving and Process," in *Handbook of Social Psychology*, II. Cambridge, Mass.: Addison-Wesley, 1954, pp. 735–85.

KELMAN, HERBERT, C., "Attitude Change as a Function of Response Restriction," *Human Relations*, VI (1953), pp. 185–214.

KING, BERT T. and IRVING L. JANIS, "Comparison of the Effectiveness of Improvised Versus Non-Improvised Role-Playing in Producing Opinion Changes," *Human Relations*, IX (1956), 177–86.

KLEIN, ALAN F., *How to Use Role-Playing Effectively*. New York: Association Press, 1959, 61 pp. A valuable introduction for beginners to the meaning and use of role-playing, partially adapted from the author's full-length book.

———, *Role Playing in Leadership Training and Group Problem Solving*. New York: Association Press, 1956.

KRASNER, LEONARD, LEONARD P. ULLMANN, and ROBERT L. WEISS, "Studies in Role Perception," *Journal of General Psychology*, LXXI (1964), 367–71.

LANDES, RUTH, *Latin Americans of the Southwest*. New York: McGraw-Hill Book Company, Webster Division, 1965.

LANE, HOWARD and MARY BEAUCHAMP, *Understanding Human Development*. Englewood Cliffs, N.J.: Prentice-Hall, Inc., 1959.

———, "Using Group Discussion and Role Playing" in *Human Relations in Teaching*. Englewood Cliffs, N.J.: Prentice-Hall, Inc., 1955, pp. 266–79.

LEE, J. MURRAY and DORRIS LEE, *The Child and His Development*. New York: Appleton-Century-Crofts, 1958.

LIPPITT, RONALD, "Cohesive Group Structure." Address delivered at Association for Supervision and Curriculum Development Research Conference, Palo Alto, 1961.

LIPPITT, RONALD (ed.), "Human Dynamics in the Classroom," *Journal of Social Issues*, II, Nos. 2, 5–6 (1949–1950), pp. 31–41.

LIPPITT, RONALD and MARTIN GOLD, "Classroom Social Structure as a Mental Health Problem," in *Educating for Mental Health*. Jerome M. Seidman (ed.). New York: Thomas Y. Crowell Company, 1963, pp. 117–40.

LIPPITT, RONALD and MARTIN GOLD, "Classroom Social Structures as a Mental Health Problem," *Journal of Social Issues*, XV, No. 1 (1959), pp. 40–49.

LIPPITT, RONALD, CHARLES E. HENDRY, and ALVIN ZANDER, "Reality Practice as Educational Method," Psychodrama Monographs, No. 9. Beacon, New York: Beacon House, 1947.

LIPPITT, ROSEMARY and CATHERINE CLANCY, "Psychodrama in the Kindergarten and Nursery School," *Group Psychotherapy*, VII (December, 1954), 262–73.

LUCE, R. D. and HOWARD RAIFFA, *Games and Decisions: Introduction and Critical Survey*. New York: John Wiley & Sons, Inc., 1964.

MACCOBY, ELEANOR E., "Role-taking in Childhood and its Consequences for Social Learning," *Child Development*, XXX (1959), 239–52.

MAIER, NORMAN R. F., *Principles of Human Relations; Applications to Management*. New York: John Wiley & Sons, Inc., 1952, pp. 87–172. Chapter 4 ("Role-Playing") and Chapter 5 ("Role-Playing in Large Groups") show how role-playing techniques may be used in solving human relations problems in industry.

MARTIN, C. P. JR., "Role Playing in the Classroom," *Grade Teacher*, LXXIII (November, 1955), 63.

MASON, RALPH E., "Education for Business Through Role Playing," *Journal of Business Education*, XXXV (May, 1960), 338–39.

MASSIALAS, BYRON, "Revising the Social Studies: An Inquiry Centered Approach," *Social Education*, XXVII (April, 1963), 185–89.

MEAD, GEORGE H., *Mind, Self and Society.* Chicago: University of Chicago Press, 1934.

————, "A Behavioristic Account of the Significant Symbol," *Journal of Philosophy,* XIX (1922).

MERRILL, REED M. and FRANK B. JEX, "Role Conflict in Successful Science Teachers," *Journal of Educational Research,* LVIII, No. 2 (October, 1964), 73–74.

METCALF, GEORGE, "Some Guidelines for Changing Social Education," *Social Education,* XXVII (April, 1963), 197–200.

METREAUX, RHODA, "Gaining Freedom of Value Choice," in *New Insights in the Curriculum.* Association for Supervision and Curriculum Development Yearbook, 1963, Chapter 9.

MIEL, ALICE (ed.), *Creativity in Teaching.* Belmont, Calif.: Wadsworth Co., 1961.

MORENO, JACOB L., *Psychodrama.* Beacon, N.Y.: Beacon House, 1946.

————, "Role," in *The Sociometry Reader.* New York: Free Press of Glencoe, 1960, pp. 80–86. A short essay on the meaning and origin of the terms *role* and *role-playing* by the originator of the sociodrama method.

————, *Sociometry.* Beacon, N.Y.: Beacon House, 1951.

————, *Who Shall Survive?* (rev. ed.). Beacon, N.Y.: Beacon House, 1953.

MORENO, JACOB L. and LESLIE D. ZELENY, "Role Theory and Sociodrama," in Joseph S. Roncek, ed., *Contemporary Sociology.* New York: Philosophical Library, 1958, pp. 642–54.

McCARTHY, WILLIAM GROVER, *A Comparison of Discussion and Role Playing as Techniques in Influencing Children's Thinking About Social Values.* Unpublished dissertation, Stanford University, Stanford, Calif., 1959.

National Training Laboratory in Group Development, *Exploration in Human Relations Training,* Washington, D.C., 1953.

NEWCOMB, THEODORE M., RALPH H. TURNER, and PHILIP E. CONVERSE, *Social Psychology.* New York: Holt, Rinehart & Winston, 1965, pp. 322–56.

NICHOLS, HILDRED and LOIS WILLIAMS, *Learning about Role-Playing for Children and Teachers.* Washington, D.C.: Association for Childhood Education International, 1960, 40 pp.

NORTHWAY, MARY L., *A Primer of Sociometry.* Toronto: University of Toronto Press, 1952.

NORTHWAY, MARY L. and LINDSAY WELD, *Sociometric Testing. A Guide for Teachers.* Toronto: University of Toronto Press, 1957.

OJEMAN, RALPH H., "Basic Approaches to Mental Health: The Human Relations Program at the State University of Iowa," in *Educating for Mental Health,* ed. Jerome M. Seidman. New York: Thomas Y. Crowell Company, 1963, pp. 218–29.

PARSONS, THEODORE, "Ethnic Cleavage in a California Community." Unpublished doctoral dissertation, Stanford University, Stanford, Calif., 1965.

PETTIGREW, THOMAS, "School Desegregation: Expanding Educational Opportunities to All Americans." Background paper for Panel B of Section IV of the White House Conference on Education, July 20, 1965.

————, *Profile of the Negro American*. Princeton, N.J.: D. Van Nostrand Co., Inc., 1964.

PRATT, CAROLINE, *I Learn From Children*. New York: Simon and Schuster, Inc., 1948.

PRICE, ROY ARTHUR, *Needed Research in the Teaching of the Social Studies*. National Council for the Social Studies, Research Bulletin No. 1, National Education Association, Washington, D.C., 1964.

RAPAPORT, ANATOL, *Fights, Games, and Debates*. Ann Arbor, Mich.: The University of Michigan Press, 1960.

REDL, FRITZ, "Crisis in the Children's Field," *American Journal of Orthopsychiatry*, XXXII, 759 (1962), 1–21.

RIESMAN, DAVID, *The Lonely Crowd*. New Haven, Conn.: Yale University Press, 1950.

RIESSMAN, FRANK, *The Culturally Deprived Child*. New York: Harper & Row, Publishers, 1962.

————, *The Culturally Deprived Child: A New View*. Opening address at the Conference on Education of Disadvantaged Children, U.S. Office of Education, Washington, D.C., May, 1962.

————, "The Overlooked Positives of Disadvantaged Groups," *Journal of Negro Education*, XXXIII, Section 3 (1964), pp. 225–31.

————, "School Culture, Learning Culture, and the Cognitive Style of the Disadvantaged." Address delivered at Training Program for Mobilization for Youth Staff, New York, September, 1962.

ROGERS, CARL, *Client-centered Therapy*. Boston: Houghton Mifflin Company, 1951.

ROSENBERG, PEARL, "An Experimental Analysis of Psychodrama." Unpublished doctoral dissertation. Cambridge, Mass.: Harvard University, 1950.

RUSSELL, DAVID, *Children's Thinking*. Boston: Ginn & Company, 1956.

RUSSELL, ROBERT D., "Interracial Marriage: An Interesting Aspect of Current Social Change." Address at San Francisco State College, July 13, 1965.

SANFORD, FILLMORE H., "The Follower's Role in Leadership Phenomena," in *Readings in Social Psychology*, (eds.) Guy E. Swanson, and others. New York: Holt, Rinehart & Winston, Inc., 1952, pp. 328–39.

SARBIN, THEODORE R., "Contributions to Role Taking Theory," Vol. I: Hypnotic Behavior, *Psychological Review*, LVII (1950), pp. 255–70.

————, "Role Theory," in *Handbook of Social Psychology, Vol. I: Theory and Method*, ed. G. Lindzey. Cambridge, Mass.: Addison-Wesley, 1954, pp. 226–58.

SARGENT, S. STANFIELD, "Conceptions of Role and Ego in Contemporary Psychology," in *Social Psychology at the Crossroads*, John H. Rohrer and

Muzafer Sherif (eds.). New York: Harper & Row, Publishers, 1951, pp. 355–70.

SCHMUCK, PATRICIA, JOHN E. LAWMAN, RONALD LIPPITT, and ROBERT FOX, "Social Science Education: A Curriculum Frontier," *Educational Leadership*, XXII, No. 5 (February, 1965).

SCOTT, WILLIAM A., "Attitude Change by Response Reinforcement: Replication and Extension," *Sociometry*, XXII (1959), 328–35.

SEARS, PAULINE SNEDDEN, *The Effect of Classroom Conditioning on the Strength of Achievement Motive and Work Output of Elementary School Children*. From a report on Cooperative Research Project, No. OE 873, Stanford University, Stanford, Calif., 1963.

SEARS, PAULINE and VIVIAN SHERMAN, *In Pursuit of Self Esteem*. Belmont, Calif.: Wadsworth Publishing Co., 1964.

SEEDS, CORINNE A., "Newer Practices Involving Dramatic Play," in *Newer Instructional Practices of Promise*. 12th *Yearbook*, Department of Supervision and Directors of Instruction. Washington, D.C.: National Education Association, 1939.

SHAFTEL, FANNIE, "Cultural Understanding in a World Community," *Educational Leadership*, XIX, No. 8 (May, 1962), 535–41.

———, "Learning to Feel with Others," *Childhood Education*, XXVII (December, 1950), 161–65.

———, "Role-Playing in Teaching American Ideals." Unpublished dissertation, Stanford University, Stanford, Calif., 1948.

SHAFTEL, FANNIE R. and GEORGE, *Role Playing the Problem Story*. National Conference of Christians and Jews, New York, 1952.

SHELLHAMMER, LOIS B., "Solving Personal Problems Through Sociodrama," *English Journal*, XXXVIII (November, 1949), 503–5. Use of sociodrama in seventh-grade English to gain insight into students' problems.

SHERIF, MUZAFER, "The Problem of Inconsistency in Intergroup Relations," *Journal of Social Issues*, V–VI (1949–1950), 32–43.

SHERIF, MUZAFER and HADLEY CANTRIL, *Psychology of Ego-Involvements*. New York: John Wiley & Sons, Inc., 1947.

SNOW, C. P., *Two Cultures*. New York: Cambridge University Press, 1959.

SOBEL, MORTON, J., "Sociodrama in the Classroom," *Social Education*, XVI (April, 1952), 166–68. For high school classes.

SOLT, M. Z., "George Wanted In," *Childhood Education*, XXXVIII (April, 1962), 374–76.

STAMPP, KENNETH, *The Negro in American History Textbooks*. California State Department of Education, 1964.

STEINBECK, JOHN, *The Winter of Our Discontent*. New York: The Viking Press, Inc., 1961.

STENDLER, CELIA and WILLIAM MARTIN, *Intergroup Education in Kindergarten-Primary Grades*. New York: The Macmillan Company, 1953.

STRAUSS, BERT and FRANCES, "Role-playing," in *New Ways to Better Meetings.* New York: The Viking Press, Inc., 1951, 91–110. Chapter 11 shows role-playing in many kinds of situations, particularly in adult groups.

SUCHMAN, RICHARD, *The Elementary School Training Program in Scientific Inquiry,* Illinois Studies in Inquiry Training, 1962. (mimeographed material.) University of Illinois, Champaign, Ill.

TABA, HILDA, *Cultural Deprivation as a Factor in School Learning.* Lecture delivered at the Merrill-Palmer Institute, Detroit, Mich., March, 1963, mimeographed.

———, *Curriculum in Intergroup Relations.* Washington, D.C.: American Council on Education, 1949, pp. 109–25.

———, *Diagnosing Human Relations Needs.* Washington, D.C.: American Council on Education, 1951.

———, "Education for Independent Valuing," in *New Insights and the Curriculum,* Chap. 10. Association for the Study of Curriculum Development *Yearbook,* 1963, 221–40.

———, *Elementary Curriculum in Intergroup Relations.* Washington, D.C.: American Council on Education, 1950, pp. 60–62; 156–60.

———, *School Culture.* Washington, D.C.: American Council on Education, 1955.

TARCOV, OSCAR, *To Clarify Our Problems: A Guide to Role-Playing.* New York: Anti-Defamation League of B'nai B'rith, 1950, 6 pp. One of the best brief guides providing step by step directions.

THELEN, HERBERT, *Education and the Human Quest.* New York: Harper & Row, Publishers, 1960.

TORRANCE, E. PAUL, *Guiding Creative Talent.* Englewood Cliffs, N.J.: Prentice-Hall, Inc., 1962.

TROW, WILLIAM CLARK, *Educational Psychology* (2nd ed.). Boston: Houghton-Mifflin Company, 1950.

TROW, WILLIAM CLARK, A. E. ZANDERS, W. C. MORSE, and D. H. JENKINS, "Psychology of Group Behavior: The Class as a Group," *Journal of Educational Psychology,* XLIV (1950), 322–38.

WARD, BARBARA (Lady Jackson), *Five Ideas That Changed the World.* New York: University College of Ghana, 1959.

WATTENBERG, WILLIAM, *The Adolescent Years.* New York: Harcourt, Brace & World, Inc., 1955.

WHITE, RALPH K. and RONALD O. LIPPITT, *Autocracy and Democracy, An Experimental Inquiry.* New York: Harper & Row, Publishers, 1960, 325.

WHITE, TOM MURRAY, "Two Weeks in Congress: Action Research with Sociodrama in the Study of Civics," *Social Studies,* XLVII (February, 1956), 43–48.

WHYTE, W. H., JR., *The Organization Man.* Garden City, N.Y.: Doubleday & Company, Inc., 1956.

WRIGHT, LULU, *A First Grade at Work*. New York: Columbia University, Teachers' College Bureau of Publications, 1932.

YOUNG, BRUCE F. and MORRIS ROSENBERG, "Role-Playing as a Participation Technique," *Journal of Social Issues*, V (Winter, 1949), 42–45. Excellent for insight into types of resistance to role-playing situations.

ZELENY, LESLIE D., *How to Use Sociodrama*, How to Do It Series, No. 20. Washington, D.C.: National Council for the Social Studies, 1955, 8 pp.

———, "Role Interaction in Small Groups," *California Social Science Review*, IV, No. 2 (January, 1965), 12–19.

ZELENY, LESLIE D. and RICHARD E. GROSS, "Dyadic Role-Playing of Controversial Issues," *Social Education*, XXIV (December, 1960), 354–58, 364.

II

materials: problem stories for role-playing

chapter 1

INDIVIDUAL
INTEGRITY

Honesty

THE
CLUBHOUSE
BOAT

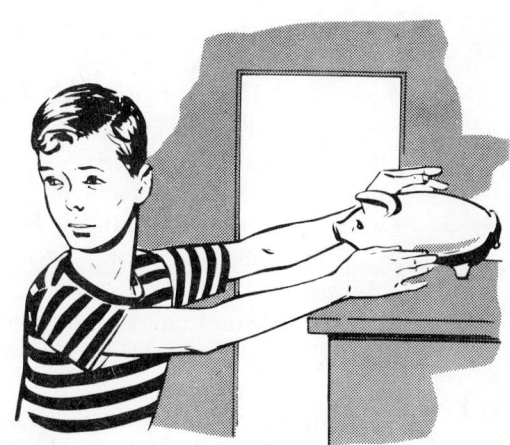

The problem:

The issue is conflict between peer-group and parental standards. To a ten- or eleven-year-old, keeping faith with his group is an all-important goal. Too often parents, in their concern for certain standards they wish to maintain for their families, ignore this need of the child to be like the rest of his age-mates. In this story, the boy's needs to be like his peer group are so hindered by his father's restrictions that the boy is forced into possible antisocial behavior in order to meet his obligations to his age-mates.

204 / Individual Integrity

Introducing the problem:

You may ask the group, "Most of you, at one time or another, have found yourself in a spot in which you had to decide whether to obey rules your parents set down for you or to do what your friends are urging you to do. It's a difficult spot to be in, isn't it? This story deals with such a problem. The story stops but is not finished. As I read, think of ways in which the story could end."

Tommy Haynes listened big-eyed as his chum Eddie Blake excitedly explained, "We *are* getting the houseboat! Listen, here's what's happened. Dave Allen's uncle has this houseboat down near the yacht harbor in Port Redwood City. He's going to give it to us, to the Pedal Pushers Club. For a clubhouse!"

"Oh, boy!" Tommy blurted.

"Only, we got to get it repaired. It leaks. He says he doesn't want to be responsible for the whole Pedal Pushers Club being drowned. But if we'll get the hull repaired, and pay the docking fee, we can have the Sea Lion! And Ed Mays says he'll bring his movie projector and keep it aboard, and my Dad says I can have our old radio to use in the club."

"Swell!"

"But we need the money to fix the Sea Lion up. There's six of us, and if we each chip in twenty dollars, we can swing it. Can you raise twenty dollars, Tommy?"

"Sure! I started delivering for the First Street Drug Store, and I make four dollars a week. I already got four dollars, and payday is tonight. I'll have eight dollars."

"That's fine. My mom says I can cash the savings bond my uncle gave me on my eighth birthday. I got to go and tell Andy Simons now."

"I'll bring the money over to Dave's house tomorrow," Tommy promised.

He rode on to the drugstore and was busy delivering until six o'clock. Mr. Ekblaw paid him his weekly wage of four dollars, and Tommy rode on home to supper.

After the meal, his dad asked, "Tommy, did you get paid tonight?"

"Yes, I did, Dad. Mr. Ekblaw's sure a nice man to work for."

"Got the money on you?"

"Yes."

"Better give it to me. I'll put it in the bank for you."

"Oh, I need it, Dad. And my four dollars I gave you last week, I'll need that too."

Mr. Haynes frowned.

"Look, Tommy, I let you take this job, though you certainly don't need it."

"Oh, I do, Dad, I do!"

"Your mother and I provide you with everything. But I figured that it would do you good to earn money, and to learn to save."

"Oh, sure, Dad. Only right now—"

"There's only one way ever to start to save, son. That's always right now."

"But, Dad, I got to have it."

"What for, Tommy?" his mother asked.

"The Pedal Pushers Club is buying a houseboat, and we each—"

"What!" Mr. Haynes exploded.

"The club is getting a houseboat from Dave Allen's uncle."

"Giving it to you?"

"Yes!"

"It can't be too good."

"We've got to get the hull repaired, so it won't leak."

"Good heavens!" Mrs. Haynes said.

"Oh. it'll be all right! Mr. Allen says so, once we get the hull fixed. Then we're going to keep it tied up near the yacht harbor. There's six bunks in it, and we'll have a radio and a movie projector. That's why I need the money. I got to put in my share."

Mr. Haynes was shaking his head.

"Listen, son. All your life there'll be a houseboat, or a car, or a lot, or an oil well that you've just got to put your money into. The best time for you to start learning that the best place to put your money is into the bank is *right now!*"

"But, Dad, the club's depending on me to put in my share!"

"Son, I'm asking you to let yourself be guided by me, out of my own grim experience. When you get your pay, you're going to bring the four dollars to me. I'll give you seventy-five cents spending money. But three dollars and twenty-five cents I'm putting into the savings bank for you. And to that three twenty-five, as long as you keep your job, every week I'll add a dollar. By the end of the year, Tommy, you'll have a respectable sum in the bank. You'll be proud of it."

"Dad, please—"

"No! And that's final. If there's anything I hate, it's coaxing. You know that!"

Tommy left the dining room, went to his own room and flung himself down on his bed.

There was dismay at the next meeting of the Sea Lions.

"Oh, gosh," Dave Allen said disgustedly, "this wrecks the whole deal! If Tommy can't put his money in, then we're shy of the full amount. We've had the repair work done, and those people want their money right now. What're we going to do?"

"Tommy, can't you get some money somewhere else?"

Tommy shook his head, his face drawn with misery.

"But, Tommy," Eddie Blake protested, "when I asked you, you *said* you could get the money. We depended on you. Now we're in a jam."

Tommy swallowed hard and said nothing.

Eddie went on, "That Mr. Bidwell, who fixed the hull—he won't put the Sea Lion back in the water until we pay him all we owe."

Pete Myers said, "Tommy, I think maybe I can raise some money to lend you. But you got to pay me back, or I'll be in trouble."

Tommy looked at their dismayed, accusing faces. Suppose he said yes? But where would he get the money if his dad took most of his pay?

"Gee, Pete, that's great," Eddie said. "Of course you'll pay him back, won't you, Tommy?"

Tommy couldn't speak. He only nodded.

Pete Myers said, "Some lady lost her purse in Dad's taxi the other night, and Mom's got it put away in the dresser drawer, until somebody claims it. There's over twenty dollars in it. I'll borrow the money for you, Tommy. But you sure got to pay me back, so I can put the money back in the purse."

"I'll try."

Tommy was in a constant agony of fright that week. Suppose he couldn't pay back the money, and the owner came and found the money missing? They'd accuse Pete's dad of stealing . . .

Tommy made a discovery Monday afternoon. He had to deliver a package of aspirin and vitamins to a house on the Lake Street hill. He was puffing and sweating from effort as he rang the doorbell, and when the kindly woman who answered looked at him, he said impulsively, "Golly, that's some hill!" She said, yes it was, and when she paid him for the drugs she gave him a quarter extra. It was his first tip and he stood there confused, staring at it. She smiled at him and said goodbye.

It gave him an idea.

On his next delivery he had to go out to the edge of town. After handing over the package to a flashily-dressed man at the given address, he stood there, sort of waiting and said meaningfully, "You sure live 'way out."

It worked. He got only a dime, but that was a tenth of a dollar.

At home he said nothing of these tips, just hoarded them carefully in his bureau drawer.

He worked hard. Tips were something he had never thought of. Tips might help him solve that awful problem so heavy over his head. He did not dally on his deliveries; the more customers he brought drugs to, during his brief working hours, the more chances for that extra piece of change.

Wednesday night he got another surprise.

The druggist, Mr. Ekblaw, grinned at him when he said good night, and remarked, "You're a hard worker, Tommy. I'm afraid maybe I'm gypping you a little on the pay. You'll get a dollar more, Friday night. Five bucks."

Tommy's eyes shone.

"Thanks, Mr. Ekblaw!"

His eyes were still shining when he got home, and Mother asked him, "Tommy, you look like the sun has come out again. The way you've been mooning around, I'd almost decided you better see the doctor. What happened?"

"Oh, nothing, Mother."

But in his room he counted up his tips. He had $1.30.

It was next evening that a Mrs. Black on Page Drive overpaid him fifty cents. He didn't know until he reached the drugstore and handed over the money to Mr. Ekblaw. Mr. Ekblaw returned the fifty cents to him.

"Tommy, you got some of your money in this," he said. "Better keep it in separate pockets."

Tommy flushed, and leaving work, he knew he should head back to Page Drive . . . but he pedaled straight home, and there was such a sick churning in his stomach that he left his food on his dinner plate. His mother's forehead knitted as she looked at him.

"You feeling sick again, Tommy?"

"I'm all right!" he said vehemently, and went to his room.

His mother shook her head and wondered aloud, "Now what's wrong? Boys sure are a worry!"

Mr. Haynes looked up from his paper, frowning.

"Tommy's working pretty hard and for just four bucks a week. You know, I think I'll stop by the drugstore and tell Mr. Ekblaw that Tommy has had his tryout now, and deserves a little raise in pay."

"Maybe that'll make Tommy cheer up," Mrs. Haynes said. . . .

It was the next afternoon at the drugstore that Tommy got an unexpected phone call. Mr. Ekblaw called him.

"Somebody wants to talk to you, Tommy. Sounds kind of urgent."

Angrily, Tommy wondered who it was. His friends knew better than to call him at work.

It was Eddie Blake, and he sounded as if he were scared sick.

"Tommy, we got to talk to you. Right away!"

"Gosh, Eddie, I'm working."

"We're waiting at the schoolyard corner. Next delivery you make, you go by there. Hurry!"

"What's the matter?"

"Tell you when you get here. 'Bye."

In Tommy's stomach was a gone, hollow feeling as he hung up.

Mr. Ekblaw looked at him as he came out of the phone booth, and the kindly druggist said, "Tommy, something wrong? You can run on home if you want."

"Th-thanks, sir, but I don't really have to."

"Well, take this stuff out to twelve eighteen Vistillas Drive. It's a big order and you ask for eleven dollars and twenty-eight cents."

The boys were waiting at the school corner as Tommy rode near. Eddie beckoned him, and they moved into a huddle on the empty playground.

"The awfullest thing's happened," Dave burst out. Tommy saw that Dave looked disgusted, that Eddie was sore, and Pete Myers looked white and scared.

Eddie Blake came right out with it. "Tommy, the woman who left that purse in Pete's dad's taxi came hunting for it. Pete's ma gave it to her, and she opened it and found twenty dollars gone. She was going to call the police, but Pete's ma promised that it would be returned. Then she asked Pete, and he had to tell his ma all about it."

Dave broke in, "And his ma says Pete's got to quit the Pedal Pushers. He can't hang around with us any more at all!"

Eddie went on, "Pete's ma told his dad, and his dad says the club'll either get him that twenty dollars by tomorrow, or he's going to see all our dads and tell them what happened!"

And Dave asked, "Tommy, you get that money for us!"

Tommy choked up; tears blurred his eyes.

"I c-can't," he said.

"Look, Tommy," Eddie went on. We've raised some of it. We got about twelve dollars. Haven't you got any money at all?"

"Four dollars."

"Good, good! But, Tommy, you just naturally got to raise four more dollars by tomorrow." His voice was very stern. "You got us into this jam. Now it's up to you."

And Dave said accusingly, "On account of you, Pete's got to quit the club. I think we ought to courtmartial you."

"I got to deliver this medicine," Tommy said.

Eddie said: "Tommy, if Pete's dad goes to all our fathers and tells them—well, there'll just be no more Pedal Pushers Club. You got to have that money for us by tomorrow."

"I'll try," Tommy whispered. . . .

He passed 1218 Vistillas Drive, and realized with a start that he had gone too far, and turned back. A white-haired man answered the doorbell and grinned at him. Maybe it was Tommy's woebegone expression, but anyway, he gave Tommy a little lift of heart after paying for the medicine, by tipping him a whole quarter, saying, "Buy yourself a Cadillac, sonny," and smiled as he shut the door.

Tommy put the change in his pocket, and straightened out the bills carefully to put them in his wallet. He got a shock. The old man had overpaid him. Given him, instead of a five-dollar bill, a ten-dollar bill. Overpaid him five dollars.

Tommy raised his hand to knock on the door.

And hesitated—that five dollars—why, it would more than make up the money he needed. With his tips it would make up the sum Pete needed to give to his dad.

Tommy stood there, arm lifted, frozen . . .

**FINDERS
WEEPERS ***

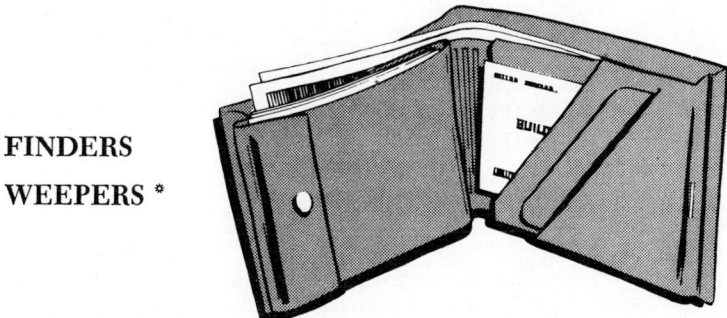

The problem:

This story concerns the dilemma of being honest when it would be easy and convenient to be dishonest in order to solve a burdensome problem.

* Adapted from *Teacher's Manual: English Grammar and Composition*, VII (New York: Harcourt, Brace & World, Inc., 1960). Reprinted by permission of the publisher.

Introducing the problem:

> Say: "Have any of you ever found a pocketbook on the street? If you have, I'm sure you wondered whether to keep it or turn it in to some lost-and-found department. Here's a story about some boys who found a wallet with money in it just when they needed money very badly. This story stops but is not finished. As I read, try to think of ways in which the story should end."

They had been told not to use the boat. Eddie's Uncle Ross had been very definite about it. "I have a good reason," he told them. "Storms come up real sudden on this big lake. You might get caught out in one and drowned. So fish and swim and hike all you want. Just leave the boat alone." But the boys had not obeyed.

They had had a lot of fun—swimming, fishing, hiking, and just loafing on the beach in the warm sun. But all the time the rowboat had rested there in plain sight, both an invitation and a challenge. Finally Pete had lost to temptation. While Eddie and Tom were in swimming, Pete had pried loose a staple that held the locked chain, and freed the boat. Then he had rowed out into the lake. Eddie had yelled angrily at him; his uncle had been very kind to invite them to stay with him for the week, and they should have respected his wishes. But, in the end, Eddie had enjoyed using the boat too.

This morning, the last day of their stay, the boat was missing. Eddie's uncle had said goodbye to the boys, and gone off to work. They had cleaned up breakfast dishes and gone out on to the beach to swim. Eddie then noticed that the boat wasn't in its usual place.

"Pete, you used the boat last night. Where did you leave it?"

"I pulled the bow up onto the sand."

"Didn't you *tie* it to anything?"

"I was in a hurry. But I had it almost halfway up onto the beach."

"So when the wind came up during the night," Eddie said disgustedly, "the waves washed the boat free. No telling how far it's drifted by now. Come on, we have to find it!"

They found the rowboat a mile away, resting drunkenly on sharp rocks that jutted out from shore. The boat was half full of water: the rocks had punched a hole in the bottom.

"That's just fine," Tom said angrily. "Pete, you have to pay for the boat!"

But Eddie said, "No. We're all in this. Anyway, I think it can be repaired."

They hauled the boat out; and got a boat-builder from nearby Lakeport to come and look at the boat. It could be repaired, he said. The repairs would cost $30. The boys added up their cash. They had, in all, $11 more than the cost of bus tickets home.

"Can we send you the rest of the money?" Eddie asked.

"Yes, but I'll have to keep the boat until you do."

After the man hauled the boat to his shop, the boys worried.

"Where'll we get the nineteen dollars we'll owe him?" Tom asked.

Eddie said, "Gosh, I'd sure hate to have Uncle Bob pay it himself, but he'll have to if we don't."

"We'll have to ask our folks for the money," Tom said.

"If my Dad hears how we broke our word, after Uncle Bob had been so good to us," Eddie said, "I'll *really* be in trouble!"

Pete said, "Now your uncle won't ever ask us here again."

"All your fault!" Tom told him angrily. . . .

It was Tom who found the wallet, on the bus station floor.

He picked it up and said, "Look!" drawing the other boys aside. "Maybe this'll get us out of trouble."

But Eddie said, "Look inside. The owner's name must be in it."

Inside the wallet were two ten- and two one-dollar bills and a check, that looked like a pay check, for $292.00.

Eddie said, "There must be a Lost and Found desk here. We'll turn the wallet in."

"You crazy?" Pete said. "This money'll pay for fixing the boat!"

"Look at the identification card," Eddie said. "This wallet belongs to a Mr. Martin Sands. The bus company will return it."

"Listen," Pete said insistently. "We'll just take the cash out, and say there was no money in the wallet when we found it. Don't you see, Eddie? Pickpockets hang around bus stations like this. The owner will figure that somebody picked his pocket, took the money out of the wallet and then threw it away, so's it wouldn't be found on him if he got searched by a cop."

"But that pay check—"

"We'll leave the pay check in the wallet. Pickpockets don't mess around with checks, they just take cash that can't be traced. The owner will be so glad to get this big check back that he won't mind losing the cash. He'll figure it's just the reward he had to pay to get his pay check back!"

"No," Eddie said.

"We'll vote on it," Pete insisted. "I say keep the cash!"

"And I say return everything," Eddie said.

"Tommy, how do you vote?" Pete demanded.

And Eddie urged, "Say it, Tommy. Keep the money? Or give it back?"

Tommy swallowed hard. Tommy said:

PAPER
DRIVE

The problem:

This story deals with problems of honesty; specifically, with the rationalization that if your opponent is dishonest, you are justified in being dishonest too.

Best used at fifth, sixth, and seventh grades.

Introducing the problem:

Say to the group: "Have you ever been in a game or a contest which you wanted to win very much, and discovered that the other side was cheating? Were you tempted to cheat too, then? This is a story about such a situation. This story stops but is not finished. As I read, try to think of a good ending for the story."

Miss Hendry's sixth-grade students were eager to win the annual Paper Drive. The classroom bringing in the most paper during the week of the contest was to be given a picnic at the Pink Horse Ranch. Hot dogs and ice cream would be free. Swimming and movies, and rides on the roller coaster and boats and ponies, too, would be free. At the start of the contest, Miss Hendry did not believe that her group had a chance to win. But each day, after school, her students busily gathered paper and tied it into compact bundles and delivered it to the big trailer waiting at the rear of the school yard. As the end of the week drew near, excitement in the classroom rose to fever pitch.

Friday morning, she had to remind the group, "You're still in school, children. Please pay attention."

"We're going to win, Miss Hendry!"

"That's fine, but meanwhile, let's get some classwork done."

"We're too excited!"

"Just calm down."

They did—a little. But this was the last day of the contest, so she was patient. At 3:30, the children rushed out, and she remained behind to work late.

She was at the back of the classroom, an hour later, when through the slats of the venetian blinds she saw three of her students bringing a heavy bale of paper to the school yard. The awkward bale was resting on a small coaster wagon they were pulling up the alley behind the school. As she watched, the wagon overturned, and the bale fell off. The cord tying it broke, and the paper came loose in a mess on the pavement. Hastily the youngsters gathered up the paper into a clumsy package again and retied it. But not before Miss Hendry, to her amazement and dismay, discovered the awful truth.

Wrapped in folds of the newspapers—which had momentarily opened to reveal their contents—were pieces of rusty iron junk. Her students were hiding heavy pieces of old iron, probably gathered from junk heaps, within the bales of paper. *To increase their weight!* So that they would deliver the heaviest amount of paper and win the contest.

She opened the window and called to them.

"Andy! Sue! You and Pete come in here at once."

They came in. They flushed uneasily as they stood before her.

"You have pieces of heavy junk hidden in those bundles of paper, haven't you?"

Andy nodded. He stared at the floor, not meeting her stern glance.

"To make your bundles heavy?"

Andy nodded again.

"Have you been doing this all week?"

"Just since Wednesday."

"You three only, or has the whole class been doing it?"

"The whole class," Sue said.

Miss Hendry sighed in despair.

"Don't deliver that bundle to the truck," she ordered. "Take it— some place and hide it!"

They scuttled out as if released from jail.

Miss Hendry sat down at her desk and took thought.

What should she do? She hated to expose her students. Her own face began to burn with shameful regret. What would the parents think of her as a teacher when word got out that her group had been cheating in an effort to win the paper drive?

If her class had not profited by this cheating, she decided that she would not expose them; instead, she would preach them a very hot sermon Monday morning on honesty. . . .

After dinner that evening, she heard local news on the radio—and learned the outcome of the paper drive. It was good news, but it left her miserable with worry.

"The sixth-grade class of Glenwood Elementary School, taught by Miss Belle Hendry," said the announcer, "has won the annual paper drive sponsored by the Junior Chamber of Commerce. The class will be given a rousing big picnic at Pink Horse Ranch as a reward. In addition, a surprise dividend for the group will be a big turkey dinner, a ball glove for each boy, and a school ring for each girl.

"Runner-up in the contest was the sixth-grade class at Wilson Elementary School, which was a close sixty-seven pounds behind in the weight of paper gathered. . . ."

Miss Hendry felt sick at heart. Her group had won—by cheating. They did not deserve this victory. . . .

What she felt must have been plain on her face when she met her class on Monday morning. The group became very quiet and tense.

"Well," she said slowly, "you won the paper drive. But you won it in a way that makes me deeply ashamed. Some of you packed pieces of iron junk in the bales of paper you brought to the truck." She paused. Nobody in the group gasped in surprise; evidently *all* knew and *all* were involved in the cheating. "You are going to write a letter, as a class, to the Junior Chamber of Commerce. You will apologize for having won the drive unfairly. You will say that the real winner is the sixth-grade class at Wilson School. Do you understand me?"

"But Miss Hendry," Sam Martin protested, "we cheated because the Wilson sixth grade was cheating."

"Oh, no!"

"Yes! Those Wilson boys were spraying garden hoses on their bales of paper. Making them wet so they'd weigh heavy. Then letting them stand in the sun so the outside would dry, and then wrapping dry paper around them. That's why we packed junk in our bales!"

"Is this *true?*"

"Yes, it is!"

"Did any of you actually see this being done?"

No one answered immediately.

"We *heard*—"

"My brother heard them talking about it," Sue Nolan said.

"But even if they *were* cheating," Miss Hendry went on, "do you think that made it right for *you* to cheat?"

"But, gosh, Miss Hendry, we didn't want them to win!" Sue blurted.

"If you make us withdraw from the paper drive, the Wilson sixth grade ought to withdraw, too!"

"But I can't go to their teacher and tell her that her class was cheating," Miss Hendry said firmly. "I have no proof. I'd just be repeating gossip and rumor. That other teacher would be justified in telling me that I'm a bad loser, and to mind my own business."

"But if you make us confess that we've cheated," Andy said, "you'll be helping that other class to win by cheating!"

"But I can't overlook your dishonesty and let *you* win by cheating," she said.

"You mean," Andy protested, "that you'll let *them* win by cheating?"

She started to answer—and could not; indecision held her silent. If she said nothing, she would be helping her students to profit from dishonest conduct. But if she made them confess their cheating, she would be helping the other group to win by dishonesty. What should she do?

BOY

OUT

ON

A

LIMB

The problem:

The issue is honesty; specifically, telling the truth about misbehavior and being punished or keeping quiet and allowing the wrong person to be blamed.

Introducing the problem:

Children are often in one kind of trouble or another over care of property. This might be a good story to use in one of those frequent occasions when adults complain of some act of vandalism committed by school children. If there is not an immediate incident to serve as a springboard into this situation, you may simply ask the children, "What was the last occasion you damaged some property while playing, when you *didn't really mean to do any damage?" After some discussion, you can say, "I'm going to read you a story about such an incident. The story stops but is not finished. As I read, try to think of ways the story might end."*

Bobby Allen's father had promised to take him fishing that Saturday afternoon. Out of excitement Bobby had risen earlier than usual for Saturday; and after breakfast, he faced a long, long wait until afternoon.

"Run outside and amuse yourself, dear," his mother urged. "But be quiet. Edie's got a bad cold and I'm keeping her in her crib so she can get a lot of sleep today."

Outside, he walked out the front gate to the street. He saw none of his friends; most of them, he knew, had already gone downtown to see the Saturday morning movie.

Abruptly the quiet street was made noisy by the racket of a motor coming from the Mapes' yard, two houses down. Oh, oh, he thought; his baby sister wasn't going to get much sleep while all that noise was going on.

He hurried down the sidewalk and saw that the roar was coming from a small cement-mixer. Two men were putting finishing touches to a new driveway for Mr. Mapes. He stayed on while they finished pouring fresh mix between the wooden forms, and watched while the men smoothed the surface of the last square of concrete. Done, they finally hitched their mixer to a small pickup truck and drove away.

Bobby sat down on the curb, and yawned. It was such a *long* wait until one o'clock.

He could go home and read, but he was too excited to do that. If Arthur and Johnny Ames were home, he could start up a ball game— Oh, no, he couldn't. Since Mike Sample knocked a ball that cracked the windshield of a bakery truck, the kids weren't allowed to play ball in the street.

And then Bobby cheered up. Al Brady was coming down the street. With a dog, by golly. Al was new on the block, and Bobby had not played with him much as yet, but now he greeted Al as if they were best friends.

"Hi, Al. Can you play?"

"I guess so."

"What kind of dog is that?"

"Red setter."

"Does he know any tricks?"

"No. He's just eight months old."

"Don't you know how to train him?"

"No."

"I'll show you. I used to have a fox terrier. Let's go into your yard."

They walked into the Brady yard, next door to the Mapes' place.

Bobby asked, "What's his name?"

"Champ."

"Here, Champ," Bobby called. "Here, Champ!"

The young setter wagged his tail furiously and came up to him, eager to play but wary of a stranger.

Bobby patted him, then said, "Sit down, Champ. Sit down!"

And with the command, Bobby pressed on the dog's flanks, forcing him to sit on his hind legs.

"See? Just practice that with him. Will he fetch?"

"Yeah, he'll go after a stick or a ball."

"But will he bring it back?"

"Yeah, sure!—sometimes."

Bobby threw a stick, saying, "Get it, Champ. Get it!"

Champ lunged after the stick, picked it up in his big mouth and lay down and worried it.

"Bring it, Boy! Bring it here," Bobby called.

Champ's ears went up and he studied Bobby—but just sat where he was.

"Bring it, Boy!"

The urgency in his tone had results. Champ came to him, carrying the stick in his mouth; but when Bobby reached for it, Champ ran across the yard and sat down and proceeded to chew the piece of wood.

"Champ!" Bobby said disgustedly. "You ought to call him Chump!"

The dog trotted over to his master, leaving the stick behind.

Bobby said, "That's because he's never been given a reward for bringing something. When he does a thing right, you should give him something. Then he'll learn. Watch." He ordered, "Sit down, Champ," and pushed down on the setter's back. Champ sat down. Bobby took from his pocket a piece of last week's licorice whip and held it out. Champ sniffed it suspiciously, then ate it ravenously.

Again Bobby threw a stick, ordering, "Fetch it, Boy!"

Champ lunged after the piece of wood.

But Bobby had thrown the stick a little too hard. It sailed over a low picket fence, into the Mapes' yard. Champ sailed right after it—down upon that new concrete driveway. Champ landed running in that last, still un-dry, square of concrete, and every lunge he took at a slant along the drive left four big imprints that looked like bear tracks.

Al breathed a gasping "Wow!" and added quickly, "*You* threw the stick, Bobby!"

Bobby stared, fright in his eyes.

"My pop will be mad," he said.

Champ found the stick and lay down and gnawed it.

"Here, Champ!" Al called urgently.

The setter cantered back toward the fence—right across the wet concrete again.

"Get him out of there!" Bobby yelled at Al.

"*You* threw that stick over there," Al repeated angrily. "Come on, Champ. Come back here!"

The setter paused, and sprang, clearing the fence but leaving final imprints like tiny bomb craters in the soft cement.

Bobby said breathlessly, "I've got to go home, Al!"

Bobby leafed through his new encyclopedia until lunch time. He didn't enjoy it much; he had a stomach-ache and he felt too hot.

At noon, his father arrived. Hurrying indoors, he smiled at Bobby and said, "Soon's we have lunch, we'll climb into the car and head for the lake."

Bobby didn't feel hungry, but he forced himself to eat.

And then the telephone rang.

Bobby knew at once what it was about. He felt sick.

"Yes, this is Allan," his father said into the phone. "How are you? ... What's that? Your new driveway? ... Oh, but look here, we don't have a dog. ... Your wife saw it? You mean actually with her own eyes? ... Oh, I see. ... Is that so? ... I'll ask him. I'll get the straight of it. I'll call you back."

And the way Mr. Allan hung up was grim.

"Bobby, I want to talk to you."

"Yes, Dad?"

"Were you playing with some dog in the Brady yard this morning?"

Bobby gulped. He looked at the tablecloth, and his stomach knotted and he felt as if he were going to upchuck his lunch.

"Dad, I—was trying to train Al's dog to fetch. I threw a stick, only it went over the fence into Mr. Mapes' yard, and the dog jumped over the fence, right onto the soft concrete, chasing the stick."

"So that's how it happened."

"Y—yes, Dad."

"All right. I'll phone Mr. Mapes to get his driveway smoothed up, and send the bill to me. And—you'll have to take your punishment, Bobby. You didn't intend any harm, so I'll be—easy."

Bobby licked his lips and didn't say anything.

"You will be confined to your own yard for a week. Maybe—next Saturday—we'll go fishing. If you haven't busted any windows or burned down any houses meanwhile!"

The afternoon began in very dull fashion. Bobby, confined to his yard, had to amuse himself alone, for neither Mike nor Arthur would come into his yard to play. They were busy on bicycles in the street.

Then Bobby got a break; his cousin Phil arrived to see him.

"Let's get a ball game started, Bobby!"

"Can't. I got to play in the back yard."

"But we can't play ball back *here!* What the heck can we play?"

"Mumbledy-peg?"

"Oh, all right. Nothing else you *can* do here!"

Phil had a Scout knife. They whipped the knife into the ground, going through the varied routine of the game.

"My brother Ned's joined the Air Force," Phil remarked. "He's going to be a jet pilot."

"Dad," Bobby said with pride, "was a pilot in the Navy."

"He didn't pilot a jet fighter. They didn't have 'em in those days!"

"Maybe not. But one time he shot down a Japanese suicide fighter just before he was going to crash into Dad's carrier. And Dad had to come in so low he couldn't zoom away in time and hit the smokestack with a wing tip and crashed into the ocean. They had to send a rescue boat to pick him up."

Phil jumped to his feet. He darted around the grassy plot of yard making noises like a jet fighter, roaring and diving with outspread arms. Bobby opened up on him with a pair of make-believe 20-millimeter machine guns. "Hrah-hrah-hrah-hrah-hrah-hrah!"

Phil stared around the place. His gaze focused on the big apple tree in the Rea yard that thrust a thick limb over Bobby's yard. "Look, Bobby, can you get a rope?"

"Yeah, we got one in the garage."

"Quick, get it!"

Quick, Bobby got it.

"But what for?" he demanded.

Phil threw the rope over the big limb of the neighbor's apple tree. Phil tied the stepladder to one end of the rope, and hauled the ladder up until it swung free, a foot off the lawn.

"You see, Bobby? This is a Jacob's ladder hanging from the side of a big carrier. You rescued me, now we got to climb up on deck!"

"But Dad wouldn't let me hang a swing from that limb. Said we mustn't damage a neighbor's tree."

But Phil was already climbing up the ladder. It swung, and swayed, and tilted, and turned, and Phil had to hang on tightly. But his dark eyes shone with delight.

"Say, this is like a rope ladder hanging under an airplane. Bobby, we're the crew of a big bomber, and three motors have been shot out and the fourth engine is spitting and choking and it's going to konk out— and another bomber comes overhead and lets down a rope ladder and we got to climb up into it! We can't just bail out because we're over a valley where cannibals live. They've spotted us and they're beating drums and grabbing their spears. Climb up, Bobby! Climb for your life!"

Bobby gingerly caught hold of the ladder, and put one foot on it, then the other. The ladder swung way back, so that the boys were leaning far over on their backs. The ladder swung and rocked, and Bobby's face lit with scared enjoyment.

He peered down at the jungle valley rising so perilously fast toward them, at the painted, mud-daubed cannibals who wore bones thrust through their nostrils and carried shiny-tipped spears and yelled to each other in the cannibal equivalent of "Come a-running! Fresh meat coming down." Already the one motor of the doomed bomber was sputtering into final silence, and the big craft was slanting earthward in a high-pitched screaming dive, bearing within it three luckless members of the crew who had not had time to climb out, and with Bobby and Phil on the dangling ladder.

Crash! The damaged bomber struck earth—

Cra-a-ck . . . and the tree limb broke under the combined weight of boys, ladder, and high excitement. The branch broke near the trunk. Ladder, boys, and high excitement plunged earthward. The ladder hit first, the boys were jarred loose, and they hit the grass separately, rope draping down around them, and the limb landing inches away and breaking into four different pieces from the impact.

Scared, knocked breathless, they just lay there a moment.

"Wow!" Phil gasped. "What a crash!"

He laughed shakily, and Bobby laughed too.

They stood up and dusted themselves off, still laughing.

But the laugh stuck in Bobby's throat as he saw the damage. That falling limb had broken a big notch in the fence, crushing a fine climbing rose. Over in the Rea yard, the thick limb had crashed down upon a big, orange-colored garden umbrella, breaking down the table below it and crushing a lounge chair; and over on this side of the fence, in Bobby's own yard, the limb had smashed flat his baby sister's playpen.

"Golly," Phil breathed, all the fun gone from his voice. "I got to go home!"

And Phil hurried off, almost running.

Bobby glanced at his mother's kitchen windows. She didn't seem to be there. Turning, with shaking fingers, he untied the rope and ladder from the broken limb, and carried them into the garage and set them in their proper places.

He wandered into the house. His mother was in the dining room, at the telephone, ordering groceries.

Bobby picked up a book, and tried to read, but the type was a blur to his eyes. . . . What was his father going to say when he saw all the damage? What was he going to *do?* . . .

What Bobby's father did say, when he returned late in the afternoon, was, "Bobby, what in the world happened out here?"

Bobby had difficulty forming words.

"D–dad, that big limb—it fell off the tree—"

"I told Rea he ought to have that old tree pruned!" Mr. Allen exploded. "I told him over a month ago. Now, when the first breath of strong wind comes along—Look at Edie's playpen! If that baby had been in it, she'd have been killed!"

Mr. Allan bent over the playpen wreckage.

"Dad—"

"I'm going over after dinner and tell Rea what I think of him. It's criminal negligence to let an old tree like that be a hazard to your neighbors. I'd *told* him to get it pruned! I'll make him pay for the playpen and for rebuilding the fence, too."

"Oh, no," Bobby gasped.

"What?" Mr. Allan said, turning to Bobby. "What did you say?"

Bobby said . . .

**LITTLE
ECHO**

The problem:

The issue is that of honesty; specifically, the "white lie." Parents often set standards of ideal behavior for their children which the parents themselves do not observe. Children, on their part, are apt to justify their own misconduct by citing the misconduct of others. In this story a child

*deliberately deceives her mother after a disillusioning experience with
"white lies" on the parent's part. This misbehavior is a consequence of a
double standard set up by adults: One code of behavior for themselves,
another for the child.*

Introducing the problem:

You may ask the class, "Have any of you ever told a lie, a little
'white lie' in order to get out of doing something you didn't want to do?
This is a story about a girl who lied, and what happened as a result. The
story stops, but is not finished. Try to think of ways in which the story
might end."

When the telephone rang in the late afternoon, Nora was busy
drying her wavy dark hair, in preparation for a party that night.

"Nora," her mother said, "it's for you. Mrs. Kyne."

Nora gasped in dismay. "Oh, my gosh, *no!*"

"Hurry, dear!"

Running to the phone, Nora asked, "Mother, is today the tenth?
It is!"

"Indeed it is!"

"What'll I do?" Nora begged.

"About what?"

"I told Mrs. Kyne I'd sit with their baby tonight—"

"Oh, *no*, Nora!"

Nora's mother held her head.

"Mrs. Kyne?" Nora said.

"Yes, Nora. I called to ask if you could possibly come fifteen minutes earlier? We have to start out earlier so's to pick up some friends."

Nora hesitated, and licked her lips, her mind racing.

"Oh, Mrs. Kyne, I'm awfully sorry!" she wailed. "But I won't be
able to come over tonight at all—"

"You won't!" Mrs. Kyne sounded aghast, dismayed, and politely
infuriated. "But, Nora, my dear, I absolutely have to have you! We have
to visit my husband's employer, and it's so late I couldn't possibly get
anyone else."

"Can't you call Beulah Allen? She usually sits for you."

"Beulah is playing at a piano recital tonight. Nora, you must come!"

"But, Mrs. Kyne, I—" Nora thought desperately. "I have a rash on
my chest and back. Mom thought it was poison oak, but the school nurse
says it isn't, and said it looks more like measles, and we're waiting for
the doctor and—"

Mrs. Kyne blurted a "Good heavens!" of despair. "Well, stay in bed, child. Mr. Kyne will simply have to go without me." And she hung up, too upset even for a polite goodbye.

Nora hung up, with a "Whew!" of relief.

But the relief curled up in smoke when she turned and met her mother's eyes.

"Nora Belle Bayliss!" Every word was underlined in an increasing surprise, shock, horror. "What did you tell Mrs. Kyne?"

"But, Mom, I do have this rash on my back—"

"You have a few miserable little hives, which you get every single time that you eat too many sweet pickles."

Nora turned red, and looked at the floor, unable to meet her mother's eyes.

"But, Mom, what could I do? I'm going to Ellen Ames's party tonight, and I just couldn't think of anything else to tell Mrs. Kyne."

"Nora, what you told Mrs. Kyne was an out-and-out falsehood!" Mrs. Bayliss' kind face was heartsick. "Nora, you have loving parents who spare no effort to give you everything you could possibly need. We try so hard to make you happy. We want more than anything else for you to grow up to be a fine person. But, my dear, to tell an out-and-out lie—"

Nora felt hot tears push into her eyes. "Oh, Mom!" she cried.

"And that's not all. You had made a date with Mrs. Kyne to watch her baby tonight. When did you make it?"

"Two weeks ago."

"And she has been counting on you all this time. Now, at the last minute, you let her down. I just can't tell you how *surprised* I am, Nora. I'm shocked."

"Mom, I'll—I'll call Mrs. Kyne back and tell her I'm coming."

"No, I don't want her to know that you had not told her the truth. I won't want people to know that my daughter—in fact, I think, Nora, that the best punishment I can give you is to *make* your story the truth." Her voice became firm. "You're not going out tonight, Nora. You're going upstairs to your own room, you're going to undress, and you're going to bed! I think that that is the best lesson I can give you."

Nora climbed the stairs, her head bent, and the steps a blur to her eyes. But not until her face was on the pillow did she let the tears come.

It was the following Saturday, in mid-morning, when Mr. Bayliss called home to say he thought he had a buyer for the house. He'd bring the people over in an hour. Could Mrs. Bayliss have the house ready to show?

"I couldn't possibly," she gasped. "But I will!"

She hung up, and grabbed the vacuum cleaner.

"Nora, darling, help me. We've got to get the house all straightened up before Dad arrives!"

"I'll vacuum, Mom. You dust."

Mrs. Bayliss was very anxious to sell their home. Here in Altadena, just under the high rampart of Mount Wilson, and some twenty-odd miles from the ocean, summer weather was very hot and dry. Besides, their house was a two-story Cape Cod type of structure and had no insulation in the roof. As a result, in summer time the upstairs bedrooms were just bake ovens. Also, there was no breakfast nook in the kitchen. And the yard was small. Mrs. Bayliss had lived with these disadvantages for ten years without serious injury to her self-respect. But, just now, she had discovered a lovely new house for sale near the beach.

Mr. Bayliss was *not* eager to sell their present home, but he had finally agreed that if they could make a good sale, he would buy the modern house which Mrs. Bayliss wanted.

"Nora, we've got to have everything just shining for these customers! So they just can't resist buying!"

"We will, Mother."

Mother dusted like fury. Nora vacuumed the living room and dining room rugs, the hallway runner, then started upstairs to do the bedroom rugs.

Through a window she saw a car stop at the curb and a woman start up the walk to the house.

"Mom! There's that Mrs. O'Manion coming to see us."

"Good heavens!" Mrs. Bayliss blurted. "She'll expect me to sit and talk over P.T.A. for a solid hour. Nora, darling, don't answer the bell. Don't make a peep!"

Nora froze, her heart pounding, as the doorbell jangled. Nora held her breath. Again the doorbell ding-aling-alinged for a long, impatient moment. Then Mrs. O'Manion rapped on the door with her knuckles, as if she suspected the bell wasn't working. Again she rang the bell, holding it down so that it rang endlessly, buzzsawing into Nora's brain like an auto horn that had got stuck.

Finally Mrs. O'Manion gave up, turning and hurrying down the walk to her car, her heels tapping wrathfully and her shoulders moving with an angry, insulted twitch.

Mrs. Bayliss waited until Mrs. O'Manion's car turned the corner before she said, even then in a whisper, "All right, Nora!"

Nora had finished vacuuming the upstairs bedrooms when all of a sudden she remembered.

"Oh, my gosh!" she cried out. "Mother! *Mother!* I'm supposed to go to Dr. Amos at eleven this morning to have these braces on my teeth fixed."

Mrs. Bayliss plumped down on a chair, as if hopelessness had drained her knees of strength.

"Nora, darling!" As if it were Nora's fault. "We just *can't* go."

"He charges if you miss an appointment and don't cancel it."

Mrs. Bayliss went to the phone; sat there a moment, frowning in thought, then dialed the dentist's number.

"Dr. Amos? This is Mrs. Bayliss. Doctor, I'm awfully sorry, but I won't be able to bring Nora in this morning. We just went out to the garage to drive downtown, and I discovered I'd left my ignition on all night, and the battery is dead, and I can't start the car. I called our garage, and they tell me they can't send a man up for another hour, so—Thanks, Dr. Amos. We'll come in Monday, then. 'Bye." And she hung up, and sat limply with a "Whew!"

She got a glimpse of Nora's face, then, and Mrs. Bayliss reddened. Getting up quickly, she hurried to the kitchen, saying, "Nora, change into your blue dress. Hurry, dear!"

Dad was well trained; he arrived not precisely on the dot, in an hour, as he'd said, but a good five minutes *past*, giving them a little lee-way. So they were dressed and ready, and the house shone like a dime that had been rubbed with quicksilver.

"Dear, this is Mr. and Mrs. McHenry. My wife, Mrs. McHenry and Mr. McHenry. And my daughter, Nora."

Mrs. McHenry was a plump, big woman, and Mr. McHenry was a plump big man. Both were graying, both had rather severe, expressionless faces.

Nora followed behind as her mother led the McHenrys from room to room. Mother was being awfully friendly, and talkative; she talked almost too much and too fast, Nora thought. Mrs. McHenry just looked; and if she felt anything about what she saw, she didn't let it stampede her into wasting a word. Mr. McHenry, though, began to thaw out.

"My, my," he said appreciatively, as Nora's mother opened the French doors at the end of the living room and let the sun flood in.

"My, my," he said, when Mother showed them the kitchen, which had cupboards on three sides, from floor to ceiling.

"My, my," he said when Mother opened the door to the basement and showed them the two hot-air furnaces, and a full concrete foundation that would baffle termites.

And he said, "My, my," again when Mother led them upstairs and showed them the bedrooms with windows on *three* sides.

Mrs. McHenry's careful armor of indifference cracked then.

"These are lovely, lovely rooms," she said, so positively that Nora almost wanted to hug her. "Tell me, Mrs. Bayliss. Upstairs rooms like these are bright and airy, yes, but in summer aren't they hot? It does get awfully hot in California, I hear. That is, in summer. Don't these rooms get stifling hot?"

Mother said, right off, "We've lived here for ten years, Mrs. Mc-Henry, and we have been entirely comfortable. There is simply nothing about this house that I personally would want to change. It just breaks my heart to think of moving, but I have to consider my husband's and my child's needs, and living across town will be better for them."

Mrs. McHenry nodded. She looked at her husband. She didn't say anything, but her husband smiled as if she had whispered in his ear.

"We like the place," he said. "We'd like to buy it. Your broker told us the price and all. We'll just go see him now and leave a deposit. I think we'll be quite happy here."

Mother said, "I'm sure you will!"

And when the McHenrys left, Mother hugged Dad, overjoyed.

Nora walked thoughtfully to her own room.

Thursday night, during dinner, the telephone rang. Mother got up from the table and answered.

"It's for you, Nora. Marylee."

Nora put the receiver to her ear and said, "Hi."

"Nora, are you coming over to study with me, tonight?"

Marylee sounded all excited. Nora said, "I was going to ask Mother if I could. Why?"

"Let's go to the State tonight! There's a swell picture showing."

"But, golly, Marylee, tonight's Thursday—"

"Aw, gee, Nora, can't you go?"

"I want to." Nora thought hard. She wasn't permitted to go to movies on a week night when there was school next day.

"Mother!" she called. "Marylee wants me to come over and—study our history. We're studying all about General Fremont and the conquest of California. Can I go?"

"Why, yes, dear. Be back by bed time."

"Okay, Marylee!" Nora said into the phone. "I'll be right over. Oh, say, I owe you seventy-five cents for school milk money, don't I? I'll bring it along."

Mother gave her the money she asked for, and she quickly slipped into her coat, grabbed her history book, and started out. At the door, however, she hesitated. Somehow she didn't feel excited and happy about going to the movie. She felt depressed. She felt worried.

"Oh, Mother?"

"Yes, dear?" Her mother smiled. "I suppose you really could study better if you stopped at the drugstore on the way over to Marylee's and bought a sack of salted almonds. All right, here's another quarter."

Nora took the quarter, but still looked uncertain.

Mother asked, "That's what you wanted, isn't it?"

"Oh, Mother," Nora said, "I—"

BOY

AND

GIRL

The problem:

The issue is honesty; specifically, our folkway, our chivalric cultural attitude, of giving advantage to girls over boys in situations requiring special consideration—and the tendency of some girls to take advantage of this privilege. In a society in which girls and women are no longer sheltered and privileged but are competing on more or less equal terms with boys and men, this ideal is an anachronism. Nevertheless, many adults insist on perpetuating this privileged relationship for girls.

Introducing the problem:

Ask, "Sometimes, in an argument with a girl, if you're a boy—or with a younger person, if you're a girl—you are asked to give in just because the other person is a girl or younger than you. This is a story about such a situation. The story stops but is not finished. As I read, try to think of ways in which the story might end."

"What's your name, son?"

"Michael Normand."

"Everybody calls you Mike, I bet?"

"That's right."

"How old are you, Mike?"

"Eleven."

"Friends, this is Mike Normand we have at the microphone, now. He's eleven, and big for his age. He has light brown hair, blue eyes, and a bashful grin. Michael, do you like to play ball, or would you rather stay indoors and read *Tom Sawyer?*"

"Depends," Michael said slowly, thinking about it. "If it's raining, I'd rather stay indoors and look at television."

"Swell, Mike! Give Mike a hand, children. All right now, Mike. I'm going to ask you the big question. Before you answer, you think about it. Take your time! Here goes: If you would put a big chunk of ice in the kitchen stove, why would your pants get warm? ... Don't hurry! Figure it out! All the time in the world!"

Michael did think about it. He was a quiet, slow-moving, thoughtful youngster. Standing up beside Mr. Dorsey at the front of the room, all the children watching him, he imagined himself at home in his mother's kitchen ... and he imagined himself putting an ice-tray full of cubes into the trash burner of the gas range, and he imagined what his mother would say and do. . . .

"If you put the ice in the stove," Michael said, "and the ice melted, dripping down on the floor with ashes and black soot, making an awful mess, why, your mother would give you a paddling—"

"And that would make your pants warm!" Mr. Dorsey yelled. "Correct, Mike! You win the semi-finals prize! We're giving you a six-room house! Furnished from kitchen to garage!"

The children whooped with excitement as Mr. Dorsey lifted the sheet which covered the low table beside his fake microphone, uncovering the presents. The six-room house was a six-room house, all right: a doll house.

Michael said, "Thanks, Mr. Dorsey!"

The party was a birthday party for Mike's chum, Pete Dorsey. All the children in Miss Webster's room had been invited. And Pete's father was making a TV party out of it.

"And it's all yours, Mike!" Mr. Dorsey said in the laughing, excited way that TV announcers use. "And now, children, next on our big Anniversary Day Program, is a Mystic Treasure Hunt!

"Everybody get out paper and pencil. But before we write down the items on the contest, I want to show you what the grand prize of this Treasure Hunt will be. I'll admit, it isn't very big, and it's something you've got to take care of. You can't leave it out in the rain, and you can't leave it lying around the living room. But if you take care of it, you can enjoy it for a long, long time."

Mr. Dorsey turned and went to the door of the rumpus room, opened it, and bent and picked up a box which he carried back to the microphone.

"Look!"

Out of the box he took a sleek, squirming little cocker spaniel and put it on the table. It looked around as the children started to whoop and yell in delight—and sneezed, nearly shaking itself off its feet. The youngsters crowded forward to pet it and hug it, and it yelped and backed away, so scared by the racket that it left a puddle on the table.

Mr. Dorsey picked the puppy up and petted it.

"His name is Benny, but if you want to change it to Thunder or Butterball, that's okay, too. All right, now! Everybody back to his seat for the big Mystic Treasure Hunt! Grab your paper and pencil.

"I'm going to read a list to you. It's a list of things hidden in the house and yard. You'll all go hunting for them. The first child who finds everything on the list wins Benny for his own, to take home and keep.

"Listen, now. This isn't an ordinary list I'm going to give you. It's a Mystic list. You'll have to figure out, from what I tell you, what each article is that you have to find. This is a puzzle hunt, really. All right, ready?

"The first thing you're to look for is: A *dog that once had a bark, but doesn't bark any more.* Write it down. Lift your hand, everybody, when you're ready for the next one. . . . Okay? Item Two: A *picture of Lincoln found in every house. . . .*

"Ready, all? Item Three: A *wing without feathers. . . .*

"Now, Item Four: *This is an object which runs. When it runs, its hands move, but its feet stand still.* Got it?

"Here's Item Five: This one is—a *dress. A dress worn by a fighting man.* Not a Scotch kilt! *It's a dress worn by a fighting man on his head!*

"And now the last item. I'll say it real slow. It's something that practically every child likes to eat. They like it very much. But get this: Though you eat this thing to the last crumb, always you leave part of it uneaten!

"All right, children, get busy. You'll find everyone of these things somewhere in the yard or in this house. You've got twenty minutes, until three thirty. Scatter, now, and start hunting!"

The youngsters scrambled out into the yard, out into the hall, scattering to poke into corners, to bend and peer under chairs and sofas, to tiptoe and stretch to see on top of mantels. Michael, though, stopped beside the box in which Mr. Dorsey had replaced the puppy. Michael got down on his knees and reached into the box and lifted Benny out and put the soft warmth against his cheek.

Mr. Dorsey smiled at Michael.

"Cutest thing in the world, isn't he? But start hunting, Mike, if you want to win him for your own!"

Michael nodded. Studying his list, he walked out into the yard.

The first two puzzles meant nothing to him. He considered Number Three a while. *A wing without feathers*. But how could there be a wing without feathers! Only birds flew, and birds had feathers. But how about *bats?* That was right. Bats had no feathers. Nor did airplanes, and they flew!

Mike turned toward Pete Dorsey's play house at the back of the yard. Mike knew that Pete kept his old and cast-off toys out there.

Nearing the little building, Mike saw Susan Barr come out of it. When she saw him she hid her hand behind her.

"Don't you follow me around and do what I'm doing!" she whispered angrily at him.

Susan Barr was big for her age, big as Mike. She had red hair and big freckles and green eyes and a pert nose. She played the piano awfully well, and she could sing, too, and she always made good grades; though sometimes Miss Webster got angry with her because she talked a lot and was bossy and restless.

Mike said, "I'm not following you."

"You'd better not!"

He entered the play shack. The place looked as if Santa Claus had emptied his big toy sack here—just after a steamroller had run over it. He rummaged around on a wide shelf, in a small mountain of tenpins and meccano parts and pingpong balls and auto racers and checkers and electric train parts and plane models and capguns and ball gloves, all slightly ruined.

Mike found a glider that once had been launched from a toy submarine. It had only one wing. And that wing Mike broke off and stuck into his pocket.

He left the shack then, and studied his list once more.

Item Four was an object which runs. *When it runs, its hands move but its feet stand still*. Mike thought about that.

He himself could walk on his hands, but not run. Not really. Anyway it was an *object* he was to look for. A table had legs. So did a chair, but they didn't run. And they had no hands.

He sighed, and decided to postpone worry over this braintwister. He looked at Item Two. A *picture of Lincoln found in every house*. Well, how about looking in the house? He crossed the yard.

He almost bumped into Susan Barr, as he went through the door. She was standing there in the hall, thinking. She glared at him, her look saying *Don't you dare follow me!* She turned violently and hurried toward the living room.

Mike walked through the rumpus room. It had a picture over the big fireplace—of Mr. Dorsey interviewing General Eisenhower, a microphone hanging between them. Mike trudged through to Mr. Dorsey's study.

Sure enough, on the wall over the desk hung a picture of Abraham Lincoln. Mike stared at it, grinning in satisfaction. His smile faded. Surely he wasn't expected to take down that picture and bring it to Mr. Dorsey? Anyway, the list said a picture of Lincoln which was found in *every* home. He'd never even seen this picture before. It wasn't in his own home. Nor in his friend Eddie's home.

No. This wasn't the right picture of Lincoln.

On the desk, then, below the picture, Mike noticed something: a little cocker spaniel carved out of wood. It looked so much like the cute puppy Mr. Dorsey was giving away for the prize that Mike reached out impulsively and picked up the carving. He turned it in his fingers, delightedly; and rubbed the polished wood, smiling. It looked so real and perfect.

Suddenly, Mike's brow puckered. He looked at his list.

Item One read: *A dog that once had a bark but doesn't bark any more.* Well, this wooden dog didn't bark any more. Only it never had barked.

Oh, but the item says, once it had *a bark!* Mike reasoned. This dog's made of wood, and when this wood was part of a tree, it had a bark on it. That's the answer. This is the right object!

He stuck the dog in his pocket.

"What've you got there?"

It was Susan asking, her voice suspicious. She had come up behind him.

"Use your X-ray eye, Superwoman," he told her, and walked back into the rumpus room.

He looked at his list again. *A dress worn by a fighting man.* Mr. Dorsey had added a hint: this dress was worn on the head. Michael thought. A dress—worn on the head. Head . . . dress. Why, headdress, of course! And what fighting men wore a headdress? Knights of old? No, they wore steel helmets. Pilots. No, they wore plastic helmets. Indians!

Sure enough, in the front hallway alcove, which Mr. Dorsey had fixed up as a little Indian museum, were woven reed baskets and food and water containers and beaded moccasins and several baby-carriers and half a dozen feather headdresses. Carefully Mike took one down.

He walked out into the back yard then. First thing he noticed was that Susan Barr also had a war bonnet rolled up tightly in her hands. She was quick in the head, that girl.

He noticed, too, that nearly everybody was clutching a doughnut in his hand. He looked around wondering.

"They serving eats?" he asked Eddie.

Eddie burst out laughing.

"Gosh, no! You asleep?"

Mike stared blankly at him. He looked at his list again.

The last item caught his attention. Something children like to eat, *though you eat this thing to the last crumb, always you leave part of it uneaten....* Why, a doughnut, of course. You ate it all, but you didn't eat the hole. That you left uneaten.

On the garden table was a big plate of sugar doughnuts. He took one. He shifted it to his left hand, and licked the sugar off of his right fingers.

Mr. Dorsey called out warningly from the doorway, then, "Children, you've got ten more minutes. Hunt hard, now!"

Mike studied his list, frowning with effort.

Two more items yet to find. A *picture of Lincoln found in every home.* And something which *When it runs, its hands move but its feet stand still.* But he just could not think of an answer to either of these two puzzles.

He wandered around the yard, peering under benches, looking into shrubbery, even drifting into the big three-car garage to look around. But nothing he saw suggested an answer to his two problems.

"Time's just about up," he realized; and he walked into the house. For the first minute or two that was left, he decided, he'd play with the puppy. Lacking two items, he couldn't win; so he'd grab this chance to play with Benny a little bit before the winner took him away.

On the mantel in the rumpus room was a small alarm clock. Mr. Dorsey had said they had until 3:30 to finish the hunt. Five minutes were still left. Mike frowned, staring at the clock.

When it runs, its hands move, but its feet stand still....

Why, golly! When a clock runs, its hands move! But a clock had no feet—oh, yes, it did! This one did. This alarm clock had little round knobs for feet that kept it from rolling, that kept it standing upright. Feet did that for people, too. The clock was the answer!

Mike lifted it carefully off the mantel.

As he turned to go pet the puppy, something on the floor that glistened caught Mike's eye. A coin. Somebody had lost a dime. Well, Mike thought, he could tell Mr. Dorsey to ask the kids who had lost a dime. Mike bent and picked it up and put it on the mantel—and stood there, looking at the coin.

For it wasn't a dime. It was a penny. One of the light-colored pennies —and it had a picture of Lincoln on it!

And that was one picture, Mike realized, that you *could* expect to find in practically any house!

Excitedly Mike reached to take the penny from the mantel. Now he had all six of the items of the Treasure Hunt. Nobody else had got six yet. So he'd won! Benny was his!

"That's mine!"

A hand grabbed for the penny. He got hold of it, and two hands clawed at his closed fingers.

"That's my penny!" Susan Barr raged at him.

"It is not!" he said furiously. "I found it, I put it on the mantel, and—"

"You give it back to me!"

She wrenched at his fingers, and almost got the penny away from him. His other hand was holding the clock and war bonnet and he couldn't use it to fend her off; so he jerked away from her as she clung, jerked away so violently that she was flung to the floor and hit her head against the leg of an easy chair. She was instantly scrambling back onto her feet, but she was wailing, she was screeching at the top of her voice.

"Mike hit me! Mike knocked me down and took my penny!"

Mike stared at her, shocked, outraged. Behind him, someone came into the room.

"Michael Normand! I'm surprised at you!"

Mrs. Dorsey, Pete's mother. Mike flushed painfully. Mrs. Dorsey folded Susan into her arms and petted her and cooed over her. "There, darling, you'll be all right. Mike'll give that penny back to you. Mike, a big boy like you. A gentleman doesn't strike a lady."

"This is my penny," he said stubbornly.

"Let's see your head, Susan. Heavens, what a bump! Mike, you might have killed her."

Mrs. Dorsey had to talk loud, to be heard over Susan's wailing. Mr. Dorsey came hurrying in, alarmed by the uproar; and behind him, children started coming.

"What's wrong?" Mr. Dorsey asked.

"Mike knocked me down and took my penny away!" Susan repeated.

"I did no such thing!"

"Mike, a boy doesn't hit a girl."

"I didn't—" Mike began; but Susan was screeching, "I dropped my penny, coming through here, and I turned around to get it—but Mike had picked it up, and then he wouldn't give it to me, and when I tried to take it he knocked me down!"

"A gentleman doesn't behave like that," Mr. Dorsey said.

"She's lying! She's—"

"Don't use that sort of language in my house! I'm surprised at you!"

"It's not fair! Just b-because she's a girl, you stick up for her!"

"I want my penny!" Susan wailed.

"Mike, give it back to her," Mr. Dorsey ordered.

Mike's throat choked up; he was afraid that if he tried to speak, he wouldn't be able to keep from crying. But he managed to blurt, "I won't!"

"Mike," Mr. Dorsey was regretful. "I'm sure you wouldn't want to win a prize by taking advantage of someone, especially a girl. Be a good sport now, and give Susan back her penny."

He thrust the penny at Susan and she grabbed it. Mike turned quickly, and hurried out of the room, down the hall and out the front door.

"Oh, Mike! Wait, Mike!" Mr. Dorsey called after him. "You're forgetting the prizes you won!"

"Don't w-want 'em!" Mike choked.

Mr. Dorsey ran after him, caught him.

"Gosh, boy, I don't want you running off like this. You shouldn't be so upset. Let's talk this out!"

Responsibility for Others

TRICK

OR

TREAT *

The problem:

    The issue is honesty; specifically, responsibility for others in a situation in which two boys, guilty of leading smaller boys into trouble, can escape all blame by saying nothing and allowing the younger boys to be punished for the misdeed.

* Adapted from *Teacher's Manual: English Grammar and Composition*, VIII (New York: Harcourt, Brace & World, Inc., 1960). Reprinted by permission of the publisher.

Introducing the problem:

> Say to the group, "Have you ever been tricked into doing something mean and hurtful to somebody else? Or have you ever been on the other side? Have you ever, without really intending to, induced other children to do something that got them into trouble? This story deals with such a problem. The story stops but is not finished. As I read, think of ways in which the story could end."

Pete's father was very firm in his stand. "I want this clearly understood, Pete. No serious damage, this Halloween. Ordinary trick or treat, okay. Have fun. But keep it just fun. No malicious mischief. I want your word on this."

"Okay, Dad. I promise."

But Pete's friend Sandy groaned when Pete told him.

"What'll we do? Wear the same old cowboy costumes that everybody else has got, and just knock on doors and collect a bag full of jellybeans?"

"That or nothing."

As Pete got dressed in the old cowboy rig Halloween night, he discovered it was much smaller than it had been last year. He was outgrowing it. Maybe, he thought, he was outgrowing Halloween entirely? Oh, well, one more time.

He met Sandy outside. Carrying bags for loot, they marched from door to door in their neighborhood, saying "Trick or treat!" and collecting handfuls of jellybeans, molasses kisses, homebaked cookies and squares of fudge, wrapped hard candy, and apples. It was a pretty dull business, Sandy grumbled over and over.

Nothing unusual happened until they ventured into the big trailer camp several blocks away. A couple of younger boys had started tagging after them. They also were wearing cowboy suits, and that enraged Sandy even more. Their masks, however, were just narrow eye-covers, and Pete recognized one of them as eight-year-old Ronnie Hites who lived on his block.

"Quit following us!" Sandy snapped at them, and they hung back for a few moments, but came on again.

Pete and Sandy started knocking on trailer doors, and were given treats. But at the fifth trailer, a sour-faced old man opened the door, and at sight of their masked faces and costumes he flew into a rage.

"Go on, beat it! Get out of here or I'll throw dishwater on you!" he shouted; and as they backed away, he slammed his door shut.

"What an old crab!" Pete said, surprised.

"No treat," Sandy said, "so he gets a trick."

"Let's soap his windows."

"Sissy stuff. No, we've got to think up a real good one for him."

Sandy noticed that a car stood in front of the next trailer, lights on and motor running. Somebody had evidently stopped, had gone into the trailer, and was planning to leave in a moment or two. Sandy also noticed that, between the trailers, lines were stretched between T-posts on which to hang drying clothes. His quick wits leaped to a possible use of these resources.

He drew a Scout knife from a pocket. Reaching up to one of the clothes lines, he cut it at his end, and then ran to the other end and cut it there. He hurried back, and started tying one end of the rope to the front hitch of the house trailer.

"Sandy," Pete whispered angrily, "no rough stuff. I promised my Dad."

"That's right," Sandy said, but he finished tying the knot. Straightening up, he looked around the dark camp. "You promised *you* wouldn't play any rough tricks. So okay. *You* won't."

"You're included! I said *we* wouldn't!"

"Okay. Hey, you!" Sandy called, low-voiced. The two younger boys, Ronnie Hites and his pal, were hovering nearby, watching. Ronnie came forward. Sandy handed the end of the rope to the eight-year-old. "Can you tie a good knot?"

"I can tie a square knot," Ronnie said proudly.

"Fine! Just tie this rope around the bumper of that car."

"What for?"

"To play a trick, that's all. You chicken?"

"I ain't chicken," Ronnie said sturdily.

He took the rope, went to the rear of the waiting car and carefully started tying a knot.

"That car'll tow the trailer away," Pete started to object.

"No, it won't," Sandy said. "It's just clothes line—it'll break. It'll just give the trailer a jerk."

"Oh," said Pete, and laughed. "The old guy'll think it's an earthquake!"

Ronnie finished his knot—then ran, for the door of the nearby trailer opened and a man came out. Pete and Sandy also crouched back in the darkness as the man got into his car. His door slammed. The engine revved up as he stepped on the gas—and then the car started forward.

The car moved ahead—and the rope lifted taut, and broke with a violent twang; but it held just long enough to give a jerk to the house trailer, a strong, unexpected forward jerk. Pete discovered something, then, that he had not noticed before; he had thought that the trailer would roll forward a few feet. But the trailer's wheels had been removed, and it could not roll. The trailer had been set up on permanent supports, on wooden blocks. And now it was jerked off those blocks: it lunged forward and crashed to the ground.

"Pete, come on!" Sandy whispered, and started running. Pete followed after him.

Behind them, the car had stopped. The trailer door had opened. Somebody was shouting angrily, *"Grab those kids!"* . . .

There happened to be no school next day, so Pete slept late. When he finally rose and went to the kitchen for some breakfast, his mother was in the backyard, talking to the next-door neighbor, Mrs. Long, over the back fence.

"It was the Hites kid," Mrs. Long was saying. "Just eight years old! The trailer was badly damaged. The poor old man'll have to pay a couple hundred dollars, maybe, to get it fixed up."

"I'm sure glad Pete stayed out of trouble," his mother said. "His father had really laid down the law to him."

Pete's appetite for breakfast vanished. He waited in dread for his mother to come inside.

"What did Ronnie Hites do?" he asked.

"Crazy little tike tied a man's house trailer to a car," she said. "When the car started off, it yanked the trailer off its blocks, and when the weight of the trailer came down on those blocks, they ripped up through the floor. The old man inside was pouring himself some hot tea, and when he was flung off his feet by the jerk he got a bad burn. That Ronnie is in real trouble. You sit down, son, and I'll get you some oatmeal."

Pete forced the oatmeal down his throat. . . .

As soon as he could leave, he went to Sandy's house.

"Sandy, what we going to do about Ronnie Hites?"

"Nothing."

"He may tell the cops that a couple of older boys told him to tie that rope to the car!"

"So what? Ronnie doesn't know who we are. We were wearing costumes and masks. He can't give us away."

"He can tell the cops we were wearing cowboy costumes—"

"So were at least a dozen other boys in this neighborhood."

"But he's being blamed for it all!"

"Sure. He tied that rope to the car."

"But it wasn't really his fault. He didn't know what might happen. A little kid like that— He just did what we told him to do."

"Now he knows better."

"We can't let him take all the blame!"

"So what do you want to do?" Sandy demanded. "Tell your father that it was all *your* fault? After you promised him? And you want him to pay for all that damage?"

Pete gulped. He wanted to do the right thing, but—

BLIND

FISH

The problem:

The issue is honesty; and, specifically, obeying rules and responsibility for others.

One of the important growth needs of middle childhood is that of learning to abide by rules. The child who does not learn this is in constant conflict with age-mates and adults in school and community.

Introducing the problem:

You may ask the group, "Most of us, at one time or another, have broken a rule set by parents or school or other authorities. Sometimes nothing happens; sometimes nothing happens to us, but does happen to other people. This is a story about such an incident. The story stops but is not finished. As I read, think of ways in which the story could end."

From the edge of the pool, Mr. Brady, the camp counselor, yelled, "Oh, Mike! Come here!"

Mike thought, *Oh-oh, I'll get it.* Reluctantly he swam toward the bank where Mr. Brady stood.

The counselor's face was stern.

"Look, Mike. You know the rules. This is the second time that you've gone in swimming here during hours when it's not permitted. Why?"

Mike pulled himself onto the rim of the pool.

"Mr. Brady, I just don't like fire-making and building lean-tos and learning the names of birds and plants. Swimming's the only thing in this camp I like."

"But do you know *why* you're not permitted to go in swimming between ten and twelve in the morning?"

"I guess you don't want anybody going in swimming all by himself."

"Why?"

"Well, if he got into trouble, there'd be nobody around to pull him out of the water and he'd drown."

"Mike, even the best swimmers sometimes get cramps. If that happened to you, and you were here alone, there'd be nobody around to help you. Come on, now, climb out. We're hiking to Crystal Cave, and if you want to come, get ready."

"Yes, Mr. Brady."

By the time Mike got dressed and came out, the dozen boys going on the hike were already in the back of the big truck parked out in front of the Camp Waterman office. Mr. Brady was giving them a short talk.

"We'll hike through the cave. I want you all to stick to the trail. There's a reason for that, and I want you to understand it right now. Underground exploring is actually underground mountain climbing, for caves are rugged, and our path will wind along cliffs and shoot down into deep pits. You could easily have a bad fall. So I'm laying down this rule: Everybody sticks with the party. We'll move in single file, and no boy is to step out of his place in the line. All right, let's go."

The truck took them halfway up the side of Mount Sherman. On a grassy flat circled by live oak and sycamores, they parked the truck. Mr. Brady led them up the bed of a tiny creek, to the back of a box canyon, where the little stream emerged from a dark hole in the mountain wall.

Each boy had a Scout flashlight. In addition, Mr. Brady had brought along four gas lanterns. He pumped them up, now, lit them, and assigned one to every fourth boy in the file.

Then, carrying one of the lamps, Mr. Brady led the file through the cave entrance into a dark, narrow tunnel. The path underfoot was soft and moist. It followed along the tiny creek, and the boys moved carefully so as not to slip and take a header into the shallow water. They bunched close, at first, and were silent, awed and a little frightened by the dark walls crowding close around them. Their flashlights seemed dim, here underground, but the gas lamps gave off a warm, reassuring flood of light.

Abruptly, the narrow tunnel ended. The boys found themselves in a cave chamber so great that they could not see the ceiling, nor the far walls.

"Turn your flashlights straight up," Mr. Brady said.

They obeyed, the slender cones of light whipping up like anti-aircraft searchlights. And, far overhead, they saw the myriad sparkles that marked the ceiling—the glistening tips of long icicles of stone that hung from the arched roof.

"Stalactites," Mr. Brady said. "That's a drop of water at the tip of each one of them."

He turned his flashlight level to the ground. Far across the lofty room they saw the opposite wall, at least a hundred yards away. It was a big cave, all right.

"All right, let's move on," Mr. Brady ordered.

He led the file across the chamber. At the far wall, a dozen corridors opened off this big central room. Mr. Brady stopped.

"Those tunnels run into other big rooms. This cave system honey-combs the mountain, and parts of it have never been explored. A man lost in here could likely wander around for days and starve to death. That's why," he said firmly, "we're sticking to this main path."

He led on, then, into a broad hallway that widened and became higher until it was like the still, echoing interior of a cathedral.

Mr. Brady said, "Gather around."

The boys crowded about him. There in the wall before them was a niche, hollowed like a bowl, which held a little pool of crystal clear water. On the bottom of the bowl were round white objects, smooth and shining, like birds' eggs, white and lovely.

"Cave pearls," Mr. Brady said. "Not really pearls, but a lime forma-tion. Come on."

Presently he halted the column once more. In a low spot at the base of the wall were shallow dish-shaped holes that held a white liquid. They looked like bowls of milk set out for kittens.

"Moon milk," Mr. Brady said. "Not really, just water full of a sort of lime mixture that hasn't hardened solid."

He led on. Mike, at the end of the file trudging after the counselor, noticed the huge shadows everybody cast on the walls. The swinging Cole-man lamps made those shadows seem to lunge and leap like giants in a crazy war dance.

Mr. Brady paused beside a cluster of stalactites that hung from the roof like giant icicles of alabaster. With his Scout knife he struck one, and it gave off a ringing tone that vibrated through the cavern in a deep, linger-ing reverberation. He hit another stalactite. It had a different tone. He tapped several others, and their humming vibrations blended in a chord that stirred up a thousand echoes.

Mr. Brady said, "I bet I could play Yankee Doodle on this stone xylophone, if I could play Yankee Doodle."

They filed on again then. Their path, following the little stream, twisted through a forest of columns and on into another high-roofed chamber. Here the creek widened into a broad, shallow lake so still that the water seemed not to be moving at all.

Mr. Brady stopped, bent down, held his lantern out over the water. The boys moved close to him. In the pool they saw a small sleek fish.

"Blind fish," Mr. Brady said. "They have never, in all their lives, seen light. Let's go on."

The boys stared at the fish, then turned reluctantly to follow Mr. Brady around the lake and on into another corridor.

Mike, at the end of the line, slowed his footsteps. Tony Pringle, next ahead of him, looked back. Mike beckoned to him, and Tony stopped, and came back.

Mike said, "Tony, let's get us some of these blind fish!"

"What for?"

"Don't you see? Bill Toland's got some guppies, and Steve Akers has some fighting betas, and Nick Barton's got some of those long-tailed, big-eyed Japanese fish. But nobody's got any *blind* fish. Bill brought his aquarium to school, for the science class, and Miss Mason made a big fuss over 'em. We'll bring in some blind fish, and that'll really be something!"

"How'll we catch 'em?"

"Scoop 'em up in a mess kit. You hold my lamp. I'll do the catching."

Mike waded out into the shallow pool. Bending, he lowered the mess kit into the water, moved slowly toward a little school of the tiny fish, and scooped them up.

"Got three of them, Tony! Here, I'll put 'em into your kit."

He caught a dozen of the blind fish.

Tony, tired of being a mere onlooker, put the fish into his drinking cup. Then, lantern in one hand and mess kit in the other, he waded into the water.

"Tony, let me carry that lantern."

"Okay. That'll make it easier—"

Tony didn't finish. It was odd. One moment he was standing in knee-deep water, turning to talk to Mike—and the next moment he was sliding, falling, vanishing down under the water. And the brilliance of the Coleman light just as abruptly died, and was followed by a surprising and shocking darkness. Mike knew what had happened: Tony had stepped into a deep hole.

Mike plunged ahead and dove—and his groping hands caught Tony. Mike headed for the surface, kicking strongly. Their heads came up into

242 / Individual Integrity

the air. Tony gasped and screamed; and his arms caught around Mike's neck and he clung with panicky strength. They went under again.

Mike wasn't frightened. "They do it every time," he thought. He got an arm inside of Tony's elbows, and as they broke surface again, he pushed back against Tony's chin, pushed his head back until Tony's hold on him broke. Dragging Tony with one arm, Mike started swimming.

His feet touched bottom. He stood erect, gasping for breath, holding Tony up. Mike got scared, then. Not of drowning, but of the darkness. It was so utterly unbroken, so solid, so heavy, so suffocating. Fumbling at his belt, Mike unhooked his flashlight, lifted it, and pressed the button. It was supposed to be waterproof, but if water had got into it—

The light came on; Mike grinned in relief. Tony was shivering now, his teeth chattering, and he began to cry.

"We're all right," Mike told him. "Here, you hold this flashlight. I've got to dive down and get back that Coleman lamp."

"I s-swallowed water," Tony sobbed.

Mike dove back into the deep hole and groped along the bottom for the gas lantern.

He had been in a sweat from hiking hard, and the water was icy cold. Something happened to Mike that had never happened before. He found himself doubling up, his stomach knotting in the awfullest pain he'd ever felt. "I'm getting cramps!" he realized. He had to get into shallow water. He had to reach shore before his muscles locked on him and he sank like a rock.

He struck out with arms, trying his level best, but was so doubled up that he couldn't use his legs at all. He got scared, panicky. He had never felt so utterly helpless in his life. He let out a yell—and strangled, his mouth full of water. *I'm going to die*, he thought. *I'm drowning.*

Then he felt rock under him. A hand grabbed his elbow, and hauled him out; he was able to gulp air into his stinging lungs.

The pain eased. He was shivering, lying on the bank and shivering.

"What happened to you?" Tony was demanding. "You sure scared me!"

"I'm all right. Just leave me alone."

Lights neared, and they heard voices.

"Hey, Mike! Tony! Where are you?"

"Here!" Tony answered, and waved the flashlight.

Charley Ames and Jeff Hollis and Georgie Parker and Fatso Landiss came hurrying down the trail.

"Say, you guys! What's the idea of dropping out of line?"

"Mr. Brady sent us to find you."

"What you doing, anyhow? Going in swimming with your clothes on?"

Tony said, "Wise guys. Look!"

Triumphantly he showed them the drinking cup with the dozen blind fish, so small and graceful, swimming in it.

"Blind fish!" Charley Ames blurted.

"Uh-huh," Tony said. "They're scarce. They're worth a lot of money."

"Where'd you get them?" Georgie demanded.

Tony jerked his chin toward the pool.

"Caught 'em."

"With what?"

"Mess kit."

"Boy, I'm going to get me some!" Charley Ames said.

"Me, too," Jeff Hollis said.

Mike scrambled unsteadily to his feet.

"Hey! Don't you go into that water," he said.

They looked at him.

Charley retorted, "You ain't gonna tell *me* what to do."

"If you can get some blind fish, I can," Jeff said.

"You guys ain't going into that water!" Mike shouted at them.

"Who's going to stop me?" Charley snapped.

"I'll call Mr. Brady!"

"You got some blind fish," Jeff said. "The rest of us are going to get some, too."

"Keep out of that water," Mike repeated. "It's icy cold, and—"

"You got some blind fish but you don't want us to have any!"

"I'm telling you, I'll call Mr. Brady!"

"If it's all right for you and Tony to catch 'em, why isn't it all right for us?"

FROGMAN

The problem:

The issue is honesty; and specifically, responsibility for others. Two boys have broken regulations to spearfish for big trout in a forbidden pool. Other boys now intend to imitate them. And if the other boys go ahead with their plan, it is very likely that they will get into serious trouble. The two boys who have already broken the rules will, if they permit their friends to imitate their behavior, probably be causing them to commit a serious breach of regulations and to get severely punished.

The story Blind Fish deals with the same issue, but is appropriate for a younger group.

Introducing the problem:

Ask the group, "Have you ever done something that was risky or forbidden, because it might be dangerous, and felt scared but excited about it afterward—and then had your kid brother or sister or other young people say that if you had done it, they could too? This is a story about such a happening. The story stops but is not finished. As I read it, think of ways in which it could end."

Mike turned the pickup truck off the highway and into the darkness under the trees, stopped, and switched off the engine and headlights.

Danny, on the seat beside him, whispered: "You sure nobody saw us turn in here?"

Mike just laughed. Slipping from behind the wheel, he jumped to the ground, then climbed into the back of the truck. Hastily he pulled off his clothes, then drew on a rubber frogman's suit. He pulled his flippers onto his feet, and hefted a "scuba"—aqualung—onto his back. Finally he picked up a waterproof flashlight and a long fish-spear with its powerful elastic "gun."

"Mike," Danny whispered, "if anybody passes over the bridge, they'll see your light in the water!"

"No traffic this late at night. But if a car does come, slap the water twice with your hand. I'll turn off my light."

"Be careful, will you? Guys've drowned wearing gear like that."

"Relax, Danny."

Mike lowered himself to the ground and walked with flapping flippers to the river edge. Danny followed. They were parked on the bank of the Truckee River, between the Tahoe City bridge and the Lake Tahoe dam.

Mike waded into the water, the flashlight beam guiding him. Danny watched as Mike sank lower and lower until the water covered his head and the flashlight beam was a weird, greenish glow under the surface. Nervously, then, Danny watched the highway. *If we're caught, we'll be in real trouble,* he was realizing.

The river, at this point, was blocked by a dam. In the pool below the dam lived many large trout. In California, fishing is not permitted close below a dam. As a result, these trout had lived long lives and grown to enormous size: up to fifteen pounds in weight. Every year, thousands of tourists stopped here below the dam to stare at the huge fish lazing in the clear water. The wise old trout seemed to know that they were safe but would be fair game to zealous fishermen farther downstream; the trout remained here in safety, never venturing downriver.

Mike Albee and Danny Ames were junior counselors at Pine Knob Boys Camp. Mike was seventeen and Danny was sixteen. Mike had an older brother who had been a frogman in the Navy. Two weeks ago Mike had a bright idea: "Let's borrow my brother's diving gear and spearfish some of those big trout in Truckee River!" he had suggested to Danny. To Danny, at the time, it had seemed like a good idea. But now they were actually doing it, Danny was scared. If a game warden or highway patrolman came along—

In the wide pool, Mike was kicking his flippered feet, slowly propelling himself along close to the bottom. The lamp strapped to his head sent a narrow cone of light ahead of him. He held his spear gun ready, nerves tensed to aim and pull the trigger when he sighted a fat trout.

Moments passed. The mountain water was icy cold, and the chill knifed through his rubber suit.

There! Into the tapering funnel of light ahead of him a long, deep-bellied trout swam lazily. Mike reacted with swift precision. He aimed the spear gun, pressed the trigger, felt the rebound of the heavy elastic. The big trout seemed to leap convulsively in the water and Mike felt a heavy pull on the line. Wishing he could yell in triumph, he hauled in delightedly on the line attached to the spear.

Danny, shaking with nervousness as he watched from the bank, saw Mike rise up out of the river and trudge toward the bank. And Mike was holding aloft a huge trout!

"Look at the size of him, Danny! Big enough almost to feed the camp."

"Yeah. Come on!"

"Hey, wait. Here. Get into the rig. It's your turn."

"I don't want a turn," Danny said. "Let's get—"

"You chicken?"

The question was blunt and cold. Danny felt his heart turn over, felt a hot flush of shame.

"All right. Give me the rig," he said angrily.

But even as he started putting on the frogman's outfit he raged at himself: Falling for that chicken stuff! Sure, you're scared. Why be afraid to admit it? More guys've got into trouble from being afraid to admit they were chicken than anything else. If you're right, let them call you chicken!

"Pull the straps snug," Mike was saying. "Get a big one. It's easy."

"Watch for cars."

"Relax. You're jumpy as a cat in a dog pound."

Danny waded into the stream. The icy water lifted around him, its chilliness burning through the suit and rising up his legs and stomach and chest. He shivered and his teeth chattered. Steadying himself, he started swimming underneath, kicking his flippered feet. Lifting the spear gun, he peered ahead into the narrow beam of light from his lamp.

Then he saw it. A fish. Caught full in the light. A trout bigger than Mike's!

Afterward, he never remembered taking aim or pulling the trigger, but suddenly the fish shot out of sight and the line from the spear was tugging him through the water. He set his feet on the bottom and pulled, and hauled the dying fish to him. Then he swam back, and staggered up out of the water, shouting to Mike, "Look! This one's bigger'n a cow!"

Then Mike grabbed his arm. Mike was yanking him up onto the bank, and Mike was whispering angrily, "Shut up, for Pete's sake! A car passed, and stopped, and is turning around. The driver must've seen your light in the water. Drop the fish. We got to run!"

Danny obeyed. They reached the trees, and clambered into the pickup truck. Mike started the motor. As he gunned the engine and swung the little truck out onto the highway, Danny looked back. He saw a man standing on the riverbank, bent as if peering down at something. The man turned and looked their way, but did not follow.

He had found the big fish, Danny realized. The spear was still sticking through the trout. The man must've understood at once what had happened. If he was a law officer, he would follow them; if not, he would probably report the incident to the Sheriff's office....

"Jeepers, what a fish!"

"What did you use for a worm? A boa constrictor?"

"Bet you had to haul 'im out with a tractor."

Mike and Danny had brought their catch into the older boys' dormitory; now a crowd of them was staring at the big trout.

"Going to have it mounted, Mike?"

"No. We'll eat it tomorrow. Let's give it to Mrs. Dade."

"She's probably sleeping."

"No, there's a light in the cook shack."

Mrs. Dade was elderly and skinny, but vigorous and a wonderful cook who liked and understood boys. She didn't sleep well, so she often read late; and if anybody was absolutely dying of starvation, he could sneak to the cook shack and bum a cup of hot chocolate and a doughnut from her.

Mike and Danny tiptoed to the cook shack, taking care not to wake Mr. Allen, the camp director, who slept in the main office.

Mrs. Dade, in a robe, was reading in her rocking chair.

"What's this?" she demanded. "A delegation to protest the hogwash I've been feeding you?"

Mike held out the trout for her to see.

"Ain't he something?"

"Looks like the one that swallowed Noah," she admitted. "You going to stuff and mount it?"

"Let's eat it tomorrow!" Danny blurted.

"Come on," she said, rising. "I'll make room for it in the refrigerator. That trout's big enough to give everybody in camp a taste. Mr. Allen will be going into town tomorrow. We'll eat Moby Dick here for lunch. But, boys, don't go back for his cousins, you hear me?"

Danny nodded, reddening. Mike just laughed....

The game warden arrived next morning while everyone was at breakfast. He was a stocky man with a pockmarked face and a worried expression. Mr. Allen rose from his chair at the head table to greet him.

"I'm Johnson, from the Department of Fish and Game," the warden said, loudly enough for everyone to hear. "Mr. Allen, we suspect that several of your boys went spearfishing in the river below the dam, last night." He turned and faced the suddenly quiet roomful of boys. "Any of you boys involved?"

Some boys shook their heads; others looked blank; nobody answered.

"We found a fish on the bank, right beside the pool, with a fish spear still sticking in him. Any of you own a spear gun?"

Again he got no answer; the faces looking at him were all still and tense.

"Whoever speared that fish will face charges of fishing with illegal equipment, fishing at night, and fishing in closed waters. He will probably pay a fine of over a hundred dollars and have to spend time in Juvenile Hall."

"Wow," somebody murmured; someone else uttered a low whistle; another boy groaned, "What a way to spend a vacation!"

Mr. Allen, who did not get mad very often, looked very upset now.

"If any of you boys were involved in this—raid," he said sternly, "I want you to stand up. Now."

Mike didn't stand; Danny didn't stand. But Danny felt that the hot flush of misery on his face must betray him as clearly as a shouted confession.

Mr. Johnson said, "I don't have a search warrant, and I wouldn't insult Mr. Allen by asking him to open every locker on the place. But I will ask you boys: Which one of you bought a fish spear at the Lake Sports Shop in Tahoe City last week? The owners tell me that such a spear was sold to a tall, dark-haired boy from this camp. I want that boy to stand up."

Danny's heart sank. Mike was tall and dark-haired; and, in fact, it *was* Mike who had bought the spear.

Then a boy stood up. Not Mike, but Lee Monahan, who was also tall and dark-haired.

Lee said: "I bought a fish spear at the Lake shop, Mr. Johnson, but I sent it home as a birthday gift to my brother, who's going down to Catalina to do some skin-diving in the ocean."

Danny almost gasped aloud. Lee was lying. Lee was a quick-witted guy, and he was covering up for Mike.

But the game warden was not easily fooled.

"Mr. Allen, mind if I look in the camp refrigerator?"

Danny felt a sickening wave of alarm come over him again. The big trout was in Mrs. Dade's refrigerator; it would furnish the final and positive proof of guilt.

"Not at all, under the circumstances," Mr. Allen answered the warden. "This way."

He started out of the diningroom. Mr. Johnson followed, and a group of boys tagged after. Mike grabbed Danny's arm and drew him along with the others. Danny felt so ill he was afraid he would lose his breakfast.

They filed into the big camp kitchen. Mrs. Dade, drinking her second cup of coffee, looked inquiringly at them.

Mr. Allen said, "Mrs. Dade, please excuse us. Do you have a big fish in your refrigerator?"

"I do. Why?"

"Mind if we take a look?"

"Help yourself. Bottom door."

Mr. Allen opened the refrigerator door, and there on a big platter was the fish. Using both hands, Mr. Allen drew out the platter and held it up for Mr. Johnson to look at—at clean, appetizing slabs of a fish that had been gutted and cleaned and cut into cooking-ready fillets. They might have been trout or halibut or cod or barracuda as far as any ordinary glance could tell.

Mr. Johnson's eyes were snapping with suspicion and frustration. "What did that fish look like?" he demanded.

"Wet, scaly, and dead," Mrs. Dade said. "What does any fish look like?"

"I mean, what kid of fish was it?"

She shrugged. "Just fish. The butcher may have mentioned, but I've got too many other things to remember."

Mr. Johnson glared at her, then turned and stalked angrily out.

Danny heard Mike, beside him, choke back a laugh; but Danny didn't laugh, didn't even feel like laughing. He was thinking that first Lee Monahan had lied to protect them; now Mrs. Dade had saved them by covering up for them. The mess was spreading like some kind of runaway infection. . . .

Then, several nights later, when Danny was undressing for bed in the tent he shared with Mike, two boys came in. They were Lee Monahan and Eddie Ames.

Lee said, "Danny, we want to borrow that frogman outfit that you and Mike used. Okay?"

Danny stared. "What f-for?" he stammered.

"What d'you think for?"

Eddie said, "We were up at the dam today. There's bigger trout than the one you guys got!"

"Where's the gear?" Lee demanded.

"It's Mike's. You'll have to ask him."

"So we'll ask him," Lee said.

"I don't think you guys ought to go spearfishing there—"

"Why not? It was all right for you, wasn't it?"

"But— Anyway, we lost the spear."

"I got a new spear gun from home today. Come on, Eddie," Lee said. "Let's go find Mike."

"You know," Eddie remarked as he turned to follow Lee, "I bet we could shoot a deer with that speargun. We could rig up a jacklight, and that would draw a deer close enough so we could hit it easy with the spear—"

Danny sat there, after they left, in acute misery, thinking . . .

Mike came in.

"Mike, did Lee and Eddie find you?"

"No. What do they want?"

"To borrow the frogman outfit, so they can go spearfishing."

"Let 'em have it."

"But suppose they get caught?"

"That's their lookout."

"You heard what the game warden said!"

"So did they."

"We're older. We're counselors."

"They're not babies."

"But we set the example!"

"So now we can just mind our own business."

"But, Mike, we can't let them get into trouble!"

"Don't see what else we can do."

"We can refuse to let them have the diving gear."

"Then everybody in camp would figure us for a couple of heels."

"Or we can tell Mr. Allen that Lee and Eddie are going spear-fishing—"

"I'm no lousy stool pigeon!" Mike said furiously. "You squeal on them and you know what the whole camp'll think about you, don't you?"

"Yeah." Danny caught an unsteady breath, then insisted, "Mike, we just can't let them have the diving gear."

"Then somebody will squeal on *us!* I don't put it past Lee Monahan to tell Mr. Allen that the frogman gear is in our locker and that we speared that big fish. Mr. Allen would turn us over to the game warden!"

Vividly, Danny foresaw the results of that eventuality. Being arrested. His name in the paper. Trial before a judge. Writing his mother that he had to pay a hundred-dollar fine. That he must spend thirty to ninety days in jail. . . .

Outside the tent, then, they heard voices and footsteps approaching.

Mike said, "That must be Lee and Eddie now, coming for the diving gear."

"Don't give it to them—that game warden is going to be watching that pool awful close. Lee and Eddie may get caught!"

"We can't help that."

Yes, Danny thought, we can. He could go to Mr. Allen. He could confess that he and Mike had speared that big fish in the refrigerator. Mr. Allen would seize their diving gear. Then Lee and Eddie couldn't get into trouble.

"Mike, let's tell Mr. Allen the whole thing!"

"And have him hand us over to the game warden? You crazy?"

Then Lee and Eddie were entering the tent. *Now,* Danny realized. *You can stop it now—if you go tell Mr. Allen what you did. If you've got the guts. . . .*

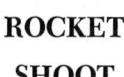

ROCKET
SHOOT

The problem:

The issue is honesty: accepting blame for a wrong committed even though someone else thinks he is guilty and has already accepted the blame. Two boys have started a fire in wheatfields by accident. A logger, who drove across the area and lost a bottle of gasoline, thinks he must be to blame and has accepted the guilt. The boys, if they keep still, will not even be suspect; but they know that the fault may well be theirs. Should they keep still?

Introducing the problem:

Ask: "Have any of you ever been in a spot where you suspect that something you did may have caused serious damage to somebody's property, but you are not absolutely sure that you are to blame? This is the problem in this story. The story stops but is not finished. As I read, think of ways in which the story could end."

Chris carefully assembled the rocket while Ronnie looked on. To the twenty-inch steel tube of the combustion chamber, Chris fastened the wooden nose cone. Then he filled the combustion chamber with the propellent—a mixture of three parts of zinc dust to one part of powdered sulphur. He tamped the charge in, working with patient thoroughness. Next, to hold the powder in, he inserted the burst-diaphragm, to which he had already attached the igniter wires. These wires he ran through the opening of the nozzle, and screwed the nozzle into place at the base of the rocket. Finally, then, he clamped the six-inch fins into place. Now the rocket was ready to blast off.

"Ronnie, you carry the launcher. Let's go!"

They rode out of town on their bikes, down a country road out into wheat fields. The rocket, Chris figured, had a range of a quarter-mile. When they were at least half a mile from the nearest house, he stopped.

"Let's set 'er up!"

Leaving their bikes in the road, they walked out into a field. They set up the launcher—a vee-shaped trough of metal with slanting braces. Chris placed the rocket on the launcher and unrolled the wires of the igniter a distance of sixty feet to a little ditch. He attached one wire to the pole of a dry battery.

"All right, Ronnie. You count-down!"

They crouched down in the safety of the ditch. Ronnie, his voice shaking with excitement, began counting: "Ten ... nine—" on down to "three ... two ... one ... *Blast!*"

Chris touched the second wire to the other pole of the battery. A long moment seemed to pass. Then the building pressure of exploding gas within the combustion chamber of the rocket burst the diaphragm; smoke and flame shot out of the nozzle, and the rocket inched up the launcher, lifted into the air twenty—fifty—a hundred feet—hesitated, wobbling as its comet's tail of fire dwindled; dropped half-way to earth—and then, as flame suddenly blasted strongly again, shot ahead once more. But it was off-course. It had veered and twisted. "She's burning uneven!" Chris shouted in dismay, for the rocket was flying parallel to the ground, about a hundred feet up. It whipped over the tops of a grove of trees and vanished from sight.

"Guess I just didn't tamp the powder down right," Chris said gloomily. "So she burned unevenly."

"It was a good shoot," Ronnie said loyally.

"Yeah, sure. We aim at the moon and hit the house next door. Fine shoot. Let's go pick it up."

But they couldn't find the spent rocket in the wheat. Finally they gave up and pedaled home.

Chris first heard the fire trucks roar down the road as his family sat down to supper that evening.

"Oh, oh," Mr. Carter said, "a fire." He hurried to the door and looked out. "Look at that red sky. Must be a big one!"

Chris looked. To the west, the cloudy night sky burned with a sullen, crimson glow.

Mr. Carter telephoned to the local paper. When he hung up, he said, "The fire's burned out over fifty acres of ripe wheat and is spreading fast. Burned a barn, too. Bet the damage will top ten thousand dollars before that fire's put out."

"Wheat fields?" Chris echoed. "Where, Dad?"

"The Bronkmyer Ranch, to the west."

That, Chris realized, was where he had fired off his rocket that afternoon. He went to his room, feeling sick and scared. . . .

At breakfast next morning, the local newspaper had a surprising story about the wheat field fire. The article said:

> Blame for the fire which burned over the field of wheat on the Bronkmyer Ranch has been definitely placed on William Hawes, who owns a small ranch adjoining the big Bronkmyer holdings. Firemen found the remains of a shattered glass jug in the area where the fire is believed to have started. Chemical tests on charred vegetation show that the jug had contained gasoline. Firemen believe that the jug, lying in the wheat, acted like a magnifying glass to focus rays of the hot sun on dry fuel to start the fire. Heat made the jug shatter and then the spilled gasoline further fed the flames.
>
> Mr. Hawes had been cutting timber with a gasoline chain saw in a grove near the fire site last Saturday. When questioned he freely admitted that he carried gasoline for the saw in such a jug. The jug, he says, must have fallen from his jeep as he took a short cut across the Bronkmyer fields on his way home.

Chris paused in his reading. He felt a happy surge of relief. He wasn't, after all, to blame for the fire!

But his relief did not last. That jug, he thought; it had been lying out in the wheat since Saturday. Why hadn't it caused a fire the first day it was out there?

Maybe it hadn't caused the fire at all! Maybe something else started the blaze. Maybe that something else was a rocket that went crazy and landed in the field still hot enough to set dry grain to slowly smoldering until a spark fanned into flame? A spark could smolder in the vegetation for hours.

Chris read on: "Mr. Bronkmyer has *No Trespassing* signs posted on his property. He has announced that he intends to sue Mr. Hawes for full damages. While the loss is less than first estimated, it is thought that it may amount to four or five thousand dollars."

Five thousand dollars!

And Mr. Hawes wasn't a rich man at all.

That sick, lost feeling came back to Chris's stomach.

"Ronnie," he said, when they met in the school yard later, "I'm wondering if my rocket started that wheat field fire!"

"Don't tell anybody!" Ronnie gasped.

"Maybe, if they find my rocket, chemical tests will show it started the wheat to burning."

"But, gosh, Chris, you'd be in awful trouble!"

"I g-guess so." His name would be in the paper. His mother would cry. He'd have to quit tinkering with rockets. Maybe Mr. Bronkmyer would even sue his father for damages.

"But nobody's found the rocket," Ronnie said. "You just keep still."

"Then Mr. Hawes will have to pay for all that burned wheat."

"You want your Dad to pay for it?"

"No."

"So what're you going to do?"

Chris said, "I think that we . . ."

A PISTOL FOR PETE

The problem:

The issue is that of responsibility for others: Eddy, a teen-ager, discovers that his young brother had committed a theft. As an older brother, which is his greater responsibility: to see that the small boy is punished for an act of wrongdoing, or to save the small boy's self-respect?

Introducing the problem:

Ask the group, "How many of you have younger brothers or sisters? Occasionally you have to babysit, don't you? You have to take responsibility for looking after your younger brother or sister—and sometimes when you're looking after them they get into trouble: they lose or break things, they fall down and scrape their knees or bloody their noses. Sometimes they get hurt in other ways, too: in their feelings. Looking after them isn't always easy. This is a story about such a problem. The story stops but isn't finished. Think of ways the story should be finished."

Eddy's birthday present from his Uncle Andrew was a sore subject in the Anderson household. Eddy's parents differed in their opinion about Uncle Andrew. Eddy's mother said that he was such a sour and crabbed character that his blood had turned to pickle brine. Eddy's father insisted that Uncle Andrew, although odd, had a heart of gold. "After all," Mr. Anderson would say, "Uncle Andrew is a seventy-three-year-old bachelor. You've got to make allowances."

Eddy had had his sixteenth birthday several weeks ago. As usual, he had received a present from Uncle Andrew. One thing about the old man: he had a memory like an elephant even if he did give forth like a mouse. He never overlooked any kind of family anniversary. "Oh, he's just building himself credit in heaven," Mrs. Anderson would say, and add "which he must need awful bad!"

The present that Eddy had received from him this year, which had made his mother boil with wrath, was the sum of fifty cents. A worn old half dollar. It had come carefully wrapped, and with it was a note that said:

Dear Eddy,

Enclosed herein you'll find a four-bit piece. I earned it myself a long time ago. It's not the first money I ever made by the sweat of my brow, but almost. I'm sending it to you with an old man's advice. Start a coin collection, boy. Not just of rare coins but of any coins—old, brand-new, any kind. When you're sitting on a pile of cash you're sitting on top of the world.

Love,
Uncle Andrew

Mrs. Anderson was outraged.

"The boy needs a winter coat and shirts and shoes, and that—that palsied old skinflint sends him advice!"

"He means well," Mr. Anderson insisted.

Eddy himself, after a first moment of disappointment, had merely laughed and made some remark about no wonder Uncle Andrew's rich. That made his mother even angrier.

"You're just as easy-going as your father," she had scolded.

Eddy had only smiled; he knew that his mother wanted him to be a famous surgeon or a lawyer who defended poor people; she had enough missionary spirit for a dozen ordinary persons.

A week later another letter had come from Uncle Andrew. And this second letter had made Eddy's mother really blow her top in anger.

"Only a mean old man who loves to see people squirm would think of a stunt like this!" she told Mr. Anderson at dinner that night.

"No, Martha, Uncle Andrew's not intentionally cruel—"

"Oh, no. He didn't have to sit up all night *planning* this—it just came natural to him! Here, son," she said, holding the letter out to him, "I want you to read this. I don't believe in shattering young people's faith in their elders, but the sooner you learn how twisted and crotchety some people can get, the sooner you'll quit wearing those rose-colored glasses you've inherited from your father."

Eddy looked up from his dessert, and took the letter. Nine-year-old Pete, finishing a second plate of Jello and whipped cream, murmured a 'scuse me and scuttled out to play in the yard.

Dear Martha,

No doubt you've wondered why I sent Eddy a mere half-dollar for that important sixteenth birthday of his. I have a reason. I always have reasons for what I do. A month from now, I'm going to write to Eddy, and I'll tell him: Lad, I sent you a half dollar for your birthday. If you've spent it by now—well, you have had four bits' worth of fun. If, however, as I advised you, you've kept that four bits, you own a rare coin worth $50, and which will likely be worth twice that some time in the future. Maybe you resent me telling you this now, and think that I should have told you the exact value of the coin when I sent it to you. I didn't tell you for a very good reason. Experience is a dear but mighty effective teacher. If you've spent that coin, you've had a lesson so expensive that you'll never forget it. If you've saved that four bits, you have a reward so gratifying that it will linger long in your memory. Either way, lad, that half dollar has helped you to do a little growing up.

Your devoted
Uncle Andrew

Eddy looked up, thinking of what he'd read.

His father said quickly, "Listen, Eddy. If you need fifty dollars, we'll find it, all right."

"You see?" Mrs. Anderson broke out. "Already you're dressing the boy's wounds!"

"But I haven't spent that half dollar," Eddy said. "It's on my bureau. I—I completely forgot about it."

"Allah be praised," his father murmured.

But his mother said, "Whether Eddy's still got the coin or not is beside the point. Uncle Andrew shouldn't have—"

"But, Martha, it's just a lesson in thrift."

"You mean to sit there and tell me you don't see how *cruel* this trick was? To tantalize and torture the boy! To make him feel like a foolish no-good—"

"Martha, you're going overboard on this thing. Eddy's all right."

"If he has spent the money, then he feels stupid and guilty. And he'll feel it all his life! Even though he forgets the actual details, he'll feel overtones of foolishness and guilt about every decision he makes!"

"But Martha, he didn't spend the four bits. He's still got it!"

"And if he still has it, then consider how smug it makes him. This experience will rob him of initiative. He'll never dare to make a move for fear he'll be squandering some opportunity he has overlooked. Either way, he's caught. Either he'll be smug and superior or timid and unventuring!"

"Maybe he won't need to be a go-getter," Mr. Anderson said lamely. "Uncle Andrew can't take his money with him."

But Mr. Anderson couldn't win. Mrs. Anderson was too insistent.

"I don't want Eddy to *inherit* money! Believe me, if Eddy can grow up with faith in himself and the courage and energy to try new things, he'll be a lot richer than if he inherits somebody else's misered-up fortune!"

"Well, yes."

By now, that four-bit piece had a lot of importance. Eddy excused himself and hurried to his room.

He looked on his bureau for the coin. He looked in the top drawer. He looked in all the drawers. He looked under the bureau; on his study table; even under the rug. Then in all his pockets. In vain.

The old half dollar was gone.

He was positive, however, that he had seen the half-dollar on his bureau just yesterday. Had he placed it in his pants pockets with his other change, and spent the coin? He thought back: he had had a malt and a sandwich at school. He had bought a notebook and drawing pencils at the corner shop. He had made change on the bus, coming home. He had gone to a movie last night, and bought a cheeseburger afterward.

"I can't trace the coin back through all that business!"

He didn't feel like facing his mother, now, and admitting that he had foolishly spent the coin. Moodily he walked out into the back yard.

Pete and his gang were playing on the lot next door pretending to be sheriff and bandits. Shooting each other full of holes and having a wonderful time. Eddy watched them a minute.

Suddenly Eddy frowned. Pete with a gun? He had no capgun. Mother, in her strong-minded way, didn't believe in kids having guns, or comic books, or secret clubs. When the family had first moved to this street, Pete had pleaded with Mrs. Anderson to buy him a ninety-eight-cent cap pistol like the other boys' weapons. She had refused. Instead she had bought him a three-dollar copy of an illustrated edition of *Moby Dick*. Later, Eddy had found Pete making a harpoon with a broomstick and a sharpened nail, an ideal weapon for punching out playmates' eyes. Eddy had confiscated the lance before his mother had taken frightened notice of it.

"Bang! Bang!"

"Bang! I got you."

"You did not. I shot first!"

"You did not! I practically had you shot full of holes before you even saw me!"

"Oh, Tommee! Come home right this minute!"

From next door, Mrs. Albee's voice rose shrill over the tumult of firing guns and warriors' shouting voices. Warfare ended.

"I got to go home," Tommy Albee said. "Pete, you've tried my gun. You pay me fifty cents or give me back my gun."

And Pete reached into a pocket, took out a coin and handed it over. Tommy ran home, leaving the gun in Pete's hands.

"So that's where my coin went!" Eddy realized. "Pete saw it lying on my bureau. And he wanted a cap gun. Wanted it so bad he just couldn't stand it. All the other kids had 'em. Poor guy!"

Now Tommy was running home with that half-dollar.

"Hey, Tommy!" Eddie yelled, and lunged into pursuit—and stopped short. What was he going to do? Tell the whole gang that Pete had stolen that four bits? Stolen a rare coin that was worth a lot of money, just to buy a junky cap gun? Make Pete out a thief in the eyes of the other kids? Pete would feel like dirt! Then suppose Mother heard of it. She'd be heartsick; she'd look at Pete as if he had been a traitor to everything she admired and respected.

But I can't let Pete get away with stealing, can I? It was partly my fault. I shouldn't have let the coin lie there in plain sight. It was too big a temptation for a nine-year-old. But, gosh, a guy can't go through life picking up anything he wants, just because it isn't nailed down! Pete's got to learn how to resist taking things. He's got to learn to be honest. Besides, that coin's worth $50.

Tommy had stopped; Tommy asked hurriedly, "What d'you want, Eddy?"

All right, tell him! Eddy urged himself.

But if I do, I'll get Pete into awful trouble . . .

HEAVY, HEAVY
HANGS OVER
YOUR HEAD

The problem:

 The issue is that of honesty; of confessing to one's guilt when some-one else is blamed for a fault of one's own. Linda, babysitting for Mrs. Mallory, tries on a string of pearl beads from Mrs. Mallory's bureau. The string breaks and some of the pearl beads are lost. Later, Mrs. Mallory accuses Linda's friend Nora of losing the pearls. Linda can clear Nora of blame only by confessing her own guilt in the matter. Involved, in addition to honesty, is integrity in friendship.

Introducing the problem:

 Say, "Sometimes you get into trouble by sheer accident, when you had no intention of doing anything wrong. Have any of you ever unintentionally broken something that belonged to somebody else and felt just sick about it? It happens to all of us. It happened to Linda in this story. But Linda's problem is more complicated because her friend Nora is blamed for the damage. Maybe some of you have been in such a spot. This story stops but is not finished. As I read, think of ways in which this story might end."

 This was Linda's first job of babysitting for the Mallory family. The baby went right off to sleep, soon after the Mallorys left.

 Linda watched television in the living room for a long while. Bored finally, she got up and wandered through the house. She had got this job with the Mallorys tonight because her friend Nora Baker had given her name to them. Nora was their regular sitter. Tonight, Nora had a bad cold and her mother had kept her at home.

 Looking into the bedroom closet, Linda gazed with a hungrily appreciative eye at Mrs. Mallory's wardrobe. Such lovely dresses and such smart suits! Linda felt an impulse to try some of them on, but checked it. She did babysitting for half a dozen different families; she never touched their belongings or opened their refrigerators or sampled cookie jars.

But the jewel box on Mrs. Mallory's dressing table was more temptation than Linda could resist. The box lay open, revealing pieces of costume jewelry that were magically lovely to Linda's eye. She picked up a string of pink pearl beads that shone with a lustrous glow. She put the string about her throat and peered into the mirror, studying the effect; and she sighed, for the beads were so shining and beautiful.

"Oh, darn!"

The string had broken. Pearls cascaded down her dress to the floor. She bent to pick them up, and gasped in alarm. Some of the pearls had fallen through an open register in the floor—the "cold air return" of the heating system. She could hear the lost pearls rolling down the long, insulated pipe toward the furnace in the basement.

And then, out front, she heard a car turn into the driveway, heard the engine race momentarily as the driver shifted gears, then die into silence as he stopped the car. The Mallorys were back!

Working swiftly, she scooped up the pearls still on the floor, thrust the partial string and loose beads into a vase on a stand in the hallway as she hurried back into the living room. Sitting down, she grabbed up a magazine and pretended to be reading. Her heart was beating so violently it seemed that the Mallorys must hear it as they entered.

But they sensed nothing wrong. They paid her, thanked her, and Mr. Mallory took her home.

As she lay in bed afterward, worry was a torment that would not let her sleep. She scolded herself bitterly; she should never have touched Mrs. Mallory's belongings.

She did try to reassure herself: a string of pearls left out in the open on the bureau like that—they were just costume jewelry. They had to be! She would go with Nora, next time Nora sat for the Mallorys, get the string from the vase, take it out and have the pearl beads restrung and pay for the job herself . . .

But she received a shocking surprise when Nora called her, several evenings later. Nora was babysitting at the Mallorys.

"Linda, Mrs. Mallory fired her cleaning woman today. For *stealing!*"

Linda gasped, "Wh-what?"

"Uh-huh! Mrs. Mallory went to put on her pearl necklace and it's gone! The pearls aren't real—that is, they're cultured pearls—but Mr. Mallory paid over fifty dollars for them in Tokyo."

Linda plumped down on a chair, strength suddenly gone from her legs.

"Have—have they looked everywhere in the house for the pearls?"

"They sure have. Mr. Mallory kept saying, Oh, they'll turn up; and anyway he wouldn't fire a poor cleaning woman without *real* proof. But

Mrs. Mallory was so mad she wanted to go down to the police station tomorrow and swear out a warrant for the cleaning woman's arrest!"

"Oh, no," Linda choked. "Nora, I'm coming over."

"Sure, come on."

For a while Linda had to listen to Nora talk. In an agony of impatience, Linda sat with Nora in the living room in front of the TV set. Then, saying, "I'm going to the kitchen for a drink," Linda walked through the house.

In the hallway, she upended the vase on the stand—and the torn string of pearls and loose gems fell into her palm.

Quickly she poured them into a covered casserole on the sideboard. There the necklace would soon be discovered.

The next afternoon, Mrs. Mallory telephoned her. In a strained voice, she asked Linda to come over that evening after dinner.

When Linda arrived, she found Nora—angry and white-faced—sitting in the livingroom with Mrs. Mallory.

"Linda," Mrs. Mallory began, "I've already told Nora what's happened. Today I found this string of pearls in a casserole on the sideboard. The string is broken and a dozen of the pearls are missing. I missed the necklace several days ago and thought it was stolen. Obviously, it wasn't. It's my guess that somebody took them from my bureau top and tried them on—that the string broke and some of the pearls were lost. And that this person then hid the remaining pearls in the casserole."

"I didn't do it!" Nora blurted. "I've told you!"

Mrs. Mallory continued right on: "Now, this casserole was empty yesterday. I know, because I used it.

"The only people who have been alone in the house since yesterday are you, Linda, and Nora. You were both here last night. Nora tells me that she has never seen the pearls before. Linda—now tell me the truth! —did you hide the pearls after breaking the string?"

"Oh, no!" Linda said. "I've never seen them before either!"

"Then, Nora," Mrs. Mallory said firmly, "you are the guilty one."

"But I'm not, I'm not!" Nora insisted. "Please believe me. I've never seen those pearls before. Not even once!" And, unable to check herself, Nora began to cry.

Mrs. Mallory's angry glance moved from Nora to Linda, then back to Nora again.

"Nora," she said sternly, "a few weeks ago, I asked you to sit for me and you told me you couldn't because you had a bad cold. But that same evening I saw you in a movie with some friends, having a gay time. Nora, I just can't take your word.

"My pearl necklace, with so many of the pearls gone, isn't worth much now. I'll discuss replacing it with your father. He may or may not feel any responsibility. As for you, I don't want you to babysit for me any more. And don't give my name to anybody as a person who will recommend you for a sitting job. Please go home now."

Nora got up to go, and Mrs. Mallory turned to Linda.

"Linda, will you stay tonight and babysit for me?"

For a moment Linda could not answer, she was so choked up. Nora, going to the door, was crying into her hands. Linda felt that she must jump up, stop Nora, turn and blurt out to Mrs. Mallory that Nora was a fine person, that Nora *was not to blame* for losing the pearls, that Nora would never lie about such a thing—

But I can't, Linda told herself. Nora doesn't need sitting jobs. I do. Her father makes good money. He can afford to replace that necklace. My folks don't have any money. I just *can't* admit I did it!

"Well, Linda?" Mrs. Mallory asked.

The Letter of the Law Series

SPELLING

BEE*

The problem:

> *Ellen, a babysitter, is asked to judge a spelling game played by a group of children she is tending. One child, Sue, has spelled the word labor as labour. The other children say she has misspelled the word but*

* Adapted from *Teacher's Manual: English Grammar and Composition,* VII (New York: Harcourt, Brace & World, Inc., 1960). Reprinted by permission of the publisher.

she insists that she is right: at home (she is a visitor from England) labor is spelled with a u, as labour. By American standards, of course, she has misspelled the word. Ellen's dilemma is this: by which standard should she rule? Should she be strictly correct by American usage and declare Sue has lost and is out of the game? Or should she be kind and considerate to a guest from another country and make allowances by ruling that Sue is correct?

Essentially, this is a dilemma in which a rigid, self-advantaging adherence to the letter of the rule or law is opposed to a flexible construing of regulations or customs in the light of probable consequences to the other fellow. Several questions are implied: Is winning by a technicality a just victory? Is the value of winning, for you, in proper proportion to the cost of losing for your opponent? At stake in such a dilemma is the open-minded and accepting attitude we imply in the terms fair play and good sportsmanship. In our legal terminology we have the expression "guilty beyond the shadow of a doubt," and our legal traditions hold that it is better for a guilty man to evade punishment than for an innocent man to be convicted. This is an attitude of "giving a break," of making allowances in areas of doubt. In our interpersonal relations, however, we do not always observe such a charitable alertness and sensitivity to fair play.

The children who insist (after an explanation that Sue is English and has been taught to spell labor with a u) that Sue has misspelled the word, are defeating her not through superior skill but on a technicality. They need, of course, to be helped to understand the unfairness of such behavior. However, you, as the teacher, must not appeal to them directly on the basis of fair play. Rather, through working with this problem-story, and with others, and with other materials, you should make it possible for them to experience the feelings of injustice and guilt aroused in the people who are involved on both sides of a contest that has been settled on the basis of a technicality or tricky maneuver. It is when young people test such an experience and become aware of their feelings that they gain insights and reach their own conclusions.

Introducing the problem:

You may introduce the problem by asking your group, "Have you ever thought you had won a game, and then discovered that you had lost because you had forgotten a rule, or didn't even know a certain rule?"

Have volunteers enact the spelling bee. The child playing the role of Ellen may decide that Sue has spelled labour correctly, giving her the benefit of the doubt.

Ask the child who played Ellen why she made her decision to allow Sue to be given credit for a correct spelling.

Ask the group if anyone would like to play the roles differently; and if you have volunteers, re-enact the parts.

If, by this time, Ellen decides that Sue must abide by our American rules, that she has not spelled labour correctly, ask the child who has played Ellen why she decided in this way. Ask Sue how she feels.

> Go on to the next step: Tell the group to suppose that the spelling game is on television, in a quiz show, and that they are all contestants; that the winner will receive for himself (or herself) and parents an all-expenses-paid trip to Hawaii, with surfing lessons at Waikiki included.
>
> Ask, "How would you feel if you were Sue, and the judge ruled that you were incorrect in your spelling?"
>
> After discussion, ask, "How would you feel if you were not Sue, but other contestants, and the judge ruled that Sue had spelled labour correctly and was the winner of the game?"

When Ellen arrived at the Becker home to babysit that evening, she was appalled to discover the size of her job. Instead of just the Becker twins, who were a lively handful, she found a dozen youngsters gathered in the livingroom.

Mrs. Becker whispered to her: "Ellen, I forgot to tell you that we're having a small birthday party. I've given the children ice cream and cake, and in about an hour their parents will call for them. Just keep them busy playing games."

Ellen gulped and said she'd try.

At first, everything went well. The youngsters were bright fifth and sixth graders. She kept them busy playing alphabet games.

Trouble came when they played a spelling game Ellen invented. All but two had misspelled words and had been eliminated and only Sue Mapes and Timmy Ross were left. Sue was given the word *labor* to spell.

"Labor," Sue repeated. "L - a - b - o - u - r."

"Wrong!"

"Timmy wins!"

"I'm not wrong," Sue protested. "I got it right."

"You are so wrong," Mary Becker said. "Labor is l-a-b-o-r."

But Pamela Becker backed Sue, declaring, "The English spell *labor* with a *u*. L-a-b-o-u-r. Sue comes from England—she's just visiting over here. She's right."

"Sure she is," Malcolm Brown said. He was a bookworm. "There're other words like labor. In England, they spell color and honor and vapor and humor with a *u*. H-u-m-o-u-r."

"But this isn't England," Mary protested.

And Timmy added importantly, "In England, you drive on the left side of the street. But you do that over here, and you'd smash head-on into a truck and kill yourself. Ignorance is no excuse."

"That's right," Eddie Nolan said. "You're supposed to learn how to do things right when you go to another country!"

But Pamela insisted. "Sue is a guest here. We've got to make allowances. She spelled *labor* the way it's spelled in her country, and we should accept it."

"No!"

"She misspelled the word, and she loses!"

"We going to argue all night?"

Timmy turned to Ellen, then.

"You decide."

"Yes," Sue said. "You be the judge."

Even Timmy agreed, "We won't ever agree. You decide."

Ellen was flustered.

"Well," she said, "I think..."

THE

TREASURE

OUT

IN

LEFT

FIELD

The second story in this group deals with essentially the same problem as "Spelling Bee" with a vital difference: there is a great deal at stake. In "Spelling Bee," the winner would gain the satisfaction of coming out best, but that is all; in this second story, the winning team will gain an important prize. The motivation for winning is far higher; and, therefore, the dilemma is a far more difficult one.

The problem:

The ethics of winning by a technicality is the issue. A junior league baseball team is tied with another team for first place, and the two teams are to oppose each other in a final game. The captain of the first team learns that, by taking advantage of a technicality, he can greatly increase his team's chances of winning.

Introducing the problem:

> Often, discussion and role-playing "Spelling Bee" will take a short time. If this has been so, go on to "The Treasure out in Left Field." You may say to the group, "I am going to read to you another story that deals with this problem of trying to decide whether to enforce rules or make allowances. This time, however, there is a big prize at stake."

Andy was carrying the garbage can out to the front curb when his mother called him in to answer the telephone. It was Tom Byers.

"Hey, Andy, I got to talk to you!"

"What about?"

"I'll come right over! You'll be there?"

"Sure, but what's so important?"

"Wait'll you hear," Tom blurted, and hung up.

Andy frowned as he hung up. Usually, Tom was a cool character. What had him jumping like this?

It had to be about the ball team, Andy realized. Nothing else, just now, was so important: the season was almost over, just one game left to play. Their team was tied for first place with the Crescent Park team, and the winner of this next game would be playground-league champions. Andy was pitcher and captain of his team; Tom was catcher.

Just as Andy came out on the front steps again, Ben Craig came running from next door. Ben was first baseman on Andy's team.

"Hey, Andy! Heard the news?"

"No, but I'm sure going to, I can see that. What's up?"

"About the game! Last year the Tenth Avenue Kiwanis Club gave the league champions new uniforms. My Dad says that this year the Neighborhood Improvement Association wants into the act. They're going to boost Junior League baseball by giving a big prize to the championship team."

"What? A big trophy cup?"

"Better than that!"

"New uniforms?"

"Better than that!"

"You been taking pep pills or something?"

"Listen, they're going to hire a big bus and send the whole team on a tour this summer!"

"Where to? Disneyland?"

"Better than that! To ten different states, to play ball against other division championship teams."

"Wow! Won't that be something!"

"Dad says the winning team will visit all the big scenic spots like Zion National Park and Glacier Park."

"You got to be kidding?"

"No! It'll be in all the papers tomorrow night. Andy, we just got to win this next game!"

"We'll try."

A shrill whistle sounded down the street. Turning, they saw Tom speeding toward them on his bike. He pulled up at the curb.

"I just heard the news," Andy called to him. "If we should just accidentally win this next game, we'll—"

"We're sure as heck going to win it," Tom yelled.

"It says so in your crystal ball? Listen, to win this next game we're going to have to play ball better than we ever played before."

"We'll breeze through it. It'll be easy as pie."

"Be overconfident, and you're licked," Andy insisted.

"Pete Larsen is the best pitcher in the League. We can't hit his fast ball. He's shut us out before, and he can do it again."

"Not this time!"

Ben snapped, "You going to guarantee Pete'll drop dead or something?"

Tom said, "We won't be batting against Pete Larsen in this next game!"

"And why not?"

"Because he won't be playing, that's why!"

"We should be so lucky."

"It's a fact," Tom insisted. "Pete won't be pitching against us."

"Why not?" Andy demanded. "Don't tell us he's got pneumonia?"

"No, he's fine, now. Last week, he *was* sick; that's why Mr. Nolan had the game postponed to this coming Saturday. Pete had the flu. So Mr. Nolan phoned Mr. Dunn, and they agreed to postpone the game. Pete was home, sick in bed—but what Mr. Nolan and Mr. Dunn didn't know was that Pete has a birthday this week. Day before we play that game, Pete will have that birthday—"

"So what?"

"Gosh, don't you get it *yet*? Pete's older than us. We play Saturday, but on Friday, the day before, Pete will be *over-age* for this division. You know how strict the rules are about age! Pete won't be able to play; he'll be *ineligible*. And without him pitching against us—"

"We'll win!" Ben whooped.

Even sobersided Andy grinned, and said, "We'll really have it easy. Their other pitcher, Willy Barton—"

"Couldn't fan a Girl Scout!" Tom said. "His fast ball takes two weeks to cross the plate. We'll knock him out of the box. Boy oh boy, we got it made!"

Then Andy asked, "But don't the Crescent Park team know this?"

"They just found out last night, when they went to see Pete. He's all right. He just had the twenty-four-hour flu and he was back in school today. Mr. Nolan is going to call Mr. Dunn tomorrow morning to see if we'd agree to change the date for the game again."

"Change it *again?*" Ben demanded; and Andy, quicker to see the point, asked, "Change it to when?"

"To the day *before* Pete's birthday. Instead of playing on Saturday, they want to set the date back to Thursday."

Ben uttered a groan.

"Then Pete Larsen *will* pitch for them. Goodbye ball game!"

"No!" Tom said. "Even if they want to change again, *we don't have to agree to changing the date a second time!*"

"Now, wait," Andy said.

But Tom blurted on, "The game is set for next Saturday, right? And now they want to change the date back to Thursday, the day before Pete Larsen's birthday, so that he can pitch for them. But Mr. Dunn told them that before changing the date again, he'd have to talk to you, Andy—you're team captain. Thursday is a weekday, and we'd have to play after school, and that might spoil our chances, Mr. Dunn said. Suppose you, Andy—or Ben here—has to go to the dentist after school? Or has to go to the doctor to get shots?"

"You're just supposing."

"Mr. Dunn said that if our whole lineup can play, then maybe you should agree to the change. But if any of our players can't play on Thursday, we won't agree to changing the date again. We play on Saturday, as set. That gives us our out! We'll play Saturday when Pete Larsen can't pitch against us—and we'll win as easy as pie!"

But Andy said, "Relax, will you? We can too play Thursday."

"No, we can't," Tom insisted. "*I* won't be able to play on Thursday. I guarantee that! And I'm the only good catcher you got!"

"Why not? What's going to happen to you on Thursday?"

"Anything's liable to happen," Tom said. "Maybe I'll have a bad allergy attack—all I got to do is eat eggs. Or maybe Miss Wimberley will keep me after school for throwing spitballs, like she threatened to do yesterday. Don't worry. I can fix it for Thursday."

"No," Andy said. "If we win, we'll win by playing ball, not by—"

"But we *will* play ball. Only it'll be on *Saturday*, when Pete can't pitch against us!"

"They'll be handicapped."

Then Ben chimed in on Tom's side: "Andy, they're pushing us too hard. We changed the date, once, when they asked. We were real cooperative, even though it handicapped *us*—"

"Sure," Tom cut in. "Last Saturday, if we had played on schedule, we'd have had Norm Lucas in left field, but he had his tonsils out yesterday, so he won't be able to play this week, and he's one of our best batters."

"So asking us to change the date a *second* time," Tom insisted, "is taking too much advantage. Andy, use sense."

"A fielder isn't as necessary as a good pitcher."

"But it's a good batter who brings in the runs. Andy, we got nothing to feel guilty about!"

"We *have* been cooperative," Andy admitted.

"Postponing the game to Saturday was all *their* idea, not ours!"

"I know."

"And don't forget, Andy," Ben urged, "that if we lose, we stay home this summer; but if we win—we get that six-week tour of the National Parks!"

"That'll sure be a nice trip."

"It's a cinch for us to win, Andy, if you just play it cool!" Tom urged. "What do you say, Andy?"

And Ben added, "Make it Thursday, Andy, not Saturday!"

Andy said:

A

LONG

NOSE

HAS

A

SHORT

LIFE

The three stories in this group hinge upon the dilemma of taking advantage of a technicality to win, or risk losing by making allowances. The "technicality" involved differs in each story; they become progressively larger in implication, in the successive stories. In the first story, the technicality was an actual rule; in the second story it was, instead of a clear-cut rule, a moral imperative—a matter of being generous in balancing advantages in a game. In this third story, the implications are larger still; the technicality is a basic element of the peer group code: You shall not betray a peer to the punishing adult. The issues at stake, too, are larger: cheating in a history test and its concomitants, on one level; and, on another level, the responsibility of the individual for involvement in other people's destinies.

The problem:

Involvement or noninvolvement is the question. In this third story, two boys are accused of cheating in a history test. One is guilty, the other is innocent. A third boy can clear the innocent person and expose the guilty one, but if he does so, he will be looked down upon by other boys as a tattletale and will have to take a licking from the cheater. He can escape both the beating and the stigma of "squealer" by simply remaining silent; moreover, to some degree, he can salve his conscience by telling himself not to be a Judas who testifies against another boy.

The crux of this social imbroglio is, of course, the question of involvement, an issue that is white-hot in public awareness now. Is the innocent bystander really innocent? Bystanders who see someone being injured and lift neither hand nor voice to aid the victim but remain silent, hidden, are themselves victims of our current "epidemic of noninvolvement."

Newspapers recently have reported a series of incidents in which witnesses have been non-Samaritan in their behavior: in New York City, a young woman was repeatedly stabbed while thirty-eight neighbors heard her outcries over a half-hour period. No one ventured out to help her; no one called police; unaided, she died. A crowd watched, without interfering, as a gang of eight men tromped two men; and in another case, a student who had been stabbed by a gang of toughs asked watching motorists to take him to a hospital—but they rolled up their windows and drove away. In California, motorists saw a taxi driver being robbed and did not bother to stop or call police. These are just a few samples of many such incidents reported in the press...

In this story, "A Long Nose Has a Short Life," the issues are confronted, defined, and alternatives delineated. The fact that when a bystander does interfere, some risk is involved, is not glossed over; the risk, sometimes, is very real; nevertheless, the responsibility of the bystander exists. Again, you, as the teacher leading the role-playing, must bear in mind that you do not put the answers into the pupils' mouths: they must respond to the issues of these stories as their own perceptions guide them.

Introducing the problem:

Ask the group how this third story resembles the others, and how it differs from the preceding two.

Ask the group how they think Raoul must have felt when accused of cheating, how Pete felt, how Barney felt, overhearing.

Ask individuals who offer solutions why they suggest their particular answers.

That morning when Barney Craig walked into the principal's outer office, he found Pete Haines and Raoul Marchant waiting there. Raoul nodded politely; Pete gave Barney a hard stare, which was all Pete ever gave anybody, unless it was an addition of lumps. Barney sat down, across from the other two.

Waiting, Barney got the feeling the two boys were worried. Raoul sat stiff and straight, but his hands kept twisting together. Raoul was new here; he was French, and his use of English was something very interesting but puzzling. In France, Barney had read, school was very strict; probably Raoul was in trouble and didn't know what to expect from Mr. Davis and feared the worst. Pete Haines was chewing gum, even here in the principal's office. Pete was big for his age, hard-muscled, and hard-headed. It wasn't just that he was a bully that made Barney leery of him, but the fact that Pete seemed to enjoy it. As far as Barney was concerned, if Pete had become extinct with the dinosaurs and sabre-toothed tiger, Barney would have been happy.

Mr. Davis opened his door.

"Come in, you two."

Pete and Raoul rose and walked into the other office. Barney sighed and settled down to wait. He was in charge of traffic patrol, and wanted to suggest some changes to Mr. Davis.

Barney did not intend to eavesdrop, but the partition wall was thin and Mr. Davis' words were distinct, especially when Barney—his attention caught—leaned his ear against the wood.

"Boys," Mr. Davis was saying to Pete and Raoul, "Miss Duncan has brought me your history test papers. She is puzzled by them. So am I. Perhaps you can explain them to me?"

Raoul said, "Sir, I do not understand. Something is wrong?"

"Yes, Raoul. This test was a review of American history reading covered by your class the past two months. You've made certain mistakes."

"I am sorry."

"Pete, the answers you gave to some questions also are wrong."

"Can't win 'em all," Pete said.

"Pete, you and Raoul sit next to each other, don't you?"

"I guess so. Miss Duncan put me there."

Raoul asked again, "Something is wrong, sir?"

"Something, Raoul, is very—puzzling, let's say. You've made certain errors in answering the test questions. Pete, you've made the same errors. In fact, *exactly* the same errors."

"Oh, now, Mr. Davis," Pete protested; and Raoul said, "I do something not right, sir?"

Mr. Davis let out a long sigh; and Barney, overhearing through the partition, snorted to himself. *He* knew what had happened! Trust good old

Pete Meathead Haines to be up to his usual tricks. When the muscle was passed out, Pete was out there with a washtub; but when the brains were being apportioned, Pete was standing there with an eyedropper.

"Boys," Mr. Davis said, "look at the questions on your papers. I've marked several—read them. *The Civil War was started when Fort Sumter was fired upon. What was the date?* Your answer, Pete, is April 12, 1867. And your answer, Raoul, is April 12, 1867. The right answer is April 12, 1861.

"Another question: *Name two presidents who were assassinated over a half-century ago.* Pete, you wrote: President Garfield, 1887, and President McKinley, 1907. Raoul, you wrote the same. But the right answer is Garfield, 1881, and McKinley, 1901.

"Another question: *When was the attack by the Japanese on Pearl Harbor?* Your answer, Pete, is December 7, 1947. Yours, Raoul, Dec. 7, 1947. The right answer, of course, is December 7, 1941. Tell me, Pete— how did you happen to make such mistakes?"

"It beats me, Mr. Davis. I just don't know."

"Raoul, don't you think it odd that the two of you made exactly the same mistakes?"

"Sir, I—do not understand. I *know* correct date of Pearl Harbor attack. 1941 it happen."

"You wrote 1947 right here on your paper, Raoul. Can you explain your mistake?"

"N-no, sir."

"Boys, I repeat: you made the same mistakes. I don't believe it was just an accident. Pete, I want the truth from you—and nothing but the truth. Did you copy from Raoul's paper?"

"Me, sir? Oh, no, sir! That would be cheating! I study hard. I don't need to copy from nobody!"

"Raoul, did you copy from Pete's paper?"

"No, sir."

"During the test, Raoul, did you notice Pete trying to get a look at your paper?"

"No, sir."

"Pete, did Raoul look at *your* paper?"

"Well, sir, you know how it is—I mean, for all I know—Well, I was too busy writing to watch."

"Then neither of you have any explanation as to why your papers have mistakes that are exactly alike?"

Barney, listening in the outer office, jumped to his feet in a sudden excited rush of understanding. *He* knew what had happened! *He* knew that one boy had copied from the other, and he knew *which* boy had copied!

Pete had copied from Raoul.

What was more, Raoul had answered those questions *correctly*—but Pete, copying them, had copied them *incorrectly.*

And what's more, Barney told himself excitedly, *I can prove it! Raoul is a good student, and he's honest; but Pete's a lazy dimwit and he's dishonest, and I can prove it!*

Those dates—1861, 1881 and 1901, and 1941—they were incorrectly written on Pete's paper as 1867, 1887, 1907, and 1947, because Pete had mistaken Raoul's figure *one* as a figure *seven*. . . . Barney's family had had a French student as a visitor; many French people wrote the figure *one* with a line slanting down from the top to the left. So it looked like our figure seven. The actual French seven had a crossbar in the middle, so that it looked like an F.

Barney then heard Mr. Davis say, "I'm marking both these papers F. Raoul, starting school in a new country and a different language is hard, I know. But cheating is not an answer to your problem. You will get a reputation that will be difficult to change."

He's accusing Raoul, Barney realized—and impulsively moved to the door, telling himself: *All I got to do is go in there and tell Raoul to show Mr. Davis how he writes the figure one. That'll prove he's honest and Pete's the cheater!*

Barney grasped the door knob—and stopped.

He would be getting himself into all kinds of trouble if he did this.

He was running tattling to teacher, that's what he was doing. Pete would blab to everybody, Barney foresaw. The gang would call him a rat fink squealer. And what would Pete Haines *do* to him? Just beat his ears off, that's all. Pete was the biggest roughneck in school. *It wouldn't be just one working-over he'd give me,* Barney foresaw. *Every day, going home after school, I have to pass the corner where Pete and his gang hang out. Every day, I'd have to run a gauntlet,* Barney realized. Every day, they'd jeer at him; they'd gang up on him. . . .

But *I'm* not supposed to know anything about this, anyway! I'm eavesdropping, and Mr. Davis wouldn't like that. Besides, if I bust in there now, I'd be squealing. Carrying tales to teacher. Sticking my nose into other people's business . . . a good way to get it cut right off. . . .

Affiliation: Integrity in Friendship Relations

BIRTHDAY
PRESENT

The problem:

The issue is individual integrity; specifically, integrity in personal relations: *keeping a promise to a friend.*

Introducing the problem:

Say to the group, "Sometimes we promise to do things with friends, and get ourselves into a conflict of promises. Haven't you ever agreed to go one place with one friend—and then unexpectedly had a chance to go to a better place with a friend you like more? Then you wish you hadn't made the first promise. This story I'm going to read deals with such a conflict. The story stops but is not finished. As I read, try to think of ways in which the story could end."

Susie Burns got a late start on her 4-H project that Saturday morning. She had had to stay home and help her mother take down the living-room curtains so that they could be sent to the cleaner. Done, finally, Susie rode her bike down Mulberry Street toward the Morton place, where she kept the steer she was fattening for the County Fair in June.

As she pedaled along, a station wagon passed and several girls called hello to her. She waved back, recognizing Dotty Burton, Ellen Hewes, and Edie Jones, riding with Dotty's father. The station wagon was pulling a boat on a trailer; and as Susie noticed the boat, she felt a pang of envy.

Dotty's father was evidently taking Dotty and her friends out to French-man's Lake. He was going to teach them waterskiing. Dotty was already good at it.

Susie wished that she knew Dotty and her friends better; Dotty might ask her along some time. Susie's family had moved to Hamilton just a month before, and she was a new girl in school. Luckily she made friends easily, or she would have been out of things entirely, like Wendy Norris.

She thought of Wendy just because she saw her coming out of the Pritchard house with little Timmy Pritchard. Wendy earned money baby-sitting. It wasn't just that Wendy was small for her age; she was a city girl who didn't know the first thing about ranch country. She was new here, too, although her family had been living in Hamilton for over six months.

Reaching the Morton place, at the turn of the street, Susie dismounted from her bike and walked back to the barn where she kept her steer. There she got busy throwing feed to the sleek Hereford and cleaning up the stall. When she saw Wendy and little Timmy walk past the barn door, headed out to the corrals, she saw no reason to warn them away.

The first clue she had of trouble was when she heard Wendy calling, "Hi, Sookie!" and little four-year-old Timmy echoing her in a shrill, "Hi, Sookie!"

Susie had picked up a brush, intending to smooth down the steer's coat. She stopped, arm uplifted, frowning.

Sookie? Sookie was the gentle old Jersey cow the Mortons owned. But Sookie had been put on a trailer and hauled out to pasture yesterday. That wasn't Sookie out in the corral now, that was—

"Good gosh!" Susie blurted. "They'll get killed!"

She dropped the brush and looked around frantically for a pitch-fork but saw none. Then she heard little Timmy cry out in fright. Susie grabbed up a horse blanket and whirled and ran out of the open door of the barn. And as she looked at the corral, she gasped in alarm. That fool kid, Wendy. She had taken Timmy right into the corral.

"Come back!" Susie yelled. "Come out of there!"

Wendy and Timmy had crawled under the bottom board of the fence and walked into the corral—had walked toward Sookie, probably intending to pet her. But that wasn't Sookie in the corral; that was Co-manche. And Comanche, now, was lowering his head, pawing the ground, and snorting his anger.

"Run!" Susie screeched. "*Run!*"

But neither Wendy nor Timmy moved; they stood frozen in their tracks, paralyzed with fright. *If only I can get there in time,* Susie gasped to herself. Already Comanche was beginning to move; Comanche was working himself into the rage that would launch him into a rush.

Susan flung herself to the ground, rolled under the fence, bounced to her feet, and ran her level best. Again she screamed, "Run!" as she passed Wendy and Timmy. She darted straight at Comanche. Her intention was to whip the blanket across the big bull's face, and this she tried to do. But the blanket caught on Comanche's horns and was torn from Susan's grasp. Susan did not waste an instant trying to clear it but kept on running her level best. If only she could draw the bull after her—

She glanced back over her shoulder fearfully—and stopped. The bull wasn't chasing her. That blanket, snagged on Comanche's horns, was hanging over his eyes, blinding him. Comanche, head lowered, was trying to shake the old blanket off his horns.

Wendy had finally come to her senses. Pulling Timmy by the hand, she was running toward the fence as hard as she could make the little boy go. Susan breathed a heartfelt "Thank goodness!" of relief and followed them. She walked at first, but then she darted into a run as she saw the blanket go flying from Comanche's horns. The bull glanced around, snorting, saw the children, lowered his head and again started into a rush.

Wendy and Timmy were at the fence. They flopped down and rolled under the bottom rail—and Susan came right after them, into safety.

As they scrambled to their feet, Comanche reached the fence, and bellowed at them, so that they jumped back in fright.

"What's the matter with Sookie?" Wendy asked Susan, stammering.

"For Pete's sake," Susan demanded furiously, "don't you know a bull from a cow?"

"You m-mean that ain't Sookie?"

"No, that ain't Sookie," Susan snapped, "that's Comanche."

"Ain't he a pet?"

"Sure, like a rattlesnake's a fishingworm, he's a pet."

"Gosh!"

"Yeah, gosh. Now take Timmy home before something else happens."

Timmy's mother had heard him crying, and had left the house and was hurrying toward them now.

"Timmy, dear, you all right?" she called. "What happened, Wendy?"

Wendy swallowed hard, still too scared and confused to give a clear answer. Timmy pointed to the bull in the corral and, as his mother reached them, buried his face in her skirt and began to yell. Susan turned away, headed back to the barn, disgusted with the whole hullabaloo.

"Shush, Timmy," his mother said soothingly. "You're all right, dear. Wendy, what happened?"

"He—went in there," Wendy said, pointing toward the corral.

Mrs. Pritchard gasped. "Oh, he's *always* getting into things. That awful bull! He might've trampled Timmy. But you got him out."

Wendy pointed to Susan.

"Susan came—she ran in—"

"You brave girls. You saved Timmy's life!"

Oh, what gush, Susan thought. If she heard any more of it, she would be sick to her stomach. She hurried into the barn to finish tending her steer.

But she did hear more of that gush.

At dinner, that evening, her mother said, "Susan, did you see the story about you and Wendy in the paper?"

"*What?*" Susan gasped.

"Listen." Her mother read from the local evening paper: "Girls save tot from bull. Susan Burns and Wendy Norris, both eleven years of age, saved four-year-old Timmy Pritchard from possibly being gored and trampled by a bull in a corral on the Morton place this morning. Timmy had climbed into the corral, thinking that the bull was a cow that the children often pet. Luckily, the older girls noticed him in time. The bull, enraged, had started toward Timmy. The two girls ran into the corral. While Wendy grabbed the tot and hurried him back to the fence, Susan distracted the bull by striking him across the face with an old saddle blanket she had snatched up. Mrs. Pritchard, who reported the incident, says that undoubtedly her little son's life was saved by the prompt action of the courageous girls—"

Susan made an inelegant sound with her lips.

Her mother said, "Susan!"

"But that's hogwash."

"You didn't haul Timmy out of the corral?"

"Yes, sure, but—Wendy didn't do nothing."

"You're going to be less generous than Wendy?"

"What do you mean?"

"According to the paper here—Wendy insisted to Mrs. Pritchard that all the credit for saving Timmy should go to Susan Burns."

"Oh."

"That's pretty nice of Wendy."

"But, doggonit, it was her fault that Timmy got into the corral in the first place."

"You sure? You saw it happen?"

"Oh, what difference does it make?" Susan said disgustedly, and gave up on the whole thing.

But it did make a difference—at school, next morning. Both Susan and Wendy were teased about being heroes by the other children. Susan shrugged it off; Wendy turned red with discomfort.

"Susan did it all," she tried to explain, but nobody listened.

Susan could have exposed Wendy; she could have told everybody that Wendy was a dope who deliberately walked into a corral to pet a prize bull; but Susan kept still. She knew how much scornful teasing this would bring down on Wendy.

Something else that was different happened: Wendy was usually left out when the girls played games. But today she was included.

Another difference was that Wendy attached herself to Susan and began to follow her around.

Formerly, Wendy's mother had taken her to school every morning in the family car. Now Wendy came to the corner where Susan waited each morning for the school bus, and climbed aboard after Susan and sat beside her. Susan didn't mind; Wendy wasn't a pest who kept talking if you wanted to sit in silence and think lazily. If you wanted to talk, Wendy talked; and sometimes she was interesting, because she was a bookworm who knew a little about a lot. Girls who liked Susan began to treat Wendy in friendly fashion. Wendy began to share Susan's growing popularity.

As Wendy became happier, her class work began to improve. She would speak up now, instead of sitting silently until the teacher called on her.

Late one afternoon when Susan got home from school, she found a strange woman sitting in the livingroom with her mother.

"Susan, dear, this is Mrs. Norris, Wendy's mother."

Susan said hello, and started to her room.

"Wait, Susan," Mrs. Norris said; "I want to thank you for what you've done for Wendy."

"But I haven't done anything."

"You've let her be your friend. Wendy hated school here, and was doing badly, although she's bright. Now she's happy with school, thanks to you."

"Actually, I'm kind of new here myself," Susan said.

"But you make dozens of friends without even trying."

"Well, I—guess so," Susan admitted.

Among her new friends were Dotty Burton, Ellen Hewes and Edie Jones. Dotty was the most popular girl in the class.

One afternoon after school, as Susan and Wendy waited for the bus that would take them home, they saw Dotty, Ellen and Edie get into a station wagon driven by Mrs. Burton. The car moved up to where Susan and Wendy were standing.

Dotty called, "Susan! You want a lift home?"

"Why, sure. Thanks!"

Not until she got in, and the car started off, did Susan realize that Dotty had not invited Wendy, too. Looking back, Susan got a glimpse of

Wendy's face, looking hurt and crushed, before the car turned a corner.

Susan said, "I usually ride home with Wendy."

"Wendy?" Mrs. Burton said. "The girl who was standing near you?"

"Yes."

"I'm sorry, dear, but I'm in such a hurry now I really can't turn back to get her."

"No loss," Dotty Burton said, and Ellen and Edie laughed.

They stopped at Susan's house to let her out.

Dotty said, "Sue, Dad's going to take us to Tomales Bay some Saturday soon, to go clamming. Like to come along?"

"Sure, that would be swell," Susan said.

Wendy wasn't at school next day. She did come the following day, however. When Susan asked why she'd been absent, she said, "Oh, I had a cold." She did look kind of sick.

"A cold? And you got over it in one day?"

"Maybe it was just an allergy," Wendy said.

But Susan's mother, when she asked her what an allergy was, wanted to know more; and when Susan told how she had left Wendy standing at the bus stop and gone off with Dotty Burton's crowd, she nodded her head and said, "Yes, that would make Wendy sick, Susan. Sick at heart."

"Wasn't my fault, Mom."

"She does count on you a lot."

"Doggonit, am I going to be saddled with that drip the rest of my life!"

"She's a nice girl, dear."

"Sure, but— Hey, I'm going clamming with Dotty and her crowd!"

"Wonderful. When?"

"Don't know yet. Dotty'll tell me."

Several days later, Susan received a letter in the mail—an invitation to a birthday party. Wendy's birthday party, on Saturday, the 14th.

"Do I have to give Wendy a present, Mom?"

"No have to about it. But don't you want to?"

"Well, sure. I'll get her a book."

"That would be fine."

On the bus next morning, Susan said to Wendy, "Thanks for inviting me to your party, Wendy."

"You'll come?"

"Sure, I'll be there. Who else did you invite?"

"All the girls in our room."

"That's nice."

So it came as a surprise to Susan—a disastrous surprise—when on Friday night she got a phone call from Dotty Burton.

"Hey, Susan, you be up and dressed at 5 A.M. tomorrow morning!"

"What for?"

"We're going to the beach to hunt clams. Remember?"

"*Tomorrow?*"

"Sure. Dad says it'll be the right kind of low tide. I told you it would be some Saturday soon."

"B-But—aren't you going to Wendy's birthday party?"

"When we could go clamming instead? Don't make me laugh. Wouldn't go anyway. She gives me a pain."

"Look, I—I think I got to go to her party," Susan said.

"Say, I invited you first, didn't I? I asked you over a week ago, and you promised you'd go."

"I did," Susan admitted. "But you said we'd go clamming *some* Saturday, not exactly—"

"So you owe it to me to go clamming with us."

"But Wendy's feelings will be hurt."

"So who cares? See you tomorrow. Be waiting for us at 5 A.M.!" Dotty said, and hung up.

Susan was so silent at supper that her mother asked, "What's the matter, dear?"

"Mother, what do you mean when you say that you have a 'prior engagement'?"

"Oh, that means—Well, somebody calls you up, for example, and asks you to come to dinner. But you've already promised somebody else you'd come to *their* dinner. That's your *prior engagement.*"

"I guess I can't go to Wendy's birthday party. I got a prior engagement to go clamming with Dotty Burton."

"Susan, dear, Wendy will be hurt!"

"But I do have a prior engagement."

"Was it definite? Seems to me you said it was *some* Saturday?"

"Whatever Saturday, I promised to go."

"You mean you *want* to go?"

"I've got to go!" Susan said wildly.

"Would you really do that to Wendy?"

"I've got nothing against Wendy."

"She'll really be hurt, Susan. She'll think you don't like her. She'll think you prefer to go with Dotty and her crowd."

"Maybe I do!"

"But you accepted Wendy's invitation. You're willing to go back on your word?"

"Oh, darn it! What *should* I do, anyway?"

"It's your decision, dear."

"I wish I'd never heard of Wendy Norris!"

"Don't get upset. Go ahead and phone. Whichever way you decide, you settle it now. You phone Wendy—or Dotty—and say you're awfully sorry, but you can't go."

Miserably Susan sat down at the telephone.

Whose number, she asked herself, should she dial? Wendy's ... or Dotty Burton's?

LOST

BALL

The problem:

> The issue is that of honesty, of personal integrity. Sometimes young people are so frightened of their elders that they lie to escape punishment for infraction of rules.

Introducing the problem:

> Say, "Sometimes you get into trouble without ever intending to, by accident. Then, trying to get out of it, you get yourself into even worse trouble. In this story I'm going to read to you, a boy breaks the rules when he was really trying hard to mind them. This story is unfinished; when it stops, I will ask you to finish it. While I'm reading, think of ways in which the problem of the story might be solved."

Johnny Lucas was idling out in front of his house, standing with one foot on the gate and the other on the walk. His father had repeatedly warned him not to swing on that gate, so he was just putting half his weight on it and keeping his other foot on the ground, so that if necessary he could say in self-defense, "But I wasn't really swinging on the gate." Johnny was bored. He was not supposed to go out of the yard when his folks weren't home, and he had no one to play with.

A streetcleaning truck went past, and behind it the gutter filled with a rapid current of water. Johnny considered making a sternwheel paddle-boat out of a cigar box, with paddles that would be slung on rubber bands that could be wound up to turn them. Trouble was, his dad didn't allow him to play in the street. Traffic came zooming downhill here. Johnny considered; it would be an hour, probably, before either his father or mother returned from shopping. Should he risk playing in the street?

He forgot the matter then, as he saw another eleven-year-old boy coming down the sidewalk. It was Lon McCassland, and he had a softball in his hands.

"Hi, Lon."

Lon looked at him. "Hi."

"I got a Superman comic—"

"Seen it."

"Let's swing on the rings."

"I can't play in your yard."

Johnny followed with his eyes as Lon threw the softball up and caught it, and tossed it again and caught it behind his back.

"Hey, Lon. Let's play Andy-Over!"

"Your Pop doesn't want me to play in your yard. *My* Pop doesn't want me to play in your yard. *I* don't want to play in your yard. That makes it unanimous."

"I mean, you stay out here *in front* of the house, and I'll go around in back."

Lon considered. He'd come down the street because he had no one to play with. He nodded. "Okay."

Johnny ran around to the rear of the Lucas home, and waited.

From out in front came Lon McCassland's high-pitched yell—"Andy-y-y-Over-r-r-r!"

Presently, high over the house, Johnny saw the ball rising, saw it slow, and arch, and come slanting down toward him. He ran back, and almost caught the ball. It tore through his fingers, and bounced against the garage. He snatched it up.

Then it was his turn.

"Andy-Over-r-r-r!" he shouted, and threw the ball high as he could over the roof of the house, and watched it rise and curve and start down on the far side, and drop out of sight.

He waited. He'd thrown pretty hard. Presently he began to have worries. If the ball had gone over Lon's head, out into the street, it might start rolling downhill, to the boulevard below, where traffic was heavy and constant. They might never get the ball if it rolled down there.

He grew tense. No yell of "Andy-Over!" came from Lon.

And then, around the edge of the house, at the driveway, he saw Lon. Lon beckoned. Lon looked scared.

Johnny hurried to him.

"Didn't you catch the ball? What's wrong?"

"Come see," Lon whispered.

Johnny followed Lon out in front. Lon pointed to the car at the curb. It was Johnny's folks' car, an old convertible.

"What happened?" Johnny demanded.

"Look!" Lon said hoarsely.

Johnny looked. In the fabric top of the car was a hole.

Lon said, "The ball landed on the car, and tore through the roof. The ball's in front, on the floor, and the car's locked!"

"Oh, my gosh," Johnny breathed. "My Dad'll just—"

"Get my ball."

"You better run on home, Lon. I'm going out in back—"

"First you get my ball!"

Johnny tried the car door.

"But it's locked."

"Get a key! I ain't going home without my new ball. My Pop'll strap me good."

"I haven't got any key."

"Go in and get one from your mother."

And tell her what happened? Oh, no!

"Can't. She's downtown, shopping."

"Johnny, your folks've got an extra key to the car. Everybody has. It's in your mother's bureau, or your dad's desk somewhere. You go get it."

"That's right."

In the tall file in his father's study . . . Johnny ran indoors. In a couple minutes he was out, with a key.

He unlocked the car door. The ball was down on the floor, under the clutch pedal. He climbed in, on hands and knees on the floor, and groped around to seize the ball.

Johnny's mother always left the car in gear on this hill, because of the steep grade, and because the hand brake didn't hold well. Dad had trained her always to cramp the wheels into the curb as well. Now, as Johnny crouched on the floor, fumbling under the clutch pedal for the ball, his shoulder nudged the gear shift lever and pushed it out of gear.

The front tire slid along the curb, and the front wheels straightened as the car started rolling.

Lon yelled wildly, "Johnny, look out!"

But Johnny was down on the floor, groping for the ball. In a moment, Lon realized, the car would be at the steep part of the sloping street. The car would gain momentum, would roll down onto the boulevard at the bottom of the hill, out into that stream of traffic.

Lon jumped onto the running board. He couldn't reach the hand brake—Johnny was on the floor, in the way—so Lon grabbed the steering wheel and jerked it savagely, twisting the front wheels back toward the curb.

But those front wheels jumped the curb.

The car careened up onto the parking strip—and crashed into a tree, coming to an abrupt, jolting halt.

Lon jumped from the car. Lon murmured, "Oh—oh!" as he looked at the front of the machine.

Johnny backed dazedly out of the door and stood up, rubbing his head, where he'd bumped against the steering column as the car hit the tree.

He walked around in front. And stopped short, and just stood there, staring, aghast. The radiator grill was smashed in; the front of the convertible was wrecked.

Lon grabbed his ball, and ran up the street toward home.

Johnny didn't notice at all. Johnny was thinking, "Oh, gosh, will I catch it now . . ."

"All right, start over, and tell it slow," Johnny's father said sternly that evening. "You and Lon were playing ball?"

"Yes-s, Dad."

"I thought I made it plain to you that I didn't want that McCassland boy on this property?"

"But we were playing out in the street, Dad."

"Oh, so that's different, huh?"

"And Lon was batting—"

"How often have I told you not to play in the street? You want to get run over by a truck? Why do you think I've bought you all the play equipment in the back yard?"

Johnny stared at the rug and did not answer.

"Well, go on," his dad said.

"Lon hit the ball, and it went up high, and it came down right on the car, and broke through the top."

"As if that isn't enough," Mr. Lucas remarked. "Then what?"

"Lon wanted his ball back, so—so I got the extra key, and—gave it to him. He opened the car door, and got in and was feeling around for the ball, and the car started rolling—"

"He must've pushed it out of gear."

"It looked like the car would roll downhill, so he turned the steering wheel, to bring it against the curb—"

"And the car jumped the curb."

"That's right."

"And smashed into the tree!"

"Well, I won't stand for it!" Mrs. Lucas said angrily. "If that harum-scarum boy were grown up, I could put him in jail. It's illegal to meddle around with somebody else's car! Ed, you go right over to see this Mc-Cassland kid's father. He's going to have my car repaired, or find himself with a lawsuit on his hands."

Mr. Lucas nodded.

"Come on, Johnny."

"Oh, Dad, I—got to do my arithmetic!"

"That can wait. This is important. It's a civic duty, Johnny. When you see somebody damage property belonging to somebody else, you're duty bound as a witness to testify and help the owner get pay for the damage done. Come along."

"But, D-Dad, I don't feel so good."

"For Pete's sake, what's *wrong* with you?"

"My stomach hurts," Johnny said, and he wasn't pretending.

"You'll live."

They walked down the block to the McCassland house. Mr. Lucas rang the bell, and the door was opened by Mr. McCassland.

"Why, hello there, Lucas. Come in, come in. Nice to see you."

Johnny followed his dad into the living room.

Young Lon was there, squatting on a hassock, watching television. He saw Johnny, and started to speak, but noticed how worried and miserable Johnny looked. Lon gulped and said nothing.

Mr. Lucas came right out with it: "McCassland, I don't know whether your boy's told you yet, or not—"

"Told me what? Sit down, Lucas. Johnny, there's a chair for you, over by Lon."

"McCassland, the boys were playing ball out on the street today—"

"That's not so good."

"And your son batted a high ball that came down onto my car and tore through the top."

"Oh?" Mr. McCassland was a big, hearty man who smiled easily and a lot. He frowned now, and it made him look sad and older. "Lon didn't mention it."

"Then, trying to—" Mr. Lucas went on; but at the same time Lon started saying, "Dad, I didn't—"

"Lon, Mr. Lucas is talking," Mr. McCassland said firmly.

"But—"

"You wait."

"Then my boy got the key to the car," Johnny's father continued, "and Lon got in and groped along the floorboards to find his ball—"

"No, that's not it! I was just—"

"Don't interrupt!" Mr. McCassland said sharply.

"And Lon must've touched the gear lever. Anyway, the car started rolling downhill."

"Good Lord!" Mr. McCassland paled. "He might've got killed! And wrecked your car, too."

"Yes, if he hadn't twisted the steering wheel, and sent the car against the curb."

"But, Dad, I was just—"

"You'll let Mr. Lucas finish!"

"And the car jumped the curb and smashed into a tree. Wrecked the radiator grill. There may be other damage."

"Did you see this happen, Lucas?"

"No, I didn't. But Johnny was right there."

"I didn't do it!" Lon burst out.

"Lon, I'll talk to you later!" Mr. McCassland was furious. "Mr. Lucas, you get your car repaired and send me the bill."

"You don't have to pay—"

"When my own son damages property belonging to somebody else, I do have to pay for it and I *will* pay for it," Mr. McCassland said. "I'm going to make sure that you remember that, Lon. You're going to be punished. You've been saving up to go to boys' camp this summer. You'll keep on saving your show money and what you earn cutting grass, but you'll use it to pay me back for repairing Mr. Lucas's car. You understand?"

Lon's lips quivered. He turned to Johnny.

And he said wildly, "Tell your Dad the truth! Go on, tell him what really happened!"

Johnny couldn't look at Lon.

Low-voiced, Johnny said, "I've already told him."

Johnny's dad shifted uncomfortably on his chair.

"I'm afraid," he said then, "that one or the other of you boys is lying. Let's get the truth of this right now."

The "Getting Even" Series: Being Fair

One of the strongest of all emotional experiences is the sense of outrage felt when one has suffered injustice. In the first wild heat of such a mood, one wants to pay back in kind for the wrong that has been inflicted. Young people, children, are especially prone to suffer burning desires to "get even." But behavior motivated by the urge to get revenge is often unwise and far out of proportion. The wronged individual, lashing out wildly in an effort to get even, too often inflicts a wrong greater than the one he has suffered. Too often, moreover, when a so-called wrong is studied dispassionately, it proves to have been something far different from the vicious act it seemed at first.

This group of stories is based upon the desire to "get even." The purpose of role-playing this material is to provide practice in *exploring the feelings and the consequences* of behavior based upon the need to strike out at someone who has wronged you.

In using these stories, the role-playing leader should help the group to analyze:

1. How an individual feels who has suffered a wrong
2. Why the individual who committed the wrong behaved as he did
3. Why people try to "get even"
4. Whether the way of "getting even" is a punishment that "fits the crime"
5. What will be the consequences of the act of revenge upon people other than the original wrongdoer
6. How the person who is getting even will feel later about his revenge

To bring the problem close to home for the individuals of your group, you may ask:

Have you ever had experiences in which someone:

1. humiliated you
2. played a trick on you
3. stole from you
4. tattled on you
5. lied about you
6. took credit belonging to you
7. laid blame on you for an act you did not commit
8. destroyed something you cherished
9. excluded you
10. could have cleared you of undeserved blame but did not bother to do so?

Younger children are especially prone to have violent desires to get even for real or fancied wrongs. It is, perhaps, a sure sign of maturity that one, when wronged, can be detached enough and analytical and cautious enough to study the unjust behavior before lashing out in an effort to get even. It is, perhaps, an even surer sign of maturity when one can recognize the reasons why an individual wronged you and sympathize with him. It is, perhaps, a still higher level of maturity when one can see a way of getting revenge for an act of wrongdoing, but can recognize that the consequences of getting even are likely to be far more evil than the injustice suffered, and can forego the satisfaction of revenge.

MONEY

FOR

MARTY

The problem:

The issue is honesty: if someone has cheated you, is it fair to cheat him in return? Bryan owes Marty fifty cents he has borrowed but not paid back in spite of Marty's repeated requests. Marty has a chance to get his money back—by stealing it in a way that will cause Bryan much trouble.

Introducing the problem:

Say to the group, "Have you ever lent something to a friend—who just never gets around to giving it back? If you have, you can remember how provoked you felt. This story is about such a happening. The story stops but is not finished. As I read, think of ways in which you might end the story."

Marty had put his foot on a shiny half dollar.

Nearby, on hands and knees, Bryan was searching through the grass, carefully parting the blades to peer between them for a silvery telltale glint.

"Marty, help me?" he pleaded. "I lost my half dollar!"

"Too bad," Marty said. "Too bad you didn't pay me what you owe me before you lost that money."

"Oh, I couldn't pay you out of *that* half dollar!"

"Oh, no?" Well, you are, chum, you are, Marty said to himself. He was really disgusted with Bryan. He had lent Bryan two bits for a movie just a week before, when Bryan already owed him for a hot dog and a coke. But Bryan who was good at mooching always managed to forget any debts he owed.

"I couldn't pay you from that half dollar," Bryan explained, "because it isn't mine. Besides, it's special. It's a coin from my Dad's collection. I brought it to school to show to Mr. Dolan. He collects coins. I didn't tell my Dad I was taking it. He doesn't like me to mess with his collection. Besides, this coin isn't worth just fifty cents. It's scarce, so it's worth a lot more. Dad'll really be sore!"

So you're in trouble, Marty thought. Well, go ahead and squirm. You got it coming to you. Then Marty thought of Bryan's father. He'd really be rough on Bryan.

Marty almost lifted his foot, almost said, "Hey, look—" but checked the impulse. Bryan needed a lesson.

But this would be so tough a lesson. . . .

TELL-TALE

The problem:

Getting even can sometimes be extremely unfair: the revenge can be a far greater wrong than the original hurt done to the person trying to get even. In this story, two boys are exposed as authors of a prank. To get even with the person who exposed them, they arrange for her to seem guilty of stealing from a lunch box.

Introducing the problem:

You may say to the group, "When you've done something wrong, and someone tattles on you, you feel very angry toward that person, especially if you were punished severely. You really want to get even. But getting even can sometimes lead you into serious trouble. This is a story about such a case. The story stops but is not finished. As I read, try to think of ways in which the story should end."

Ken had worked out a clever plan to arouse some excitement. They were bored, and just aching for something to happen. Ken's big idea promised to be a lot of fun. But Ken needed Jimmy to help because Jimmy wasn't afraid of snakes.

During the morning recess, they carefully stole back into their classroom. Their teacher, Miss Moffatt, was busy doing playground duty. At the rear of the classroom, on a long work table, was a natural history exhibit the class had been preparing. Jimmy opened a cage, reached in, grasped a young gopher snake just back of the head, and took it out of the cage. He wasn't afraid of it; in fact, he had caught the snake in his own backyard and brought it to school just a week ago.

Ken leading the way, they hurried into the cloakroom. Ken glanced along the rows of lunchboxes set on shelves.

"Here. Put it in Lenore's."

Ken opened the lunchbox, and Jimmy carefully stored the snake inside.

"I'll bet she screams like she was bit by a rattler," Ken whispered.

"She'll probably think it *is* a rattler," Jimmy said scornfully. "Okay, close the box."

"Come on, let's get out of here."

They met Dora in the doorway to the hall. She looked at them suspiciously but said nothing.

"Think she saw us?" Jimmy whispered.

"No," Ken said, making his voice confident because he wasn't, but wanted to be.

At lunchtime, Lenore performed as well as the two boys could have hoped. In fact, she even surpassed their expectations.

Rain had started to fall outside, so Miss Moffatt had asked the children to eat at their seats. "No commotion, *please*," she had requested. Everyone got his or her lunchbox; everyone had gone back to his or her seat; everyone had started opening his or her lunchbox with eager appetite. Only Jimmy and Ken had delayed; taut and aquiver with expectancy, they waited for the excitement. It came.

Lenore opened her box—and as the little snake reared its head up, tongue forking redly from its mouth, Lenore screamed. Lenore had a strong pair of lungs and a sturdy voice box, and she really put her heart into the effort, for she was scared—she was sincerely, profoundly, and wholeheartedly scared. She screamed as if a lion had leaped at her with wide-open jaws. She shrieked and jumped from her seat and flattened back against the wall, and uttered screech after screech.

Several other girls screamed too; but the boys, after one look at the cause of all the uproar, slumped back in their seats and howled with laughter.

"Children! Children!" Miss Moffatt's stern voice finally clamped control on the hullabaloo. Guffaws dwindled to chuckles and silence.

Some of the boys spoke up then.

"Miss Moffatt, there's no reason for Lenore to bawl like that. It's just a gopher snake."

"A little one. Like the one in our cage."

"It *is* the one from our cage," Dora said shrilly. "Miss Moffatt, Jimmy and Ken put it in Lenore's lunchbox. I saw them in the cloakroom during recess."

Miss Moffatt looked at the two boys.

"Aw, we didn't mean to scare her silly," Jimmy said.

And Ken added, "It was just a joke, Miss Moffatt."

"But how was Lenore to know it wasn't a poisonous snake?" she asked. "Practical jokes can do serious harm."

"I'm sorry, Miss Moffatt," Jimmy said.

"I think," the teacher said soberly, "that you two boys should give some serious thought to the possible consequences of such mischief. You'll stay after school each day for the rest of the week."

"Oh, no," Jimmy gasped.

And Ken said, "We got a Little League game to play! Jimmy's pitching, and I'm catcher."

"Shouldn't you have thought of that before you played your trick on Lenore?"

"But Jimmy's our best pitcher," Ken protested unhappily. "Besides, I got a birthday party tomorrow after school!"

"I suspect that the best birthday present anyone could give you, Ken, is awareness of how important it is to look ahead to the possible consequences of your behavior," Miss Moffatt said. "All right, it's one o'clock. Everybody to work."

Jimmy and Ken smoldered as they served their time after school. Miss Moffatt had them wipe off the chalkboards, clean out the cages of the little wildlife exhibit at the rear of the room, and stack books neatly in the cupboards. Then she gave them each a book to read at their desks. While they supposedly read, they griped, low-voiced, to each other. She heard their mumbling but made no effort to gag them.

"That Dora! I'm going to fix her good," Jimmy said.

"We ought to put her in a barrel of cement and dump her into a river," Ken suggested.

The big idea came to Jimmy as he and Ken were walking home.

"Say, I know how to fix that Dora!"

"How?"

"She got us into trouble. Okay, we'll get her into a big mess, and see how she likes it!"

"What'll we do?"

Excitedly, Jimmy told him. . . .

Next day, at recess again, Jimmy and Ken stole back into their classroom, to the shelves on which the lunchboxes were kept.

"There's Brenda Norton's lunchbox."

"What's she got in it?"

"Look—two hardboiled eggs, a liverwurst sandwich, and a jam sandwich and a thermos of milk and a big, thick slab of cheese cake and a red apple."

"No wonder she's so fat."

"Take the eggs?"

"No. Anybody might have eggs. We'll use the liverwurst sandwich and the cheese cake. She'll miss them. She'll really scream if those are stolen."

"Yeah. Now where's Dora's lunchbox?"

"Find it, quick! She might come walking in early again."

"You really think that everybody'll believe she really *stole* the stuff?"

"Sure. Those Webber Street kids'll steal anything."

"Here's Dora's lunchbox."

"Open it."

Ken obeyed. The box looked almost empty. Inside were just two thin peanut butter sandwiches; nothing else.

"Plenty of room," Ken said.

Jimmy leaned over to place Brenda's liverwurst sandwich and thick cheese cake inside.

"You really think," Ken demanded, "that Miss Moffatt will believe that Dora stole this stuff?"

"Sure she will!" Jimmy insisted. "Dora has stolen stuff out of lunchboxes before. Miss Moffatt knows it. In the fourth grade. You weren't here then."

"Maybe Dora was hungry?" Ken said. "Maybe that's just a story and she never really did it?"

"Look, she tattled on us, didn't she?"

"Yeah."

"She needs a good lesson, doesn't she?"

"Yeah," Ken admitted. "Hey, hurry, will you! Somebody's coming down the hall. Put that stuff in and let's go!"

Jimmy reached to lower the liverwurst sandwich and slab of cheese cake into Dora's lunchbox. He hesitated.

Frantically Ken whispered, "Quick, we got to leave. Put that stuff in and shut the box. Well, are you or aren't you?"

Jimmy said:

EYE-WITNESS

The problem:

The issue is personal integrity: the problem is one of controlling the violent urge to 'get even' for a wrong done.

Introducing the problem:

Ask the group, "Has someone ever played a joke on you that hurt your feelings so badly that you wanted to get a very punishing revenge on him (or her)? This is a story about such a case. The story stops but is not finished. As I read, think of ways in which the story might end."

It happened during the afternoon recess. John was wearing his gray slacks and blue jacket—the new clothes Mrs. Latham had bought him just a week ago. It was the first time he had worn them. Mrs. Latham had urged him to wait until after school to dress up, but he was so impatient to be ready when his Uncle Walter came for him that he had insisted on putting on his good clothes. The evening would go fast enough as it was; too fast, in fact. But dressing up before school was a mistake, and John realized it when he reached the school yard.

"Hey, look at John. All dressed up."

"Where you going, John? To a funeral?"

He just grinned and did not try to answer. The reason he was dressed so nicely was too important, too wonderful, to share just yet; later, perhaps, he'd feel like talking about it.

The remarks had continued during the noon hour, and started again at the afternoon recess. Now something worse happened.

"Hey, John. Come over here," Andy Byers called to him.

John walked over.

Andy was the biggest boy in the sixth grade and very popular. John had started school here just a month ago, and so far Andy hadn't paid much attention to him.

"John," Andy began, in a serious, confidential way, leaning close and speaking in a low tone, "do you know what the man said to the shovel? *Hit the dirt!*" And Andy pushed John, pushed John hard.

John went over backwards—flipped back over Tony Barnes, who had kneeled down behind him. John fell over backwards, legs flying up—flat onto his back on the ground. Andy and Tony and the other boys standing around howled their laughter.

For a moment John did not move. He wasn't hurt, just numb with surprise. The laughing made him flush with humiliation, and he started to get up. He put his hands down to raise himself—and his hands sank wrist-deep into mud. Then he felt dampness at his back.

He scrambled to his feet. He twisted his neck to look around, and felt of his back and his pants. He had fallen flat on his back into a muddy spot left by the sprinklers on the school lawn.

The stricken look on his face made the boys laugh all the harder. Blindly, John turned and swung his fist at Andy. But Andy, a head taller, merely caught his arm and pushed him again. Then the bell rang; recess was over, and everybody ran to enter the building.

Fighting back tears, John went to the boys' room, took off his jacket, and tried to wipe the mud off with paper towels. Presently he gave up; the coat was a mess; his slacks were a mess; he was a mess.

He went to the school office and asked permission to use the phone. Calling home, he said, "Mrs. Latham, I won't be home right after school. Tell Uncle Walter I can't go with him."

"Why not, John?" Mrs. Latham wanted to know; she sounded a bit shocked.

"I—got into a fight."

"I hate to write your father that you couldn't come to see him because you were kept after school for bad behavior," she said disapprovingly. "He's going to be terribly disappointed."

He said goodbye and hung up, biting his lip. Mrs. Latham provided a foster home for John. His mother was dead, and his father was a seaman on an oil tanker that got into San Francisco but two or three times a year. John's younger sisters, twins, were in a foster home in Redwood City. When their father made port, young Uncle Walter, who was unmarried, gathered them all up and rushed them to the city for dinner and a show or a ball game with their father. Tonight, they had planned to see the Giants play. The whole family would have been together. Now, John realized, he'd probably have to wait six months to see his father. . . .

The rest of that afternoon was wasted; he could not focus on studying. His thoughts seethed. That was such a dirty trick they had played on him! Any other day, it wouldn't have been so bad. But to dump him into the mud *today!* During the several weeks he had been at this school, he had got along well with everybody, except Andy, who had mostly ignored him.

Usually, John went straight home after school; Mrs. Latham believed a boy should have duties around a house, like mowing the lawn, sweeping the walks, and washing windows. But tonight John delayed, to make good his story that he had been kept after school.

Andy and Tony and Pete—biggest boys in the sixth grade—horsed around on the play equipment in the school yard, until finally a teacher shooed them homeward. John, having nothing else to do, followed them.

A new road was being constructed across the side of a hill near the school. Earth-moving equipment was parked there now; the workers had just quit for the day.

To the big boys, this equipment was a challenge. They climbed aboard the big dirt carry-all, the enormous roller, the big tamping machine that seemed studded with railroad spikes. John watched, frowning. They had been warned, at school, to stay off the big machines.

Andy, on the seat of the big tractor, twisted the steering wheel and shifted the gears, making a roaring sound with his mouth as he pretended he was taking an enormous Sherman tank across a battlefield, ramming enemy tanks, capsizing them, crushing them, as his main cannon blasted enemy pillboxes and his turret gunner knocked down enemy planes trying to strafe him.

He'd better not go off and leave the emergency brake loose, John thought. And when, finally, Andy jumped down and followed Tony and Pete on home, John climbed aboard the tractor. *Huh,* he snorted, *what a dope!* For Andy *had* left the brake loose. . . .

Reaching home, John mowed the lawn before entering the house for dinner. Mrs. Latham looked sharply at him but did not scold.

"Maybe your father'll put into San Francisco again soon, John," she said reassuringly.

He just nodded. But he could not sleep well, that night. Disappointment made him jittery and restless. When he did finally doze off, the heavy drumming of rain on the roof woke him. He felt headachy when he left for school.

In mid-morning, his teacher, Miss Allen, was called out of the room, and was gone for a long ten minutes.

When she returned, several people were with her—a policeman, a burly man carrying a construction worker's hard hat, and a fourth-grader named Mamie Anderson.

Miss Allen said to the class: "Boys and girls, as you know, you have been asked not to play on the road construction machinery making the new street south of the school. Yesterday, several of you disobeyed that rule. The result is that an accident has occurred. Luckily, nobody was hurt.

I say luckily, because somebody might easily have been killed. What happened was that a boy released the brake on the tractor parked on the hill, the tractor rolled during the night and left the road. Now tell me—did any of you boys release the brake on that tractor?"

She studied the group. The policeman and the construction worker eyed the pupils. Then Mamie Anderson turned to the policeman and whispered something to him.

Miss Allen continued: "The tractor started rolling down the roadway, went over the edge, and slid down the bank and turned over and slammed into a garage. The garage wall was caved in, and the side of a car parked inside was also caved in. If the tractor had rolled a little farther, it might have crashed into a bedroom of the house, in which people were sleeping. I'll ask you again—Which one of you boys played on that tractor after school yesterday?"

No one spoke up; each boy sat rigid. John finally glanced at Andy, thinking, *Serves him right. He's got it coming to him. I'm glad of it.* Andy was biting his lip and staring fixedly at his hands knotted together on the desk before him.

"Miss Allen," the policeman said then, "we know who the boy is. Mamie has recognized him. She doesn't know his name but she can point him out. I'm sorry to interrupt your classwork, but I have to take this boy down to Juvenile Hall."

The construction man added: "His parents are going to have to pay for the damage done. We've chased kids off those machines until we're tired of it. We've got to make an example now."

Miss Allen said: "Please don't blame the whole group for one boy's misbehavior." She looked at the class. "Whoever it is—I'd like him to come forward of his own free will."

Slowly Andy stood up. He looked sick, he was so scared.

John, unable to keep still, blurted out: "I know what really happened!"

Andy turned and looked at John. Everybody stared at John. And Miss Allen asked, "What do you mean, John?"

John swallowed hard, trying to sort out his racing thoughts. *Be quiet! Andy's got this coming to him. Why should you do anything to help a guy like him? . . . But Andy wasn't really to blame for the tractor accident.*

Swiftly, John thought how he could explain the accident to the policeman. Sure, Andy *had* played on that tractor. And Andy had let loose the tractor brake, and had shifted the gears, pretending he was driving the darn thing. And when he had jumped off the tractor, he had left the brake loose.

But I climbed onto the tractor after Andy left, and I set the brake. That's not all. I put the gear shift into reverse.

That tractor never could have rolled by itself—the rain had come down hard last night. The tractor was standing on the soft shoulder of the new road, right at the edge of a drop-off. The road had just been graded and the dirt was soft. The rain had loosened that dirt. No other way to figure it! What happened was that the edge of the road shoulder caved in, just washed away, and the tractor tipped off balance and then dropped down the slope. *I'll bet it never rolled forward at all*, John reasoned. *And there's a way to prove it!* Look at the brake. See if it's still tight. Better yet, look at the gear shift. If it's still in reverse, that'll be positive proof that the tractor never rolled forward. It just couldn't have! *I'll bet anything that gear's still in reverse!*

But after what Andy had done to him, why should he bother to help Andy? Why in the world should he even say a word to clear Andy of blame?

"John," Miss Allen repeated, "do you know anything about the accident?"

"Well, I—I did see Andy playing on that tractor," John said slowly, and hesitated.

"So? Is that all you've got to say?" Miss Allen pressed.

Just nod your head, John told himself. *That's all you've got to do....*

YOU'RE

NOT

INVITED

The problem:

The issue is the problem of controlling the urge to "get even" for being slighted; specifically, the problem is acquiring the judgment to weigh how vastly disproportionate taking revenge on someone for hurt feelings may become—and recognition that "getting even" can hurt both victim and perpetrator.

Introducing the problem:

> Say, "Sometimes somebody says or does something to you that hurts
> your feelings very deeply. It happens to all of us, and when it does, it is
> only human to want to get even. This is a story about such a happening.
> The story stops but is not finished. As I read, think of ways in which
> this story could end."

Alice was the only girl in the classroom not invited to Millie's party.
Alice kept hoping as days passed, sure that Millie meant to include her,
that the lack of an invitation was just an oversight. Actually, Alice was
not a close friend of Millie, but then, neither were half of the girls who
were invited.

Alice felt worst about being left out when Luella, her closest chum,
suggested that they go to the party together, and Alice had to say, "I'm
not going."

"But everybody's going!"

"I'm not."

"You mean," Luella gasped, "that you're not invited?"

Alice nodded and turned away, too choked up to answer.

But why, she kept asking herself. Why was she, of all the girls in
the class, the only one not included?

She could not hide her feelings from her mother. At dinner, the
day before the party, her mother asked her, "What's wrong, dear?"

"Oh, nothing really important, Mom. Millie Bailey's having a party
and didn't invite me."

Her mother's pretty face saddened.

"We're still new in this town, dear. Be patient."

Later, after Alice had gone to bed, she heard her father and mother
talking, low-voiced, in the dining room. The house was very quiet; her
parents did not realize that even their careful, soft-toned speech could
be heard by Alice.

"Maybe I'm wrong," her father was saying, "but Alice sure looked
down-in-the-mouth tonight."

"Yes, she's really low."

"Why?"

Her mother told about Millie's party, and ended, "The only reason
I can think of why Millie didn't invite Alice is me. I work as a waitress at
a drive-in, and I make slangy talk with the truck drivers. In this town,
that means you're dirt."

"So that's it," Alice's father said.

But my mother's a fine, decent person! Alice told herself, in outrage. They've got no right to think she isn't as good as they are!

Her father was saying, "Maybe you'd better quit your job."

But her mother said, "I can't, just yet. We couldn't carry the payments on the house and the hospital bills."

"Change to another kind of job."

"Nothing else I can do would pay as well, counting the tips. Besides, it makes me mad! I'm doing a decent job."

"A waitress in a highway cafe ranks pretty low on the social scale."

"But the Baileys, of all people. Putting on airs. Telling everybody that their boy is in the army overseas when he's in prison for drunk hit-and-run driving!"

"Ssh."

"Oh, nobody can hear us."

"We don't spread gossip."

"It's not gossip; it's a fact."

"We're not supposed to know it. You found out only because I'm in the Sheriff's office. If it got around, the Sheriff would guess that there had been a leak in his office."

"Just the same, I resent the whole thing! The Baileys have really got something to be ashamed of. We haven't."

"And they really are ashamed," Alice's father said thoughtfully. "They wouldn't have spread a lie around if they weren't terribly upset about their boy."

"That's right. It's a heartache."

Alice lay awake for a solid hour, thinking hard; and gradually, she saw a way she could get even.

They were such *nice* people, Millie Bailey's family! Her father was the manager of a big new chain store in the little town and her uncle was running for mayor. Really nice people. But their older son got drunk and caused a car accident, and ran away. Didn't stay to take his medicine and to see if he could help anybody he might have hurt. Just drove away; probably speeding, too. A fine character. But so stupid that the cops caught him, anyway; and now he was in prison somewhere. And the family were so ashamed they lied about it. Spread a story that he was in the army overseas. *That* was what would make people really disgusted with them. That they had lied about it. If they hadn't lied, but let the truth be known, people would've gossiped about it and enjoyed it in a way, but in the end they would have been sorry for the Baileys. But the Baileys had covered up, as if they were too good to have any black sheep troublemakers among them. Now people would sneer at them.

Alice saw just how to handle the news. She would tell the story to Joanie Lucas. Everybody called Joanie a blabbermouth. Joanie was always drawing you aside to give you a present of some big secret. She'd whisper the worst kind of gossip in your ear and beg you not to tell anybody ever—and then go and tell it herself to everybody she met. Telling her a confidence was really broadcasting.

Finally Alice fell asleep. For the first night in almost a week, she slept well.

After eating a good breakfast, next morning, she called Joanie Lucas. She asked Joanie if she'd go to the movie with her that night; it was Friday night.

"Movie?" Joanie said. "But aren't you going to Millie's party?"

"I should say I'm not," Alice answered. "Don't tell me that *you're* going."

"Sure I am. But why aren't you?" Joanie demanded.

"You mean you don't *know?*" Alice gasped.

"Don't know *what?*"

"It's the *awfulest* thing—" Alice said, lowering her voice to almost a whisper. "But, gosh, I don't *dare* tell you over the phone. Wait till I get to school."

"Gosh, *hurry!*" Joanie whispered back.

As she walked to school, Alice began to have some misgivings. If she knew Joanie, the broadcasting had already begun. Spreading this story about Millie Bailey's brother—wasn't it spreading gossip of the worst kind? But it's not just gossip; it's true! Yes, but wouldn't a lot of people be hurt? Millie, her parents, her brother . . . But haven't I been hurt by the way they're treating me? And they haven't any reason to treat me like this! And wasn't she broadcasting something she had *overheard?* She was being left out of a party, true; but she'd get over it, all right. But how about Millie's folks? They'd be so terribly ashamed. . . .

Joanie had already been talking. Alice realized that as soon as she reached the schoolyard, for Joanie and Millie and a knot of angry girls turned toward her as she approached.

"There!" Joanie said triumphantly. "Alice'll tell you! Alice, tell them why you're not going to Millie's party."

But Millie Bailey broke in furiously, "She's not coming to my party because I haven't invited her, that's why!"

"Even if you had, she wouldn't have come," Joanie retorted. "Tell them why, Alice!"

But then an interruption occurred: their teacher, Miss Carter, joined the group. She was stern of face.

"I overheard some of this talk," she said. "You girls know how I feel about spreading malicious gossip."

Joanie said: "But it's not just gossip. Is it, Alice? You said it was *awfully* important—"

But Miss Carter said very firmly, "Alice, you have evidently told Joanie something that is mean, spiteful, and probably untrue. I shall ask you first, to apologize to Millie. Then you are to stay after school to explain your behavior to me, and to give me a good reason why I should not report this whole incident to your mother."

"Tell her, Alice," Joanie urged. "Tell her!"

"Sure," Millie said scornfully, "go ahead, give your imagination a workout. Tell us, tell everybody."

But Alice stood taut, silent. Speak up? Here? Before everyone?

Miss Carter said, "I'm waiting, Alice, for your explanation or your apology."

Alice said:

MR.

EVEN

STEVEN

The problem:

> The issue is that of getting even. So often, all of us have a wild but very human impulse to get even with someone who has wronged us. This impulse can lead us into very destructive and unjust behavior.

Introducing the problem:

> Say, "Have you ever had somebody do something to you that was so inconsiderate, so mean, that you wanted to do something really awful to him by way of getting even? This story deals with such a problem. This story stops, but is not finished. As I read, I'd like you to try to think of ways in which you might end the story."

Bob's father was very angry with him.

"I thought you were a responsible kid. When I helped you make that go-cart, I was sure that you had the good sense to handle it properly."

"What did *I* do?" Bob demanded, surprised.

"You know what you did!"

Mr. Ames wasn't exactly shouting, but he was really upset and angry. Bob thought frantically. I haven't set fire to anything. I haven't broken any windows playing ball.

"I haven't done anything," he insisted again.

"Mr. Scanlon's new driveway?"

"What about old Scanlon's new driveway?"

"You drove right across it in your go-cart. Right after he got through smoothing fresh concrete."

"Oh, no!"

"You left tracks in that concrete four inches deep. He didn't discover it until the concrete had set. Now he has to rip out a big section and pour new concrete. He's so mad he's threatening to sue me."

"Dad, I didn't do that!"

"A neighbor saw you."

"*Nobody* saw me. Because I didn't do it."

"Mrs. Holzer saw you from her front porch."

Bob gasped. "She's a liar!"

"Bob!" His father never used that tone unless he was deeply aroused.

"But, Dad—"

"I've told Mr. Scanlon to have the driveway fixed. You'll pay for it. I get off work at two today. We'll go down to the bank and draw out your savings. If you haven't enough money to pay for the repair, you'll sell your go-cart to make up the difference. Meanwhile, don't use the go-cart at all."

And that was that. . . .

A little later, Bob looked at Scanlon's driveway; and as he looked, he wondered how in the world Mrs. Holzer had got the notion that she saw him running his go-cart across the fresh concrete. He had not done it. But someone had certainly left two deep ruts, just the width of the go-cart's wheels, across the width of the driveway. Mrs. Holzer had evidently seen it happen. But she was short-sighted. She wore glasses with lenses that looked half an inch thick.

"It wasn't me. She saw someone else do it," he realized.

But who? Who else in this neighborhood owned a go-cart? Then Bob remembered. Russ Adams had just got a brand-new one. From a store. He and his father had not bought parts and a lawnmower motor and assembled them, as Bob and his dad had done, working together long evenings for several months. Instead, Russ's father had paid a lot of money to buy him a go-cart ready-made and all set to go. Russ lived on the other side of this block. Maybe Russ, Bob reasoned, had been circling the block; he had come barreling down the sidewalk and without even slowing up had crossed old man Scanlon's new driveway. Scanlon was a chintzy guy. He probably had a box standing in the middle of the walk with a penciled sign saying *Keep Off*. He was a bossy old coot who was used to giving orders without bothering to explain. So, naturally, if Russ had noticed the sign at all, he had merely glanced around to see if Scanlon was watching—and not seeing him, had rolled right on across the driveway. Then, discovering that the concrete was soft and he had rutted it, Russ had probably raced away as fast as his go-cart could roll.

"'Course, maybe it wasn't Russ at all," Bob reflected. "But then, who else *could* it have been?"

Worrying, he walked around the block to Russ's house and turned down the driveway.

Sure enough, Russ was in the garage, tinkering with a new Hurri-Kart. Oh, oh, Bob thought—maybe his wheels'll show fresh concrete on them.

Russ's dog, Trigger, came up to him and nuzzled his hand with a big wet nose. Trigger was a large Boxer, thick of chest and powerful, but very good-natured with people.

"Hi, Russ," Bob said. "Hey, that's a swell-looking wagon."

"Uh-huh." Russ did not seem especially pleased to see him.

"Russ, did you drive this thing across old man Scanlon's fresh-laid driveway?"

"His what?"

"He just had concrete poured for his driveway. Did you drive this go-cart across it?"

"Heck, no!"

He said it loudly, nervously, and did not look Bob in the face as he spoke.

Bob examined the go-cart's wheels for specks of clinging concrete. The wheels and tires, however, were spotless; so shiningly spotless, so free even of dust, that they glistened.

"You just *washed* this thing?"

"So I washed it! What's it to you?"

"Look. Old Lady Holzer saw a kid drive a go-cart across Scanlon's driveway. She thought it was me, and told Scanlon. He told my father. They both think I did it, and I've got to pay for having it fixed. But I didn't do it. Did you?"

"No!"

"You're a liar."

"I tell you I didn't!"

Russ was almost crying, and was scared; but Bob was positive that he was lying.

"I've told you," Bob said, "that I'll have to pay for it if you don't own up that you did it."

"Get out of here. Go on, get off this property!"

Bob looked at him, realized argument was useless, and turned and left. Trigger followed him.

"Go on back," Bob angrily told him, but the big Boxer just licked his hand and trotted comfortably on ahead, settling into a steady zigzagging walk down the street. The husky dog was so sociable that he went for a walk with almost anybody who passed the place.

Moodily, as Bob started home he wondered what to do.

Russ was afraid to tell the truth. Probably his old man had not really wanted to give Russ a go-cart, and had agreed to it only after Russ had begged and begged; but he had probably warned Russ—You get into trouble with that thing *just once*, and I'll sell it! So Russ was scared.

He stopped. He was passing the big Dorfmyer place. Mr. Dorfmyer raised chickens. Often, after mowing his huge lawn, he would open the chicken runs and let the white Plymouth Rocks out to wander over the grass to feed on the freshly mowed greens. The trim white chickens were now scattered all over the wide yard, clucking contentedly, their heads nodding down in a stitching motion as they pecked at the ground.

Bob looked across the street at Trigger, who was looking through a fence bemusedly at a small but frisky terrier who felt safe enough, with the fence between them, to growl threats at him. Trigger, though so nice to people, was a chicken-killer. In fact, Russ's father had brought him in from their little ranch because Trigger had made enemies for him among his neighbors. Here in town few people still raised chickens; but Mr. Dorfmyer was one of them, and he and Russ's father had already had a run-in over Trigger. The Boxer had already had a taste of Dorfmyer pullets. Mr. Dorfmyer had made threats, and Russ's father had made threats right back. But Russ's father *had* warned Russ to keep Trigger out of trouble, or Trigger would be sent to the pound.

Bob saw his chance. Russ liked Trigger. Liked him a lot. And Russ was so afraid of his old man that getting into trouble with him would be a real punishment.

Bob called, "Here, Trigger!"

Obediently the big Boxer trotted across the street and came to him. Then Trigger sighted the chickens through the fence, and stuck his blunt muzzle between the upright pickets and whined with eagerness, drooling.

Bob looked around warily. He saw no one close by on the quiet street. All he had to do was open the gate and say, "Go get 'em, Trigger!" And then the feathers would really fly! The chickens would squawk like crazy; neighbors would pop out of houses all around; Old Man Dorfmyer would run outside, and shake his fists and screech at Trigger, and maybe rush back inside and come out with a shotgun, or go to the telephone and yell for the police, and then he'd phone Russ's father and swear and say he'd get his lawyer busy and sue for thousands of dollars, and Russ's father would say he could sue his head off; but when Russ's father got home, then Russ would really be in hot water.

That's what Russ is doing to *me!* Making my father raise Cain with me. Letting me pay for the damage he's done. So okay! Now he'll get a taste of his own medicine. He's got it coming to him!"

Bob took a step to the gate. Trigger followed, pawed at the gate, whining with eagerness. All Bob had to do was open it, and say, "Get 'em, Trigger!"

Bob heard a long-drawn distant whistle: wheet, wheet, whe-ooo!

It was the clear long note that his mother whistled when she wanted him or his brother to come home. It meant, Bob realized, that his father was home, waiting to take him to the bank to draw out his money to pay for having Mr. Scanlon's driveway fixed. He had to hurry home.

But it would take just a second to open the gate, to give Trigger a push, and run—

Personal Integrity: The Individual Versus the Group

Often a young person faces a most difficult kind of choice: whether to cooperate in a decision of his group or to resist it.

It is very hard to say no to one's friends. Yet it is vitally important for an individual to have the courage to say no to his cronies when, in his best judgment, no should be his answer. On this base rest responsibility and self-respect; without this integrity, it is impossible to function as a conscientious citizen.

But saying no *does* take courage. For anyone to stand against the desires of his close friends, especially when the group expresses its desires in concert, requires an unusual degree of conviction and hardihood. Among children, such dissent is all too often rewarded with abuse and rejection.

When *should* an individual cooperate with his group? When is cooperation just abject surrender? When is refusal to cooperate an act of unworthy self-indulgence—and when is it an act of courage and wisdom? The answer varies with each instance, of course; according to the special circumstances of each case; deciding upon that answer requires a serious and insightful evaluation of the issues involved.

It is all too human for the individual to stifle his qualms and go along with the crowd. A group of boys may be planning a prank that, in the judgment of one member, may do someone serious injury. This member may even voice an objection, but the group is enthusiastic, and his objection is raucously pooh-poohed. He foresees that if he persists in saying no, he will be jeered at and told to go home to his mother. Similarly, a group of young girls may be mistreating a newcomer by ignoring or ridiculing her; one member of the group, out of sympathy for the newcomer, may want to charge her friends with callous bad manners. Again, this inwardly dissenting individual will, too often, stifle her good impulse for fear that she, in turn, may be made to suffer by the group.

Of course, on occasion just the opposite kind of dilemma confronts the individual: he wants something, wants something with an overwhelming wholeheartedness, but his group asks that he participate in a venture which makes it impossible for him to realize his own goal. His desire may be utterly selfish; the group project may be a good one, perhaps idealistic and truly worthwhile. Too often, the individual may give lip service to the group project, but actually sabotage it out of sheer inability to relinquish his own cherished purpose.

Young people need help in acquiring the good judgment to evaluate the alternatives of such dilemmas: to decide which course is the more ethical and humane. Young people need help to acquire the courage to make a choice and to stand by it in spite of abuse or disappointment. Young people need help to acquire the inner stability and security to weather such emotional storms without crippling damage to their self-esteem.

The group, too, should be imagined as an entity that also needs guidance in learning to accept and support the dissenting individual. Perhaps, in the last analysis, individual integrity cannot exist without group responsibility for understanding and respecting the member who says no to its yes.

To reach such levels of social maturity as are implied by the terms *personal integrity* and *group responsibility*, groups need many opportunities to face up to and cope with crucial issues.

Some types of individual-versus-group choices can be roughly described as dilemmas in which:

1. The individual has a worthwhile personal goal, but the group has a frivolous purpose.
   If the individual cooperates with the group, he will lose his own serious goal (for example, see the story entitled "Sacrifice Hit").

2. The group has a serious and worthy purpose, but the individual has a self-indulgent goal.
   If he cooperates with the group, he will fail to gain his selfish goal. (See the story "Shutter-Bug.")
3. Both the individual and the group have serious, worthwhile goals, but they are in conflict; if the individual persists in resisting the group decision in order to gain his own purpose, the group goal will not be achieved, and vice versa.
4. The group may be planning some action which may possibly cause serious hurt to someone. The individual wishes to prevent this happening, but if he objects or interferes, he may be rejected by the group. (For examples, see the stories entitled "The Menace in the Tree," and "The Junior Cavemen.")

Can a general rule be laid down to guide the individual and the group in making choices between such conflicting personal and group issues? Perhaps it is valid to say this: that the more worthwhile purpose should be honored. It is not always easy, however, to decide which is the more worthwhile purpose. Sensitive judgment is required, and must be cultivated. Practice can be of help in acquiring such judgment, or at least in setting precedents that can be of help in coping with difficult value choices.

To elaborate: young people can be helped to learn to deal with crises of decision making by living through such dilemmas at a remove: by *practice* in confronting choice-demanding situations, by practice in defining the issues and alternatives involved, by practice in foreseeing the consequences of their choices, by practice in recognizing their own emotions, by practice in making decisions that they can live with afterward with self-respect. Practice in making decisions with-or-against the group can help young people to build the confidence and inner security that will enable them to be more ethical and humane in their choices.

The responsibility of the group to understand, respect, and support the dissenter is, of course, a vital necessity. How can it be achieved? Part of the answer may lie in this fact: that the group which *makes an active effort* to understand the emotional crisis of the dissenter in its midst, even in an imaginary situation, acquires some degree of empathy for the dissenter; that, as each individual in a group experiences a dissenter's role, he is sensitized to it and made sympathetic. It may well be that the group which practices solving dilemmas of the individual-versus-the-group will increasingly acquire the maturity that provides it with the empathy and wisdom to respect and support differences of perception and purpose.

DEEP

SNOW

The problem:

The issue is that of conflicting demands of peer group and adults in authority. The peer code says that you must not tattle, must not report a playmate to people in authority. Adults, confusingly to children, pay tribute to this concept of loyalty to one's fellows; and yet, people in authority demand that youngsters be sensible enough to report activities of their age-mates that may result in serious consequences. Knowing when not to tattle is sometimes too difficult a matter of discrimination for young people. Often it is not possible to foresee when mischief can become serious misbehavior.

Introducing the problem:

Ask the group, "Have you ever seen someone you know doing something that is silly, or wrong, or dangerous that you thought ought to be reported—and yet, felt that you could not go running to grownups to tattle on your friends? This is a story about such a problem. This is an unfinished story: it stops before the ending. As I read, I'd like you to think of ways in which you would finish the story."

Eddie Adams was furious as he hurried into the camp director's office.

Mr. Lorton grinned at him. "A dormitory on fire? Or is there a bear in camp?"

Eddie flushed. He was a well-mannered boy ordinarily.

"Sorry to come rushing in, but Toby Enright stole a box of candy my mother sent me!"

"Easy, boy. The box is probably just misplaced."

"No, sir! I hid it in my bunk and now it's gone."

"You've searched carefully?"

"You bet I have! Toby s-stole it. I know he did."

"Have you actually seen the candy in Toby's possession?"

"No, but he was the only boy I told about getting the candy. So he's got to be the one who took it!"

"Let's go ask Toby."

They left the office and took the path through a half-foot fall of snow toward the dormitory cabin in which Eddie and Toby Enright were assigned. Camp Conifer was a camp in the Sierras which was operated by the public school system of a coast city. Every fifth- and sixth-grade child in the city got the chance of a turn at a two-weeks stay in Conifer. The camp was open not just in summer but all year round, to give the youngsters a taste of mountain life in every kind of weather.

Entering, Eddie and Mr. Lorton found Toby alone, lying on his cot and reading a book. Toby was a few months older than Eddie, taller and heavier, and much quicker with a laugh and a smart retort than Eddie.

"Toby," Mr. Lorton began, "Eddie tells me that somebody took a box of candy from his bunk. Do you know anything about it?"

"He told me he'd got it in the mail. That's all I know."

"You stole it!" Eddie burst out.

"Like heck I did."

"You went to my bunk while I was out at breakfast and took it!"

"I didn't, and I can prove it, Don," Toby said to the counselor. "Eddie says he got that candy in the mail just before breakfast. Well, I left camp before breakfast! Ned Eby and I hiked up to the lookout tower and stayed there until just a little while ago. You can ask Ned. So I was gone from camp when Eddie's candy was stolen!"

"That seems to settle the matter." Mr. Lorton's gaze became stern as he looked at Eddie. "Come back to the office with me, Eddie."

As they left, Toby shot Eddie a look of triumph. . . .

Back in the office, Mr. Lorton said, "Eddie, what've you got against Toby?"

"Something he did. My Dad gave my little brother Danny a cocker spaniel pup. Toby came over and played with the puppy. I had to go to the store, so I put the puppy back in the yard and shut the gate. After I left, Toby opened the gate and the puppy got out into the street and a bus ran over him. My Dad asked Toby if he had let the puppy out of the yard, and Toby said he didn't. But Mike Chartok from 'cross the street *saw* Toby do it! But my Dad blamed me. I had to save my Saturday show money all summer to buy Danny another puppy."

"So you've got a grudge against Toby."

"But Toby did steal my—"

"You dislike him, and you want to get even with him. You were just too ready to jump to conclusions that he stole your candy."

"But he did!"

"He couldn't have. The fact is, you haven't one item of proof. You haven't anything but a grudge. I don't like tattle-tales. I think a person who carries tales," Mr. Lorton went on, "is pretty low and mean. Eddie, I want you to learn a lesson, so I'm going to punish you. You will not attend any evening movies while you're here. After supper, every evening, you will go straight to your cabin."

Eddie said, "Yes, sir," and walked out, his lips pressed tight to keep back sobs of humiliation.

The supper bell rang. Toby was going out as Eddie entered their cabin. Toby whispered "Sucker!" But as Eddie whirled toward him, in fury, Toby ran on toward the mess hall. Eddie flopped down on his cot, his stomach a cold sick knot inside him.

Toby had lied. Eddie was positive of that. But he had no proof.

He did not go out for supper. After a while he undressed, and crawled into his blankets, and fell asleep.

Don Lorton had been teaching the sixth-graders to ski. Some of the youngsters had learned before coming to Camp Conifer. The counselor had promised to take the five most capable skiers together on an overnight trip to Clouds Rest with a snow-surveying crew. Eddie was among those five, and so was Toby Enright.

At five next morning, they had an early breakfast; and then the boys gathered out in front of the office, all five wearing ski pants and windbreakers and stocking caps and carrying their skis.

The snow-mobile was already waiting for them. It was a sort of truck that ran on caterpillar treads. It had an enclosed and heated cabin in which the driver and the two men of the snow survey crew were riding. Behind the snow-mobile was a freight sled.

Mr. Lorton introduced the boys to two snow surveyors, lanky Mr. Craig and short, thick-set Mr. McGaa, who were hydro-engineers for the county water department. Mr. Lorton explained that the surveyors made this trip up into the Sierra once every month during the winter to measure the amount of snow on the ground. Then Mr. Lorton and the boys clambered aboard the freight sled.

They started off, the snow-mobile roaring like a tractor but traveling, in spite of its bulk, surprisingly fast on level snow. It was cold, but the boys huddled down into a pile of tarpaulins on the freight shed and were comfortable.

The snow-mobile clattered some twenty miles across Squaw Basin. At Goose Creek it slackened pace, dipped down onto the ice, then lurched up on to the opposite side and tore on through a patch of brush to the base of Granite Ridge.

Here the snow-mobile stopped. Everyone got off and strapped on his skis. Mr. McGaa, the older surveyor, led off up a narrow trail to the plateau above. The others followed Mr. McGaa in a single file. The counselor took his place at the middle of the line, to be close to help Neil and Dick and Pete, should any of them need it. Because Eddie and Toby were the most skillful, Mr. Lorton let them come along right behind at the end of the file.

Eddie's father had had a photography shop in Yosemite Valley until Eddie was nine, and Eddie had been able to ski from the time he was seven. Toby's father had taught him to ski on trips to Lake Arrowhead in wintertime.

Toby came last in line, behind Eddie; and Eddie felt that this was a chance for mischief that Toby would never pass up.

The trail zigzagged up the slope of Granite Ridge and was so gradual that no one had trouble making progress. Mr. Lorton watched the boys carefully and when they were panting for breath, he called on Mr. McGaa and the long file paused for a brief rest.

On up the party shuffled, pushing back on their ski poles, and "herringboning" where the going was steepest.

They reached the top of the ridge presently, coming out on a level plateau. Before them lay a high mountain meadow on which grew scattered clumps of fir and pine. No path or roadway was visible upon the dazzling unbroken snow, but Mr. McGaa confidently led the way due eastward and the party strung out after him.

It was a brilliant day and the snow and mountain ramparts glistened sharply in the clear cold air. The exertion of moving along kept Eddie warm, and he felt excited and happy—until the snow ball hit the back of his neck.

Anger fired up in him. He had an impulse to whirl and to pounce on Toby. But he knew that a fight would upset Mr. Lorton very much. So Eddie did not even turn his head, just kept going.

"Hey, Eddie!" Toby called in a jeering whisper. "What makes your ears so red?"

Mr. McGaa led the way toward a marker sticking up out of the snow. It was an iron pipe with square metal sign on top which read "Granite Meadows, #1."

"This is the first 'snow course' on our route today," Mr. McGaa explained. "We'll take our first snow samples here."

He and Mr. Craig took the canvas packs off their backs. From his pack Craig took out 30-inch lengths of Duraluminum pipe. These sections he screwed together until he had a single pipe taller than he was. This "sampler" was open at both ends but had a cutting head on the bottom, and in the sides were narrow slits which had markings beside them.

Meanwhile Mr. McGaa had taken a weighing machine from his haversack. A Mt. Rose Balance he called it. He hung the balance by a thong over the handle of a ski pole. Craig placed the empty sampling tube on the "cradle" of the balance, swung it carefully to point into the wind, and noted the weight.

Then Mr. McGaa took the sampling tube, straightened it up, and drove it into the snow, turning it in his hands as it went down so that the teeth of the cutting edge at the bottom would bite a way through the hard-packed ice layers. The boys watched, surprised at how far down he pushed the shining tube. All the way to the ground beneath the snow he drove the sampler. Then he lifted it out.

He looked at the slots in the side of the tube and read off, "seventy-three inches" to Mr. Craig, who wrote the figure on a pad he carried. Next, they weighed the tube on the balance again. From this weight they subtracted the weight of the empty tube, and Mr. Craig said, "Forty ounces."

Mr. Lorton explained, "Boys, the snow here is seventy-three inches deep. But when this snow melts, it'll melt into forty inches of water. Every ounce of snow inside that tube will melt down into an inch of water."

The two snow surveyors moved on, then. Every fifty feet along a straight line from this marker toward the next one, a thousand feet away, they took another "core" from the snow field. Finally the party stopped in a clump of tall, snow-laden firs for a rest and to eat a sandwich.

While they ate, Mr. Lorton told the boys: "From the information that Mr. McGaa and other crews gather in the mountains, agencies like the Weather Bureau and the Department of Agriculture learn how much water will melt from the snow in the coming spring. Do you see how this information can help farmers?"

A boy said, "Yes, farmers can tell whether there's going to be floods or low water in the spring."

"Exactly! Farmers can...."

Eddie didn't hear the rest, for the sky fell on him, or so it seemed. He'd been standing under a tree. He heard a swishing thud—and then snow crashed down upon him, blinding him, covering him, burying him. He yelled in fright and threshed wildly with his arms to dig out of the cold, smothering cloud that blotted out all light about him.

"We'll get you out, Eddie!"

Hands dug the enveloping snow away. He was pulled out from under the tree and lifted to his feet.

"That tree dropped its load of snow on you, Eddie. How do you feel? Hurt anywhere?" Mr. Lorton asked him.

"I'm all right," Eddie gasped.

"Sure you are!" Mr. Craig said. "Golly, trees've dumped their snow on me a dozen times." He grinned at Eddie.

But Eddie was looking at Toby. Eddie was realizing that Toby was choking back laughter. And Eddie suspected what had happened: Toby had been molding a hard snow ball when Eddie had been watching him. Toby had pitched that snowball into the tree, and the slight jar had been enough to cause the heavy load of snow to fall upon whomever was below. Eddie felt sure that this was what had happened. But he said not a word. . . .

Following the two snow surveyors, the boys crossed Granite Meadows and climbed up onto another lofty flat, Clouds Rest. The surveyors sampled two more snow courses. And by the time they finished, it was late afternoon.

"We're almost to the cabin, now," Mr. McGaa said. "I bet you boys don't want to sleep out in the snow tonight, huh?"

"Gosh, no!" Pete said.

"We aren't wolves," Toby added.

"Don't worry. We'll sleep snug under a roof."

But the boys did worry as they followed the surveyors toward the foot of an anvil-shaped ridge shouldering up out of Cloud Rest Meadows. For the boys saw no cabin.

"Well, here we are," McGaa said suddenly, and stopped.

Eddie looked around, puzzled. Everybody else was looking around, just as flabbergasted as he was. They were near the foot of the hogback. But they saw no cabin and no sign of any cabin.

"These little shrubs sticking up out of the snow," Mr. McGaa said, "aren't just bushes. They're the tops of trees."

He was studying those "bushes." He turned toward one which held a flat black object. The object was a shovel wired to the branches. He freed the shovel, then carefully faced west and measured twenty feet, and started digging.

Two feet down in the snow, he hit something. He took a bunch of keys from his pocket, selected one, and bent down. The boys, crowding around the hole, saw him unlock and lift a wooden trap door.

"We call this a 'Santa Claus chimney'," he said. "All right, everybody follow me, one at a time."

Eddie, when it came his turn, lowered himself into the hole, onto the top rungs of a ladder that led straight down through a wooden passageway. A black stove-pipe lifted inside this passage. Carefully Eddie climbed down twenty ladder rungs. He found himself, with the other boys, inside a spacious log cabin. A coal oil lamp had been lit. Mr. McGaa was starting a fire in a stove. Mr. Craig had unlocked a frost-proof cupboard in the floor and was taking out cans of food. Along the walls were four bunks on which blankets and sleeping bags were neatly arranged. Mr. Mc-Gaa looked around at the staring boys, and laughed.

"I told you we'd sleep snug tonight!"

Soon after supper everybody started yawning. It had been a rugged day. The boys drew lots for the bunks. Eddie and Toby won a bunk. The men and Pete spread sleeping bags on the floor.

Eddie stretched out in his bunk and instantly dropped off to sleep. He woke with a start. Don Lorton was shaking him. "Get up. It's morning and we're leaving."

They had breakfast. Then, one by one, the party climbed up through the Santa Claus chimney, out into the dazzling sunlight on the snow above. Mr. Craig and Mr. McGaa said goodbye, and started northward on their skis to the next snow course.

Mr. Lorton led the boys west, on their backtrail, homeward bound. Everyone felt good. The air was so crisp and clear, the sun so bright, and the view of the valley and range had a clean, exciting loveliness. The party made good time. Without trouble of any sort they reached the brink of the steep face of Granite Ridge.

The path left yesterday by their skis marked the zigzags of the trail switching down the high slope of snow. Mr. Lorton started down at a careful pace; and the five boys, strung out in a long line, followed behind him.

"Hey, Eddie!" Toby called from behind, low-voiced. "Let's make a snowball and roll it down. It'll get bigger and bigger and when it rolls down on Dick and Neil, it'll make 'em jump!"

"Oh, gosh, no!" Eddie protested.

He looked around. Toby had paused and was packing snow into a big ball. Up here, on a zig of the trail, they were almost directly above Mr. Lorton and the two leading boys on a zag of the pathway below.

"Don't do it, Toby," Eddie insisted. "Mr. Lorton's told us, 'No tricks when hiking in the mountains. Snow is dangerous.' "

"Ah, you're just chicken. Even if I hit 'em with this soft snow, it wouldn't hurt 'em!"

Eddie reached out with a ski pole and smashed the big snowball. Toby glared at him in outrage.

"What'd you do that for, doggonit!"

"You can't tell about snow. Something might happen."

"I ought to pop you good!"

Eddie just turned away. He felt a prickly crawling at the back of his neck. He expected Toby to jump him or to hit him in the back. But nothing happened.

That is, nothing happened to him.

The file of boys zigzagged down the mountainside behind Mr. Lorton following the switchbacks of the trail. And presently again Eddie and Toby were directly above the leaders below.

Eddie, from the corner of his eye, saw something move past him, off to one side. He whirled. It was a snowball rolling down-hill. A big globe of snow that had started above him—where Toby stood watching and grinning now. The ball was rolling swiftly down, wrapping snow about itself like a thick bandage as it turned, leaving a trough behind. Already the ball was a thick wheel, two feet in diameter and getting fatter, taller, every instant. By the time it reached Neil and Dick and Pete and Mr. Lorton below it would be big enough to knock a boy down and bury him!

Eddie stood petrified, breath chocked back, watching. He tried to shout, in warning, but his throat seemed locked and he got out only a hoarse gasp. He tried again, crying shrilly, "Look out!"

But already it was too late. It was too late for the counselor and the boys to jump aside, too late for them to do anything, even if they had been warned, even if they had been alertly watching.

For the whole side of the mountain now was moving, falling, sliding, plunging away toward the ridge bottom.

A snow slide! The weight and movement of that big, thickening snowball had been enough to jar a wedge of the unstable snowpack into slipping down hill. Eddie himself was safe, and behind him Toby was safe; but below them, that rushing slide was widening, growing in depth and breadth as it hurtled down upon Mr. Lorton and the other boys. Already in its swift descent the avalanche was flinging up a shockwave of icy spray in the air, and noise of its passage over the rock was a rumbling roar.

Mr. Lorton heard it. He whirled to look up at the slide, and then he was waving his arms and shouting to the boys. It blotted them from view in the uprush of icy spray at its front. It swept them on down-slope. It plunged onto the foot of the ridge with a shock that came through the granite to Eddie's feet.

For a long instant he stood where he was, straining to see into the cloud of snow dust that hid the scene below.

He jerked his head around. Toby had not moved either. Toby was staring down, his mouth open, his eyes sick and stunned.

"I told you not to do it!" Eddie raged at him. "Now you've killed them all!"

And Eddie started recklessly down the mountain side.

The snow dust was blown away by the wind. At first Eddie saw no human movement as he neared the bottom of the slope. Then he noticed arms threshing in the snow. Mr. Lorton was digging himself out of the drift. Mr. Lorton was unhurt!

Eddie called to him and Mr. Lorton turned and saw him and beckoned for him to come. Then the counselor lunged, wallowing deep in the soft snow, toward a spot a dozen feet away and started digging with half of one of his broken skis.

Eddie reached him and Toby came up. "Dig!" Mr. Lorton commanded. "I think Neil's down here."

They heard Neil then, and it sounded as if he were trying to shout and cry with fright at the same time. Then Toby yelled and pointed off to the left. There an arm was sticking up out of the snow—stiff and unmoving.

"Get him out! I'll take care of Neil!" Mr. Lorton ordered.

Eddie, Toby helping him, dug Pete out. While they were working they heard Dick calling. He had cleared snow away from over his head. So Dick and Neil were at least alive, Eddie thought; but Pete, as they lifted his still body out of the snow, was heavy and limp in their arms giving no sign of life.

"He's dead!" Eddie gasped.

Pete wasn't dead. He had been knocked senseless as the churning snow swept him downhill. Mr. Lorton felt his wrist, then said to stretch him out comfortably. Presently Pete sat up and shook his head and looked around. His wits were hazy with shock.

"How do you feel, Pete?" Eddie asked him anxiously.

"Like I'd been through a concrete mixer."

"We're all of us pretty well shaken up and bruised," the counselor said. "But so far there doesn't seem to be anybody with broken bones or internal injuries. We're lucky. We might," Mr. Lorton said, looking sternly at Eddie and Toby, "have been killed. Do either of you boys," he asked, "know what caused that snow slide?"

Eddie didn't speak, just looked down at his feet. He felt his face turning red and hot. As if he were guilty! . . . Toby sort of sighed and said, "Gosh, we—were just moving along, and then—it happened."

Toby was covering up. Toby was lying out of it!

Eddie bit his lip. He wasn't going to say a word. He wasn't going to get bawled out and punished again for being a tattle-tale!

Mr. Lorton said, "Boys, this is a very serious thing. I want the whole truth. Did you two start this snow slide down onto us? Eddie, I'm asking you a serious question. Answer me!"

THE
MENACE
IN
THE
TREE

The problem:

The issue is that of conflict in group–individual relations: Should the individual surrender to group will against his own inclinations and sense of right? In this story a group of three boys are playing a prank. Jimmy wants to call a halt when it seems to him that their victim is someone who may be hurt by their mischief; the other boys insist on going through with their prank.

Introducing the problem:

Ask, "Have you ever been with a bunch of friends who wanted to do something reckless that you did not really want to have a part in, and you were too afraid of being called "chicken" to make objections? Perhaps your friends' plan wasn't reckless but just wasn't sensible, and they all seemed to want to go ahead with it—and you didn't want to be the only person who wasn't cooperating. This story deals with such a problem. The story stops but isn't finished. As I read the story, try to think of ways in which the story should end."

The three boys crouched in the dark shrubbery at the back of the garden. They had been waiting, tense and eager, for long minutes.

Jimmy, keenest of hearing, heard footsteps on the sidewalk.

Jabbing Pete, he whispered, "Somebody's coming!"

"Sounds like two or three people!"

"Okay, okay. I'm ready."

The tree-lined street was dimly lit by a street lamp, blue in the distance. Few cars passed on the quiet residential avenue. An occasional couple or group of boys and girls, returning from an early movie, had sauntered past at intervals. It was for such a group that the three boys waited.

Here, hidden in the bushes a hundred feet from the sidewalk, they felt safe from discovery and pursuit. Pete held a ball of kite string. Tom crouched beside him, and Jimmy kneeled behind them.

The kite string, invisible in the darkness, stretched at a long slant to the middle of an elm tree that loomed over the sidewalk, bent over a bough, and hung straight down, suspending a bag of waxed paper containing water.

When somebody passed beneath the tree, Pete would let go of slack in the string: the bag of water would drop. It would startle the passerby. He would think something was up in the tree and making an attack on him and he would jump, and blurt out in surprise. If the passerby were a woman, she would utter a shriek; if a bunch of giggly girls, they would scream and chatter like crazy. If the bag hit somebody on the head and split, that somebody would think a miniature cloudburst had used him for a target. If the victim happened to be a big, husky man—well, no telling what might happen.

"He's getting close," Tom whispered.

"They. Two men."

"Oh, boy! We'll have to run."

The two men, talking earnestly, were walking at a brisk pace and drawing quickly nearer.

Jimmy felt a dart of fear. Two men. If they got mad, they'd be good and mad.

"They'll chase us."

"For gosh sake, stop shivering!"

"Don't be so chicken."

Closer the men came, almost to the tree—

"Now!" Tom whispered.

Pete let go the coils of slack in the string.

The bag of water dropped until the string was tight.

"Hey!"

"What's that?"

The two men had jumped back and stood tense now, peering up into the darkness of the foliage above their heads.

"Just a bird, prob'bly."

"Maybe a cat."

They moved closer, straining to see among the branches.

Pete carefully pulled the kite string, drawing the bag up into the darkness of the leaves.

One of the men—the younger one—strode decisively to the tree trunk and started climbing up.

"Careful, Jack. If it's a cat, it might claw you," the other man warned.

"Might be a raccoon. I'd like to catch it."

Hearing this, Pete chuckled. Tom choked back a laugh, but Jimmy was too nervous to think it funny.

He whispered, "Maybe they'll see the string."

"Too dark," Pete said confidently.

And he was right.

"Come on down, Jack," the older man said. "I want to get home."

The young man delayed a bit, straining to see among the leaves, then gave up. He climbed down, rubbed his hands together, and brushed off his clothes.

"Whatever it was, it isn't moving now."

"Maybe just a branch fell. Let's go."

The two men left, walking on down the street.

Jimmy finally let out a long breath of relief, but Tom and Pete were somewhat disappointed.

"Pete, we're not letting the bag fall down far enough."

"I'll let out more slack."

"But it'll hit somebody smack on the head," Jimmy pointed out.

"Sure. That's the idea. Hey, here comes somebody."

"Sounds like two people again."

"No—just one."

It sounded like more than one, Jimmy realized, because this person was using a cane and tapping along at a slow shuffle.

"Somebody old," he whispered.

"Maybe it's Old Lady Corbin," Pete said.

"Good!" Tom added.

But Jimmy stirred uncomfortably. Old Lady Corbin was a mean old witch, sure. If you passed her house on roller skates, she came out and screamed that you were making too much noise. If you batted a ball into her fenced yard, it was goodbye ball; if you climbed over her fence to get it, she'd yell murder and phone your parents to complain that you had trampled her flower beds; then she'd come hunting for the ball and if she found it, she'd keep it.

But she was real old. She was using a cane because she had had a fall and broken a hip that had never mended right. She had a weak heart; Jimmy's mother had said she'd pop off one day in one of her rages.

Suppose, now, when the bag dropped down over her head from the tree, she got such a fright that she jumped back and fell down and broke her hip again. Or suppose she got so mad she screamed and tore around more than was good for her!

"You ready, Pete?" Tom whispered. "She's almost—"

"But maybe that's Old Lady Corbin," Jimmy blurted.

"Nobody ever saw her out at night," Tom said, "except on her broom, maybe—"

"But maybe it is," Jimmy insisted.

"You chicken or something?" Pete snorted. "If you don't like what we're doing, beat it on home."

Jimmy gulped. What should he do? He could warn her—he could yell to the old lady to watch out. Or he could grab hold of the kite string and prevent the bag from falling. But if he did, Tom and Pete would despise him. They'd tell him to stay away from them: to go on home and play with dolls. But if they *did* drop the bag and the crippled woman *was* Old Lady Corbin—

"Pete—"

"Shh! She's almost there!" Tom said.

And Pete said, "Right . . . on . . . target!"

He could grab the string, Jimmy realized. He could stop the prank. But if he did . . .

THE
JUNIOR
CAVEMEN

The problem:

   The issue is that of cooperating with the group, or standing against it. In this instance, the group is behaving badly, but to stand against the group would mean rejection. A bunch of boys are out on a hike and are playing pranks on an unpopular member. The pranks are becoming progressively crueler and one boy is outraged. But if he protests and resists, the group may reject him, and he is a newcomer who wants very much to have a secure place with these boys.

Introducing the problem:

Ask the class, "Have any of you ever been with a bunch of boys or girls who kept picking on you, making you the fall guy for a lot of jokes that were funny to them, perhaps, but very unpleasant to you? Or, have you ever been with a bunch who were so busy picking on one person that they were making life miserable for him? Maybe you wished, at the time, that you could stop it, but you didn't know how. This story deals with such a problem. The story stops before it s finished. While I am reading, try to think of ways in which you would end the story."

When Ben walked into the house, his mother looked at him and realized at once that he was feeling happy.

"Who gave you a million dollars?" she asked.

He stared at her.

"What million dollars?"

"You're feeling good, aren't you?"

"Uh-huh."

"Why?"

"Oh, nothing much— Going on a hike."

"Okay, give. When, where, who with?"

"Giant City Game Refuge—all day Saturday."

"And who with?"

"Ted Dolan and his friends."

"Ted's the boy who's such a good soft ball pitcher?"

"Yeah. How'd you know, Mom?"

"You've been talking about him and his friends for weeks. They're big-shots at school, huh?"

"I guess so."

His mother smiled at him.

"Okay, you can go. You'll need chow for—two meals?"

"Yeah. Lunch and prob'bly we'll cook up something before coming home. By rights, we should stay overnight, but those kids' folks won't let them." Ben's voice held a note of superiority. His father was a State Ranger, now in charge of the Giant City state park. In the few months since the family had moved to this new job, Ben already knew every part of the rugged park. He wouldn't have minded sleeping out in it over night, even alone. "Their folks probably think there're grizzly bears and timber wolves hiding in the caves."

"You can walk off a cliff in the dark, Ben. Well, I'll fix up a pack for you."

"Thanks, Mom."

He went to his room, and Mrs. Cagle breathed a little sigh of relief. Her husband had been transferred to this job at the beginning of summer. In the short time that they had been here, Ben had had little chance to make friends and had been very lonely. He was a sociable boy; back in Colorado he had had many friends and been very popular. She knew, too, that starting at a new school could be very hard on one. But now, finally, Ben was making friends; and for that she was grateful. . . .

Giant City, far down in southern Illinois, is a wilderness of limestone cliffs and caves and stony corridors and rock slides, much of it overgrown with brush and dense timber. It is easy to imagine that, long ago, a tribe of brawny, primitive fighting men used this maze of lofty stone walls and narrow passageways and caverns as a fortress from which they darted forth in sudden raids to steal women and robes and horses from more peaceable tribes, racing back to lose themselves in this labyrinth of twisted corridors and rockfalls. Here, in the narrow passages between cliffs and caverns, a few men could trap myriads, ambushing them, rolling avalanches of stone down upon them, then vanishing into craggy recesses, safe from vengeance.

Saturday morning, Ben guided the group of boys into Giant City. This area, privately owned, had been closed to the public until the state bought it and converted it into a park.

"Boy, what a mess of scrambled geography!" Ted Dolan said, as they eyed the cliffs reaching up from the roadway.

"Ben," Syd Gold asked, a little anxiously, "you got a compass and map with you?"

"Don't need 'em."

"We could get lost awful easy."

"Not if you knew the place like I know it."

"You must have built-in radar."

"My Dad taught me how to get along in the hills."

The five boys, respecting his knowledge and woods skill, followed him into the stony maze of Giant City. He led them along new trails that his father's crew had opened up, and into areas of craggy beauty none of them had ever seen before.

"Say, this is really something," Ted said.

"Hey, wait," Syd begged. "I got to get a picture here."

Ben liked the group. Ted was a fine athlete and the natural leader of the group. Syd was the brainy, talkative one: on hikes he was the one who lectured the rest on mushrooms and grasshoppers, on solar eclipses, on the habits of ants and bumblebees and lizards. Andy was quiet (like me, Ben thought); but he always pitched in when work had to be done, always doing more than his share. Tom, the biggest boy, was strong but awkward, so uncoordinated that he was poor at athletics; but he was good-humored, always making jokes at his own expense. The only boy in the group Ben did not immediately cotton to was Joey Bayne. Like himself, Joey was a new member of the group. Joey talked a lot, mostly about himself; Joey had a loud, rough voice, and used a lot of gutter language. He took offense easily, and was quick to use his fists. Ben wondered why the boys had ever included him in their group. Probably the boys' Sunday school teacher had urged them to befriend him. They didn't, however, seem to like him. What happened at lunch time showed that.

"Here, Joey, try one of my sandwiches. I got some extra," Ted said.

Joey had eaten the one slim sandwich he'd brought, so he took Ted's thick sandwich and bit into it ravenously.

Something odd happened.

Joey's eyes suddenly grew huge and round with horror. He gasped. He choked. He spluttered food in a shower over his shirt front.

"It b-burns!" he gasped.

"Here. Drink this."

Syd handed him a camp cup full of water. Joey took a huge mouthful—and then he really was sick. His face turned white and green. He jumped up and ran into the woods and was sick—upchucking all he'd eaten.

"What's wrong with *him?*" Tom asked, amazed.

Ted and Syd couldn't answer; they were guffawing, laughing their heads off.

Andy, grinning a little worriedly, said, "Red peppers. Mexican peppers in his sandwich."

"And drinking water full of s-salt," Ted gasped, trying to choke back his laughter, "didn't help at all!"

So the whole thing had been planned and prepared in advance, Ben realized.

"Think you're so funny, don't you!" Joey quavered. "For two cents—"

He had to turn and heave once more, and the boys again doubled up in laughter. He did look funny, Ben thought; but not to himself. Another minute, and he'd clout somebody.

Ben took his canteen to him.

"Here, drink this, Joey. It's good water." And, turning to the group, Ben said, "Let's get going. Lot to see."

He led the group into a newly opened part of the refuge.

Here, in this region of limestone cliffs near the Mississippi River, rainwater seeping down through the rock had eaten away many caverns; and the various geologic forces that erode and split rock had created many passageways, and rock slides had added confusion to the labyrinthine puzzle. It was as though a cluster of huge skyscrapers had fallen flat to earth and cracked and shattered and crumbled over many square miles of ground. The result was a crazy jumble of cliffs and chasms and gloom-filled, echoing caverns and passages that seemed like huge corridors and chambers, once inhabited but now moldering in ruin, lonely and haunted.

Ben showed Syd the best vantage points from which to take pictures. Ben also showed Tom and Andy where to dig—in sites that had been camp-fire sites—to find old arrowheads. Ben led the way through tunnels and over rockfalls and along paths slanting up the face of cliffs.

"This trail is like poison," Joey Bayne said. "One drop'll kill you!" And he laughed at his joke.

At least, Ben thought, he's getting over being mad.

It was then that Syd saw a slender body moving across the path before them.

"Hey, look!" he whispered, catching Ted's arm. "A coral snake!"

"No," Ben said, "just a king snake. Nonpoisonous."

"Let's catch it," Ted said. "We'll put it in Joey's lunch box and when he opens it—"

"No," Ben said.

Ted and Syd looked at him, their faces suddenly angry.

"You telling me what I can't do?" Ted demanded.

Ben wanted to say: Lay off Joey; he's having a bad time. But instead he said, "This is a game refuge, remember? My Dad's in charge."

"That's right," Syd said.

Ben led on and Ted said nothing more.

Nobody paid much heed to the passing of time, they were all so interested in exploring. Hunger, finally, made Syd look at his watch.

"Hey, it's past five o'clock. It'll be dark before we find our way out to civilization!"

Ben said, "Doesn't matter. I know the way. Let's eat."

He built a camp fire in the mouth of a huge cave. Its light cast their shadows in huge distortion upon the back wall—as if they were giants, of long ago, sitting in council. Outside, sunset dimmed into gloomy dusk; and the wind fretted through the twisted passageways of Giant City, moaning like a lost ghost.

It was night by the time they finished eating; and it seemed abruptly, and menacingly, dark when Ben poured water onto the camp fire to quench all embers.

"I sure hope you know the way home," Syd said to Ben.

"Look, if I had to, I could lead you out blindfolded, and I'm not bragging."

"But let's not try it," Ted said.

The accident happened soon after they started hiking. Ben led, the rest strung out in single file on the trail. As they walked along, he was thinking that he liked these boys. They were a good bunch. Of course, they did let Ted boss them too much. Given time, Ben figured, he could manage Ted; he could make them more sensible about going along with some of Ted's wild ideas—like riding Joey so much.

It was then, at the rear of the file, he heard Joey yell: "Hey, wait—Help! Help!"

The boys stopped, hurried back along the trail.

Andy was crouched at the cliff edge, shining his flashlight down.

"That Joey," Andy said disgustedly. "Draw a line on the floor and he'd trip over it."

"What happened?" Ben demanded.

"He slid off the trail. Listen to 'im holler."

"Help me up!" Joey was screeching.

Ben examined the slope below. It was almost straight down, for its upper half, then sloped out; and the slope, covered with thick shrubs, had cushioned Joey's fall. From the strength of his yells, he hadn't suffered anything but fright and scratches.

"You all right, Joey?"

"Yeah, but help me up!"

"Can't. Got no rope. Anyway, you can just walk along the bottom of the cliff there. You'll come to a break, where you can climb back up to the trail. We'll move along right above you. Use your flashlight."

Ben's calm soothed Joey.

"All right, I'm starting."

And then Ted got another of his wild ideas.

"Hey, Ben! Syd! You guys," he whispered. "This'll be good! Keep real quiet. Let's move fast, now—and leave Joey behind."

"He'll get lost," Ben said sharply.

"That's right!"

"You mean, leave him out here alone all night?"

"Sure, he won't freeze or anything. Ain't no bears or wolves around to hurt him. Weather ain't even chilly!"

Andy chuckled. "Serve him right for lagging behind. Next time he'll keep up."

"He'll be scared."

"And how," Ted said. "He'll sure remember this night!"

"I mean, he'll be *really* scared—"

"You chicken or something?" Ted demanded.

"I'm just saying that—"

"You don't like anything we want to do! Well, you just don't need to have any part of what we do."

"Come on," Andy urged. "Let's get off a way and make noises like howling wolves—"

"He'll be shaking like a leaf!" Syd said.

"Come on, then!" Ted commanded. "You coming, Ben, or aren't you?"

Ben hesitated. *I could teach the bunch of them a good lesson,* he thought angrily. He could easily, in the darkness, slip away from the group —and join Joey. He could lead Joey out of Giant City to the highway to town, while the rest of them wandered around in the dark passageways, lost. They'd be lost the minute he left them. They'd discover what it was like to be lost at night in the woods!

But if I play this trick on them, Ben realized, they'll be through with me. I won't have any friends but that no-account Joey—

"You coming, Ben, or not?" Ted demanded.

Ben said . . .

SHUTTER-BUG

The problem:

The issue is a problem of the individual and his group: whether to cooperate or to stand against his close friends. Sometimes a member of a group finds himself in strong opposition to the emphatic, united wishes of the rest of the group. Such opposition is especially difficult for the disagreeing individual when the group consensus is focused on a worthy goal and his own conflicting purposes relate only to himself and might, in some instances, be considered mere self-indulgence.

Introducing the problem:

Ask the class, "Have you ever wanted something very badly, then discovered that somebody else needed that thing just as badly as you did? This story deals with such a problem. Listen carefully as I read. The story stops before it is finished. Think of ways in which you might end the story."

It was a treasure to Jimmy Norton: a twenty-year-old press camera. It belonged to his Uncle Tod, who was a veteran news cameraman. With that camera he had taken historic pictures of flood damage, of forest fires, of gunmen being tear-gassed into submission, of oil tanks blazing in a lightning-caused fire, of troops landing on D-day, of earthquake ruins, of visiting statesmen in the hall of the United Nations center.

Jimmy, at twelve, was quite a good photographer himself. He hoped some day to be a crack photo-journalist who traveled around the world for *Life* or *Look*, taking pictures of events that caused headlines in the press. By that time, of course, he figured that he would have a whole battery of fine cameras, but, at present, he wanted nothing so much as that bedraggled old press box of his uncle's.

Right now, Jimmy and two of his friends, all members of his Scout group, were on a sort of scavenger hunt. They were combing their neighborhood for "white elephants." Their church was going to hold a rummage sale to raise funds to buy an organ for a mission church overseas. The plan was to ask people to donate articles for this sale, articles that, while no longer of real use to their owners, were still useful enough to find a buyer at a rummage sale where prices were irresistibly low. People were glad to donate, for a really worthy cause, such items as old radios and broken-down sewing machines and vacuum cleaners and coffee grinders and abandoned toys—all broken but mendable.

So far, Jimmy and his friends had had good luck in their hunt: they had gathered in an old TV set, five old table-model radios and one old console that looked as big as a juke box, a power lawnmower that needed a new motor, two sets of cowboy boots that were scuffed and twisted but honorable with use, a Civil War rifle, a portable phonograph that needed a new tone arm, a tired cavalry saddle, and a grandfather clock.

"Hey, Jimmy," Pete asked, "isn't this your aunt's house?"

"Yeah. She'll give us something sure. She's real nice."

His Aunt Mary answered the bell, and beamed at the three boys.

"Hi! Come in—come in. I've been baking. You fellows don't think that some fresh cookies and lemonade would be out of order just now, do you?"

Their ear-to-ear grins were sufficient answer to that.

As they munched and guzzled in the kitchen, Jimmy explained that they had come for "white elephants" for the church rummage sale.

"I've got just the thing for you!" she said, rising from her chair. She hurried into another room, and came back. "Here. Look at this!"

"Boy!" Ed gasped.

And Pete said, "Hey, that's something! It'll really sell."

Jimmy said nothing; he couldn't. He just stared, his heart a sick, heavy lump in his chest.

His aunt had brought out his uncle's old press camera.

She said, "This isn't all. More junk goes with it. I'll get the rest."

Junk! Jimmy's face grew hot with outrage as his aunt brought in the accessories that went with the camera—a flash gun, tripod, separate backs for roll and sheet film, wide angle and telephoto lenses. Junk worth its weight in money!

"Gee," Ed breathed in delight, "what a haul!"

And Pete said, "I'll bet that'll sell for real money."

"B-but, Aunt Mary," Jimmy protested, "this stuff is too good to j-just give away!"

"Oh, no. Your uncle finally got the fine new camera he has been daydreaming about for months. He doesn't need this stuff any more."

"This outfit's good enough to put up for auction, at the sale," Ed said soberly.

And Pete added, "I'll bet it'll bring in over fifty dollars. That'll sure help a lot toward buying the organ for the mission."

"Aunt Mary," Jimmy insisted, in desperation, "you've got to check with Uncle Tod first—"

"No," she said comfortably, "I heard him say he was going to give all this stuff away."

"To me!" Jimmy blurted. "He promised it to me."

Aunt Mary looked suddenly stricken.

"Oh, Jimmy! I didn't *know*. Boys, I—I'm sorry. I hate to disappoint you, but—"

"Aw, heck, Jimmy," Ed protested, "you already *got* a good camera. Nobody in the gang gets as good pictures as you do!"

And Pete added: "Look what a big, awkward thing that old box is, anyway. I can just see you packing it up Mt. Baldy. It'd break your back."

"Besides, think of the money it'll bring at the sale," Ed went on.

"Fifty bucks, at least," Pete said. "You know how much the mission needs that organ. You heard what Reverend Michaels said: the gift that counts most is the one that the giver wants most."

Aunt Mary broke in, "But if Jimmy really wants this camera, it's his, of course."

"Aw, Jimmy, how crummy can you get!" .

"I'd hate to live with that on my mind." Pete snorted.

"Now, boys," Aunt Mary said.

"Aw, come on, Ed," Pete said, "Leave 'im here with his loot."

But Ed pressed, "Jimmy, think how much that fifty dollars would help. What d'you say?"

Jimmy caught a shaky breath, and said:

THE
UN-INVITATION

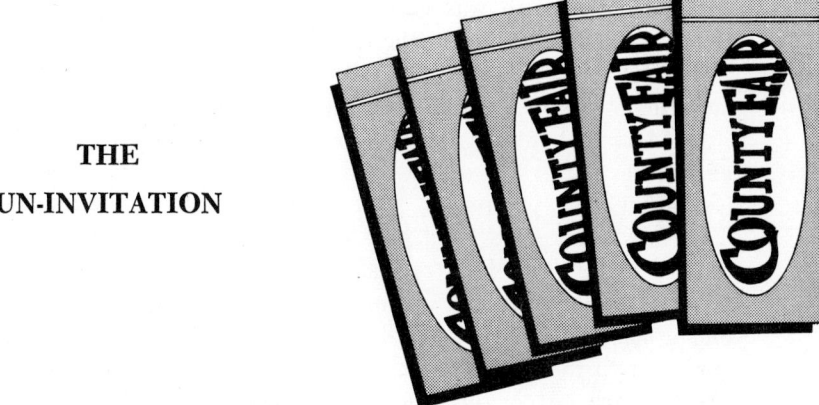

The problem:

The issue is that of integrity in human relations: Should pleasure for a group be bought at the price of pain for an individual? Mary has invited six girls to go to the Fair with her on her birthday. But, for the seven of them, she has, she discovers, only six books of tickets. Someone has to be left out. Who? Should one person's feelings be deeply hurt so that the rest of the group can have a fine time at the Fair?

Introducing the problem:

Ask your group, "Has your family ever decided to go to a movie or on a picnic or on a trip, and then discovered that someone will have to stay home to take care of something—a sick person, or the pets, or to open the house to repairmen, or something of the sort? It happens in all families. Sometimes it happens when you have arranged to go someplace with friends. How do you decide what to do then? This is a story about such a problem. The story stops but is not finished. Try to think of ways in which the story should be finished."

When Mary realized what she had done, she felt just sick. It had been unintentional. She had no desire to slight anybody, to hurt anyone's feelings, but now she saw no way out of it.

"Mother, what shall I do?"

"About what, dear?"

"I've invited all the girls to my birthday party—and now there's one too many!"

Mrs. Neilsen laughed and said, "Is that all that's worrying you?" And then she understood, and she gasped, "Oh, my goodness!" And just stood there, stricken, trying to think what to advise Mary.

"I've got to talk to Beth and Nancy!" Mary said.

She ran out of the apartment, down the three long flights of stairs to the front areaway, and around to the back, to the laundry room where she knew that Beth was helping her mother. She found Beth moving clothes from the washer to the drier.

"Beth, listen!" She drew Beth into a corner. "Something awful has happened," she began, and explained.

Mary had invited her six closest friends to her birthday party—all girls in her sixth-grade class who lived in this apartment house. Mary and her mother had planned to hold the party in their apartment—to listen to records, play games, and have ice cream and cake. But her father had phoned home a half-hour ago, and changed all that. Mr. Neilsen drove a taxicab for the Reynolds Company. He would take tomorrow afternoon off, he had phoned Mary. In his cab he would drive the whole birthday party out to the Fair Grounds. He had six books of tickets for the Fair, one for each girl in the group: each book would admit one girl to the Fair Grounds and provide tickets for the rides, the big show, and a fine dinner. The public relations office of the Fair had given the ticket books to cab drivers who had been bringing people out to the Fair, and Mary's father had persuaded some of his friends to give him their tickets for Mary's party.

"Beth, I was so excited," Mary explained now, "I didn't stop to think. We've got six books of tickets, but there's seven of us girls. One too many!" And, as Beth just stared at her, Mary wailed, "Don't you *see?*"

"Well, I guess somebody can't go."

"But who?" Mary demanded. "I can't just un-invite somebody I asked to my party!"

Nancy arrived then, carrying a hamper of clothes to be laundered. Mary beckoned her to their corner and told her the exciting but upsetting news.

Nancy, at first, was too delighted with the treats in store to be worried.

"You mean we all get into the Fair, and we get to ride that big ferris wheel and the rolly-coaster and eat in the revolving dining room on the tower and—everything?"

"And ride in the spaceship," Beth added, "and in the submarine gardens and—"

"But we can't all go!" Mary interrupted. "That's just it. We've got one too many people!"

"Let's chip in and buy another book of tickets—"

"They cost too much."

"Anyway, Dad says there's no more available. Besides, we couldn't get another passenger in the cab."

"Then we've got to leave somebody out."

"But *who?* Gosh, I—maybe we'd better have the party at home."

"And waste all six books of tickets? Oh, no!"

"But who can I leave out?"

They thought hard for a moment.

"Leave out Nora. She's new here. She's the girl you know the least, Mary. Tell her the party is called off."

"Then suppose she sees us all leaving together? Then I'm not only mean but a liar, too."

"Leave out Ruth," Nancy suggested. "She doesn't go to the same Sunday school we go to."

"Or Edith. She's colored," Beth said.

"You've had a quarrel with Lucy," Nancy pointed out.

"Ruth's been sick so much, this past year," Beth then reminded them. "She hasn't been running around with us—"

"Or doing much of anything else," Mary said. "Don't forget: I *did* invite her."

"But, Mary, somebody has to be left out," Beth said, "or none of us can go!"

And Nancy added, "It's your party, Mary. You've got to decide. Who'll it be?"

Mary hesitated, and her voice trembled as she said...

SACRIFICE
HIT

The problem:

    The issue in this story concerns the often difficult task of deciding when to cooperate with your close group of friends and when to stand against them. Should you do what your group wants you to do, although you would much prefer not to? The problem of this story deals with a youngster's difficulty in trying to make up his mind whether to cooperate in a group project when doing so will require a real sacrifice on his part, or to refuse and accept the penalty of being disliked and belittled.

Introducing the problem:

>Ask the group, "Have you ever been a member of a bunch that voted to do something nice for somebody—something that was very difficult for you to take part in? Perhaps it required you to put in money you didn't have, or to do something forbidden by your parents. Whatever it was, remember what a spot you felt you were in? This story deals with such a problem. This story stops but is not finished. As I read, try to think of ways in which you would end the story."

Danny was having a nightmare—again, the same old nightmare. He was pitching for the sixth grade against the seventh-grade team. His side was one run ahead. It was the last half of the last inning. He had just tried his fast ball, and the batter had hit it—but the ball had soared almost straight up in an easy pop fly. So easy! All Danny had to do was stand right in his tracks and wait for the ball to drop into his glove, then throw the ball home to catch the runner from third, and the game would be over with his side as winner.

So he stood there, waiting for the falling ball to plop into his glove. But it didn't. Sunlight dazzled him. Sunlight was a blinding flare in his eyes. The ball slipped through his upstretched fingers and struck him on the forehead and glanced to the ground. Half-dazed with pain, he stood there a moment before realizing that the onlookers were shouting, that the batter was running toward first, that the man on third was streaking toward the home plate—

"Pick it up! Heave it—*heave it.*"

"Head for third, Pete!"

"What a butterfingers!"

Groggily he saw the ball on the ground, where it had rolled. He bent to snatch it up, and bumped headfirst into Pete Byers, his own shortstop, who had come running to get the ball. Pete fell flat on his face. Danny snatched up the ball and flung it toward home plate, but the ball went wild over the catcher's head—and the seventh-grader got safely home for the winning run.

Danny woke up, heart pounding, his face damp with sweat.

This was just a nightmare, but the game had really happened just as he had dreamed it, a week ago. He had lost that game—and he would lose the next one, if he pitched for his team.

He ought to quit playing ball, he told himself dismally. He was still the best pitcher on his team, and he was a good batter. But he ought to quit because, no matter how hard he tried, his playing was going to get worse and worse. Unless—

"Danny, you all right?" his mother called.

"Sure," he answered.

"Time to get up."

Before dressing for breakfast, he opened the bottom drawer of his bureau and took out the old toy cash register that he used as a bank. He counted the coins it contained. He had exactly $14.50. He needed $11.50 more. How could he get so much money in time to be of real help?

Danny had this problem—

He was a fine athlete, but his eyesight was defective. He needed glasses. He had reading glasses. But he did not have glasses for distance vision.

His eye doctor had suggested that, in time, he be given lenses that would not only correct his vision for distance but would be tinted so that they would protect his eyes from sunglare, as well.

Wearing such glasses, he would easily snag a pop fly instead of letting it slip through his fingers to smack him on the head. With such glasses, he could recognize birds in a tree top, he could tell a DC3 from a Boeing 707 in the air. With such glasses, he could continue playing baseball; he could go rabbit and quail hunting.

He didn't want to ask his parents to buy the glasses just now; they couldn't spare the money. He figured that getting the distance glasses he wanted, but didn't absolutely *have* to have, was his own responsibility. He had been saving for them.

At lunch, that day, Pete Miller stopped him.

"Danny, I want the team to meet after school, at my place."

Pete was captain of their ball team; his folks' garage was the usual meeting place for the group.

"What for?" Danny asked.

"Something's come up."

That was all Pete would say, and Danny worried all afternoon.

After school, the group gathered in the Miller garage.

Pete explained why he had called them together.

"You know what happened at batting practice, two weeks ago," he began.

Danny's worry sharpened. Their second-baseman, Tom Eads, had socked the ball clear out into the street. The ball had struck the windshield of a passing car, shattering it. The car belonged to Fred Turner, a young mailman. The boys had had to chip in to buy him a new windshield. It had cost them $7 apiece. For Danny, taking that $7 out of his carefully saved-up hoard of dimes and quarters earned by running errands and mowing lawns had been almost unbearably painful.

"Well," Pete said now, "I've discovered that Fred Turner paid more for a new windshield than he told us. They're expensive. But that's not all. He could have reported the accident to the insurance company and they would have replaced his windshield for nothing. But they would have reported the accident to the police and the park director."

"Oh, no!" Tommy Eads groaned.

"You know what the park people have told us. If playing ball in the park causes anybody to get hurt or any property to be damaged—off we go. No more ball diamond."

"And no more games," Tommy echoed.

"Darn nice of Mr. Turner not to squeal on us," Ed Norton said.

"That's right," Pete agreed. "I say we got to thank him. When people do you a favor you've got to show appreciation, or you're a slob."

"And they stop doing you favors," Ed said.

"Sure, we appreciate what Mr. Turner did for us," Danny said, uneasily. "So let's thank him."

"Here's what I think we should do," Pete said. "Mr. Turner's car is a hot rod. On weekends he runs it on the drag strip. So let's give him something he'd be darn tickled to get."

"Good idea!"

"Sure."

"But what, for instance?" Danny demanded.

"You know how drag racers dress up their engines. Let's give Mr. Turner a set of chrome air filters for the carburetors of his engine. And maybe a chrome cover for the generator."

"He'd sure like that!" Tommy agreed.

"But what would it cost us?" Danny asked.

"Maybe five or six bucks apiece would be enough."

"Wow!"

"We got to be *that* appreciative?"

"We can't be chintzy!" Pete insisted.

"But we paid seven bucks apiece just two weeks ago," Danny protested, "and now you say—"

"Okay, okay, we'll trim the deal down to just chrome air filters," Pete conceded. "That's the least we can do—four bucks apiece."

"*You* get an allowance," Ed said. "Some of us earn our spending money."

"So earn it. Let's take a vote."

"Pete," Danny protested, "it takes a lot of jobs mowing lawns at four bits to make four bucks—"

"Mr. Turner saved our ball park for us. Everybody in favor," Pete commanded, "raise your hand!"

Everyone but Danny and Ed raised their hands.

"Come on, Ed," Pete said. "I know you sold your bike last week."

"Yeah, but—okay, okay."

Now only Danny hadn't raised his hand. Everyone looked at him. He felt his face grow red and hot. Still, he did not raise his hand.

"Aw, come on, Danny," Pete insisted. "You know the club doesn't do anything important unless the vote is unanimous. You ain't a chintzy guy."

But Danny just sat there, mute, unmoving. All he could think of was those tinted eyeglasses he needed. He just couldn't spare another four dollars!

"Doggonnit, Danny, you're not going to be the only guy holding out, are you?" Pete said angrily.

"You want it unanimous—you think it's really unanimous when you *make* everybody vote the way you want?"

"Never mind all the argument," Pete retorted. "You with us or ain't you?"

And Ed said, "If you're going to stay with a team, you got to co-operate, Danny!"

"Yeah. Yes or no? Give us your vote!" Pete insisted.

Danny said . . .

chapter

2

GROUP RESPONSIBILITY:
TO RESPECT AND
SUPPORT THE INDIVIDUAL

Accepting Others: The Deviant

BANDIT

CAVE

The problem:

The issue is accepting others; specifically, the responsibility of the group to accept and support the individual who is "different."

Recent studies of child groups have increased our sensitivity to the sufferings of the youngster who is rejected by his age-mates. Not only must teachers and parents help children to acquire ways of behavior and skills that are acceptable to their peers, but the child group itself must be helped to acquire more democratic attitudes toward children who are different. This is a story of a boy who was left on the fringe of play activities to watch other children instead of participating with them.

Introducing the problem:

An opportune time to use this story is after an incident in the classroom group in which a child has suffered rejection by his fellows. This story is particularly useful as a follow-up to "The Squawk Box" after such an incident. You may introduce the story by saying, "I'm sure you all know how it feels, once in a while, to be left out of activities your friends are taking part in. When they're starting up a game, are going on a trip, if you're not included, you feel hurt and rather miserable. This is a story about such an incident. The story stops but is not finished. As I read, think of ways in which the story might end."

Johnny Whelan and Dick Barry sat on the grass, watching the other boys playing softball. Mr. McCann, on his way from the office to inspect the camp dormitories, stopped for a moment.

"Why aren't you boys playing ball?"

Johnny said quickly, "I turned my ankle yesterday and it still aches."

But Dick, more frankly, revealing the puzzled hurt he felt, said, "They wouldn't choose me, Mr. McCann. I can't play good enough."

The counselor understood, then. For a moment he studied the two boys. Johnny Whelan was red-headed and freckled and big for ten, but chubby and soft-looking, and evidently was too clumsy to play softball or tag football well. Dick Barry, on the other hand, was small for his age; dark-haired, dark-eyed, but with a paleness to his skin that two days at camp had not yet covered with sunburn. He looked frail, as if he had lived indoors too much.

Mr. McCann said, "I'm sure glad you aren't tied up just now. I need two boys to go into town on the supply truck and do some errands for me. Would you fellows help me out?"

"Oh sure," Johnny said. He was quick and bright enough. "Be glad to help you out."

Dick just sat there, letting Johnny do the talking.

So Mr. McCann sent them into Hampton in care of Mack, the driver, with a list of items to buy, and permission to see an afternoon movie while Mack had a new radiator mounted on the truck.

But then Mr. McCann, very troubled, reported to the camp director.

"Johnny and Dick have been left out of games so much that they're beginning to hate camp."

"Why?" Mr. Calhoun asked. "Are they unpopular?"

"No-o. I've asked around. The other boys don't dislike Johnny and Dick. But they can't play ball. Any side they play on is bound to take an awful licking. So, when the boys choose up sides, they leave Johnny and Dick out."

The director nodded. "Johnny's father is dead, and his mother's a concert violinist. She travels on tours, playing engagements. She has kept Johnny with her, and the result has been that he has lived in hotels and on trains and just never played with kids very much. He's had a tutor, so he's kept up his school work all right, but—"

"He's never had a chance to play games."

"That's it. And Dick hasn't either, though for a different reason. Dick had rheumatic fever when he was six, and he's had to take it easy for a long time. He's all right now, though."

"Steve, you question the two youngsters. There must be *some* sport that they're good at."

"Yes, sir."

Mr. McCann managed to have some casual talks with Johnny. He asked Johnny about himself. Where he'd been, what he'd done. The camp counselor smiled to himself, pleased by what he learned, and hopeful. His talk with Dick Barry, however, brought him increasing worry.

"Johnny," Mr. McCann said the next evening, when the whole camp was sitting about the big outdoor fire for the evening sing and stunts, "show us how you make a spinning rope, will you?"

Johnny rose to his feet, flushing and self-conscious.

"Y-yes, sir," he stammered. "Only you need some spot cord—"

"Like this?" Mr. McCann held up a coil of cotton rope.

"Why, yes, that's right," Johnny said surprised. "And you need a hondo and string—"

"Like this, maybe?"

Everybody laughed. It was almost like a magic act, the way Mr. McCann whipped the stuff out from under his jacket. He had, of course, come prepared.

Johnny took the rope, and fitted it around the groove of the hondo —which was an "eye" of brass—and fastened the hondo snugly into the rope by wrapping twine around the $\frac{3}{8}$-inch cord. Then he coiled a snug layer of string around the far end of the rope, as well, to keep the threads from raveling.

Everybody watched, quiet and absorbed.

Johnny worked deftly, his gray eyes intent, forgetting his audience and his self-consciousness.

"The rope is twenty feet long, Johnny," Mr. McCann said.

"That's about right."

Johnny held up the long end of the loop, and threaded it through the eye of the hondo. Then he took the loop in his right hand, and coiled the slack in the other hand. He held his hands up.

"To spin your rope, start by holding it like this," he said, "so that the loop will stay open and so's you can let go of it. And see that the slack will play out. Keep the far end tight under the last two fingers of your left hand."

He whipped the loop over his head, letting it down around him, and kept turning the rope with his right hand. The loop widened out as it spun in a steady, graceful ring around his body, suspended by the "lead" from his right hand held over his head.

Abruptly he lowered his right hand, then whipped it up, deftly timing it so as not to foul the "lead" around his body—and the hissing loop lifted high over his head, spinning flat out for a second or two before it lowered down around him again. He let it come almost down to the ground, then whoosh! he lifted the spinning loop up high over his head once more. Down, then up, down and up, he snapped the whirling circle. The onlookers burst out clapping and cheering.

Blushing with pleasure, Johnny worked on through a whole list of fancy tricks. He laid the spinning loop so low that it slapped the ground with reports like a lashing whip as it spun—and he danced over the turning spoke of the "lead" as he kept it revolving from his right hand.

He brought the flat loop up shoulder high, and spun it faster, faster, *faster*, until it was screaming as it whirled. Then, very gradually, he tilted the loop from its flat position. Slanted it higher, higher, until finally it was spinning straight up and down like a giant wheel. Then, startlingly, he whipped the loop sideways and jumped clear through it. Then back he leaped. Back and forth through the vertical loop he sprang, whipping the spinning rope from side to side. The watching boys applauded.

He had to stop finally, sweating and gasping for breath. It was very hard work.

"How do you do it, Johnny?" they kept yelling at him.

"Where'd you learn, Johnny? Out on a ranch?"

"No," he said. They grew quiet, to hear. "Funny thing, but real cowboys don't know how to spin rope. When my mother was playing violin in a movie, a movie cowboy taught me how to spin. He used to spin rope in vaudeville. There's just one secret to it besides practicing a lot. That's to keep the rope, where you're holding it, twisting just as fast as the loop is spinning. You keep it twisting with your fingers, so that it never kinks up. Once it kinks, it's closing time."

"Show us how, Johnny!"

Mr. McCann grinned as Johnny showed them. Johnny was going to be popular ... but Mr. McCann's face got serious again as he noticed that little Dick Barry sat on the edge of the crowd of boys, saying nothing; not trying to push up close to see how Johnny kept the spinning rope from kinking, just sitting, quiet as a mouse. ...

Beside the swimming pool next morning, Mr. McCann started talking to Dick.

"Ever play tennis, Dick?"

"No, Mr. McCann."

"Call me Steve, Dick. Ever learn to play the mouth organ?"

"No, sir."

"Can you run pretty fast, Dick?"

"I don't think so . . ."

"Ever play basketball?"

Dick just shook his head, and swallowed hard.

"Or make model planes?"

Again Dick answered with an apologetic, hopeless shake of the head.

"Maybe you've collected stamps?"

Dick gave a shaky little laugh. "Guess I just never did anything."

"Dick, you're going on the hike with us, tomorrow, to Bandit Cave— aren't you?"

Dick nodded. "I'd like to go, sir."

"Better jump in, now, and have a swim, Dick."

"I—I ain't allowed to, Steve. I got bad sinuses."

"Oh, I see. Well—"

Mr. McCann stalked away, shaking his head and his lips compressed. In the recreation hall, during the rest period before dinner, Dick settled himself away from the other boys, in the library corner. He was halfway through a book that fascinated him. Its title was "Camels, Caves and Cavalry," and it was a gossipy history of Southern California. During his long illness, he had whiled away endless tedious months in reading. There was a whole shelf of books about early California here, but most of them Dick had already read. His father, now dead, had been a travel writer. The book Dick held had been his father's first published work, and it had been out of print for twenty years. Dick actually had never seen it before. He pored over it now, remembering his father with painful vividness.

Twenty boys went along on the hike with Mr. McCann next morning. The tall, smiling counselor kept the pace easy, for Dick's sake. Time and again he had to caution the boys to slow up. They were excited at the thought of visiting a Bandit Cave, and impatient to reach it. Mr. McCann became uneasy. The youngsters would be disappointed when they discovered that a hole in the ground was just a hole in the ground.

In a box canyon, on the left wall, and at the base of a dry waterfall, they found the cave. The youngsters crowded up close and peered into it, silent and expectant and wondering.

"Shucks," Bill Callen said.

"Couldn't any bandits hide in *that* little old place."

"Bandit Cave. Huh! Gyp Cave."

"Mr. McCann, why is this place supposed to be something we ought to see?"

The counselor wiped sweat from his lean face with his bandana, and frowned in thought. "Well, I guess horse thieves probably camped here. It's a famous spot, only I don't seem to recall all the details."

Bandit Cave? Dick Barry studied the hole in the cliff, his thoughts milling excitedly. Once it had been a deep cave. Flowing through it had been a clear stream of water and a current of cool air that told of a winding system of great dark caverns far within the mountain. That had been over a hundred years ago, when California was still part of Mexico, before Fremont and Sloat and Kearny had raised the United States flag over the territory. That had been back in the days of the missions and the big ranchos, when California was a sleepy paradise, troubled only by the occasional foray of thieves who came out of the desert to rob the missions and ranchos of fine mules and horses. "Chaguanosos," the Californians called these raiders, "thieves of all nations." They were Paiute Indians, and a variety of white renegades. It was on moonlit nights that they swept down Cajon Pass, riding fast and hard, rounding up stock and driving them swiftly before them in a wild rush to whip through Cajon and into the Mojave before the rancheros could catch up with them. The "silver nights" became dreaded nights for the Californios. They learned to keep vigilant guard. They armed themselves and slept lightly, alert for signals in the night that would summon them to seize lance and musket and mount their finest palominos to ride against the raiders.

And, being watchful, once they almost caught the leaders of the Chaguanosos, a white man called Pegleg Smith, and a Paiute known as Walkara, "Napoleon of the Desert." The raiders had split forces in an effort to shake off close pursuit. Walkara and Pegleg Smith and several of their wounded men had finally taken refuge here in the cavern.

The rancheros had not dared to charge into the cave after the raiders, knowing they would enter an ambush. Instead, the Californios had built a fire in the cave mouth, in an effort to smoke out the raiders and shoot them down as they popped out of the hole like rabbits out of a burrow. The trick didn't work.

For Walkara and Pegleg Smith and their men retreated far back into the cavern. The stream of clear water and the unceasing flow of cool, sweet air saved them.

In chagrin, the Californios used their gunpowder to blast down the roof of the entrance passageway, sealing it shut, locking the bandits inside it forever! Grimly satisfied, then, the Californios returned to their ranches.

That's why the cave now looks so shallow, Dick thought. *All we can see is just this end, where the roof was blasted down to shut the bandits up inside. The cave really extends way back. The hole inside of the mountain is just a honeycomb of tunnels and big, weird, ghostly rooms.*

Not that Pegleg Smith and Walkara were ghosts, now, haunting the cavern. For they had not died inside. By torchlight they had explored the winding limestone passages. They were worried, all right. They were scared and shaken. But the fact that the air flowed through the jagged tunnels, in a current that they could feel, gave them hope. They noticed, too, that there were many bats in the cavern. And that the bats seemed to leave the cave; and after a long interval, would return in big numbers. As if they were flying out of the cave at twilight, and returning at dawn.

So they watched the bats. They followed the passages that the bats seemed to be flying through. And that way, climbing high to the top of the wall of a big room, they found a narrow outlet through which the wind sucked hungrily. It was a tight squeeze, but out of this coyote hole the bandits all escaped. Dick could imagine how they looked and felt when they stood in the glaring sunlight again. How they grinned at each other, and wiped their faces, and looked blinkingly at the sun and let its warmth beat upon their heads.

"To tell the truth, boys," Mr. McCann was confessing, "I don't really know why this cave is supposed to be anything special. Looks just like another hole in the ground."

"Mr. McCann," Dick began. "Steve—"

"Well, let's eat," Mr. McCann said. "Don't use all the water in your canteens. You'll want a drink on the way back."

"Steve, I know—"

"Mr. McCann!" Bill Lyle yelled. "Let's build a camp fire in the cave. Just like the Indians! Let's fry some bacon!"

"Good idea. Scatter and look for firewood. Small stuff, for a cook fire."

"Steve," Dick said. "A long time a—"

"Mr. McCann," Peter Akers called. "Johnny Whelan brought his spinning rope. Can he show us some tricks while we eat?"

"That's a good idea. Feel like it, Johnny?"

"Soon's I eat one sandwich," Johnny agreed.

Dick turned away . . .

That night after the evening meal, Dick was called to the office. There was a phone call for him, from his mother.

"Are you enjoying camp, dear?" she asked.

"Well—no."

"Would you like to come home?"

He did not answer.

"Son," his mother repeated. "I can drive out to get you tomorrow. Shall I? Do you want to stay—or do you want to come home?"

Dick said . . .

THE
SQUAWK
BOX

The problem:

The issue is accepting others; specifically, the responsibility of the group to respect and support the individual who is different.

Children can often be cruel to one another, and the group can be especially cruel to the youngster who is "different." An aspect of this problem is the frequent tendency of a group to choose for an honor a child who, though not meriting the specific recognition, is popular and a leader—meanwhile ignoring (and thereby rejecting) the individual who does merit the honor because he is not accepted by them.

Introducing the problem:

You may say, "This is a story about a boy who is somewhat different from his playmates. Because he seems odd to them and lacks the abilities they respect, he is unpopular; and because he is not liked, he is not elected to offices he is really very able to fill. This story stops but is not finished. As I read, try to think of ways in which the story could end."

Andy Eaton remembers the day that police cornered the mad dog out in front of the school gym. Andy has big reason to remember it. . . .

The boys were choosing up sides for a ball game when Andy came to school that morning, early. He stood by as Neil and Jerry took turns naming the fellows each wanted. Neil got five on his side. Jerry had just four. And Andy was the only boy not yet chosen.

"I don't want Andy," Jerry said. "He can't play ball."

"You've got to take him. There's nobody else."

"Ah, he couldn't catch a fly ball if it had handles on it."

Andy blushed. He knew that he was clumsy and slow. He wasn't very good at baseball or football, or any of the games the boys played. But he was a year older than most of the group, and bigger too.

"I beg your pardon," he said angrily, "but anybody could play ball if they practiced."

"Oh, I beg *your* pardon, but you couldn't bat your way out of a paper bag! Anyway, here comes Pete Neylor. Neil, I choose Pete!"

"I was here first," Andy insisted. "It's not very sporting to pass me up—"

"Sporting yet!" Neil hooted. "My word, Reginald, you'll get those sissy clothes mussed up if you play with us!"

"I mean it's not fair," Andy said. But he couldn't correct his clothes. His father had sent from England the gray flannel slacks and the smart blazer Andy was wearing.

"Aw, come on, let's play," Neil said. "We bat first!"

They all turned away from Andy, leaving him standing alone, ignoring him. Andy's fist clenched. He was mad enough to fight Neil and Jerry. Then he realized how upset his folks would be.

When the bell rang and the fifth-graders all trooped into the classroom, their teacher had a surprise for them. Everybody crowded up front to look at the surprise on Mrs. Chandler's desk.

"What is all this stuff?" Neil asked.

"That's a record player," Andy said, "and an amplifier and loudspeaker and a microphone."

"What's it for, Mrs. Chandler?" Jerry inquired.

"For our program this afternoon. Children, the record player wouldn't be loud enough to use in the gym for our pageant, so I borrowed this equipment to use."

"Our music'll be plenty loud, now," Andy said. His brown eyes were shining with excitement. "That's a dandy Marvel-tone amplifier and a swell twelve-inch speaker. That set'll give a ten-watt output and that's plenty for our gym. Mrs. Chandler, the set's not hooked up. Please, can I hook it up for you?" he asked eagerly. "The loudspeaker has to be connected in back here with this round-pronged plug, and the mike line is screwed onto this connection, here. Your turntable has two wires and they have to be put on at these terminals in back and the screws turned down tight."

"Oh, do you know how to run it, Andy?"

"Yes, ma'am, my Dad's taught me. This tone control here—you keep it set at ten for natural tone, unless you get feed-back. Then you can fiddle with the setting to cut it out—"

"Show-off!" Elsie Bates whispered.

Andy shut up, turning red.

"Thanks for explaining it, Andy," Mrs. Chandler said. "All right, children, back to your seats. We've got to plan."

That afternoon the class was to perform a Pageant of the West in the gym. The other classes were to be invited to watch. The pageant would show a wagon train moving along the Santa Fe Trail. Then abruptly the scene would shift to a tribe of Indians holding a big medicine smoke. Chiefs would argue about the danger of the incoming white men and the loss of buffalo. Older chiefs would counsel peace; but young hotheads would make shrill demands for battle, and would start a war dance around their camp fire.

"Remember, children," Mrs. Chandler reminded them, "we want to change from the wagon party to the Indian tribe very quickly. The shades will be drawn in the gym, and we'll have a spotlight on us. When the square dance ends, the light will go out. All of you pioneers run to the east doors and go outside. The children who are the Indians will then run in from the west hall. The light will come back on—and the Indians are to be sitting around a camp fire in front of their wigwams. We want to make the change very quickly. So remember. Soon as the music ends, pioneers run for the exit door—and Indians come running in."

Andy put up his hand. Mrs. Chandler nodded.

"Excuse me, Mrs. Chandler, but you've got to have somebody at the turntable to start the records and to change them, and somebody to run the amplifier."

"You're right, Andy. I'll handle the records myself. We'll have to choose a sound engineer."

"Let Jerry be the sound engineer," Neil called out.

"Jerry, do you know how to handle the equipment?" she asked.

"Well, some," Jerry said hesitantly.

Andy waved his hand, trying to get permission to speak again, but Sam Balch spoke up, "Yes, Jerry'd make a good engineer!" and Susan Kyle said, "Let Jerry do it."

Jerry was very popular. He was good at sports, and had a lot of ideas about games to play and talked and laughed a lot.

"Please, Mrs. Chandler," Andy said, "if I may, I'd like to be engineer."

"Children," Mrs. Chandler said, "why not have Andy as engineer—"

"We want Jerry!"

"Let's have a vote!"

"All right," Mrs. Chandler said, "those in favor of Andy raise your hands."

Andy sat in front. He could see no raised hands. Two hands were raised behind him.

"Those in favor of Jerry," Mrs. Chandler said.

All but two of the children raised their hands.

"Jerry, you're elected. Andy, you'll help Jerry, if he needs it, won't you?" Mrs. Chandler said.

Andy wanted to say, "Sorry, but I certainly won't," but instead he swallowed hard and nodded.

"All right, now we'll have a rehearsal," Mrs. Chandler said.

The show was really a pantomime; that is, the children out on the gym floor would act everything out, would do their marching and dancing, while one person would explain everything going on through the microphone for all the audience to hear. Susan was the commentator who would do all the talking.

She began, "It was the spring of the year 1846—"

She stopped. Her voice wasn't coming from the loudspeaker.

Jerry was bent over the amplifier, turning the knobs.

Andy said, "I'm very sorry, but turning the phonograph knob doesn't turn on the microphone. Anyway, it's smart to wait until the tubes get warm before you turn up the juice."

"Sarcastic," somebody whispered.

Andy flushed. But he added, "Takes just a minute for the tubes to warm up."

"All right, Susan," Mrs. Chandler said, "start over."

Susan began again. The children settled back in pleased surprise as Susan's voice came full and rich and loud from the speaker, carrying clearly to every corner of the room.

"A-and at St. Louis and Independence wagons were being outfitted for the spring trip over the Trace to New Mexico and Cal—"

Squawk-howl-screech-meeow-rawr-wow!

Susan's voice was lost in the rumbling yowl that shrilled deafeningly from the loudspeaker, like the shriek of a giant panther wounded by an Apache arrow. Mrs. Chandler said something to Jerry, but the racket was so ear-filling that nobody could hear her words. Jerry looked at her, at Susan standing with her mouth open, at the amplifier, and didn't know what to do.

Andy reached over and gave the mike control a quick twist and the awful noise ended as if it had been chopped off with a hatchet.

By that time, the school principal, Mr. Bayley, had the room door open and was looking in, his face surprised and alarmed.

"What in the world was that?" he asked.

Mrs. Chandler pointed at the loudspeaker.

Andy said, "Feed-back."

"Feed-back. What's that?"

Andy didn't answer. He looked at Jerry. Jerry was the sound engineer.

"Whatever it is," Mrs. Chandler said, "it's awful. Jerry, what happened?"

Jerry looked at the amplifier, and edged away from it a little bit, as if expecting a dinohippopus to reach out of it and bite him.

Andy said, "If Jerry knew very much about a public address system he'd know that you get 'feed-back' inside a room, especially a small room. You don't have to, though, if you watch your controls."

"I was watching them," Jerry said angrily.

"I'm sorry, but keeping your eye on them isn't enough. You have to keep your hands on them too."

"Andy," Mrs. Chandler asked, "will you please show Jerry what to do?"

"Yes, ma'am. Jerry, you had your volume control up too high. Turn it lower, whenever she first starts to howl. Or turn your tone control down. Sometimes that'll head off a howl."

Mrs. Chandler said to Mr. Bayley, "I believe everything's under control now."

The principal shut the door, still looking doubtful.

"All right, Susan, start over," Mrs. Chandler said.

Susan wet her lips and lifted the microphone, shifting to a more comfortable position against the table.

But before she opened her mouth at all, before she spoke even a single word, from the loudspeaker came a whistle like a police siren screaming at the top of its voice. It was deafening, and growing shriller every instant.

The children clapped their hands to their ears. The room door was pushed open, and Mr. Bayley was there again, his mouth working as he yelled something which nobody could hear until Mrs. Chandler reached down and pulled the amplifier plug out of the wall connection. That wild whistle faded out like a rope jerked through a knot hole.

"—heavens, you'll blow the roof off this building!" Mr. Bayley was shouting.

"Jerry, did you turn the wrong switch?" Mrs. Chandler said.

"No. Susan hadn't even started talking," Jerry protested.

Everybody looked at Andy then.

Andy raised his hand and waited until Mrs. Chandler nodded. Then he said, "It's really very simple. If Susan will just be careful not to step right in front of the speaker with a hot mike in her hand, she won't cause that noise again."

Susan backed away from the speaker as far as the microphone cord would allow.

"We're learning," Mrs. Chandler said to the principal.

He nodded, his mouth tight.

"Trial and error. Or should I say 'trial and terror'?" he murmured, and shut the door.

"Jerry," Mrs. Chandler suggested, "don't you think we'd better let Andy run the sound system?"

"Oh, no. I know all the tricks, now," Jerry insisted.

The rest of the rehearsal went off all right, then. Jerry watchfully squeezed off every howl as it began by closing down on the volume or tone. Mrs. Chandler nodded, satisfied.

"Fine. Put the equipment away, Jerry. Let's finish the costumes now."

Jerry looked at Andy and whispered, "The big expert! It doesn't take any brains to run a P.A. System."

"You certainly proved that," Andy retorted.

"Wise guy!" Jerry said.

Mrs. Chandler said, smiling, "With your help, Andy, I'm sure that Jerry has that wild microphone tamed so it won't howl this afternoon."

"I'm sorry, Mrs. Chandler," Andy said, "but that microphone won't howl this afternoon—and it won't talk, either. It's going to be an awfully dead mike. We won't be able to use it."

"But why not, Andy?"

"Jerry's put it on that window shelf, over the radiator. That's a crystal mike, and the Rochelle Salt crystals in it can't stand heat. Leaving it over a radiator like that is a sure way to make junk out of it."

"Jerry—"

But Jerry was already moving the mike to a wall cupboard.

"Wise guy!" he whispered at Andy. "Ain't you smart!"

The mad dog was a fine big Doberman Pinscher, a very well-mannered lady dog who came often to the school grounds. The children loved to pet her. However, she had not been inoculated, and somewhere, unluckily, she had picked up a rabies germ. And the germ had grown, spreading itself, until today the dog was doomed. Mrs. Weaver, who lived across the street from the school, saw the Doberman coming down the street, her jaws flecked with foam, carrying her head at a funny angle, saw her turn into the school grounds. Mrs. Weaver, alarmed, phoned the police. Then Mrs. Weaver had a second thought and phoned the school principal's office.

But Mr. Bayley and all the teachers and children were in the gym, watching the fifth grade's Pageant of the West.

From the loudspeaker was coming music made from a record on the turntable which Mrs. Chandler was tending. To that music her children were performing a square dance. Mrs. Chandler was smiling; her class had done very well.

Mr. Bayley's secretary came through a side door and hurried to Mrs. Chandler's side.

"Mrs. Chandler!" the secretary whispered. "Tell everybody to stay in the gym. Nobody's to go outside. There's a mad dog on the school grounds. She's out on the east side of the play yard!"

Mrs. Chandler nodded. "When this record ends, I'll just announce it over the loudspeaker," she said. And then Mrs. Chandler had an awful thought.

This was the music for the dance now being played. When the record ended, the wagon train party was to run to the east doors and go outside—while from the west hallway, the Indians would come into the gym to take their places. When this record ended, her fifth-graders would immediately go out those east doors!

"I can't stop the music!" she thought. "I don't dare shut off this music!" But the record was almost over. The needle was very close to the last grooves at the center of the disc.

"*Children!*" Mrs. Chandler shouted. "*Stay inside the gym! Don't go out those doors!*"

She hadn't been heard. The music was so loud that her voice hadn't a chance to carry over it.

Jerry, beside her, reached to turn down the volume of the music. Andy said, "No!" and stopped him. Andy seized the microphone, standing on the table before Susan. Andy turned up the mike volume control, but did not touch the phone volume control.

"Listen, Neil and Kenneth and the rest of you kids!" Andy said— and though the music had not diminished at all, his voice soared loud and clear over the dance melody. It traveled through the microphone and amplifier and out the loudspeaker with the music, so that everyone in the gym heard it plainly. "This dance is almost over," Andy said. "When it ends, stay in the gym. You are not to go out, but stay right in the middle of the floor where you are!" And then his voice seemed twice as loud, for the music had come to the end of the record. "Ellen!" Andy called to Ellen Barnes. "Mike, Barry! *Stay—where—you—are! Don't anybody leave the room!*"

By now, Mrs. Chandler was running to those east doors, so that she could stop any children who tried to go out.

It wasn't necessary. They all stood where they were, surprised and wondering.

"Don't be frightened, children," Mrs. Chandler said. "We're to stay where we are for awhile."

Now that the music had stopped, the Indians came rushing in, right on cue. They slowed up and stared, puzzled at seeing that the wagon train people were still on stage in the middle of the floor.

And then, outside, sounded the hard bang of a pistol shot.

Everybody's head jerked around to look at the east doors. Somebody cried out, as if scared. Mr. Bayley started toward those doors to see what was going on. Mrs. Chandler called to him.

"Wait, Mr. Bayley! Don't go outside!"

He hesitated and while he paused, the door opened. Pushed open, from the outside. It was a tall policeman who came in. He looked surprised when he saw so many people staring at him.

"We've got the dog," he said. "Mr. Bayley, it's all right to go outside now."

Later, Mrs. Chandler talked to Andy alone.

"Andy, I just can't thank you enough."

"Why, you're welcome, Mrs. Chandler. But it wasn't much," he said honestly. "I just knew how to use that mike, and I did, that's all."

Next day, Mr. Bayley sent word that he'd like to have the fifth grade put on their pageant for the Wilson Grade School, across town. The class voted to do it.

Mrs. Chandler said then, "Children, let's elect a sound engineer to serve for this performance."

"We've already elected Jerry."

"Sure, let Jerry keep on being engineer."

"But," Mrs. Chandler said, "Andy knows so much more about the job! Don't you think he'd make a good engineer?" she asked.

Accepting Others: Surmounting Prejudice

NO

TRESPASSING

The problem:

The issue is accepting others; specifically, the problem of surmounting prejudice.

This story typifies the classic human relations problem of exclusion because of race, creed, or nationality. Young children show few tendencies to discriminate against others for the usual social reasons until the adult culture influences them by example or pressure. By the time they are ten years old, most children do reflect the social patterns of discrimination of their family and class and community.

In this story, a boy is discriminated against on the basis of prejudice: anti-Semitism. The story, however, could also represent anti-Negro bias, anti-Italian bias, anti-Mexican, or anti-Puerto Rican, or any form of bigotry against people.

Introducing the problem:

This story involves such a controversial problem in our American scene that it is not possible to make simple and positive suggestions for treating it. You will have to estimate the meaning this story has for your pupils and community. If you teach in an eastern city that has a large Jewish population, this problem may be a very real and bitter one for some of your children. In some communities in the Middle West, on the other hand, there may be no incidents of anti-Semitism in the experience of your pupils.

One of your difficulties will be not to embarrass a Jewish child in your classroom, not to isolate him through this role-playing session. If there are only one or two such children in your group, it may be wise to change the nationality or religion of Syd in order to impersonalize the issue. You may make him a Chinese or Mexican or Indian boy. However, if there are a sizable number of Jewish children in your class, they probably are acquainted with the problem, and an honest, sympathetic approach through this story may help them to accept themselves, and may help the rest of the group to consider the consequences of discrimination.

Important to your success with this story is the task of meeting the problem so that children can see that people discriminate against others for various reasons, none of which is entirely rational.

The sign on the fence said very plainly, KEEP OUT!

Syd pointed to it. "Look."

"Oh, heck with it," Joe grunted. But Eddie walked closer and carefully read aloud the rest of the sign, "Private Property of Gray Hawk Military Summer Camp. Trespassers will be prosecuted to the full extent of the law."

"Maybe we better not go in there," Syd said. Dark-haired, ten years old, he was the smallest of the three boys. He wore glasses and tan gabardine trousers that weren't meant for hiking through brush. "We might get caught."

"Gosh, Syd," Joe complained, "you always worry!" Joe was bigger and chunkier than the other two. He had unruly red hair and freckles like paint splotches, and his clothes looked like hand-me-downs from an older brother. "You wait here, and if you see cops coming you send up a signal smoke."

Eddie said, "You got Wagon Train and The Untouchables mixed up, Joe." Eddie and Joe were eleven. Eddie was as tall as Joe, but slimmer. Eddie had sandy hair and gray eyes and an easy grin. Spreading apart two strands of the barbed-wire fence, he said, "Syd, crawl through."

Syd climbed through and ripped a big tear in his pants.

Joe said, "You're going to be sunburned in a funny place."

Joe followed through the fence.

"Shh," Syd warned, "I hear voices."

"Flat on your stomachs," Eddie commanded, "and pipe down."

Their pulses beating with excitement, they crawled up a slope of brush to the edge of a big level field on which was a fenced enclosure. Inside were a dozen boys on horseback, taking a riding lesson from a big gray-haired man on a restless palomino.

"Look at the fancypants!" Joe sneered.

"Shh!" Eddie commanded.

But Syd whispered, "He's teaching them stunt riding!"

"I don't like these stuck-up military schools," Joe said.

But his scorn was as envious as Syd's wistfulness. The Gray Hawk boys did look awfully smart in their gray whipcord riding breeches and shiny riding boots and light gray shirts with the hawk-shaped red patch on the shoulder. The Gray Hawk Academy was an expensive boys' boarding school.

The instructor gave some orders and the riders dismounted and took off their boots, then got back into the saddle. The man gave further orders and the boys separated and started going through stunts.

It was a good show to watch. The Gray Hawk boys practiced riding standing on two horses, one foot in each saddle. They did that with a boy sitting on the shoulders of a boy standing up. Then two boys, each standing on a horse, would carry a third boy standing between them with a foot on their thighs. Several boys practiced riding standing up and doing "gainers"—turning and lighting on their feet in the saddle again.

"Wish I could ride like that," Syd murmured.

"Practice enough and you could," Eddie said.

"Fancy stuff," Joe snorted. "Let's go somewhere else."

"We'll go to the lake," Eddie decided. "Follow me in single file and *no* talking!"

They did a real Indian job of snaking through the brush toward the water edge. Fawnskin Lake was an artificial reservoir, but big enough for sailing and outboard racing. Eddie stopped, peered through a fringe at the boathouse just beyond them and at the big raft fifty yards from shore.

Gray Hawk boys were diving off a high board on the raft. Others were in boats, using double paddles to speed along in kayaks made of tear-shaped droppable fuel tanks for airplanes. Other boys were pedaling contraptions made of fuel tanks rigged in pairs with a bicycle frame between them on which a boy could sit and pedal, turning a paddle wheel below him. Still other boys were coasting down a tall slide built on the bank—lying on their stomachs on a sled fitted with skates which zoomed down the slide and shot away out into the water.

"Look at that," Syd whispered, "I bet that's fun."

But Eddie said, more excitedly, "Look at that!" and he pointed out into the lake. "That's *more* fun."

Out in the middle of the lake were a couple of motorboats racing along at a speed that sent a bow wave slanting back on each side higher than the boat itself. And out behind each craft, being towed at the end of a long line, was a boy on water skis.

"Lucky, lucky," Eddie said. "Al Burns goes to Gray Hawk. His Dad's a doctor."

"So's Ned Warren at Gray Hawk," Syd said. "His Pop sells cars."

Joe insisted, "Come on, let's go home!"

Syd was slow about turning. "They sure have fun," he murmured.

They crawled for some distance, then stood up and elbowed their way through the bush. It was hard work and when they came out upon a narrow path they followed it with relief. It led away from the lake toward the highway, winding down a slope through the high greasewood.

Suddenly Eddie whispered, "Hide, quick!" and dived into the brush. Syd and Joe plunged after him for they now heard the approaching clatter of a horse coming up the trail. Flat on their stomachs they lay frozen, straining to see through the foliage.

The horse trotted into view its sides heaving and its neck lathered. A rein had come undone from one bit and was dragging along the ground and the sorrel was stepping on it and scaring himself. There was a saddle on his back but nobody sat in it. The horse was riderless.

As the animal passed Eddie said, "Wait! Maybe his rider's chasing him."

Moments passed, became a minute—two minutes. The horse had gone out of sight and out of earshot. Nobody came up-trail.

"Maybe the horse ran under a tree and the rider got knocked off?" Syd suggested.

"Shucks," Joe said, "the rider just tied him up and the dumb horse pulled and pulled until he broke the rein and got loose."

Eddie was looking left and right off the trail, frowning as he led hurriedly down the path. Syd was almost stepping on Eddie's heels but Joe lagged behind.

"What's the rush?" he complained. But presently he quickened his own stride because the sun was lowering behind a ridge to the west and it was getting cool and dark in the thick chaparral on the valley floor.

It was Syd who sighted the two buzzards circling high in the air and who gasped and said, "Eddie, look!" and pointed to them.

Eddie looked. "No, Syd. Too far, I'd say."

They came around a bend then and Eddie saw the shiny tan boots a half-dozen yards from the trail. Syd saw them too and stopped, but Eddie plunged into the brush.

"Syd," Eddie called. "Joe! Come here!"

The boy in the whipcord riding boots and gray shirt with the red hawk emblem on the sleeves was lying on his stomach in the grass, perfectly still. He might have been sleeping, except that one leg was twisted awkwardly and his arms were crooked as if he had tried to pull himself along on the ground.

Joe gasped, "Is he dead?"

Eddie bent down, took hold of the boy's wrist and felt for the pulse.

"Look at his head," Syd said.

Eddie nodded. "Looks like he hit a rock when he got thrown."

"He's bleeding a lot!"

"But I can't feel any pulse," Eddie said.

Syd took a small mirror from his pocket, pulling out a comb at the same time. The comb fell to the ground, but Syd didn't notice. He bent and held the mirror before the boy's open mouth.

"Look! The mirror's clouding over. He's breathing. Let's run for help!"

But Eddie said, "We can't leave him. It'll be dark. We might not even be able to find our way back here until morning."

"I don't think we should leave him here all night—not while he's bleeding."

"Well, then, we've got to carry him out."

"Carry him? Gosh, he's bigger than any of us—"

"We're carrying him!" Eddie said sharply.

He put his hands under the senseless boy's armpits and Syd picked up the boy's legs and they started down the trail. They hadn't gone fifty feet before they had to put him down.

"Gosh, we'll never get him out to the road this way!"

"We'll have to make a litter. Two poles and a couple of jackets."

"What jackets?"

"We'll use our shirts," Eddie said and took his off. Syd and Joe stripped theirs off, too.

"Look at my goose bumps," Joe complained; he had no undershirt on.

They found several slim saplings of tree tobacco not far from the trail. Joe had a Scout knife and with it he laboriously cut the saplings into two rough poles. They stuck the poles through the sleeves of their shirts and made a crude stretcher. Upon it they placed the hurt boy.

The makeshift litter was such an improvement over carrying that they started out confidently with the boy. But after the first dozen yards it was surprising how much heavier the hurt youngster got with every additional step.

"Let's stop a minute," Joe panted. They halted and set the stretcher down.

"My turn," Syd said eagerly and took Joe's place.

A little further on Eddie stopped again. "Gosh, I'm tuckered," he gasped.

"My turn again," Joe said, and took hold of the front end.

"Look!" Syd blurted. He was gulping for breath and his slim legs were shaking with weariness. "He's moving, he's trying to talk!"

The hurt boy was stirring, was mumbling something, but it didn't make sense, and when Eddie asked him, "How're you feeling?" the boy didn't answer and gave no sign that he heard at all.

Syd quavered, "I d-don't like the way his head is bleeding. It isn't stopping at all."

Eddie bent and pressed fingers against the boy's temples. That seemed to lessen the seeping flow.

Syd said, "Losing too much blood. That's awfully bad."

"Let's hurry, now!" Eddie ordered.

Twenty steps farther and Syd stumbled with weariness; a sob broke from his lips. "Gosh, I nearly dropped him!"

"Here, my turn again; you press your fingers against the sides of his forehead," Eddie ordered.

Fifty feet farther on Joe stopped and swayed in his tracks. "I'm— I'm pooped out," he admitted, and his voice ached with shame. "Just this little ways and I'm dropping!"

"My turn again," Syd said.

"Maybe we'd better rest. Just for a minute," Eddie said.

"We got to get him to a doctor," Syd said.

"I know it!" Eddie snapped. "Come on!"

Syd made it another fifty feet and then choked out, "Joe!" and Syd fell to his knees. He tried to hold the litter up but could not, and when it dropped the hurt boy rolled off. Syd began to cry.

"I d-dropped him! I dropped him!"

Eddie bent and helped Syd get up and said, "Gosh, Syd, nothing to feel that bad about! I'm falling off my feet too!"

"Look, Syd," Joe said, "my fingers are so stiff I can't press them against his head right. You do it, Syd. Eddie and I will do the carrying!"

A little farther on they reached the highway. Getting the hurt boy through the fence was a hard job. They braced the bottom wire up with a stick and Eddie crawled under and then had to push the hurt boy through.

Cars whizzed past on the highway and in the twilight their headlights were dazzling winds of light that flowed over the boys. One car, however, did not roar past, but stopped, pulling off the shoulder. A spotlight turned and shone full on the boys, blinding them.

An angry, bossy voice demanded: "What're you boys doing in there? Can't you read those NO TRESPASSING signs?"

Joe whirled, looked, and gasped: "They're cops. Highway Patrol. Run!" Joe bent his head and plunged off into the brush alongside the road.

Eddie gave Syd a push and whispered, "Run, Syd, run!"

Then Eddie slowly walked straight into the spotlight glare, toward the Highway Patrol car.

"There's a hurt boy here," Eddie said, his voice breaking. "I want to report a hurt boy!"

Two minutes later the police car was racing down the highway, siren screaming, toward the Emergency Hospital in town. Eddie had never ridden so fast in his life. But he wasn't enjoying it.

It was the next evening that Eddie's Dad answered the door bell after supper and saw a big gray-haired man waiting there.

"My name's Nichols," the man said, "I'm looking for a youngster named Eddie Malloy."

"Why, this is Eddie's home. Come in, sir," Eddie's father said.

Eddie, doing his homework beside the radio in the living room, felt his throat tighten up. They were looking for him!

"I'm Eddie's father. What did you want to see Eddie about?"

"Why, last night the police picked up a boy named Eddie Malloy. They saw him coming from the grounds of the Gray Hawk Military Academy. He had another boy with him who was hurt and the police rushed the injured lad to the hospital. But while they were carrying the hurt boy into the hospital, Eddie ran away."

And now they've come after me! Eddie realized. In his mind was that sign on the Gray Hawk fence: *Trespassers will be prosecuted to the full extent of the law.*

"The policemen knew his name," the man went on, "because they had questioned him while driving to the hospital. He told them two other boys had been on the school grounds with him. I'm looking for them, too. Your boy wouldn't give their names to the policemen."

"Oh, he wouldn't?" Eddie's Dad said. He didn't sound angry, exactly, more like he was proud, or something.

"I want to find all three of them," Mr. Nichols went on. And his voice had an odd, shaky unevenness in it. "You see, my boy, Philip, is a student at Gray Hawk. He—my wife died five years ago. Philip likes horses. He's a great little rider. Well, yesterday, he says, he was riding this new horse, Chappo, down through the brush and a quail flying up suddenly scared Chappo into bucking and a rein broke. Phil got thrown. He doesn't remember much after that, but the doctor says the horse must have kicked him in the head."

"Good Lord," Eddie's Dad said, "that's awful!"

"Yes, I—" Mr. Nichols coughed kind of hard, and didn't finish.

"How is the boy?"

"The doctor thought at first it might be a fracture, but now he's decided it's just concussion. But Mr. Malloy, if Philip hadn't been found he'd have lain out there all night. He'd lost a lot of blood, and probably —if your son and his friends hadn't carried him out to the highway, he'd be dead now."

"Oh, no, I don't think—"

"That's exactly what the doctor says." Mr. Nichols' voice was getting kind of loud. He shut up abruptly, as if realizing it. "My boy means an awful lot to me."

"Of course."

"I'm not really a wealthy man, Mr. Malloy. I keep Philip in Gray Hawk because he has such a swell time there and I can manage it. Now, I can't just say thanks to your son and his two friends. I'd like to do something for them."

"Oh, that's not necessary at all, Mr. Nichols!"

"Yes, it is, sir. For me. Now, I had this idea. Tell me what you think of it. It's summer time, it's vacation time—and your lad and his two chums were trespassing on the Gray Hawk summer camp. I don't blame them for that. It's a wonderful place. What I'd like to do, sir—I'd like to have Eddie and his two friends become members of Gray Hawk for two weeks. To spend two weeks up there as my guests, swimming and riding and having all that fun. What do you think of that idea, Mr. Malloy?"

Eddie's Dad's voice was soft as he said, "Mr. Nichols, I think those boys would love it. But suppose we ask them." And Mr. Malloy called, "Oh, Eddie! Come here!" Eddie came running in. One look at his excited face told his Dad and Mr. Nichols that he had overheard.

"You'd like to go, wouldn't you, Eddie?" his Dad said.

"I would, Dad, I sure would!"

"How about Joe and Syd?"

"Can I go call them, Pop?"

Mr. Malloy nodded, and Eddie shot out of the house. Syd lived next door and Joe lived across the street. A few minutes later Eddie was back, bringing Joe and Syd.

"Mr. Nichols," Eddie blurted, "I told them, but they just can't believe it's so."

Mr. Nichols smiled at them. "It's true, boys. Would you all like to spend two weeks at the Gray Hawk camp?"

"Gosh, yes!" Joe almost yelled, and Syd said breathlessly, "Yes, sir!"

"All right, then, it's settled! I'll telephone Major Arnott in the morning and at two o'clock tomorrow afternoon I'll come for you and I'll take you there. I'll have to give Arnott your names and addresses." He took a pencil from his pocket and opened his wallet to write in it. "Eddie Malloy ... and Joe—Joe Harris ... and Syd—is that Sydney?"

"Yes, sir, Sidney Goldberg."

"Sidney Gold—oh. G-o-l-d-b-e-r-g?"

"Yes, sir."

Very slowly Mr. Nichols wrote the name out, letter by letter. His face got very red and his forehead was sweaty, as if the room had suddenly become very hot. After finishing Syd's name he stared at the paper, frowning, as if trying hard to see something that had become very dim.

"I'll call Major Arnott first thing in the morning," he repeated, almost as if talking to himself. He glanced up at Mr. Malloy suddenly, an odd, baffled, worried look in his eyes, almost as if he were asking Mr. Malloy for help. But Mr. Malloy didn't say anything, though he, too, was looking strange now. His lips had shut tight and his eyes had a bright, steady glint as if he were suddenly angry, but he wasn't going to let the faintest hint of it escape him.

"Look, Sidney," Mr. Nichols said. "Have you—have you got a bicycle?"

"Why, no, I haven't, Mr. Nichols," Syd said.

Mr. Nichols seemed suddenly to cheer up. "Sydney, what do you think of this— I'm going to get you a brand new Columbia bicycle! You know, one of those fancy models with a klaxon and an electric light and racing tires and—would you like that, Sydney?"

Sydney looked puzzled. "Are you going to give Joe and Eddie a bike too?"

"Oh, no!" Mr. Nichols was very bluff and hearty now. "Instead of a bike, I'll take them up to the Gray Hawk camp. You'll be luckier than they are! After the two weeks are over, you'll still have a bike, while they—"

"But you said *all* of us were to go to camp?" Eddie reminded him, and at the same time Joe was saying, "Syd would rather go to camp. I know he would!"

Mr. Nichols wiped his face with his handkerchief and looked miserable.

"Boys, I—Mr. Malloy! Won't you—"

Eddie's Dad said briefly, "Tell them yourself."

"Well, you see—believe me, boys, I don't like this, but the Gray Hawk School is a very special kind of place. Believe, me, I've had nothing to do with making the rules—"

"Tell them," Mr. Malloy repeated.

"The Gray Hawk summer camp won't take Jewish boys."

Eddie and Joe did not understand at first. They stared at Mr. Nichols. But Syd said, "Oh." And Syd got a white, sick look on his face.

"But why not?" Eddie demanded. And then Eddie said, "Wait, Syd!"

for Syd had turned and was walking out of the room. Eddie started after him.

Mr. Nichols said, "Boys, Gray Hawk won't take Negro boys, either, or Chinese, or—listen, just because one of you can't go to camp, that's no reason for the other two fellows to lose out, is it? I'm sure Syd wouldn't want you to miss a fine vacation just because he can't go. Wait, Eddie, let's talk this over!"

KEEP
OUT:
THIS
MEANS
YOU

The problem:

The issue is accepting others; specifically, the problem of surmounting prejudice.

This is another version of the "No trespassing" story, for use with somewhat older children, and for use with groups for whom it is better not to use a Jewish boy as the object of exclusion. In this story, the boy being discriminated against is of Mexican-American background.

This story, as does "No Trespassing," deals with the problem of exclusion because of race, creed, or nationality.

Introducing the problem:

You may say to the group, "Have you ever wanted to go to a movie—or into a private park or swimming pool—and been told that you can't enter because you are too young, or because you don't have a proper guest card or you're not on the list of eligible people? If you have, you can probably remember how you felt: you were frustrated and annoyed and probably angry. This is a story about such an incident. The story stops but isn't finished. As I read, try to think of ways in which the story might end."

A barbed wire fence blocked the way for the three boys. Andy stooped to crawl under but Ben stopped him.

"Don't. Look at that sign."

On a tree nearby a sign warned:

PRIVATE PROPERTY

KEEP OUT: THIS MEANS YOU

TRESPASSERS WILL BE PROSECUTED

Sierra Beach Recreation Club

Pete said, "Guess that finishes our short-cut. We'll have to go back to the highway and take the long way back to camp."

"Aw, that sign isn't legal," Andy said angrily. "You can walk along the edge of any navigable waters. The law says so."

Ben said, "But maybe this isn't navigable water?"

"Oh, no? Is that a boat out there, or a whale blowing his nose?"

"It's a boat, but—"

"And it's navigating this lake. I'm going ahead," Andy said, "and if you're scared, you can go back. Come on, Pete."

Andy flopped down and crawled under the fence. Pete looked at him, looked at Ben, and sighed.

"You're probably right, Ben, but—here goes." He bent and stooped quickly under the wire. "This is like eating green apples. I know I'm probably going to be sorry."

"Okay, let's go, Pete," Andy said.

But Pete looked across the wire at Ben and said, "Ben, the vote's two to one against you. Come on."

"Let 'im be stubborn," Andy said.

Ben gave in. Dropping flat to the ground, he rolled under the strands.

"We got to walk along the water edge," he warned the others.

They started walking warily along the lake shore.

The Sierra Beach resort, they realized presently, was a dream place for fun. It made their Scout camp look like a meager pigpen.

A big clubhouse stood near the beach. Behind it, in the shade of towering pines, were attractive log cottages. In front of the clubhouse was a beach and a big swimming area with a diving tower and a tall slide. Out beyond was a line of rafts to which boats were tied.

"Boy, what a fancy place!" Pete said.

Andy snorted. "I don't like these stuck-up resorts."

Ben said, "Say, just look at those water skiers. Those boys are sure good."

"They ought to be, after all the practice they get!"

Out beyond the rafts, a ski competition was taking place. A double line of buoys bearing flags made a slalom course. One after another, a boy on a single ski, towed by a fast boat, would go racing through the course, making swift, graceful turns to left and right around the successive markers.

"Hey, we go this way, so we won't be spotted," Andy ordered, and led the others around to the back of the resort, through the trees. Farther on, they returned to the water edge.

Here a group of small tree-covered islands stood near the shore. The water between islands and shore was stippled with stumps.

"Somebody's coming!" Andy cautioned suddenly and crouched down behind a bush. Pete and Ben flopped down beside him.

From the direction of the resort, a boat came roaring into the stump-strewn channel between the shore and the little islands. The boat was a fast outboard driven by a single passenger. The boat towed a water skier, who swerved from side to side, dodging stumps like a slalom racer.

"They're crazy," Andy gasped. "If he hit a stump—"

"Gosh, he's good!" Pete said. "Look at him! Not even wearing a life jacket!"

"They're breaking the law," Ben said. "You're supposed to have at least two people in the boat when pulling a skier, so one is always watching—"

"Unless you've got a panoramic rear-view mirror for the driver," Andy butted in. "Hey, look!"

The boat was roaring straight at a sandy spit that jutted from the shore out into the water. The boat hit the obstacle—but slid right over it, and raced on. The skier, approaching, hunched and jumped, launching himself into the air, leaping over the sandspit. Then the boat veered right toward a wooden ramp in the water that looked like a raft set at a slant. At the last possible moment, the boat turned slightly, barely missing the ramp. The skier did not turn: he swooped up the inclined ramp and into the air. He kept his balance and landed upright on the water again, and kept right on going behind the boat. The boat curved around a nearby island and swept out of sight, the skier following in a wide, whipcracker swing.

"Gosh, did you see that?"

"Darn good way to break your neck."

"Hey, here comes another!"

A second boat was following the first, as if they were playing follow-the-leader. This boat in turn zigged and zagged through the puzzle of stumps, the skier skillfully swooping left and right around the hazards. The boat drove right on over the same sandspit, slid across, motor kicking up behind; and the skier leaped the barrier. This boat also raced close past the inclined ramp.

But the skier was coming out of a turn when he hit the ramp. He hit the ramp at a bad angle, whipcracking in a swooping turn at the end of the long rope. He had too much momentum and too much torque: he was flung as if from a sling. He went up into the air, somersaulting, losing his ski, whirling head over heels and coming down onto the water in a smacking bellybuster that made the watching boys wince in sympathetic shock—and he disappeared under the surface.

Andy, Pete, and Ben—all shouted at the fellow driving the boat. But the driver didn't hear over his engine noise and hadn't noticed what had happened to his tow: the boat roared on around the end of the island, and vanished from sight, the tow rope and handle skittering over the wake behind him.

"That dumb—"

"Going off and leaving that guy in the water!"

"Maybe he doesn't know what happened!"

Taut, the boys watched, waiting for the skier to rise to the surface and strike out toward shore.

But they saw no sign of him.

"He's sure staying down long."

"That guy in the boat ought to be coming back."

"He must've been looking ahead and never saw what happened," Andy said. "Come on!"

Andy started running down the beach. At the water edge he paused just long enough to kick off his shoes, then he splashed in and flung himself into a flat dive and swam out as fast as he could stroke.

Pete said, "But suppose the fellows in the boats come back and catch us here?"

"So they send us to Juvenile Hall," Ben said. "We can't let somebody just drown!"

Pete jerked off his shoes and ran into the water, following Andy. Ben started after him, then swerved toward a tree near the water's edge and pulled himself up into the branches.

"Andy!" he shouted, "to your right. To your right!"

Andy had stopped swimming, was looking for the skier. Hearing Ben, Andy turned to the right, then kicked his legs up and went under water in a dive. Moments passed, stretching almost into a minute. Andy came up, gulped for air, gasped, "Help me, Pete!" and went down in a second dive. Pete, nearby, also dived. Again Andy came up—and this time he had hold of the skier.

"Pete—help!"

Pete reached him. Together, pulling the limp body of the other boy, they worked toward shore.

Ben climbed down from the tree and ran into the water.

"Help, Ben. I'm pooped," Andy gasped.

"I got him!"

They brought the boy ashore.

"Look at his head. Bleeding. Must've hit something," Andy said.

"Gosh, he's dead," Pete said.

"Maybe he's just senseless," Ben said. "Come on."

The boy was about their own age, twelve, and light. They laid him on his stomach across a log, to empty his lungs of water, for a few moments.

"Now. Flat on the ground. On his back," Andy said.

He knelt beside the boy, tilted his head back, opened his mouth wide, pinched his nose closed. Then, leaning down, Andy breathed into the senseless boy's mouth. Raising his head, Andy caught a full breath of his own, gave the senseless boy's lungs a chance to exhale, then bent down and breathed into the boy's mouth again. Over and over he repeated the process.

"Too fast," Ben warned. "Time it to a count of five—the manual says twelve breaths a minute."

"Gosh, he sure looks dead," Pete said.

"Spell me!" Andy commanded.

Pete spelled him; then Ben took a turn working on the boy.

"Where's the driver of that boat?" Andy wondered aloud angrily. "You think he still doesn't know he lost his skier?"

Ben said, "He doesn't know *where* he lost him."

"This kid would sure be drowned by now."

"Don't see how he could be any deader."

But the boy moaned, then, and stirred.

"Hey, he wasn't really dead!" Pete marveled.

"Only slightly," Ben said. "Keep working on him."

Presently the boy opened his eyes and demanded, "Wh-what happened?"

"You tried to push a hole in the bottom of the lake with your chin," Andy said. "You're all right now."

The sound of motors came from the lake.

"Now they come," Pete said. "We better scram."

The two boats were moving slowly. Then their passengers sighted the group on the beach, and the motors revved up and the boats came roaring up toward shore. Shutting off their engines, the drivers beached the boats and jumped up and came running.

"Hey, leave that boy alone!" one shouted.

They were big boys, older boys, teen-agers; probably counselors at the Sierra camp.

"What are you doing to him?" one demanded.

"Saving his life," Andy said. "Any objections?"

Several days later, after dinner in the evening, Andy's father got up from his easy chair in front of the TV set to answer the doorbell. A tall, gray-haired man was at the front door.

"My name's Borden," he said. "I'm looking for Andy Hollis."

"He's here. Come in, won't you? I'm Andy's father."

Andy, doing his homework on the diningroom table, overheard, and was startled. Somebody coming for *him?*

"What did you want to see Andy about, Mr. Borden?"

"Why, a couple of days ago, some boys climbed through the fence into the grounds of the Sierra Beach resort. They were seen, and two of the counselors talked to one of them, who said his name was Andy Hollis. While the counselors were carrying an injured boy to the clubhouse, Andy and his friends ran away."

And now they've come for me, Andy realized. The sign just outside the resort fence blazed clear in his mind: TRESPASSERS WILL BE PROSECUTED. His stomach churned with fright.

"Two other boys were with your son, Mr. Hollis. Your boy wouldn't give their names to the counselors."

"That so?" Andy's father didn't sound displeased exactly, but his voice did become serious as he asked, "They were trespassing, were they?"

"I want to find all three of them," Mr. Borden went on, his voice a little unsteady. "You see, my boy Tom is staying at Sierra Beach this summer. He—my wife died a few years ago, and I have to travel in my business. Tom—well, he gets lonely. He likes water sports, so the resort is fine for him. He's a good water skier. Well, the other day, he says he was running through the obstacle course, as they call it—and had an accident. He hit the jump ramp at a bad angle and crashed into the water. His forehead hit a ski edge and he was knocked out. He wasn't wearing a life belt, either; and the boy driving the boat was looking ahead and never even saw what had happened. Just kept right on going."

"Good gosh!"

"Yes, I—" Mr. Borden could not speak for a moment. "I have no other children."

"What happened? How's your boy?"

"Your son and his friends saw him take that awful spill. They dived in and brought Tommy out. Even then, he'd have died if they hadn't revived him."

"Oh, now, I imagine—"

"No, the big boys in the boats were looking in the wrong places for him. They might never have found him. They admit it. Now, I just can't only say thanks to your son and his two friends. I'd like to *do* something for them."

"Oh, that's not necessary at all, Mr. Borden."

"Yes, it is, sir. Now I had this idea. It's vacation time. Your lad and his two chums were trespassing on the Sierra Beach resort grounds. Obviously, the place attracts them. What I'd like to do, sir—I'd like to have Andy and his two friends be guests at the resort. To spend two weeks, swimming and riding and water-skiing and all the rest of it. What do you think of the idea?"

"They'd love it, Mr. Borden," Andy's father said enthusiastically. "Why not ask them? Oh, Andy. Come in here, will you?"

Andy came in. One look at his excited face told the two men that he had overheard.

"You'd really like to go to the resort for—"

"I sure would, Dad!"

"How about Pete and Ben?"

"Can I go call 'em, Dad?"

Mr. Hollis nodded, and Andy ran out of the house. Pete lived next door, and Ben lived across the street. A few minutes later Andy was back, with his friends.

Mr. Borden smiled at them.

"It's true, boys. Would you all like to spend two weeks at Sierra Beach, as my guests?"

"Gosh, yes!" Pete almost yelled; and Ben said breathlessly, "Yes, sir."

"All right, then; it's settled. I'll have to give the manager your names and addresses." He took a pencil from his pocket and opened his wallet to write on a memo sheet.

"Andy Hollis. I have this address."

"Pete Bailey, sir," Pete said. "226 Morton Road."

"And Ben—"

"Ben Gonzales, 2259 Morton Road."

"Ben . . . G-o-n-z-a-l-e-s?"

"Yes, sir!"

Slowly, letter by letter, Mr. Borden wrote out Ben's name. Mr. Borden's face got red, and his forehead beaded with perspiration, as if the room had become hot. After finishing Ben's name, he stared at the writing, frowning, as if trying hard to remember something.

"I'll call the manager, first thing in the morning," he said, but his mind did not seem to be on what he was saying at all. He looked at Andy's father with a deeply troubled expression, as if he were asking Mr. Hollis to come to his help. But Andy's father did not say anything although he too had an odd look now. His lips had shut tight and his eyes were angry.

"Look, Ben," Mr. Borden said. "Have you—have you got one of these new go-carts?"

"Why, no, sir, I haven't," Ben said.

Oddly, this seemed to make Mr. Borden cheer up.

"Ben, I'd like to do something special for you. How'd you like a brand-new Hurri-kart? It's got a two and a half horsepower motor, ten-inch wheels with real pneumatic tires, a roll bar like a real racer, and a top speed of thirty miles an hour? Would you like that, Ben?"

Ben looked puzzled.

"Are you going to give Andy and Pete a go-cart too?"

"Well—no. I'll take them up to Sierra Beach for a vacation. You'll be luckier than they are! After the two weeks are over, you'll still have the Hurri-kart, while they—"

"But you said all of us were to go to Sierra Beach," Andy reminded him, and at the same time Pete said, "Ben would rather go to the lake with us!"

Mr. Borden wiped his face with his handkerchief; he looked as if he were in acute discomfort.

"Boys, I— Mr. Hollis, won't you—"

Andy's father said, "Tell them yourself."

"Well, you see— Please believe me, boys, I'm unhappy about this— but the Sierra Beach resort is a sort of—exclusive place. Believe me, if I had anything to do with making the rules—"

"Tell them," Mr. Hollis insisted.

"Sierra Beach won't take Mexican boys."

Andy and Pete did not understand at first; they stared at Mr. Borden. But Ben said, "Oh!" and looked as if the bottom of the world had dropped out.

"But why not?" Andy demanded. And called, "Wait, Ben!" for Ben had turned and was walking out of the room. Andy started after him.

"But, boys," Mr. Borden said hurriedly, "Sierra Beach won't take Negro boys, either, or Chinese, or— Let's be sensible; after all, just because one of you can't be a guest at the resort, that doesn't mean that the other two should give up such a fine chance, does it? Ben wouldn't want you to miss out on such a swell vacation just because he's not along. Wait, Andy! Pete! We've got to talk this over!"

SECOND

PRIZE

The problem:

The issue is discrimination on the basis of color, creed, or nationality; this story deals with a subtle aspect of segregation.

Introducing the problem:

You may say to the group, "All of you know what a great effort is being made today to rid ourselves of bias against people who are of different color than we are. This is a story dealing with the problem of prejudice. The story stops but is not finished. As I read, think of ways in which the story might be finished."

Edith, Tom, and Lucia were puzzled and a little worried as they walked down the hall toward the principal's office. Edith was president of the sixth-grade class, Tom was secretary, and Lucia was treasurer.

"Why did Mr. Watson send for us?" Tom asked.

"You worry too much," Edith said. "Nobody's busted a window."

And Lucia said, "It doesn't have to be something *bad*."

"Mr. Watson doesn't call us in unless it's for something important."

As the students entered the office, Mr. Watson looked up from his desk and smiled at them. They relaxed; the principal was obviously pleased about something.

"Hello. Thanks for coming down so promptly. I've got an important job for you."

"What is that, sir?" Tom asked.

"I want you three to act as a special committee. I want you to select the boy or girl whom you believe to be the Best School Citizen of the Year.

"I'll explain. You remember, last month, when five-year-old Pete Doyle was lost in the park along Deer Creek? All you sixth-grade boys helped search for him. It got freezing cold that night, and if you boys hadn't found Pete he'd have probably died. His grandfather wants to show his appreciation by doing something for the sixth grade. I suggested that we could use a record player. He said sure, he'd give the school a good one. But he'd also like to give something nice to just one student. Something that would be his or hers to keep; and yet, would give recognition to the school too. We decided to make it an award to the Best School Citizen of the Year."

"That's a good idea."

"What is the award, sir?"

"I can't tell you that; it's to be a big surprise. We're having Field Day on Friday, and Mr. Doyle will bring the present here and will give it to the winner himself. I'll tell you this much, though: it's a pretty wonderful surprise. It's something that'll be enjoyed for years, and will make the winner mighty happy."

"Sir, can't you tell just the committee?"

"We'll be staying up nights, trying to guess—"

"Mr. Doyle wants it to be a surprise," the principal repeated firmly. "He says he wants to see everybody's eyes pop out when he unloads it. Well, I'll leave you now. You three are now in session as the selection committee. Pull your chairs up to the table and start balloting."

"It's not going to be easy, sir," Tom said.

Mr. Watson walked out. The students leaned their elbows on the table and frowned in concentration.

"Best School Citizen of the Year," Tom echoed. "Say, how about *you*, Edith?"

"Sure," Lucia said. "You got elected class president. You're our top citizen."

"I'm out. So're you two. We're the nominating committee."

"How about Sam Baker, then?" Lucia asked. "He ran the paper drive for his room last month, and they brought in the most paper."

"But that paper drive," Edith objected, "wasn't nearly as important as the milk drive!"

"That's right," Tom agreed. "Sending milk to refugee camps in Asia is more important."

"You think maybe it's a television set?" Edith asked.

"What is?"

"The prize, the prize!"

"Will you quit crying about the prize," Tom snapped, "and get to work?"

"But, gosh, Mr. Watson said it's something you'd enjoy for years—"

"How about Toby Anderson?" Lucia suggested. "Everybody likes him."

"But what's he ever *done?*" Tom demanded. "This isn't a contest for who's *liked* the most."

"Toby's good at baseball."

"So's Joey Stevens and Ralph Nix."

"Say, how about Joey Stevens?" Edith said excitedly.

"That's right."

"But what's Joey ever done?" Lucia asked.

"Well," Tom started to explain, "that day there was a fire on his block—"

"You missed it, Lucia," Edith put in, "you were absent that week."

"So what happened?"

"It was after school," Tom began, "and Joey was home . . ."

Joey saw the two small boys turn from the sidewalk into the weed-grown lot next door. At the time, it did not worry him. Kids had used that lot for a playground until the city had built a real playground a block away that had swings and slides and traveling rings and a baseball diamond and a director who provided bats and balls and kept the big boys from bullying the little boys too much. Now the lot was usually deserted. A crop of weeds had grown over it. In spring the weeds were pleasantly green but now, after a hot summer, they were dead and dry.

People who lived in the shabby tenement flats on each side of the lot often dumped rubbish in it: baby carriages too worn out to use even for carrying junk; mattresses with rips that oozed stuffing; broken chairs, boxes, bottles, excelsior, trunks, and so on. An old wagon and a truck without wheels rested in peace at the back of the lot. Occasionally a hackie living next door would run his old cab over the curb onto the lot and wash the car or leave it there overnight.

Joey, sitting at the front window of his mother's flat, was busy doing his arithmetic homework. After looking up as the two small boys turned into the lot, he bent over his book and paper again.

He smelled smoke a minute or two before actually realizing what it was. Then he heard a crackling noise like strings of firecrackers popping. Faintly against that noise he heard a kid yelling.

Abruptly he jumped up, remembering. Those two small boys who had walked onto the lot—

He ran out the front door and around the corner of the house onto the lot—and saw the fire.

Tall weeds at the back of the lot were tonguing flames a dozen feet into the air.

"Those kids! I bet they started it."

But where were they? He could not see them. He heard them, however. One was crying, the other yelling. Through his mind streaked an explanation of what had probably happened. They had brought matches from their mother's kitchen. Maybe a couple of wieners, too. They had come out here to play at camping; maybe planning to put wieners on the ends of sticks to roast them. But, of course, the fire had got away from them. Once started in these dry weeds, it would spread like an explosion.

Where were they?

He saw them, as a gust of wind bent the smoke flat. They were on the other side of the fire, against the wall of the sheds behind them. Trapped. And scared into senseless panic.

Joey didn't stop to think. He ran. He started through the smoke over ground burned black, through the curtain of fire where it was thinnest.

Reaching the two kids, he lifted one six-year-old—hoisted him up onto the roof of the low shed.

"Run!"

Bending, he grabbed up the second boy. This youngster was heavier but Joey somehow boosted up the boy onto the roof of the shed.

Smoke swirled around Joey's face; smoke was a scorching torment in his throat, and he choked. Reaching up, he caught the edge of the roof. Heat struck his back like a slashing whip. He tried to climb, but his muscles lacked strength. A small hand grabbed his wrist. The fool kid was trying to help him! "Run!" Joey gasped. "These sheds'll burn too!"

Joey rested a half-second, and made another hard try—and got his elbows over the roof edge. Heat licked at the backs of his legs, and drove him into frantic effort. He swung a knee up, got it onto the roof, and rolled over into safety on the roof top.

Both small boys were there, staring at him with big eyes.

"Come on!" he yelled angrily at them.

They climbed down the far side of the shed, ran through the hallway of the tenement in front to the far side of the block.

"Go on home," Joey told the two kids, and ran home himself.

The backs of his shoes and jeans were scorched black. As he took them off, he heard the siren of a fire engine. He didn't run out to watch, but stayed in the bedroom, hiding. His legs were red and the skin blistered, and the blisters were beginning to hurt so much that he had to choke back whimpers of pain.

When his mother got home from work an hour later, she took one look, and said, "Come on, Joey! You can tell me what happened on the way." By cab she took him to a hospital dispensary three blocks away...

All that had happened over a month before; and the voices of the committee members were grave with respect as they discussed the incident.

"That was a pretty brave thing Joey did," Tom said.

"Sure was," Lucia agreed.

"I think," Tom decided, "that we ought to pick Joey for Best School Citizen of the Year."

"I agree."

"I vote for Joey too!"

Field Day came on a Friday. The whole school, from kindergarten through sixth grade, took part, singing on the school lawn and doing folk dances to music from a loudspeaker. Parents and friends looked on.

The last event of the afternoon was the presentation, by the principal, of the surprise award. Mr. Watson was smiling as he picked up the microphone at the stand and faced the crowd of children and parents. Everybody became quiet.

"And now, friends," Mr. Watson said, "I'm going to make the presentation of the award for our Best School Citizen of the Year. First now, I'm going to let you see the prize, which has been kept a secret. Then I'll name the winner." He looked around, toward the corner of the building, and shouted, "All right, Mr. Doyle! Bring it on!"

A car came down the school driveway, from around the corner of the school, towing a trailer. The rig stopped opposite the crowd. Mr. Doyle himself got out of the car, walked around to the rear of the trailer, opened its door, and carefully eased a pony out of it onto the ground.

Sight of that pony made a gasp go up from the crowd. Someone started clapping, and everybody applauded and whistled.

"What a beautiful pinto pony!" someone said, near Tom. And that was what Tom—and practically everyone in the crowd—was thinking. The pinto pranced as Mr. Doyle led him around in front of the children. The pony wore bridle and saddle made of fine hand-tooled leather and studded with silver conchas that glistened in the sun.

Mr. Doyle led the pony to the stand.

"Here he is, Mr. Watson. Whom does he belong to?"

Into the microphone, so that everyone would hear clearly, the principal said: "The youngster who has been chosen to receive this award as our Best School Citizen of the Year is—*Joey Stevens!*"

The crowd applauded heartily, some of the young people whooped until others shushed them. It was a popular choice.

Mr. Watson called: "Joey! Where are you? Step up here, son."

"I'm coming, Mr. Watson."

People made way for him, as he hurried forward; as he passed, friends patted him on the back and said, "Hurry, boy!" and "Nice going, Joey," and "Are you ever lucky!"

Mr. Watson shook hands with him, and held out the reins.

"Here, take the reins, boy. He's all yours, Joey! Climb aboard and ride 'im!"

Joey swung into the saddle in a way that showed he knew something about horses. The pinto stepped out lightly into a trot. Joey rode back and forth before the crowd, beaming with delight as everyone applauded. . . . Only Mr. Doyle stood dour and silent beside the principal, biting his lip as he stared.

"Mr. Watson," he said, his voice low but sharp, "I want to have a talk with you!"

On Monday morning Tom and Edith and Lucia were called to the principal's office again.

They found Mr. Watson looking very solemn and upset.

Tom said, "Good morning, sir. You sent for us?"

The principal nodded. "I'm sorry to have to tell the committee that Mr. Doyle isn't pleased with the way we awarded the prize for our Best School Citizen."

"Why not?" Tom asked. "It was a unanimous choice. We all three agreed on Joey Stevens."

"Mr. Doyle says he didn't know we had Negro children in our school. He says that he never intended for the pony to be given to a Negro boy."

"It wasn't given," Tom said angrily. "Joey won the pony—by being our best citizen!"

"I know." The principal sighed. "Mr. Doyle says Joey can keep the pony. Joey is our best colored citizen. However, Mr. Doyle says he has another pony just as fine as this one; a pinto, too. Mr. Doyle wants us to pick a *white* boy or girl who's our best school citizen, and give him or her this second pony."

The students just looked at Mr. Watson for a moment.

"That's odd—" Edith said.

But Tom demanded, "What did *you* say, sir?"

"I told Mr. Doyle that I'd leave it up to this committee. Shall we accept this second pony and choose another Best School Citizen?"

"But we've already picked him—it's Joey!" Tom insisted.

"But, Tom," Lucia said impulsively, "what's the harm of having another pony to give away? It's just extra good luck. Let's choose another lucky winner!"

"No," Tom said. "We've made our choice—and it's a good choice, and I'm sticking with it!"

"But I don't see the harm—" Lucia insisted.

Mr. Watson looked from Tom's face, to Lucia, and turned to Edith.

"Well, Lucia votes yes, and Tom votes no on choosing another Best Citizen. Edith, your vote will make a decisive two to one. How do you vote, yes or no?"

Usually Edith was quick to make up her mind; but a long, breath-held moment passed before she came to her decision. She said:

JOSEFINA

The problem:

The issue is that of discrimination on the basis of color, creed, or nationality. Josefina is Spanish-American. Her great-grandparents moved to Southern California long ago; her mother and father still speak Spanish in the home. In this story she meets a nice boy whose family have just moved to town from an eastern city. Josefina likes Ted, but he is an Anglo. When he asks her for a date, she is very troubled. If she goes out on a date with him, she foresees that the Anglo young people will snub him—and her Spanish-speaking friends will snub her. This story is for junior high or high school level.

Introducing the problem:

Say to the group, "Dating is a many-sided problem for most of us. Not only parents, but your friends, too, influence you in your choices of whom you'll ask to parties or whom you'll agree to go with. This story deals with one aspect of the matter. As I read, think of ways in which you might solve the problem of the story."

The big white rabbit hopped around the corner of the house onto the front lawn. He wasn't supposed to be there; he belonged in a hutch in the backyard. Josie Ruiz, seeing him from her bedroom window, sighed and realized that she'd have to go down and shoo the dumb brute back where he belonged. At dinner she'd tell her kid brother that he'd better put a lock on his hutches or he'd lose some of his pets. Josie pulled on a sweater and started brushing her hair.

Meanwhile, the rabbit hopped a little farther across the yard. He was a huge New Zealand buck with ears that looked big enough to catch baseballs in, a nose that wiggled constantly, hind feet that weren't really as big as snowshoes but were enormous, just the same, and a wide powder-puff of a tail. He sat down on that puff and looked around, his big ears swiveling to sample the breeze, like twin radar antennae. He heard nothing alarming, but he did see and smell a plot of pansies which Josie's mother had put out the day before, and he galumphed over to the bed and started putting down a square meal.

Josie saw, and thought, "Oh, gosh, mother'll have a fit!"

She delayed a moment, to finish brushing her hair—and then she heard the dog: the shrill, excited ki-yi-ing of a small dog that was chasing something. She glanced out of the window again and saw a small black and white dog starting across the street toward the rabbit.

"For goodness' sake!"

She slammed her brush down on the bureau and ran out of her room.

As she came out the front door, she heard somebody yell, "Spot! Spot! Come here!" She saw the big rabbit lift his head and look at the dog. She saw the dog, running across the lawn now—and a young fellow chasing after the dog.

She darted at the dog, crying "Git!"

The dog sat back on its haunches. The young man sprang at him and caught him. Holding on to the pooch, the young fellow looked at Josie.

"Hey, you oughtn't to let your rabbit run loose like that," he scolded. "Golly, I'd hate to have Spot kill it."

That little pooch kill Gargantua? Josie almost laughed out loud. The dog was a small terrier. Oh, he was probably full of fight, all right, and Gargantua was only a rabbit, but—

"You know, they use packs of terriers like this to hunt bears," the young fellow was saying. He smiled at Josie. "It's sure lucky I saw Spot start to cross the street."

Lucky for Spot! Josie thought. Oh, sure, Gargantua was just a big, fluffy-looking rabbit, but what he would have done to Spot would have been just plain murder, that's all. With those big hind feet, Gargantua could kick like a pile-driver—and those feet were armed with claws like sickles. Spot would have thought he had tangled with a combination tiger-and-mule that was kicking him to pieces and tearing him apart at the same time. Spot *was* lucky that he was still in one spot and not scattered all over the yard like confetti.

But Josie didn't say this to the young fellow; he was too nice. He was about her own age, fifteen or sixteen, and he had blue eyes and wavy brown hair and he really was good-looking. And the way he smiled at her showed that he liked what he saw, too.

So Josie just said, "Thanks." And then she didn't know what to say; she was shy with new people, especially with Anglos.

"I'll help you catch the rabbit," he said.

They herded Gargantua into the back yard—and he hopped up into his own hutch by himself, so that all they had to do was shut the door. Spot whined at sight of all the white rabbits, but the young fellow held the dog in his arms.

"My name's Ted Anderson," he said. "We moved in across the street just last week. I've seen you on the high school bus."

"I'm Josie Ruiz," she said. "We've always lived here."

"I'm a junior at high."

"I'm a soph."

"What's Liston High School like?"

She almost said, "Oh, I hate it!" but checked herself.

"Oh, it's all right, I guess—if you have friends."

"I've made a good start," he said, smiling. "Well, got to get home and practice. See you on the bus tomorrow, Josie."

Next morning, Josie put on a new plaid skirt and her favorite sweater, and tied a new nylon scarf about her dark hair.

When she came down to breakfast, her kid brother, Ramon, stared at her and said, "Gosh, Sis, you look neat!"

Josie flushed with pleasure. Ramon was usually far more apt to say, "Hey, what rock did you crawl out from under?" than to give compliments.

As she waited on the corner for the school bus, Ted Anderson walked up, carrying a musical instrument case. He smiled and said, "Hi." He wore tan slacks and a gray shirt, and he was just about the best-looking boy she had ever known, she realized.

There were plenty of vacant seats on the bus, but Ted sat down next to her.

"Got to finish a theme," he said. "I have band practice, first period, so I can't do it then."

He opened his instrument case. She saw the trumpet inside—and several books and some papers. He took paper out and started writing. In spite of the swaying of the bus, his handwriting was swift and readable.

Even while he worked, he looked up often to say something and smile at her.

"I'm writing a theme on the role of Spanish people in bringing civilization to our Southwest," he explained. "I never knew how important a part they played! In fact, back in the little town in Illinois I come from, I never knew any Spanish-speaking people at all. Moving here is a big thrill for me. I've been doing a lot of reading and making discoveries. The Spanish people were great Indian fighters. They were the first farmers and cattle-raisers and miners in our West. Why, our '49'ers learned how to mine gold from the Spanish miners who came up from Mexico! I bet you are proud of your people's history."

Proud? Josie thought a moment. Proud of their past, yes; of their present history, no.

Each time the bus stopped, other young people came aboard. Most were Anglos; some were Spanish-American. Many nodded hello to Josie. In grade school she had been close friends with many of the Anglo girls; but when they had moved up into high school, something had happened that cooled the friendship, that put a distance between her and the girls she had played with so often. At the same time—perhaps because of it—she had become closer to the young people of the same Spanish-speaking background as her own.

"Can you dance the Jarabe?" Ted asked her.

"Yes. I can do the Twist, too," she said.

He laughed. People across the aisle looked at them. Josie knew what they were thinking. The Anglo girls were wondering how she rated this good-looking new boy. The Spanish-speaking girls were wondering if she was busy social climbing.

They were clannish, the Spanish-speaking kids; they stuck together. There had been a time, not so long ago, when they even wore a kind of uniform to proclaim that they were separate and different—the girls wore long hair and short skirts and the boys wore jeans and heavy boots and leather jackets and duck-tailed hair-dos. Most of that was forgotten; but they were as clannish as ever. Very rarely did one of them go on a date with an Anglo boy or girl.

If you did, the other Spanish-speaking students decided that you thought you were too good for them. They stayed away from you, then; among themselves, they said sarcastic things about you. You were an outcast from your own group. Josie had seen this happen several times.

And the Anglo group did not take you in. In fact, the Anglo kid who became chummy with a Spanish-speaking youngster would soon discover that he wasn't being invited to Anglo parties any more....

Ted finished writing his theme as the bus drew up in front of the high school.

"I'll walk you to your class," he said, as they rose to leave the bus. "Say, isn't there a rally at noon today?"

"Yes," Josie said.

"Let's sit together, okay?"

"Why . . . yes," she said.

"Fine!" he said. And when they reached her classroom, he said, "I'll meet you here, Josie!" and hurried off toward the gym.

But as Josie sat down, her mind was very troubled. She had made a mistake, she told herself; she should not have made this date with Ted.

All morning she brooded over the matter. At noon, coming out of her English class, she realized she had to make a decision. She could wait here for Ted. Or she could avoid him by hurrying to the cafeteria to eat her lunch. Which should she do?

Sensitivity Training

Many expressions common in our language reveal bias in our culture:

"That's real white of you."
"Don't be an Indian-giver!"
"I jewed him down."
"So that's the nigger-in-the-woodpile!"
"He's too Scotch."
"Nobody here but us chickens."
"White man speaks with forked tongue."
"Real clever, these Chinese."

Such sayings reveal a set, a stereotype of belittlement for particular minority groups. These expressions are used quite commonly, and often with no intent to hurt the feelings of anyone within hearing. Nevertheless, these expressions do imply a contempt for the minority group referred to, and they *do* hurt.

Young people who are alertly sensitive to the feelings of others will not use such expressions. Children can be helped to become aware that using such stereotypes, even without the intent of offending anyone, does hurt other people's feelings and contributes to a sense of being separate and inferior and rejected.

Role-playing stories involving the use of these "hurt words" can help to build this kind of sensitivity to other people's feelings.

The problem:

Two stories follow: "But Names Will Never Hurt Me?" and "Eeny-Meeny-Miney-Mo." The first deals with direct namecalling; the second with the use of "hurt words" in expressions that are not deliberately used with intent to hurt anyone's feelings.

The teacher of a class that contains a large number of minority group children (Negro, Mexican, Indian, etc.) may find that there is considerable contention in the class, with namecalling. When using one of these stories, make the application indirect: change the minority group referred to. If the minority group children in the class are Negro, change the minority referred to in the story to Mexican, or Puerto Rican. The reason for this tactful measure is to avoid putting children so directly on the spot.

A problem should be considered at this point: Will the point of the story come home to the whole class? Will a "transfer" of meaning occur? Some children, of course, will immediately see the application of the principle and will come at once to a generalization: they will understand that using labels that belittle another group of people always hurts. Other children will fail to make this transfer; they will see only the specific example shown: that to use the expression "jew him down" offends a Jewish child.

Introducing the problem:

It is part of the teacher's role to provide a series of experiences that give the class a variety of applications of the general rule so that the children will, on their own, achieve the "Aha!" experience of suddenly seeing the general application of the various instances they have dealt with. The generalization will come home to them without being presented by the teacher.

The teacher can help the class to arrive at the generalization and insight by asking such questions as the following:

"Can you think of other 'hurt words' that might offend children you know?"

"What kinds of names make you mad?"

"Why do you suppose some people use such words?"

"How do you suppose people feel when they are called names or overhear name-calling talk?"

"Have you ever been called such names? Or overheard expressions like 'He's too Scotch' that could refer to you? What started it? How did you feel? What happened? What did you do?"

Some groups may be quite unfamiliar with such language. In other groups, listing offensive words may often cause tittering and embarrassment. The teacher should recognize this embarrassment and accept it without censure, and lead the group on to serious discussion.

When discussing "But Names Will Never Hurt Me?" the teacher may ask, "Why do you think these little girls were calling each other such names?"

The group may or may not have a realistic appreciation of what often lies behind such behavior. They may say, "They don't like each other."

The individual's estimate of himself—his self-image—is in large part a reflection of the way people around him feel about him and respond to him. Minority group individuals are prone to have a self-estimate that reflects the opinions of them held by the dominant group. As a result, Negro and Puerto Rican and other minority group youngsters, when angry with one another, will use the insulting labels they have heard applied to them by members of the majority group. Such names, of course, reflect their conditioned dislike of being minority group members, their own self-hate.

BUT NAMES
WILL NEVER
HURT ME?

Lorna had just left the apartment and was walking into the playground behind the housing project when she saw her sister, Ellie. *Heard* her, too. Ellie was crying. Loudly.

Lorna hurried toward her and brushed Ellie's matted blond hair out of her eyes and put her arm about Ellie's shoulders.

"What happened?" Lorna demanded. "Why're you crying?"

Ellie was a third-grader, eight years old. Lorna, who was eleven and big for her age, was a sixth-grader.

"They slapped me!" Ellie wailed. "They t-tore my dress!"

"Who did? Show me!"

Ellie turned, and led Lorna toward a group of three small colored girls playing hopscotch in a corner of the playground. They looked up, and grew silent, their eyes big, as they saw Ellie approaching with her angry big sister.

"They did it!" Ellie shrilled. "They hit me and kicked me and tore my dress!"

They stood stiff and silent as Lorna's outraged glance swept their faces.

"Three of you," she said scornfully, "ganging up on one kid! I ought to slap your faces. Maybe I will."

"She called us names," one child said.

"Yeah," another said. "She called me a monkey. A black monkey."

Lorna caught a sharp breath. She looked at Ellie.

"*Did* you?"

Ellie nodded, her eyes filling with tears.

"B-but they were doing it too! I just said what they were saying. Lucille called Betty a—what they said."

Lorna looked at the three girls.

"Is that true?"

They nodded.

Lucille burst out, "But *she* can't call us that!"

Lorna turned.

"Come on, Ellie."

Ellie stood stubbornly in her tracks, her small face ugly with anger.

"Ain't you going to hit them back?" she demanded. "Go on—hit them!"

EENY-MEENY-MINEY-MO

Martha asked, "You kids ever play Duck-on-a-Rock?"

"No."

"What's that?"

"Let's play, let's play!"

"Hold on. You can't play a game until you know what it is. Listen."

The faces of the third-graders were respectful and eager. Martha, a big seventh-grader, felt very grown-up and important. This was a new kind of arrangement being tried by the city schools—using some responsible seventh-graders to help with primary grade children. The six- and seven-year-olds were delighted to have the big eleven- and twelve-year-olds thinking up games for them, playing with them, helping with their lessons.

Martha explained, "You take four of these wooden blocks and pile them up straight, like this," she said, building a straight column. She did not explain that when boys played Duck-on-a-Rock on a vacant lot or in a back alley, they did not use wooden blocks but half-bricks. "Then, everybody stands back here, back of a line, and takes turns throwing a block at the pile. When the pile is hit and knocked down, everybody runs and hides—except the kid who is *It*. He has to run to the blocks and stack them up straight again—and count to thirty. Then he starts hunting the others. Everybody who can run past him and touch the pile without his tagging them is free. But if he tags someone, that person is *It* for the next game."

"That'll be fun!"

"Who's It?"

"John's It!"

"No, Lena's It!"

"No," Martha said. "We'll draw lots."

"Too many," Lucy said. "I know! Everybody stand in a circle. We'll find out who's It." And as the kids grouped around her, she started chanting, "Eeny, meeny, miney, mo—" and as she spoke each word, she pointed to a different child, moving around the circle, "catch a nigger by the toe—If he hollers, let him *go!*—You're It, Sammy!"

But then something happened.

Toby Jones smacked Lucy's face.

For a startled moment, the group stood frozen in shock. Then Lucy burst out crying, and a chorus of angry words exploded from the rest.

"You crazy? Why'd you do that?"

"Why'd he hit her?"

"You can't play with us!"

"Martha, don't let him play with us!"

Toby had turned away from the group. He was leaving, his dark face set and defiant.

"Wait, Toby!" Martha called.

"Oh, let him go, Martha!"

"But why did he slap her?"

"We don't want him around."

"Wait," Martha called. "Toby, don't go!"

"What got into him?"

"Hitting a girl!"

Dora, the other Negro child in the group, had run after Toby and put her arm around his shoulder and was going off with him.

"Why did he hit me?" Lucy was wailing.

Martha said, "Wait here," to the group, and started to go after Toby and Dora.

The other children said, "Oh, let him go!"

"We don't care—we can play without him."

Martha said:

SEED

OF

DISTRUST

Betty was all excited when she ran into the apartment.

"Mother, will you iron my green dress tonight?"

"I was planning to do it Saturday night, honey, so you'd have it for Sunday School."

"But I'll need it!"

"What's the rush?"

"Nora's invited me to a party tomorrow after school."

"Oh, I see," her mother said slowly, as if thinking hard. "Nora's the little girl on the second floor?"

"Yes. She's real nice."

Betty's sister Lucy, who was a sophomore in high school, asked, "Does her mother know?"

"Know what?" Betty asked.

"Nora's white, isn't she?"

"Sure!"

"Does her mother know she's invited you?"

"Of course! I m-mean, I guess so."

"Does her mother know you're Negro?" [1]

"Sure!"

"You mean—you *think* so?"

"Y-yes," Betty stammered.

"Better make sure," Lucy said, and turned back to the math she was studying.

"I'll iron your dress, honey," Betty's mother said reassuringly. "You'll look real nice."

"Uh-huh," Betty said dully. "Thanks, Mom."

And then, next day, after lunch, the thing happened—

Nora met Betty in the hall, outside the fifth-grade room.

"Betty, I've been hunting for you," Nora said urgently. "Listen. My aunt Dorothy phoned last night. She's arriving today for a visit. My grandma's coming over to see her, and mother's making a dinner for the whole family, cousins and all. You see? We've got to postpone my party. Until next week, maybe. I'll let you know!"

Betty looked at her, blank-faced.

"Don't bother," Betty said. "Don't bother at all." And Betty turned and walked away, her back very straight.

For an instant Nora just stood and stared. Then she ran. She caught Betty's arm and stopped her.

"Betty, what's the matter? Why're you talking like that?"

---

[1] Or Mexican, or Puerto Rican, etc.

chapter

3

SELF-ACCEPTANCE

Outside, Looking In Sequence: Wishing You Were Bigger, Better

Basic to good mental health is self-acceptance.

How can we help young people to realize that, for many, lack of self-acceptance is a problem that makes for inner conflict? Respect for one's abilities, and awareness of and calm acceptance of one's limitations, all help toward freedom from anxiety and toward venturesomeness and creativity. It is said that before one can "accept" others, one must be at peace with oneself.

How can we help young people to identify their strengths and limitations or to find satisfaction in cultivating their areas of competence, to gain confidence and self-reliance and resourcefulness? How can we help them to accept and minimize their areas of handicap?

Role-playing specific problems of self-acceptance—with all the attendant discussion and discovery and enactment—can help.

In the following stories, the attempt is made to bring a problem of self-acceptance to an acute focus in a dilemma. This is not an easy dilemma to construct; the area of concern is so very subjective and relatively subtle. The method of these stories consists of presenting a young person with a dilemma involving a chance to secure a longed-for role that is, actually, beyond his capacities—or accepting the reality of his limitations. This chance to gain a coveted role can be made possible through a variety of means. The role is presented as a great kindness on the part of another person; or is made possible by a mistake; or is earned through sheer accident; or, although earned, will call for capacities beyond the individual's actual capabilities.

What are such coveted roles?

Most of us yearn for strengths to compensate for our lacks. The shy, homely girls long to be lovely and sought after.

Boys are especially prone to wish they were fine athletes who are admired and respected by their peers. Such longings for status and achievement beyond their innate potential are especially keen on the part of youngsters who are least successful; the happier, most successful people are usually more reality-oriented individuals whose aspirations are not too far out of proportion to their abilities.

Troubled youngsters often wish intensely they were athletic or popular or very pretty or gifted in music or art or writing or acting or ability to lead others. Such longing leads to much indulgence in fantasy, of course. For emotional balance, such individuals need help to measure frankly their areas of daydream and to assess their real strengths.

Most of us do have areas of strength. Some 50 per cent of even the mentally retarded have some strengths. Identifying such capacities, refining and reinforcing them, is a process of positive improvement for the individual.

But with it must go a calm acceptance of limitations and handicaps, of assessing them as much as practical in their true measure of deficit for the individual.

The range of individual differences is, of course, infinite. And yet many types of disadvantage are common to vast numbers of people. So many of us are short and chubby; so many of us have a heritage and cultural background at variance with the coveted white-Anglo-Saxon-Protestant type that our culture values most. To be American also means to be Negro, Japanese, Catholic, Jew, Seventh-Day Adventist, Mennonite, and so on. Some of us are physically handicapped: we limp, for example, we have bad eyesight, we have asthma, or severe allergies. Some of us lack muscular coordination. Some of us find working with our hands far easier and more satisfying than coping with books. Some of us are homely, red-headed, endowed with a bad skin.

To achieve a reasonable degree of happiness, each one of us must look at his dissatisfactions, decide that he cannot let them corrode his emotional stability and creative potentialities; each of us must identify his strengths and cultivate them to win a measure of confidence and pride.

In this group of stories the individual is given a chance to realize a highly coveted role. But full awareness of how inappropriate this coveted role is for him (or her) is established. The dilemma is presented: to accept the long-desired role—in the light of possible consequences not only to oneself but to others—or to reject the coveted role in acceptance of one's actual limitations? The more sensible goal remains: to nurture and reinforce one's *actual* strengths.

What are the real dilemmas of self-acceptance? Essentially, perhaps, and in most cases, the dilemma consists of either accepting one's shortcomings and reducing one's aspirations to a realistic level—or engaging in a futile struggle against them and living with resentment and disappointment.

And if the latter course is taken, the individual becomes a difficult person to live with: He tries too hard at an unreal level. And he overcompensates. He competes furiously, he brags obnoxiously, he derides others, out of envy, belittling others' efforts and sometimes even actively working to hamper and defeat others' successes.

The more wholesome course for the individual is, naturally, to face up to one's limitations and go on from there. Studies show that the most successful students are those who have set realistic goals for themselves. In practice, this means managing disappointment instead of withdrawing in hurt and anger. It means cooperating with the leader who got the job you wanted. It means relinquishing a task that is beyond your abilities to someone who does have the capacity to handle it well. Even more important, it means estimating your capacities exactly as possible and finding the tasks that you can perform satisfactorily and tasting to the full the rewards of competence that such tasks offer.

One caution, perhaps, is in order here: the individual must estimate his capacities and potentials correctly and *fairly*; that is, he should not *underestimate* himself. The teacher can do important counseling service in helping young people to avoid mistakes of underestimation as well as of exaggerated evaluation of their capacities.

FAST

BALL

The problem:

Becoming reconciled to one's limitations and focusing on improving one's abilities are facets of a problem we all face. Learning to accept one's deficiencies, nevertheless, is something that we all find difficult.

Introducing the problem:

Say, "All of us have strengths, all of us are good at something or other; and all of us have weaknesses and lacks—there are activities for which we have no ability. Learning one's strengths and weaknesses, and being sensible about them, is a problem we all must face. This is a story about a boy who faced this problem. This story stops, but is not finished. As I read, try to think of ways in which you might end the story."

Eddie's team won the toss and was first at bat. Eddie led off; limping to the plate, he got ready for the pitch. He knew he wouldn't reach first, even if he got a hit, but of course he had to try.

The other team, warming up, tossed the ball around. And as Eddie watched, he felt a longing and envy more intense than he had ever felt before. This other team was good. The boys whipped that ball from first to second and home with a real snap. And they *looked* good. They wore brand new Little League uniforms and peaked caps and real baseball shoes with spikes. Eddie glanced down at his own faded jeans and torn sneakers. He felt like a tramp. His own team was just a scrub neighborhood gang. Compared to the Little Leaguers, they looked pretty sad.

"Play ball!" the umpire, Mr. Bonner, shouted.

The first ball was fast, but high. Eddie let it pass, and Mr. Bonner called "Ball one!" But the next pitch came straight for the plate, and

Eddie swung. Bat met ball with a sharp crack and the ball went driving between second and third. Eddie started for first. He knew it was no use, but he lunged along as best he could.

The third baseman snagged the ball, straightened up, and took his time to snap it accurately to first. Eddie was not even halfway to first when Mr. Bonner shouted, "You're out!"

Eddie grinned as he limped back to his team. His right foot was twisted and underdeveloped; he had had polio when he was four years old.

"That was a good hit, Eddie!"

"Gosh, Eddie, if somebody could just run for you!"

Eddie's next teammate was put out on strikes. The next batter hit a two-bagger, and the next man up drove him in. But the next batter fouled out, and the first half of the inning ended with a score of one to nothing, in favor of Eddie's team.

"We'll beat 'em, Eddie. Don't let a one of 'em get a hit!"

Eddie just nodded, and flashed his big smile as he walked out to the pitcher's mound. He was short, but strongly built, all except for his shrunken leg. In fact, he had had to use his arms so much, lifting himself around, that he was unusually well muscled in arms and shoulders. He was not muscle-bound, however; he was a skillful pitcher.

The opposing team came in from the field to take their turn at bat. Eddie studied their gray and blue-edged uniforms. Really neat, he thought. On the back of their shirts was printed the name of the donor: *Ames Shoes,* and a figure of a Tiger. The team called themselves The Tigers. They looked so smart and sharp! *I'd like to be on a team like that!* Eddie mused; but he knew how foolish such a wish was. A cripple like him? Why, he couldn't even run to get under a pop fly, let alone steal bases, or jump to snatch up a fast grounder. He couldn't make it to first when he hit a three-bagger. So he'd never be asked to join a *real* team.

"Batter up!" Mr. Bonner yelled.

The hard ball felt good in Eddie's clever fingers. He got his grip on it, wound up, and pitched. The ball sizzled straight and bullet swift across the plate, smacking into the catcher's mitt with a clear hard rap.

"Strike one!" Mr. Bonner called.

The batter blinked. He hadn't even swung. The ball had been too fast. He did swing at the next pitch—too late; the ball was already in the catcher's mitt. Tightening his lips, he swung more quickly at the next pitch; but Eddie had expected this, and sent over a teasing slow ball.

"Strike three. You're out," Mr. Bonner yelled.

The next batter was a bigger boy. He eyed Eddie with grim determination. Eddie grinned at him, and Eddie settled down to work. Again he whipped the ball straight over the plate—whipped it over so fast that the batter swung so late that the onlookers laughed. A second, and a third time, Eddie threw his fast ball.

"Batter out!" Mr. Bonner called.

The third batter up hit a foul, on the first pitch, that the catcher caught, and was called out. With just seven pitches Eddie had retired the other side.

"Atta boy, Eddie!" his teammates yelled.

"You're going good, boy!"

The Little Leaguers walked out on the field, and looked at him very thoughtfully. Eddie just grinned; Eddie glowed with happiness. . . .

Eddie's side, at bat again, got two men on base but never scored before their half of the inning ended.

Again Eddie, pitching, fanned three batters, one after the other. They just could not hit his fast ball. He seemed absolutely invincible. He did not fool himself, however. His fast ball was his best pitch. Batters who practice against fast pitching would, after a while, start hitting him. To be a good all-around pitcher, he would have to develop different kinds of pitching. But, meanwhile, he had more speed than these Little Leaguers had any hope of handling.

Next inning, his side scored a second run. The Little Leaguers got one man on base, but did not score.

The game finally ended, two to nothing, in favor of Eddie's scrub team. His teammates were so delighted that they threw their gloves into the air, they jumped up and down and whooped and hollered. They'd beat the snappy-looking Little Leaguers in their fancy uniforms. . . .

The boys began to scatter homeward; some of them were already late for chores. Eddie had to return his ball glove to Steve, a neighbor boy from whom he had borrowed it, so he started home.

"Eddie!"

The Little League team had gathered at the curb and were climbing into the truck in which they had come. Two of them, with Mr. Bonner, their coach, were hurrying after Eddie.

"We'd like to talk to you a minute, Eddie," Mr. Bonner said. "Go ahead, Pete."

"I—well, you see, Eddie," Pete began, stammering a little in earnestness, "the bunch of us just talked this over. You're a good pitcher. You're awfully good. We haven't got anybody that's in your class at all. What we'd like— Would you join our team?"

"Who, me?" Eddie gasped. "You mean—wear a uniform like you got, and everything?"

"That's right. What d'you say, Eddie?"

"And pitch for you?"

"You'd be our first-string pitcher."

Eddie stood there, his thoughts milling.

"How about it, Eddie?"

"B-but I can't run bases—"

"We want you just the same."

And I can't jump to grab a high throw. Even if I knocked a fly clear over the fence, a fast fielder could climb that fence and throw to home before I'd make it!

"What do you say, Eddie?"

There are real good teams in the Little League. This team needs good all-around players to compete....

"Say yes, Eddie. We need your pitching!"

Eddie said, "'I—'"

THE
BIG
COMIC

The problem:

The issue is that of self-acceptance. Sometimes the difficulties seem too great to surmount.

Introducing the problem:

Say to the group: "Many of us have private worries we don't like to have other people discover; or, if it's something that can't be hidden, we don't like to talk about it. If you stutter, you try not to talk at all when among strangers. If you have a birthmark on your neck, you wear something to hide it. In this story, a boy hides a handicap he has, although hiding it may cost him something he wants very much. As I read the story, which stops before it is finished, try to think of ways in which the story might end."

Every student in the class quit working when the stranger came into the room. Tom heard somebody whisper excitedly, "That's Eddie Morgan!" and Tom stared in sudden interest at the small, muscular man. Eddie Morgan was a movie comic, like Bob Hope and Milton Berle, only not so important. Tom had heard him often on radio and also seen his television program a couple of times when he had been allowed to stay up later than usual.

Mr. Williams, the teacher, shook hands with Eddie Morgan and then turned to the class.

"I'm sure that you boys and girls have all heard Mr. Morgan's TV program. Most of you may know, too, that Mr. Morgan was once a student here at De Haven Junior High. He would like to talk to you a minute. Mr. Morgan."

Eddie Morgan grinned at them, and they couldn't help smiling back. He was a nice guy.

"I not only went to school here, I even graduated," he told them so proudly that they couldn't help laughing. But then he became serious. "Look, kids, I need your help. Your principal, Mr. Haines, has asked me to be the guest star, this year, on your annual Hi Jinks program. I'm proud and happy to be invited, and I want to put on a swell show. But to do that, I'll need your help. Can any of you kids sing or dance, or do any sort of stunt that I can spot in the show?"

"Tom Bailey can."

"Tom can do rope-spinning, Mr. Morgan!"

Tom felt his face grow red, and he slumped down in his seat. Just the thought of talking to Eddie Morgan in front of everybody scared him so that he wanted to sink through the floor.

"Rope-spinning?" Eddie Morgan said delightedly. "Wonderful! Tom? Where are you?"

The kids around Tom pointed at him and Mr. Williams said, "Tom, come up here, won't you?"

So Tom had to sit up, had to get to his feet, had to start to the front of the room, feeling like a Daniel in a cage of lions. But Eddie Morgan walked down the aisle to meet him, and put his arm about Tom's shoulders, and that made it all easier.

"Tommy, we can make up a good act. Both of us spinning yarns! You making with the rope, and me with the corny gags. Will you help me out?"

Tom managed to stammer, "S-sure."

"Great! Look, you meet me in the boys' gym in an hour. Get your spinning rope. I've got to look in on other classes and scare up some more talent." He smiled and patted Tom on the back. "Be there, boy. I'm counting on you!"

He waved to the class and left the room. Tom walked back to his seat. "Gosh, are you ever lucky!" he heard somebody say, and realized that the other boys envied him.

An hour later, Tom met with Mrs. Hale, the reading specialist, in her office. He explained about Eddie Morgan, and she excused him. He hurried to the gym.

Eddie Morgan was already there with a half-dozen other boys.

He explained: "We've got to work fast, boys. I'm so tied up with my radio and TV programs that two days were all I could take off. The Hi Jinks show is tomorrow night. Today is all the time we've got to re-hearse, but it's enough! Now, the kind of show I want to whip up is this—lots of gags, lots of action. Corny, sure, but moving so fast that nobody's got time to stop laughing and throw rotten tomatoes." He looked at Tom. "Tommy, could you spin a big rope while you're standing on my shoulders?"

"I guess so."

"We'll try it. I got a swell act in mind. Al, and you, Pete—I'll want you boys standing on each side of me, inside the spinning rope. You'll juggle your Indian clubs—while we tell the gags. You see the act? Rope spinning, Indian clubs whirling—and all the time we're telling jokes. Tom," he demanded, "where did you learn to spin ropes?"

"My father showed me how."

"Where did he learn?"

"He used to travel with a Wild West Show."

"In show business, huh?"

"He runs a gas station, now."

"And eats regular! Okay, let's go. Tommy, hop up onto my shoulders!"

Mr. Morgan bent at the knees and took hold of Tom's hands; he stepped onto Mr. Morgan's knee, then onto his left shoulder and onto his right. Morgan straightened up, steadying Tom with his hands; and when Tom was upright, Morgan moved one hand and then the other to the back of Tom's calves, and held him securely in place. Tom had tucked his spinning rope into his belt. He shook out the rope into a loop, swung it, started it circling in a wide loop around him and Mr. Morgan.

"That's the stuff, Tommy. That's fine," Mr. Morgan said. "Ed and Pete—when Tommy makes the loop lift up into the air, you run inside it and stand beside me, Ed on the left and Pete on my right."

With extra force and a sudden lift, Tommy made the wide loop rise up as high as his own head, and that gave the two boys plenty of time to dart in to take their places beside Mr. Morgan. They carried their Indian clubs with them, and started juggling the clubs. One of them hit the lead of Tom's spinning rope, and that brought the rope into a snarled stop.

"That was just fine for the first time," Mr. Morgan said. "Ed, keep your Indian clubs lower—"

"I can keep the rope spinning higher," Tom said.

"Good. But not too high. We want the loop to be circling us. Boys, this is going to be a swell act! We'll smear the rope and the Indian clubs with luminous paint, and we'll have the stage lights turned off, so all that the audience will see will be the rope and the clubs spinning and twisting like gobs of fire! That'll be a swell finale for the act! We'll paint skulls and crossbones on our suits, too, to glow in the dark. It'll be great! Jump down now, Tommy. Let's read over the gags."

They sat down on chairs. He gave each one a sheet of paper filled with closely typed lines.

"I'll ask the questions. You'll take turns answering. We do this while Tommy is spinning the rope around us, and you boys are juggling the clubs. You'll have to memorize the lines today. Don't worry about not remembering—I'll have a teleprompter—we call it an 'idiot board'—that you can glance at when you feel uncertain. All right, let's read these through. I'll start by asking—Tom, why is the letter *F* like a cow's tail?"

Tom, staring at the sheet of paper before him, blinked and grew red and did not answer.

"Because it comes at the end of beef," Mr. Morgan said. "It's there—the second line, Tommy. This has to be said fast, lad, so don't lose time coming in with the answer, any of you. Pete, the second gag—Why is a room full of married people empty?"

"Because there isn't a single person in it," Pete replied quickly.

"That's the speed! Al, your turn—What's the difference between a blind man and a sailor in prison?"

"One can't see to go and the other can't go to sea."

"Good! Okay, Tom—line 10 for you, now—"

Tom's face burned red with shame. *No use telling me the line!*

"Tommy—Why is a pretty girl like a hinge?"

Tommy's lips trembled; sweat beaded his forehead.

"Go ahead, Tommy—read it."

But Tommy did not answer.

"You got the right sheet of paper?" Mr. Morgan asked, and leaned over, and pointed with his finger.

"There it is—I ask, Why is a pretty girl like a hinge? and you say, Because she's something to adore. See it?"

Tommy nodded. *I can see it but I can't read it!*

"You come in real fast, next time, Tommy. Okay, Al—What's the difference between a husband and a guy who's been jilted?"

"One kisses the missus and the other misses the kisses."

"Fine! That's coming right back like I want it. Pete—Why do hens usually lay eggs in the daytime?"

"Because at night time they become roosters."

Sure, sure, I can see it but I can't read it! But Tommy didn't say this aloud; miserably, his head bent, he said, "Mr. Morgan, I—I can't be in your show."

Mr. Morgan blinked with shocked surprise.

"Tommy, lad, we *need* you. Don't you want to be in the show?"

More than I want anything in the world! Aloud, Tom said, "I'm sorry, Mr. Morgan, I—just remembered that tomorrow I got to go to my aunt's—"

"Tommy," Mr. Morgan was a bright, sensitive man, "What's wrong, son?"

I can't read, that's what's wrong. I never did learn to read like other people do! I've got to have special help to learn, and it's going slow. Aloud, Tom said nothing.

"Tell me," Mr. Morgan insisted.

Tell him? In front of everybody? Say it out loud so that everyone would hear? *I can't read!* I'd just make myself look silly, and spoil the show for the rest of you—

"My aunt's giving a big—"

"What's wrong, lad? I wish you'd tell me," Mr. Morgan interrupted. "Maybe we can fix it up. Tell me."

Tom caught a shaky breath, and said:

NORA ADAMS
EDITOR-IN-CHIEF

BIG

SHOT

The problem:

The issue is that of self-acceptance. Nora, a newcomer at school, is unknown to the other students. At her former school, she had been a leader; she wants desperately to become a "very important person" here. She gets a chance at a prestige position which, in her heart, she knows she really does not deserve. Junior high or high school level.

Introducing the problem:

Say to the group, "Have you ever wished you were an important person at school? Someone that everybody looked up to? This is a story about a girl who wanted to be a leader, and who won a chance to become a "big shot." This story stops before it is finished. As you listen, think of ways you might end the story.

Nora Adams sat daydreaming at her study desk—daydreaming herself into trouble. Her family had moved to Westport just two months ago, so she was a newcomer to the Latham School. Back in Fresno, she had been a leader at school, but here she was still a nobody, and it hurt.

She was realizing that if she could get herself appointed to the editorial staff of the school paper, she'd be somebody. Mary Brooks, for example; Mary was pretty, and smart, and the most popular girl in the eighth grade. She would probably be made editor because she was so all-around capable. She could get grown-ups to treat her with respect, to take her seriously. She'd have no trouble gathering news stories. She was good at writing about topics of the day, so she would write editorials. And she was quick and sharp in seeing the faults in other people's writing and in correcting such mistakes. Because people liked and admired her so much, she could be very good at giving orders, at deciding which members of the editorial staff should go after stories, and who should do rewrites in the office, who should do lay-out, and so on. No doubt of it, Nora thought, Mary would be editor. Steve Cagle was a natural for sports editor. Sue Kearny should probably be art and drama reporter.

I should be a feature writer, Nora decided. I should be the kind of roving reporter who does her own column and has her name and picture at the top.

Nora could write tart, clever, little stories about such things as interesting signs, people with odd hobbies, interesting accidents, strange doings of animals. She really was clever; she could write verse and little sketches that made people laugh and say, "Golly, this kid's got a gift. She's smart!" But Nora wasn't disciplined, and she knew it. She couldn't write to order. She could write only when she was all excited about something. I guess, she decided, I'm just a gossip columnist at heart.

"I better get busy," she scolded herself then.

Everyone who wanted to be on the paper staff was required to hand in a sample of his or her work tomorrow morning. A committee of three teachers and the principal would select the staff from these samples.

Nora decided to write a sample column. She wrote:

THE PROWLER . . .

Overheard:
> Pete Naylor went to the dentist yesterday. He gave the dentist a piece of advice: "Your office," Pete said, "should be called the drawing-room." *Tch, tch.*
> Irene Mosely says the mosquitoes are religious insects. They sing and prey over you.
> Yesterday, on the playground, Johnny Hoyle got into an argument with Mr. Bates, who was coaching the ball team. Finally Mr. Bates said, "Look, Johnny, are you coach of this team?" "No, sir." "Then don't talk like an idiot!" Mr. Bates said.

Daffy Definitions:
Hug: a roundabout way of expressing affection.
Hospital: a place where people who are run down wind up.
Usher: one who takes a leading part in the theater.

Conundrum:
Why is Ireland such a rich country?
Because its capital is always Dublin.

Nora flung down her pencil in exasperation.
"This stuff just isn't good enough!"
She almost cried in vexation. Abruptly, then, an idea came to her. Why not write a story about her great-grandmother who was captured by

the Indians? Actually, she hadn't been kidnapped: she ran away and joined them. The Indians were not the fierce, bloodthirsty Plains Indians who burned settlements and scalped soldiers, but the peaceful Yokuts of California; and they did not harm her but took fine care of her and brought her home. The only harm she suffered was a spanking from her own father. But she *had* had a thrilling time with the Yokuts.

Nora wrote a title: *Captured by the Indians.*

She went on to write the story. Vivid details flowed swiftly from her pen. She told where the Yokuts lived: in the south end of the big Central Valley of California, which was desert but contained a huge, shallow, inland sea in a sump that gathered overflow water from rivers that ran wild in spring but dried up in summer: Tulare Lake. The Indians had not lived in tepees but on big rafts made of bulrushes. Each raft held a small cabin made of reeds. A mud fireplace was located in the middle; and a blind set up in the pointed front of the raft from which the Yokut warrior shot at ducks and geese. The wild fowl were so plentiful that they blotted out the sun when they rose in flight. The Indian women gathered clams which were so numerous that they practically paved the lake bottom near shore, and turtles that also were immensely abundant. From a hole in the raft the men speared fish. Ashore, the men hunted antelope and held jackrabbit "surrounds." Once in a while they fought a grizzly bear that emerged from his underground burrow. . . .

In details that were vividly real, Nora wrote the story—swiftly, because it was all so familiar to her. All during her early childhood she had heard these stories of her great-grandmother, and after she had learned to read, she'd pored over her great-grandmother's diary until she almost knew it by heart.

When Nora had finished writing, she knew she had done a good job. The piece was better than anything she had ever written before; better than anything she could ever write until she herself was grown up and had had important experiences of her own. . . .

Next morning, she turned the composition in as a sample of her work to the committee that would select the editorial board of the school paper.

The selections of the board were announced the following Friday morning by Miss Brameld, Nora's English teacher.

"Reporters will be: Tony Moore, Dan Leeds, Esther Bonner and Tim Morris. You accept the assignments?"

The students nodded. Nora's heart sank. She wasn't considered good enough even to be a reporter!

"For Sports Editor, Steve Cagle. Okay, Steve?"

"Sure! I m-mean thank you, Miss Brameld."

"You're welcome. For Art and Drama Reviewer, Sue Kearny."

"Hooray!" Sue exclaimed, clapping her hands. Everybody laughed.

I knew she'd get it, Nora thought. Sue deserved it. Maybe I can contribute pieces once in a while, she tried to reassure herself. Why wasn't I born bright?

"For Student Events editor, Mary Brooks. You accept, Mary?"

Mary nodded, smiling, "Yes, thank you."

Nora's stomach felt sick and hollow. She hadn't made the staff at all. If Mary, who was so very gifted, was just an assistant editor, Nora told herself, then I haven't a chance to be anything!

"And for Editor-in-chief," Miss Brameld went on, "we have a person with far more ability than anyone on the committee expected to discover. Her writing shows so much maturity, so much awareness, such a vivid eye for detail and for story values that— Well, on the basis of the samples presented, there was just no question: the outstanding writer among the candidates, and the person selected to be our Editor-in-chief, is—Nora Adams!"

Oh, no! Nora thought, almost gasping it aloud. But that should be Mary Brooks' job! She's so neat and orderly and punctual, I'm helter-skelter. Mary can get people to do things for her. Mary can write *every-thing*—and she can see the faults in things other people write, and she can help them correct things without making them sore. This job should be Mary's. Giving it to me's a mistake—why, what I wrote was really my great-grandmother's—

"Nora," Miss Brameld was saying, "this is a big job you'd be taking on. Do you accept the responsibility?"

Yes, it was a big job! She'd be important around school. She'd be going around with the best kids here, with Mary and Sue and Steve—But—but—

"Well, Nora?"

Nora gulped, and stammered, "Miss Brameld, I—"

WINNER
TAKE
ALL

The problem:

Acceptance of self—learning to be comfortable with one's limitations as well as one's strengths—is difficult for all of us. This story deals with such a problem.

Introducing the problem:

Say to the group, "All of us wish we were better than we are. We envy fine athletes, if we're boys; we envy lovely movie actresses, if we're girls. Most of us, unfortunately, are more aware of our weaknesses than our strengths. Learning to appreciate our abilities and to get along with our limitations is difficult. This is a story about such a problem. The story stops before it is finished. Try to think of ways in which the story should be finished."

Miss Clanahan stopped Lucia in the hall.

"Lucia, I don't see your name on the list. Aren't you entering the contest?"

Lucia looked at her in surprise.

"*Me* in a beauty contest?"

"Of course. Don't underrate yourself. It'll take more than just looks to win this one, Lucia. We're scoring big on talent. That you have."

"But it is, actually, a beauty contest, isn't it?"

"Yes. I'll put your name on the list. Okay?"

Very reluctantly, Lucia nodded.

"But Ella Warner will be in it, and Terry Norton, and Dorothy—"

Miss Clanahan patted her shoulder reassuringly.

"I'll be pulling for you, Lucia."

"But they're all so awf'ly pretty—"

"Lucia, you know what the winner will receive?"

"Gosh, yes!"

"Think big, dear," Miss Clanahan said, and walked on.

The loot, Lucia reflected, *would* be big. This junior high school contest was backed by several local service clubs. The winner would get an outfit of clothes from the Junior Miss Store, a full set of matched luggage from the Mercantile Mart, a camera from the Photo Shop, an all-expense trip for her mother and herself to Disneyland.

Golly, if only I did have a chance to win, Lucia daydreamed.

Her father had sung in opera; now he was a voice teacher at the nearby State College. Lucia had inherited some of his talent; she sang beautifully. Moreover, he had helped her develop her voice and had taught her a number of fine songs. She decided that she would prepare for the contest by practicing on a group of English folk songs and ballads.

The beauty contest took place on the last day of a three-day Pioneer Festival held in the town late in May. The first half of the beauty contest came in the afternoon.

As Lucia walked out onto the big stage in the school gymnasium with the other contestants, she was stiff and awkward with stage fright. She was a shy girl, to begin with; she suffered such agonies of self-consciousness that it was torment for her to get the attention of people. This painful self-awareness would, her father kept telling her, pass as she grew up; meanwhile, it was a severe handicap to her in winning the liking and admiration of people she wanted as friends.

When she looked at the other contestants, her heart sank. They were so lovely! So very lovely. She had no right to be on the same stage with them. At fifteen she was still—well, skinny; but the other girls had good figures. Of the twenty girls, she alone wore thick-lensed glasses. She had to wear them for her left eye was slightly crossed. The glasses corrected the condition and corrected her short-sightedness. Your eyes are a lovely violet, her mother kept telling her; someday we'll get you contact lenses, and you can get rid of these specs.

The audience applauded generously as the girls arranged themselves on the stage.

The first contestant to perform was Terry Norton, a redhead. She did dramatic imitations, like Sammy Davis imitating Jimmy Stewart, James Cagney, Marlene Dietrich, Bing Crosby. She won hearty applause. After her, Ella Warner played the piano. She began with a heavy treatment of the Rachmaninoff prelude—slow and thumping and grim and highbrow; then abruptly she changed into a rock-and-roll version that sent a wave of delighted laughter over the audience. Her applause exceeded Terry's.

Dorothy Blake, on next, did a skillful tap dance. She wasn't very good, but she was exceedingly pretty and popular; her applause topped

Ella's. Mona Allen, next, whistled: she imitated birds, then combined their calls into a song medley that was clever; but the applause was less than Dorothy's.

So it went. Lucia was almost last on the list.

She made no attempt to ingratiate herself with the audience by singing something timely or popular, or by a tricky dramatics of pace. She simply sang a half-dozen old songs—*Greensleeves* and *The Minstrel Boy*, and others of the same kind. Her voice was pure, strong, soaring in its reach, vibrantly alive and infectiously rich with feeling. The crowd grew quiet the moment she started; grew intensely quiet as she went on; and when she finished, the audience exploded into wild applause. It was far greater applause than any contestant had received before. Moreover, the crowd would not let her go. She had to do two encores.

The remaining contestants were but half-hearted in their performances; both sang songs, but they seemed so amateurish and untalented, after Lucia's performance, that the audience applauded them just for trying.

Well, anyway, Lucia thought, I'm probably still in the running for the finals tonight.

She was. The principal announced the finalists, and Lucia was among them. They would perform at the evening show. . . .

At 8:30 that night, Lucia went into the big dressing room behind the gym where the contestants did their final primping before going on stage. Della and Terry were there. Della left, but Terry hung back, and came over to Lucia.

"Well, I hope you're all set for your trip to Disneyland," Della said bitingly.

Lucia looked at her, surprised at her unfriendly tone.

"What do you mean?"

"You're going to win the beauty contest. It's all settled."

"What in the world are you talking about?"

"The judges have already decided to make you the beauty queen."

"That's not very funny!"

"I think it's a howl. You—a skinny broomstick with specs—our beauty queen! Oh, well, this isn't a beauty contest, it's a *talent* show. Hope you enjoy your trip to Disneyland."

"I still don't know what you're talking about," Lucia insisted, on the point of tears.

"All right, I'll tell you. Miss Clanahan persuaded the two other judges to give you the prize."

"I don't believe it!"

"The janitor heard them in the principal's office. He's my uncle, you know. He told my dad, who told me."

"But—if that did happen—why would Miss Clanahan do a thing like that? Anyway, the other judges wouldn't agree to it!"

"She said you lack self-confidence. That it's such a handicap to you that it may keep you from being the really great singer you have promise of being. She said if you started having success now, by the time you grow up you can really be somebody big. She said you needed to win." Della shrugged. "Maybe she's right. Winning this contest wouldn't be really important to any of the rest of us. Don't worry—I won't tell anybody. Besides, I'm going to Disneyland and Hollywood this summer, anyway! My dad's taking me."

She walked out.

Lucia sat there, stricken, trying to get control of her feelings.

She heard the band begin to play. It was time for the contestants to parade out onto the stage.

She stood up, walked to the door. But in the hallway she stopped, tormented with indecision. The way to the stage was down the hall to the left.

But she didn't have to go there. The door to the street was down the hall to the right. She could run now, get to that door, rush outside, and hurry home before she was even missed. . . .

Inside, Looking Out Series: Anticipation of Rejection

The problem:

The issue is an aspect of self-acceptance, of being comfortable with oneself; specifically, these stories deal with the problem of the uneasy self-concept: the individual who expects rejection, sometimes unnecessarily.

All of us have times when we feel unliked and unwanted; times when we think that people are treating us unfairly. Such moments are a natural and human reaction to difficulties we may encounter in our relations with others. Some people, however, feel this kind of doubt about themselves much more often than is necessary or justified.

Children need to be helped to explore such experience, to confront and analyze their feelings. Were they too quick to judge the situation? Were all the facts in? Is it possible that they made a mistake? Often, when we act as though we expect mistreatment, by our behavior we invite such response.

Introducing the problem:

You may say to the group, "All of us have times when we feel un-liked and unwanted, when we think that people are treating us unfairly. Can you recall such times? . . .

(*Allow time for response.*)

"Sometimes when we have problems, it is easy to feel that someone is treating us in a way that is unfair.

"I am going to read you three short stories about people who felt that they were being treated unkindly.

"The first two stories are finished. When I read the third, I am going to stop, and ask you how that story might be ended."

JUDY MILLER

Something peculiar was going on. Judy noticed it as soon as she walked into the schoolyard that morning. First thing that happened was that she saw Marta and Nancy talking busily together. But when she turned toward them, when she called "Hi!" they shut up in a hurry. They glanced at her, and Nancy gasped and covered her mouth with her hand in a guilty way, and she and Marta both giggled oddly. Marta leaned close and whispered quickly to Nancy, and Nancy turned and hurried off as if she had something important to do on the far side of the yard. Marta did turn to meet Judy, then, and Marta said, "Hi!" in an ordinary way, pretending that nothing had happened.

But Judy told herself, "They've got a secret. They don't want me in on it. They're leaving me out." And Judy felt upset.

She and Marta had been best friends. But that had been two years ago, in the fourth grade. Then Judy's family had moved to Fresno. Judy had not liked going to school there. When the family moved back here, to Newton, Judy had been wildly happy, thinking that she would be back again with old friends whom she had missed so terribly. But things were not the same after these two years. Marta and Nancy and Edie and Nora and the others—they seemed to have changed. Almost a week of school had passed, and Judy still felt like a stranger with her former friends. She felt pushed out, set apart.

The bell rang, and the children in the schoolyard moved into the building. As the hours wore along into recess, and lunch, the day proved to be an odd kind of time; she felt a kind of electric tingle in the class-room. The boys were not part of it; they seemed unaware that anything unusual was going on. But the girls seemed to be making a hard effort to hide a rush of excitement that was making them chatter in rushed whis-pers and choke back nervous giggles that bubbled from their lips. Not just Marta and Nancy were sharing secrets, Judy realized; most of the girls seemed to need to get together and make guarded, hurried talk.

But when *she* approached a pair whispering together, they glanced at her and turned quickly away. All the girls seemed to be in on the secret, whatever it was; she alone was left out. Her sense of being friendless grew steadily harder to bear.

She discovered the big secret as school let out. Unintentionally, she overheard Marta whisper to Della Ross: "I'll come by for you at seven. What dress are you going to wear?"

"My new white one."

"Like Dora's?"

"Yeah, but she isn't going to wear hers."

"See you later!"

A party! That was what everybody was so worked up about. And all the girls were going. Even Doris Gard, whom nobody liked very much. "Everybody's invited," Judy realized, "but me. They don't want me."

As she walked home, her thoughts were heavy with gloom. I don't have friends any more, she told herself. I'm not invited to that party be-cause the girls don't like me. Why should they? I'm not pretty; not really; not like Alice and Nancy. I don't have nice clothes. My folks aren't im-portant. And when you go to a church with an odd name, and attend Sunday school on Saturday—why, you just can't be part of the crowd. You're treated like something was left out of the recipe when you were baked.

She tried to be sensible, then. She tried to get rid of her unhappy thoughts. She told herself that the girls of the class used to like her; be-fore long she would be part of the group again. She should be patient.

But she could not shake off the disappointment and loneliness that put a sick, all-gone feeling in the pit of her stomach. . . . When she got home, she went to her room and lay down on her bed. For a minute or two she cried; very quietly. Carefully, then, she washed her face; she didn't want her mother to guess that anything was wrong.

But at dinner her mother did seem to sense that she was miserable, for her mother stared at her with a worried look on her face.

When Judy started to help with the dishes after dinner, her mother said, "Dear, I asked Mrs. Jeffers if she'd fix the hem on your red dress tonight. Would you take it over to her?"

Judy nodded. The red dress was fairly new, and she usually felt dressed up and gay in it; but, over the summer, she had grown and the dress needed to have the hem lowered. She put the dress on and walked two blocks down the street to Mrs. Jeffers' house.

An hour later, Judy returned home. The house was dark, she saw as she approached; and she guessed that her parents had either gone for a walk or to a movie.

Walking inside she switched the livingroom lights on—and gasped in sudden shock. The room was crowded with people—

"Surprise! Surprise!" they were all shouting, and laughing at the amazed, wide-eyed look on her face. Marta was here, and Nancy, and Alice, and all the other girls in her class, even Dora. Everyone! All were crowding around her. All the girls who had been invited to that party she hadn't been asked to— But of course they hadn't invited her, she realized now, with a great lift of happiness: they couldn't invite her. But they hadn't left her out. They hadn't invited her because it was *her* surprise party ... to welcome her back among her friends again.

JOHNNY
KOTOWSKI

Johnny wasn't eavesdropping; he didn't intend to overhear what Mr. Morton was telling the boys. Johnny's first thought as he realized that the Little League ball team was already assembled in Mr. Morton's yard was *Gosh, I'm late, and I thought I was arriving early.* He started to hurry down the path beside the garage to the patio where the team was meeting. Then he heard Mr. Morton mention his name. The coach was talking about him. Then, as Johnny heard what Mr. Morton was saying about him, Johnny stopped short, frozen in his tracks. The boys couldn't see him, because of the high patio fence, and for this Johnny was suddenly grateful.

"Before we vote for either Johnny or Mike," Mr. Morton was saying, "we should take some thought about the candidates. Being captain of a team is an important job. Besides ability, it demands something that we call character. Now, Johnny Kotowski—"

So that was why the team was here, Johnny realized. Mr. Morton had asked him to come at 10 o'clock. So that he would arrive *after* the voting, Johnny decided. He knew that he and Mike Nolan were the two candidates for team captain.

"Well, Johnny's a little guy," Mr. Morton was saying. "Smallest boy on the team, I guess, and he's not a natural athlete. Sometimes he's so awkward he trips over his own feet." This drew a laugh from some of the boys: and Johnny, listening, felt shame and misery. "And sometimes Johnny's hay fever gets so bad he has to stay out of a game. Also, he happens to be red-headed, and he's very touchy about being teased. In fact, he's got a quick temper and loses it awfully easily. Also, he gets excited in a game, and he has to fight from getting rattled. I guess that's why sometimes he stutters so badly you can hardly understand him—"

"B-Boys, let's g-g-g-get g-g-g-goin'—"

Pete Ames mocked Johnny's stutter, and some of the boys guffawed; but Mr. Morton interrupted, cutting the laugh short. "Pete, that's enough. To go on. Johnny's stubborn. He argues. He'll argue until you sometimes want to wring his neck, and—"

Johnny could not bear to hear more. He turned, blinking back tears and hurried out the way he had come—out of the yard, down the street toward home.

Talking that way about me! Mr. Morton! He's just like everybody else. If your mom and pop talk some language besides English, and if the food you eat has a lot of garlic—then you're queer. You're different. You're somebody to laugh at and to play jokes on. Nobody gives you a fair break. You're the one who's always *It* when they play games. You're the one who gets left out of parties. You're the one they think of first when something gets stolen. It's just not fair.

The more he thought about it, the deeper grew his misery. I haven't any friends, he told himself. I'm just a runt of a redhead who trips over his own feet. Why should anybody care a darn about me? I'm no good for the team. I argue, get into fights, and get all shook up when we're in trouble. They put up with me when I tag along, but they don't really care what happens to me.

Reaching home, he walked around to the backyard. Here he had built rabbit hutches. He had six does with litters.

He got busy cleaning out the hutches, working with a quiet fury in order to numb the misery that was so intense a hurt within him.

"Johnny!"

Pete McInness was calling him. Johnny's first impulse was to run indoors and not answer. He knew why Pete had come for him. It was almost time for the Little League game with the Centreville team. Jimmy's team had two pitchers—himself and Andy Roth. But Andy had just got out of bed after an attack of flu and was still pretty weak. If I don't pitch, Johnny realized, we'll lose the game for sure. What do I care, he thought angrily.

Just the same, he walked around to the front yard.

"For gosh sake, did you forget about the game?" Pete demanded, but his voice was relieved. "We thought you must be sick or something. Come on. Everybody's waiting for you."

"Let Andy pitch."

"He's too weak. Besides, we want you to pitch this one. You just got to, Johnny. Come on—run! Where you been, anyway? You missed the meeting."

"So what?"

"You should've heard what Mr. Morton said about you—"

"Yeah, I'm a little runt who falls all over his own feet and gets into fights and argues—"

"Yeah, but how'd you find out so quick? And he said you get rattled and you try to play ball sometimes when you've got hay fever so bad you ought to be home. You got all those handicaps, he said, but you rise above them!"

"Wh-what?"

"Yeah. He said you got handicaps that would make most guys quit, or make 'em impossible to get along with. But not you. He said you overcome your handicaps by guts and determination. He said that you study any sport you get interested in, until you know more about it than most guys. And he said you got real team spirit—you don't grandstand, you think about the team, and you're always working to give everybody else a chance to shine. He said you got what a team captain needs most, so that's why we elected you captain. Come on, it's time for the game to start!"

"Who g-got elected c-captain?" Johnny stuttered.

"For gosh sake, I *told* you. *You* did. Come on, we got to run!"

Johnny ran.

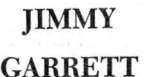

JIMMY GARRETT

The sign in the drugstore window said: BOY WANTED. Jimmy, hurrying past, stopped short. A job. Just when he wanted one so badly! He read the small writing at the bottom of the sign: *To make deliveries after school. Must have bicycle.* As Jimmy read this, his heart sank. He had no bike. One big reason he wanted a job was to save up money to buy a bicycle.

But I do have a bike I can use, he reminded himself.

He turned to go inside the store, then hesitated. *You ought to look nice,* he warned himself. *Get washed and dressed up!*

So he went home, running most of the way. His mother, who worked —Jimmy's father was dead—wasn't home, but he found a clean shirt, and he washed, put on his best pants and the shirt and a sweater. Then he went out to the shed in back and brought out the bike. It wasn't a wheel that would make anybody jealous, but it worked. He dusted it carefully with a rag, thinking that after he had received some pay he would buy new tires and a springy saddle for it. Maybe even paint. Done, he mounted and rode back downtown, hurrying.

As he dismounted in front of the drugstore, he discovered that he had a rival. Keith Lucas, who was in his class at school, was leaning his bike against the curb. He glanced up, saw Jimmy, and his mouth opened in surprise.

"What're you doing here?" he demanded.

Jimmy did not answer, pointedly ignoring him. Keith's freckled face reddened and he took a step toward Jimmy, but Jimmy didn't back away. Keith was two inches taller than Jimmy, and a dozen pounds heavier, and he had taken advantage of his bigger size to push Jimmy around; but Jimmy, although he got the worst of it in a fight, always fought back. Keith decided that this was no time for a ruckus, and stopped.

"Where'd you get that bike?" he demanded.

Jimmy retorted, "Where did you get yours?" and turned and started toward the door of the drugstore.

Keith darted past him. Jimmy did not run; neither of them would get the job if they scuffled here. He followed Keith inside.

Mr. Dormyer, the owner, smiled at them.

"So, two applicants for the job. What're your names?"

"Keith Lucas."

"Jimmy Garrett."

"Live near here?"

"I live at 43 Berenda Way," Keith said.

"Nice neighborhood. You, Jimmy?"

"At the end of Mulberry Lane."

"Pretty far from here. Well, I guess I'd better interview you separately. Who got here first?"

"I did," Keith said.

"Come into my office, Keith. Don't go away, Jimmy. I'll talk to you, too, presently."

The minutes passed. Jimmy fidgeted nervously. Finally Keith and Mr. Dormyer came out of the back office. Keith shot Jimmy a look of triumph, and swaggered out.

Mr. Dormyer said, "Come in, Jimmy," but his face was thoughtful.

"Sit down, boy. Well, now ... Jimmy, this isn't a big store, and the business isn't big, either. But I do need a boy after school to deliver stuff ordered by telephone. Things like ice cream and hand lotions and medicines. People pay for the stuff when it's delivered. Medicines can run to ten dollars and over, so naturally, I—I need a boy I can rely on, who's responsible, and—honest."

So he just takes a look at me and decides I'm not honest, Jimmy told himself. Aloud, he said merely, "Yes, sir."

"You've got a bike?"

"Yes, sir."

"Brand new?"

"Second-hand."

"Where'd you get it?"

"I guess I—just borrowed it, sir."

"Who from?"

Jimmy felt hot all over; his throat was tight and his lips trembled. "I don't know his name, sir."

"Where does he live?"

"I don't know."

"Well! Does he know you—borrowed his bike?"

"I—don't know, sir. I—"

The bell over the front door tinkled as a customer entered the drugstore. Mr. Dormyer looked up through the open officer door and got to his feet.

"Got to serve this customer. Jimmy, I'm sorry," Mr. Dormyer said, and his voice sounded sincere, "but I'm afraid I can't hire you."

He hurried forward to take care of the customer. Jimmy followed into the store, hesitated, then realized, *It's just no use!* and walked out of the store. Out of Mr. Dormyer's sight, he could not control his feelings; tears came to his eyes.

He mounted his bike and started home. His churning thoughts transmitted their troubled fury to his legs so that he bore down hard on the pedals.

I shouldn't have tried for that job, he told himself. I should've known what would happen. The minute he looked at me he was against me. Soon's he saw the color of my face, I lost any chance for that job. . . . But he did seem so nice to me at first. Then maybe Keith told him some lies about me? Oh, quit fooling yourself. You're crazy if you think people are going to be fair to you.

"Jimmy," young Mrs. Logan who lived next door, called to him across the fence, as he was putting the bike into the shed. "I thought I'd better tell you. A policeman was driving around here today. He was asking people if any of them had seen a boy with a red-and-yellow-trimmed bicycle. It's an old bike, he said, with a siren that runs off the front wheel and a bulb horn on the handle bars, but no mudguards. Mrs. Akers told him she thought she'd seen a bike like that, but didn't remember just who had it. The policeman said he'd be back later. Just thought I'd mention it," she said worriedly, and turned away.

Jimmy swallowed hard. A policeman. Asking about his bike. It was the same bike, all right. No question of it. But a policeman....

I shouldn't have taken the bike home, he told himself. *Now, I'm in trouble....*

He went into the kitchen and sat down. He was shaking. He tried to reassure himself, to calm down, to think sensibly, to decide what to do next.

One thing he could do, he decided. He could take the bike back to McCrary Dam. He could let it roll down into deep water. Then, when the cop questioned him about it, he could say that he did not know anything about such a bike. If the bike were ever found—well, it was in the lake, where it should be. Nobody could prove anything different. Nobody had seen what he'd done that day. Nobody could fix any blame on him.

You'd be lying, he told himself. *You'd be just as bad as they think you are!*

So what if I am! he thought. *Look how they're treating me!*

[Here the teacher stops to start the group role-playing. See Introducing the Problem. After the role-playing, the teacher reads the ending to the class.]

Jimmy's mother arrived home from work usually at five-fifteen. Jimmy guessed that the policeman would be back, looking for him, just about that time too.

He could just see the stricken look on his mother's face when a big officer in uniform knocked on the door and asked, "Does Jimmy Garrett live here?" And Jimmy couldn't bear to meet that ordeal. He left the house. He'd hike out into the country, he decided, and come back late, when he was sure the policeman had gone.

But first he went to the back shed and got the red-and-yellow trimmed bike. He left it in front of the house, leaning against a tree near the curb, where it could be seen instantly by anybody passing in a car.

Then he walked restlessly down the road, out into the country. He went to McCrary Dam. There, he idled away time, skipping rocks across the lake surface. He was scared and he was angry. Sensibly, he tried to argue himself into a calm state of mind. He wasn't the only person who got treated unfairly. If you had a funny-sounding name—like Pete Hogg— you got kidded. If you stuttered like Joey White, boys imitated you for laughs. If you had holidays when everybody else had to go to school, the other kids made something big out of it. Shucks, even if you had cross-eyes or a limp or a bad birthmark, you were the butt of a lot of stupid jokes. So relax, he told himself; don't be so touchy; grin and bear it.

But jokes are one thing, he told himself; not getting a job he needed was something else; and having a policeman hunting him for what he had done—that made him so mad he wanted to break things.

At sunset he started home. It was dark by the time he arrived.

The old bike, he noticed, was no longer leaning against the tree near the curb. This meant that the policeman had been back and had taken the bike.

His mother was home. The aroma of frying chicken was a warm invitation when he entered the kitchen. His mother, in the next room, heard him come in and called worriedly to him.

"Jimmy, that you?" When he answered, she said: "Mrs. Davis from across the street says a policeman was here, hunting for you. You in trouble, son?" she demanded, coming into the kitchen.

Jimmy spilled the whole story, then. Day before yesterday, he told his mother, he had hiked to McCrary Dam to go fishing. As he neared the dam, a boy he didn't know passed him, going the same way. The boy was riding a bike, and Jimmy had wished he had one.

Arriving at the dam, Jimmy climbed up onto the concrete arch. There he saw a group of four boys, none of whom he knew, although he recognized one as the boy who had passed him on the bike a little earlier. The other three were bigger boys, thirteen or fourteen years old. They were teasing the smaller boy on the bike.

"Why ain't you home practicing the piano?"

"Your momma know you're out?"

"Better not talk mean to him—he'll tell his daddy!"

The boy being teased did not talk back. He was scared. Swinging onto his bike, he started to leave. One of the bigger boys was carrying a stick. He threw it now as the younger boy rode past—threw the stick in the front wheel. It caught in the spokes and, as the wheel turned, came up against the fork, locking the wheel tight. The bike up-ended: somersaulted forward. The boy was flung face down onto the concrete.

He lay there prone, not moving, not talking. The boy who had thrown the stick muttered, "Aw, get up. You ain't hurt!" But the others ran to the fallen boy and bent over him.

"Blood on his face."

"I don't think he's breathing."

They stood up, and now *they* were scared. They looked at each other, then one of them ran to his own bike. The others followed. Straddling their wheels, they fled away.

Jimmy called, "Hey! You can't just leave him lying there—"

The other three did not even look back. Reaching the end of the dam, they swerved down onto the highway and headed back to town, standing on the pedals to make speed.

"Of all the mean, dirty tricks!" Jimmy exclaimed.

He bent over the hurt boy. Blood was coming from his nose, which seemed twisted and flattened; and his chin was laid open as if by a knife and from it blood was streaming down his neck and over his shirt. He was breathing, however, catching short, choky gasps; and his eyes were open and staring, though he did not seem to see Jimmy at all.

"You hurt?" Jimmy asked.

The boy did not answer; he moaned, and his chin quivered.

"You better go home and have your chin bandaged."

The boy did not answer, he did not seem to hear or see Jimmy at all. He was almost knocked out, Jimmy realized. He needed help—needed it right away.

Jimmy glanced around. No one else was fishing on the dam or swimming near the beaches beyond.

I can't just go off and leave him here, Jimmy told himself. Maybe nobody'll come along until tomorrow. He can't lie out here all night. He's bleeding; and it gets cold after dark. He'll be awfully scared. His only injury was the bad cut on his chin; it would be safe to move him.

Jimmy bent down. He picked up the hurt boy in a "fireman's carry" —by grasping one wrist, putting his other arm between the boy's legs and heaving him across his shoulder. Luckily, the boy was small.

Staggering, Jimmy started toward the highway. Almost at once he was gasping for breath; the boy's weight seemed to double with every dozen steps. Several times Jimmy almost dropped him. If I do, he warned himself, I won't be able to pick him up again.

Just as he reached the highway, a car came rolling past. It stopped with a sudden shriek of brakes, then backed abreast of Jimmy as he put the hurt boy down.

"Good heavens, what's happened?" the woman driver called to Jimmy.

"He—fell off his bike—"

"Look how he's bleeding! Quick! Let's get him into the car. He needs a doctor."

She got out, and together they lifted the boy onto the floor of the back of the car. The woman got in behind the wheel.

"Wait. His bike!" Jimmy said.

"Never mind! We've got to rush him to the doctor."

"But it'll be stolen!"

"Haven't room for it. We're wasting time!"

"Okay, I'll ride it to town."

Behind him, as he ran along the dam, Jimmy heard the car start off, motor roaring. He continued to the bike and picked it up. The stick was still in the front wheel and he had to pull it free. Three spokes were broken, but otherwise the bike was undamaged.

Not until he started riding back to town did he realize that he did not know where to take the bike. He did not know the injured boy, did not know his name, nor where he lived; he did not know where the woman was taking him, did not even know the woman's name.

There was just one thing for him to do, Jimmy decided: ride the bike home. And this was what he had done. . . .

"So now," he told his mother angrily, "all the thanks I get is that everybody thinks I *stole* that bike! It isn't fair. If I were Eddie Gordon or Tom Allen, I wouldn't be treated like this!"

"I guess," his mother said worriedly, "I should've told you to take the bike to the police station. But it's such a junky bike. When you came home with it, I thought you'd found it on a rubbish heap somewhere. Guess I've been too tired to keep close track of what you're doing. Anyway," she said, and hugged Jimmy, "you just relax. We'll work this out."

"How can we, with that policeman hunting for me," Jimmy said hopelessly.

Jimmy's mother sent him to the market on 7th Street for groceries. Returning home, then, he saw people in front of his house. Nearing, he saw that his mother was there—with Mr. Dormyer, the druggist, and a man in uniform, a policeman. Jimmy's throat choked up. *He's waiting to grab me*, Jimmy warned himself. He had a sudden wild impulse to run and hide; but he made himself walk straight on, although he could not help slowing his pace.

The policeman was leaning over the old bicycle, working the pedal action. *Checking to see if I ruined it! But that bike was junky when I brought it home.*

They heard him approaching, then: they turned and saw him. The policeman stepped forward and came toward Jim and reached out his hand. But the policeman was smiling, and he took Jimmy's hand to shake it. Mr. Dormyer was smiling too.

The policeman said, "I had a hard time tracking you down, Jimmy. After I'd been asking all around the neighborhood, Mr. Dormyer finally gave me a clue. He told me about a boy who had applied for a job and who had a borrowed bike but didn't know the name of the owner. I guessed that you were the boy I was hunting for. Jimmy, I owe you more thanks than I can say."

"Wh-what?" Jimmy stammered.

"That boy who got hurt on the dam Wednesday—the boy you carried to the highway—his name is Pete Jones. He's my son."

"He didn't die?"

"No, Jimmy. He might have, if he'd lain out on the dam, bleeding all night. He had double pneumonia a few weeks ago. In fact, Wednesday was the first time he'd really gone out by himself since he got sick."

"He had a bad fall," Jimmy said.

"Yes, his nose was broken and had to be set, and that cut in his chin needed a lot of stitches. But, thanks to you, he'll be back in school Monday."

"That's good," Jimmy murmured.

"Now, about this bike," the policeman said. *Now*, Jimmy thought. *Now he arrests me.*

"Sure needs a new saddle," Mr. Jones said. "I know where to get one for you. The way the paint's peeling off the frame sure makes it look crummy, but we can sand the paint off and put a couple of coats of fresh enamel on. I suspect that the coaster brake needs taking apart and oiling, but that's not hard. I'll show you how to do it. What you really need is a good luggage carrier for the handle bars, so you can deliver things on your bike."

"Wh-what?" Jimmy gasped, for the second time.

"Jimmy," Mr. Dormyer said, "my friend Mr. Kagle, who has a drugstore on First Street, decided that he could use a delivery boy after school, too. Now that you've got a good bike of your own, why don't you apply for the job?"

"But I haven't got any bike!"

"Jimmy," Mr. Jones said, "I talked it over with Pete, and we both want you to keep this bike. It isn't much, just a small way for us to begin to thank you. Believe me, if I had the money, I'd buy you a brand new one."

"But—you mean you ain't arresting me?"

"Gosh, no, boy, I'm trying to thank you."

"Jimmy," Mr. Dormyer said, "you going to ask for that job?"

Jimmy didn't jump up and down and yell with delight, he didn't kick his heels and let out a warwhoop, but he sure felt like it. And all that he felt was in the happy way he said, "I sure will, Mr. Dormyer. I'll be there, tomorrow, right after school."

Practice Sessions

The point that is made by the *Inside, Looking Out* stories is just this: Often, in our relations with other people, things are not what they seem. People may seem to be slighting us when actually they have no intention of hurting our feelings. There may be a good reason for the way they are behaving which we do not know; and, until we do learn that reason, it is important for us not to jump to conclusions.

Just for practice in withholding judgment about behavior until we learn the actual reasons for it, answer the questions raised in the following problem situations.

1. Your best friend is away on a long visit to relatives. You have written a letter to him (or her). Several weeks have gone by, and you are upset because you have had no answer to your letter. You think that your friend is angry with you. Actually, your friend is *not* angry with you.

    List three reasons why your friend has not answered your letter. These must be good, sensible reasons. Remember, your friend is not angry with you.

    (For example: Your friend has not answered because he (or she) has never received your letter; you put the wrong address on it.)

2. You answered an ad in the paper, applying for a job (such as boxing groceries in a market, or babysitting with a young child.) You did not get the job; the people have not telephoned you.

    List three good reasons, that have nothing to do with you personally, why you have not been hired.

    (For example: you gave your age, which is thirteen; but you have to be sixteen to be employed in some grocery chains.)

3. Your aunt wrote to your parents, asking if you or your older sister could accompany her and her daughter on a vacation trip. Your parents decided to send your sister. You are very upset and resentful; your parents were partial to her, you think.

    List three good reasons that have not been influenced by any partiality, why they should have sent your sister and not you.

    (For example: your sister is three years older than you and is thus the same age as your cousin with whom she'll travel; and they both dote on long-hair music, while you like popular music.)

4. Your classroom is putting on a play. You had hoped to be selected to play the lead, but you were not. You angrily wonder if the teacher has something against you.

   List three good reasons why she was right in not choosing you for the lead in the play even though she likes and admires you and thinks you have real talent.

   (For example: you are a star pitcher on the baseball team and are getting a lot of attention and admiration. Your teacher wants to help other members of your class show their talents, too.)

5. Your Boy Scout group has selected a team to put on an exhibition of signaling, or gymnastics, or rescue work at the County Fair. You were left off the team. You are angry because you think you should have been on the team.

   List three reasons why not putting you on the team was wise.

   (For example: you've just recovered from a long bout of the flu and are not yet physically up to your usual strength.)

4

MANAGING ONE'S FEELINGS:
"ACTING OUT"

**PARTY
DRESS**

The problem:

The issue is managing one's feelings; specifically, *not allowing feelings of anger and frustration to drive you into immature behavior, into "acting out" your fury in a destructive lashing out at things around you.*

Introducing the problem:

You may say to the group, *"Have you ever gotten so angry at your brother or sister that you've done something very hurtful or damaging? That is what happens in this story which I am going to read to you. As I read, try to think of ways in which you might end the story."*

When Mona got home from school that day, her mother and father were in the living room, admiring the plaster cast on her sister Ellen's leg. Ellen had had her right leg fractured in a car accident a couple of months ago. Ellen, who was fourteen, two years older than Mona, was in junior high, and was popular. She had lots of friends and every last one of them, it seemed, had either written his name on Ellen's cast or drawn a picture on it.

"It's just what the men in the Army hospitals do, Mona," Ellen explained.

Mona said, "You ought to get movie stars to autograph it."

"I have, Smarty," Ellen said. "Look."

Mona bent over the thick white casing on Ellen's leg. Sure enough, scrawled in bold letters was the name *Bob Hope*. And beside it, a hasty profile of Hope showed a nose like a bulldozer.

"Oh, no, not really!" Mona said.

"Really. He came to our junior high benefit," Ellen said. "He made a joke, too, when he wrote his autograph for me. He said, 'Oh, so you got half your legs broken. Be thankful you aren't a centipede!' "

"You have all the luck," Mona said.

And she really meant it. Mona, in time, would be a tall, lovely young woman. But just now she was thin and lanky, she still had braces on her teeth, and she wore glasses. Ellen, on the other hand, was very pretty. Ellen had vivid red hair and big brown eyes. She not only made good grades in school without seeming to try hard, but she danced well and played tennis and was on the girls' basketball team, and was president of the girls' honor society.

"Oh, sure, I have all the luck," Ellen said. "We drive to Aunt Bertha's for Christmas. You fall asleep in the car. A truck hits us. You don't even wake up. *I* get a broken leg. *I* spend Christmas in the hospital. You go to Disneyland with Aunt Bertha, and she gives you a wrist watch—"

"It's not worth half the pearl choker she gave you!"

"Children," Mrs. Martin said. "Mona, how about a glass of milk and some cookies?"

In the kitchen, as she munched the cookies, Mona said, "Mother, Sue Boyer has invited me to a big party she and her sister Linda are giving Friday night. Can I go?"

Mrs. Martin put her hand to her forehead tiredly and thought.

"You wouldn't want to go in your old blue dress, Mona, and I can't buy you a new one. Not just now. No, dear, you'd better stay home."

Mona sighed. Ellen's broken leg had cost Dad a lot of money for hospital and doctor bills.

"All right. I'll tell Sue I can't come. She'll want to know why. She's nosey."

"I'm sorry, honey."

"It's all right, Mom. I'll live through it."

When Mona got home from rehearsing a play after school next afternoon, she found Ellen in the living room, practicing a "Chalk Talk." Their father was a commercial artist, and they had some of his talent. Their pet parlor trick was to draw quick, funny silhouettes of people. The secret of making good "chalk talks," their father had taught them, was to get pictures of people who'd be at the party where you would draw profiles, and practice drawing them ahead of time.

Ellen had her junior high yearbook open and was studying the pictures. Mona looked at her, and frowned.

"Why're you practicing, Ellen?"

"Linda Boyer invited me to the party she and Sue are giving Friday night, and she asked me to make a chalk talk."

Mona gasped. "You m-mean, you're going?"

"Sure I'm going."

"Did Mother say you could?"

"Of course. Why shouldn't she? Even if I'm a cripple, I'm not something you have to keep locked up in a back room."

Mona whirled and ran toward the kitchen, yelling in outrage, "*Mother!*"

"I'm in here. Not so loud. You'll take the roof off."

"Ellen says she's going to the Boyers' party!"

"Well, yes—"

"She can go, but I *can't!*" Mona burst out furiously.

"Shh! Mona, lower your voice."

"Ellen gets anything she wants! But when I—"

"She hadn't even been invited then."

"No, but the minute she *was* invited, you said yes. But me—the minute I get invited, I *can't* go!"

"That's not the case at all, Mona. If you got invited, we knew Ellen would be invited too. It was simply that Dad didn't see how he could buy new dresses for both of you."

"Oh, now Ellen's getting a *new dress,* too!"

"Try to understand, honey. Ellen's had a pretty bad time these last few months. You realize she hasn't been to a single party since the accident?"

"Just because she can't dance."

"This is the first time she's been willing to go. And she does need a new dress."

"Don't I?"

"We felt that if she did go in a new dress, she'd be happier about everything. I'd been planning to explain it all to you—but I've been so distracted lately, and I just forgot."

"She always gets better things than I do!"

"Oh, no. Tell you what. You phone Sue and tell her that you can come to her party, after all."

"You mean I can get a new dress, too?"

Mrs. Martin sighed and shook her head.

"No, but maybe we can fix—"

"Then I won't go to the party. I won't go at all!"

In her own room Mona flung herself on her bed and cried until her wild feelings were spent. She heard her father drive into the garage. She stayed in her room until she heard him talking in the livingroom. Slowly she got up, washed her face, and walked downstairs.

"My, Ellen, that's awfully clever!" her Dad was saying.

And Mother was adding, "I want to laugh right out loud every time I look at it. You've got Danny Baker down just perfectly, Ellen."

"Pop, you think someday I might make a cartoonist?" Ellen asked.

"Better than that, honey, a caricaturist. It's the same thing, only you get paid more money."

Ellen grinned at her Dad, her eyes shining with pleasure.

Mona stepped up beside Ellen and stared at the drawing, her head bent to one side.

"It's Danny Baker, all right. You can tell that," Mona said, "if you look hard." She picked up the chalk from the easel ledge. She made some sharp, telling marks on the picture. "Dad's always told us that the ears and the mouth, more than anything else, gives a person away. Especially Danny's. His ear lobes stretch out like somebody's been lifting him by them, and his mouth always looks like he's just pulled out his thumb and forgot to close it. See?.... But Danny's nose is kind of special, too. The way it's bent, it looks like he smells around corners. And his hair always looks like he'd combed it with an egg beater. There!"

She stepped back. The picture, now, really was Danny Baker.

But her mother and dad didn't praise her. They were awfully quiet.

And then Ellen was angrily, furiously, throwing her own chalk down on the floor and violently turning her wheelchair away.

"That's so much better than I can do! I won't give the chalk talk. *You* give it, Mona!" And Ellen was crying, the tears running down her face.

"Oh, Ellen, honey," her Dad said. He bent over Ellen, put his arms around her; the look he gave Mona was furious.

And Mother said, "Mona, I'm surprised at you. Showing off! What a hateful thing to do!"

Mona gasped, and cried out, "Everything Ellen does is fine, but anything I do is awful!"

"No, Mona," her father said slowly. "It's just that—"

"You love Ellen," Mona said. "You love her and you just *hate* me!" And she turned and ran to her own room, and slammed the door.

She heard her mother coming upstairs, and she fastened the door catch. When her mother tried the knob, and said "Mona, honey, let me in," Mona refused.

"Go away! Leave me alone!"

Mona didn't sleep well, and woke up feeling tired. At school, next day, for a while she forgot her upset. Her class was studying early California history, and were planning costumes for a pageant. Mona made sketches of the costumes for the class—of the hidalgo garb of the men: the leather hat and leggings, the velvet jacket and pantaloons trimmed with silver lace at the knee. Her teacher praised Mona's drawings, and that made Mona hum to herself as she finished them.

But her good mood didn't last long.

As she walked home with Nina Tate and Edie Barton, they asked her what she was going to wear to the party at the Boyers' that night. When she said, oh, she didn't think she would go, they looked at her in surprise.

"But Mona, we always have such a good time at Sue's parties!"

That was true. Thinking about it, by the time she got home Mona was feeling very sorry for herself. Her mood got worse when she walked inside and saw Ellen and her mother opening a package from the Junior Miss Dress Shop. It was Ellen's new dress.

And a lovely dress it was, of shimmering yellow-gold nylon that would be gorgeous for Ellen with her coppery-red hair and big brown eyes. A dream of a dress, with a low neckline and a long skirt. Ellen was just beaming as she held it against herself and looked in the mirror.

"It's just *right*, Mother!"

"It's beautiful, Ellen."

"Oh, the skirt! It's wrinkled!"

"Just crumpled from being in the box. I'll give it a quick press, Ellen."

Mona passed them without a word, and went on upstairs to her own room. She slammed the door shut behind her. She was being rude, mean, bad-tempered, and she knew it; but she couldn't help it. She had an awful impulse to break something; to lash out and hit somebody hard.

She went down to dinner, though she felt little hunger. Ellen was a bit late coming down. Ellen had brushed her red hair until it shone, and now had it combed back in a long bob, the ends rolled over, and had tied around her head a yellow ribbon as gorgeous and shimmering as her new dress, and on each side of her hair had put in a comb trimmed in yellow metal.

"Gosh," Dad said. "Are you a knockout!"

Ellen glowed. "Thanks, Dad."

"She takes after my side of the family," Mother said.

"Thank goodness," Dad said.

They laughed. Mona didn't. The others were careful to act as if they didn't know how she was glaring at her plate.

So I take after Dad's side of the family. I'm skinny and homely. Well, I don't care! ...

After dinner, Mrs. Martin got busy ironing Ellen's new dress. Mona did the dishes, her back to her mother. And Mona was furious, inwardly boiling with hurt and resentment. They were going to let her stay home. They were going to take Ellen to the party and leave her alone in her room.

Ellen called from upstairs. Mother answered, "Coming, dear!" and hung the new dress on a hanger and left it hanging from the door while she went upstairs.

They've always been partial to Ellen, Mona brooded. *Maybe they've never even wanted me.*

The dishes washed, she stacked them in the rack, then wiped the silverware, working carelessly, and unaware of it. Then she poured Clorox on the dishrag and cleaned the sink.

It wasn't fair! Sue Boyer would see Ellen, and Sue would wonder. Why couldn't Mona come? She'd ask Ellen. And Ellen would shrug and say, Oh, she wasn't feeling good. Ellen wouldn't say that Mom and Pop would do anything for Ellen, but not for Mona. Oh, no, not for Mona!

"I could wear an old apron or something pulled off a scarecrow, for all they care! They don't care *anything* about me! I could just die and they wouldn't mind!"

Hot tears blurred her eyes. She turned, her throat choked up.

There was Ellen's new dress, hanging from the edge of the dining room door, so bright and shimmering and new—

Angrily, frantic with rage and disappointment, Mona threw the sopping dishrag at the dress.

The dress fell, crumpling onto the floor.

Mona caught a sharp, stabbing breath, and stood taut, staring at the heap of bright cloth. ... It was getting wrinkled. And soiled from the wet dishcloth. She took a couple of quick steps forward and bent and snatched up the garment. She hung it back in place, and smoothed its sleek length. It *was* damp in spots, from the dishrag. But the spots would dry out.

She turned back to her work, and hurried to finish. Wiping the sink. Taking out the garbage. But before she finished, her mother came back into the kitchen.

"Thanks, Mona, dear. You're a big help."

Mona busied herself filling the sugar bowl. Behind, her mother turned to the new dress. Took it off the hanger.

"What in the world? . . . Why, it's damp, it's—" And then Mrs. Martin gasped in startled surprise, in dismay, in stricken anger. "Good heavens! This dress is *ruined.*" Then Mrs. Martin turned. Mona felt her gaze. "Mona! Look at me. Did you do this?"

Mona turned, shrinking back against the sink.

"Do what, Mother?" she stammered.

"Look at this dress. Look at these spots! It's simply ruined!"

Across the front, in a long line down the length of the shining yellow cloth, were faded smudges and blotches. Aghast, Mona stared at them.

"What did that, Mother?"

"You tell me, young lady!"

And then Mona gasped as she understood what had happened. That dishrag she had hurled at the dress—that dishrag was soaked with Clorox! And Clorox was a bleach. It was eating the color out of the dress material!

"I d-did it, I guess. I got Clorox on it."

"You've ruined Ellen's new dress, that's what you've done."

"I don't care!" Mona said wildly. "You've all been so mean to me!"

Her mother looked at her with a sudden startled awareness on her face; and Mrs. Martin sat down on a kitchen chair, as if the strength had abruptly gone from her legs, and tears filled her eyes.

"Mona, dear, listen to me. We wanted Ellen to have such a good time tonight. We've tried so hard to make her happy. Mona, Dr. Balch is going to take Ellen's cast off next week. But he's warned us. There's a chance that Ellen's knee may be stiff. Probably, he says, she'll be all right; but just the same, there *is* a chance she won't ever be able to walk normally. And if *that* happens— Can't you see how she'll feel? Dad and I wanted to get her other things to think about. We wanted to make her feel that people loved her and she'd be happy in spite of—anything. And now— You see what you've done?"

Mona's lips quivered, but she cried out, "I don't care! You've all been so mean to me. I don't care—I don't care!"

INDEX